Taking Stock of Homicide

EDITED BY KAREN F. PARKER, RICHARD STANSFIELD, AND ASHLEY M. MANCIK

Taking Stock of Homicide

Trends, Emerging Themes, and Research Challenges

TEMPLE UNIVERSITY PRESS
Philadelphia • *Rome* • *Tokyo*

TEMPLE UNIVERSITY PRESS
Philadelphia, Pennsylvania 19122
tupress.temple.edu

Library of Congress Cataloging-in-Publication Data

Names: Parker, Karen F., editor. | Stansfield, Richard, 1985– editor. |
Mancik, Ashley M., 1989– editor.
Title: Taking stock of homicide : trends, emerging themes, and research
challenges / edited by Karen F. Parker, Richard Stansfield, Ashley M.
Mancik.
Description: Philadelphia : Temple University Press, 2024. | Includes
bibliographical references and index. | Summary: "This book orients
readers to the major topics and challenges for the next generation of
homicide research, including methodological issues and challenges and
emerging subfields"— Provided by publisher.
Identifiers: LCCN 2023025398 (print) | LCCN 2023025399 (ebook) | ISBN
9781439921401 (cloth) | ISBN 9781439921418 (paperback) | ISBN
9781439921425 (pdf)
Subjects: LCSH: Homicide—United States.
Classification: LCC HV6524 .T35 2024 (print) | LCC HV6524 (ebook) | DDC
364.1520973—dc23/eng/20230828
LC record available at https://lccn.loc.gov/2023025398
LC ebook record available at https://lccn.loc.gov/2023025399

♾ The paper used in this publication meets the requirements of the
American National Standard for Information Sciences—Permanence
of Paper for Printed Library Materials, ANSI Z39.48-1992

Printed in the United States of America

9 8 7 6 5 4 3 2 1

Contents

Taking Stock of Homicide

Introduction

KAREN F. PARKER AND RICHARD STANSFIELD

Introduction

Homicide, the intentional killing of a human being, is the most serious of crimes and the focus of much attention. The definition of homicide can take on complexity, from legal distinctions (first degree to manslaughter) to variations in context (organized crime, intimate partner violence, or drug market activity). The meaning of homicide also varies across countries, capturing differences in the circumstances of the act and other important elements. Often, homicide research adopts this level of complexity; one study might investigate the changes in homicide over time, while another may focus on the specific contexts in which homicide occurs. The interests of homicide researchers, along with their choices of methodologies and perspectives, have varied the study of this serious crime in numerous and important ways. We know more about this offense as a result. The reader might ask: Why write a book that *takes stock* of homicide now? What is to gain from such a comprehensive examination?

Well, unsurprisingly, the answer is complex too. If we had to offer a quick, simple answer, we would say it is time to get back to scholarship. The challenges facing scholarly work and academicians pursuing scientific knowledge are at an all-time high. Fake news and misinformation combine with politics, suspicious motives, and social and media filters designed to verify false information over facts and true narrative. The lines between real and fake are blurred. To us, producing a coherent and sustained body of research on homicide is important in the presence of today's misrepresented and distorted climate. Additionally, the COVID pandemic impacted our lives in many ways, in particular by greatly hindering scientific work. Funded research halted as scholars were unable to participate in research via interviews, observational work, and other data collection efforts. Universities restricted access to not only classrooms but also research labs and offices—and rightly so, due to the seriousness of health concerns. Many of us hunkered down in our homes with limited resources, watching and waiting for more optimistic, safer times. After a lengthy quarantine and an emerging "new normal," we felt it important to break ground on new research as well as to return to key themes and core issues of homicide. If nothing more, COVID allowed us to see more clearly. This volume is an opportunity to move forward with purpose and clarity.

Last, homicide is in a period of tremendous growth and attention. This attention has come with a realization that homicide deeply affects families and communities, as communities living with rising rates of premature death face growing health burdens. Homicide is the most serious crime, and it is historically the best recorded and accurately documented. Scholars have established the American crime drop, during which homicides and other violent crimes declined considerably across cities and towns throughout the United States. And while we were caught off guard by the crime drop in the 1990s, much scholarly literature has explored its causes and consequences. Today, homicides are increasing and, as shown during the pandemic period, shifting not only in frequency but also in circumstance and type. There has yet to be a volume capturing these important elements of homicide in the academic literature. We seek to address that.

Homicide is truly the most serious and compelling of behaviors. The very reality of homicide adds to the richness of our research. Getting a handle on—or taking stock of—homicides to better understand trends and causes remains essential to scholarship on crime and violence. This statement has never been more relevant than today, as we emerge from major drops in homicide trends and the pandemic. In fact, both contemporary trends and the serious nature of this crime compel us to question what we know, the relative merits of homicide data in use, and what areas of research have yet to be identified. We believe it is time to explore homicide for these reasons and more.

The study of homicide is at a crossroads, and the approach taken in this volume reflects that. We advocate for scholarship that considers new and old questions with fresh eyes. The chapters composed here take a broad view of homicide and, at times, offer topics not yet explored in the literature. We have asked authors to take stock of homicide research in their area of specialization and identify the challenges that hinder our understanding of this behavior—basically, what we know and what needs to be accounted for to move knowledge forward. While there are other recent volumes on homicide in print, this volume offers more than a summary and overall glossary of content. Rather, it addresses the challenges facing leading scholars investigating homicide and requires them to share what they know and what is missing in the literature. This volume offers a comprehensive review of major areas of homicide research by scholars who are leaders in those areas in the hope of challenging our own work and mapping the way for future knowledge. Only by critically exploring issues in homicide will the study and knowledge advance. This volume, then, serves as a toolkit for that purpose. As we said, it is time to get back to scholarship, and focusing on homicide seems like a very good place to start.

Purpose of This Book

The purpose of this volume is to take a critical look at homicide from the context of the research being conducted. From the eyes of the homicide researcher, this volume takes stock of current knowledge and seeks to identify areas of uncertainty in the hope of specific outcomes—more knowledge, a return to scholarly endeavors, and new directions in research. The path this book takes, then, provides leading scholars a way to review and discuss key issues they encounter when conducting homicide research in their specific area and address the challenges they face in their work. The following pages provide a comprehensive and systematic look at key areas of homicide research, including areas that will emerge in the next decade or so, and a dialogue with key scholars on how they recommend the field address methodological issues or challenges in future homicide research. Broadly, we call on researchers to guide the way.

Organization of This Book

Each chapter offers original work by scholars who are actively engaging the field. The volume is organized around major themes and areas in homicide literature. In selecting the topic for each chapter, we conducted an extensive review of homicide research using major databases (Web of Science, Criminal Justice Abstracts, etc.) and leading books published on homicide in the last three decades. In addition, we considered contemporary trends in the criminological literature for areas of research that might influence how we study homicide. Finally, we assessed work and collected information on how scholars engage topics, considering calls for more scholarship in peer-reviewed papers, areas of debate, and citation counts on which topics are being investigated most often in the homicide literature and why. In the end, the chapters offered here reflect areas that leading homicide scholars have identified as fundamentally important to understanding homicide or suggested as important in future work, as well as our own assessment of the current state of research.

The book is separated by major themes. The first part of the book addresses fundamental areas of interest to all who want to understand homicide. To begin this section, Randolph Roth builds on his book *American Homicide* (Harvard University Press, 2009) to discuss the importance of data for testing narratives created by historians on the history of violence. History matters, but more data are needed to understand the circumstances that increase or decrease homicide, and few scholars are answering that call. Roth offers a look at four major databases, including the Historical Violence Database, which he cofounded, in hopes of helping other historians overcome data issues in the historical context. Incorporating history is important not only for understanding contemporary patterns and trends but also for providing a critical lens. Criminology has grown increasingly interested in capturing the historical backdrop, from the history of carceral policies in the United States to the role of slavery on racialized violence in antebellum South. The success of these efforts to merge the work of humanists with social scientists is dependent on the quality of the data, which Roth so well illustrates in this chapter. In addition to a historical lens, this section includes a review of trends and patterns in homicide by Berg and Rogers, a look at major data sources by Regoeczi and Jarvis, and an overview of the current state of work using a cross-national perspective by Rogers and Pridemore. Throughout this section, we see how the data we use to study homicide is of great significance and can offer fresh insights—but not without challenges. For example, in Rogers and Pridemore's review of major data sources for cross-national homicide, we see how revealing homicide levels are of different nations and their cultures.

The next theme is the scope of homicide, ranging from structural dynamics driving high homicide rates to the impact of the deaths of young black men from a public health perspective. Macrolevel and neighborhood/community-level work on homicide has been a long-standing interest among scholars. In this section, Tuttle, McCall, and Land build off the seminal work of Land et al. (1990) to give us the current state of macrolevel work; they also remind us of the pitfalls facing scholars conducting aggregate-level work today. After reviewing common methodological challenges, they evaluate a number of structural covariates incorporated in homicide research. Hipp and Luo take the topic further by examining methodological challenges in community-level work specifically, such as small homicide counts and the difficulty of identifying a proper ecological unit. Offering a spatial strategy, they propose "egohoods" as a neighborhood unit able to overcome methodological issues and stimulate the longitudinal research that has long been desired in criminology. They provide two examples and demonstrate how egohoods produce more robust models than more traditional neighborhood units. Shifting away from the macro in a timely and unique way, Brookman and Jones illustrate the value of a qualitative approach to studying homicide investigations. Statistics and quantitative methodologies have dominated much of criminology as a field, while qualitative analyses have played a more limited role in homicide research. Brookman and Jones give us a look at the benefits of conducting qualitative work on homicide investigations while expanding our understanding of the challenges and opportunities of doing this work, such as difficulties taking field notes, complexities of collaborating researchers, and lack of access to people or places, to name a few.

Following Brookman and Jones, Sharon Jones-Eversley and her colleagues draw our attention to the impact and risk factors associated with high rates of premature death among young black people. Using a public health lens, they skillfully illustrate how a primordial prevention approach acknowledges underlying factors, such as the structural characteristics of places mentioned by Tuttle et al. in this volume, and how structural factors are linked to individual risk factors associated with health and safety. These scholars use Baltimore as an example to demonstrate this connection, highlighting how the homicidal deaths of young black men reflect the overall wellness of the black community and, more universally, the health of the criminal justice system. All in all, this section documents the relatively large scope of work on homicide as well as the unique questions scholars confront when conducting this work. As researchers respond to calls for time sensitive data strategies, crime mapping, spatial data to better estimate homicides in smaller geographical units like communities or street segments, other scholars offer ethnographies of homicide, which provide new accounts of homicide events. As qualitative work on homicide continues, exciting research areas are worth developing, such as in-depth accounts of the impact of homicide on communities, police-resident relations when homicides occur, and residents' points of view. To our knowledge, this volume is the first to link the structural study of homicide to narrative-style accounts and public health outcomes.

Next, we offer a section that explores the nature of homicide and offers an examination of the circumstances, types, and variations in homicide essential to representing this behavior. While homicide is the most serious of criminal behaviors, it is not a monolithic event. This section engages the reader on several core aspects of homicide that illustrate key patterns and variation in our knowledge. They include intimate partner homicide, gang-related and motivated homicide, and the involvement of drugs or guns in homicide, just to name a few. Documenting the pervasiveness of intimate partner homicides (IPH) with female victims throughout the world, Williams,

Ragan, Magnus, and Gonzalez provide a careful and methodologically detailed study of a risk assessment instrument designed to predict risk of lethality. Only by identifying risk factors linked to IPH, or "red flags," can such incidents be prevented and the "dark figure" of intimate partner violence be revealed. Then, we get a look at how gang homicides differ from other forms of homicide, as Sanchez and Pyrooz demonstrate measurement, data, and prevalence aspects encountered when studying gang violence specifically. We learn, for example, about distinctions between gang-related and gang-motivated homicides as well as how data sources on gang homicides have been key to grasping these differences. Controversies remain about labeling an incident as "gang related," and data limits the ability to map gang homicide trends nationally.

These challenges are also faced by scholars examining drug-related homicides. Focusing on the European experience, Rabolini, van Breen, and Liem outline the most pressing methodological issues facing the study of drug-related homicides and offer some next steps for this line of scholarship. While we find that recent data collection efforts, such as the European Homicide Monitor (EHM), have greatly improved the quality of data on drug-related homicides internationally, such optimism does not translate to the study of gun violence, as shown by Griffiths and Semenza. In fact, gun violence is bound not only by the cultural and legal context of the United States but also by the lack of record keeping systematically tracking firearm ownership or registration. Dependence on proxies for measuring gun ownership and other data issues hinder our knowledge of this type of homicide. After providing one of the most extensive and careful reviews of literature on gun violence to date, Griffiths and Semenza offer a set of recommendations with hopes of improving the research on firearm homicides. As a result of the efforts of contributors to this section, our knowledge of homicide is magnified and diversified. In the end, these scholars challenge others to take on research and overcome data issues.

Following these chapters, our examination of the nature of homicide shifts to emerging areas in homicide research. While variations in homicide by race, gender, age, and ethnicity have long been documented, building on this literature requires researchers to seek new approaches. In this volume, approaches include intersections in homicide, immigration, and changing demographic patterns in the United States. Compiling mortality data on thirty-year (1990–2019) trends in homicide victimization by race, ethnicity, and gender, Gaston argues that researchers have yet to fully consider intersections in homicide in their work. Gaps and changes across groups and inequality are key challenges, especially in data collection. While Gaston calls on researchers to establish a historical foundation, the pursuit of intersectionality in future efforts, such as exploring the concept of "intersectional disadvantage," is core to her arguments. For example, she draws attention to the need for research to center work on black and native women, who are at great risk of being killed. Data constraints also obscure our understanding of immigration and homicide, as illustrated by Light, Boisten, and Kim. How do immigrant homicides compare to rates among the native born? Is the homicide rate different among the undocumented? And do these rates change over time? These questions, along with gaps in our knowledge, are addressed in their chapter. We are reminded that ignoring disparities and existing inequalities does not advance our intellectual efforts and, while methodological challenges are inescapable, producing scientific knowledge is at the heart of what we do. Changing demographics in recent decades are also promising areas of research on homicide trends. Orrick, Guerra, and Piquero take a deep dive into the study of homicide trends and demographics, such as immigration status when using the incarcerated for homicide data from the state of Texas. This section, like the ones before it, builds on the premise that scholarly work is needed more than ever, especially in the face of the divisiveness in public discourse that has largely mired the study of immigration and crime. Scholars have only begun to recognize the importance of an intersectional lens, such as examining interconnections between race, ethnicity, and gender (as shown by Gaston) or accounting for immigration status along with other core characteristics and/or forms of disadvantage. This is the first volume we are aware of that brings all of these fundamental and contemporary issues together.

The last section assembles important aspects not yet addressed and often ignored in homicide research. For example, while considerable time and resources are devoted to investigating homicides, many cases go unsolved. What is the latest knowledge about solving homicides? Regoeczi and Jarvis provide a thorough examination of factors that influence whether or not a homicide case will be cleared, outlining some of the key challenges in this specific area of research. Lack of data and measurement issues are clear themes in their chapter, but they also acknowledge the impact of police technology, police practices, and existing tensions between police and communities. Braga makes connections between police and community more apparent when reviewing practices and evaluating evidence on focused deterrence strategies. What results is a compelling chapter that reviews scholarly efforts to link public health and focused deterrence approaches to homicide prevention. These two chapters remind us that our goal is not only to understand the prevalence and nature of homicide, but also to evaluate and assess efforts to solve and prevent such events.

This book is a complete and comprehensive examination of homicide that takes a balanced approach, offering original scholarship with the goal of providing information about challenges that occur when doing this work.

We provide leading scholars who study homicide and violence an opportunity to take stock of the work and explore avenues to overcoming challenges facing future work. Core themes are covered, such as data sources, homicide trends and patterns, and structural explanations, as well as the role of gangs, firearms, and drugs. Emerging topics, such as historical study, qualitative approaches, immigration, and intersectional views of homicide, are presented. Some chapters focus solely on homicide data and trends in the United States, while others offer a European or more global view. This volume expands our knowledge of homicide while offering a toolkit for future research on this serious, violent behavior. We hope you find it helpful to your own work and are reminded that the pursuit of scholarship in the most political and divisive of times advances not only our understanding of homicide but also the public's.

I

Fundamentals of Homicide

1

Data Drudges Unite!

Taking Stock of Historical Studies of Homicide

RANDOLPH ROTH

The history of crime, criminal justice, and violence is vibrant. Historians of homicide work within this broader field, which has produced stunning scholarship on criminal justice, policing, prisons, capital punishment, criminal enterprise, drugs, domestic violence, sexual violence, sex work, sex trafficking, and other topics of vital concern. Historians who study homicide are few, however, as are specialists in every subfield.[1]

We are nonetheless ambitious. Bretschneider et al. map out the field's agenda beautifully in their introductory essay to the twentieth anniversary issue of *Crime, History, and Societies* (Bretschneider et al. 2017), envisioning a global history that can inform public policy. But we need more time, money, and researchers at a moment when teaching obligations are increasing, grant agencies are stressed for funds, and history departments are being downsized.

There is a pressing need for data to test the competing narratives that historians have created of the history of violence. Best known is the civilization thesis, first articulated by Norbert Elias in the late 1930s. It posits that all forms of interpersonal violence, including homicide, have declined in Europe since medieval times because of the growth of powerful states and criminal courts, which suppress lawlessness and deter impulsive behavior, and improvements in manners and the extension of the market economy, which encourage self-control, cooperation, and regard for others. According to this theory, the civilizing process has reversed from time to time, but the trajectory has been toward stronger states, self-control, mutuality, and lower homicide rates—even in the United States, where rates remain higher than in other Western nations because of a weaker state, a premature democracy, lenient courts, crude manners, and a culture that values defense of personal honor over self-control (Elias 1982; Gurr 1981; Lane 1979; Monkkonen 2001; Spierenburg 2008; Ylikangas, Karonen, and Lehti 2001).

Most historians who have been doing the grunt work of creating datasets on the history of homicide, however, are having fits over the dominance of the civilization thesis in public and scholarly debate. One need only read the recent issue of *Historical Reflections* in which historians respond to Steven Pinker's *The Better Angels of Our Nature*, the latest statement of the civilization thesis (Pinker 2011; Mitchell, Micale, and Dwyer 2018). Among the criticisms, "data drudges" in the profession disagree with the civilization thesis's exaggerated view of violence in medieval Europe; its failure to explain the sudden drop in violence across Western Europe and its North American colonies in the late seventeenth and early eighteenth centuries, during which homicide rates lowered to near post–World War II levels in many areas; its neglect of the staggering homicide rates in the Russian Federation and most of its former satellites after the fall of the Soviet Union; and its refusal to acknowledge that the era from the mid-1880s to the early 1950s may have been the most violent in history by the proportion of humanity killed. Most of all, data drudges complain about the painful misuse of their data by scholars who fail to consider the strengths and limitations of the primary sources from which sets of data are drawn. It is a stretch to say that an early modern time series drawn from indictment records alone represents a substantial decline in violence from a medieval time series drawn from gaol records, Eyre court records, and coroner's rolls. But such misrepresentations of the past and of historical scholarship occur frequently among proponents of the civilization thesis.

The most influential alternative theories, developed independently in the 1990s by Gary LaFree, Manuel Eisner, the late Roger Gould, and me, might be gathered under the umbrella of the nation building thesis (Eisner 2001; LaFree 1998; Gould 2003; Roth 2012). This thesis recognizes the importance of state building and political stability but emphasizes the affective side of nation building and community formation—the feelings and beliefs that help human communities cohere, cooperate, and dampen the hostile, defensive, and predatory emotions that lead to homicide. What about trust in government and the officials who run it and belief in their legitimacy? What about patriotism, empathy, and other feelings arising from religious, ethnic, or political solidarity? What about faith that the social hierarchy is legitimate, that one's position in society is or can be satisfactory, and that one can command the respect of others without resorting to violence? These phenomena are hard to measure. But where they can be measured, especially with the help of humanistic histories that bring worlds of the past to life, these feelings and beliefs track well with the ups and downs of homicide rates in the broader European world over the past four hundred and fifty years.

Nonetheless, the nation building thesis may apply only to homicides among unrelated adults. Intimate partner homicides appear to follow shifts in the balance of power between women and men; homicides of children by parents or caregivers appear to vary with the degree to which the world gives young parents an opportunity to realize their ambitions for themselves and their children (Roth 2012). But we do not yet have enough data to be sure.

And both the civilization thesis and the nation building thesis leave questions unanswered about homicides among unrelated adults. Do different forms of political organization—hunter-gatherer bands, chiefdoms, ancient empires, medieval kingdoms, or today's transnational alliances, such as the Eurozone—encourage different patterns of cooperation and aggression? Within modern and early modern nation-states, did homicide patterns take shape across every region and community or only in the aggregate, with wide variation among individual locales? Why were some peoples who were incorporated by conquest into larger empires, including the French Canadians of British Quebec and the Sinhalese of the Sri Lankan interior, able to maintain relatively low homicide rates? Was it because their conquerors left property and institutions relatively undisturbed within ethnic enclaves, preserving a degree of governmental legitimacy and social solidarity at the local level (Fyson 2009; Rogers 1987; Wood 1961)? And why did some oppressed peoples, including Catholics in nineteenth-century Ireland and enslaved and newly freed African Americans in the United States, murder one another at lower rates than their oppressors did? Was it because they forged a sense of solidarity elusive to other oppressed peoples (McMahon 2013; Roth 2012)? Why have homicide rates in the United States diverged by age since the mid-1970s, after decades of varying in synchrony? Why have rates for persons ages ten to twenty-four bounced up and down in recent years while rates for older Americans have declined steadily (Roth 2017)? There is no universal or timeless pattern. History matters. But if we are to understand the circumstances that increase or decrease homicide, it is essential to determine when and where the rates of various kinds of homicide and their correlates differed.

To answer such questions—what is new, enduring, or particular to a time and place—we need more data. That is why I am writing about the four projects that I believe are the most likely to provide the data we need: to encourage historians, sociologists, and criminologists to engage in the necessary primary research.

The late Eric Monkkonen invited an international group of scholars to meet in 2000 to discuss creating an archive for historians of crime and violence to share their data in whatever form they had created it—a "data zoo," as Eric put it. He hoped to develop templates for conducting and sharing violence research with an eye to creating historical datasets compatible with the National Violent Death Reporting System (NVDRS).[2] Deborah Asrael of the Harvard School of Public Health (now associate director of the Harvard Youth Violence Prevention Center) and Jim Mercy of the Centers for Disease Control (now director of the Division of Violence Prevention) kindly agreed to meet with members of the Crime, Criminal Justice, and the Law Network of the Social Science History Association so we could learn about their effort to launch the NVDRS. We discovered that we shared a common vision: we felt it vital to consult multiple sources on each homicide, examining homicides from multiple points of view and using capture-recapture mathematics to estimate the number of homicides missing from databases (Eckberg 2001; Roth 2001). We also felt that narratives of each incident were vital for future researchers to be able to classify cases in novel ways and study violence from humanistic as well as social scientific perspectives.

To that end, my colleagues and I launched the Historical Violence Database (HVD),[3] sponsored by the Criminal Justice Research Center at Ohio State University (Roth et al. 2008). It is, as Eric had anticipated, primarily a zoo for datasets our colleagues have been willing to share in whatever format they use. Some appeared on notecards or paper worksheets, which we scanned, and some appeared as coded spreadsheets.

Those of us who created the database launched a simultaneous effort to encourage the creation of quantitative and qualitative datasets that include all information available in surviving sources on each homicide. It takes months to work through the papers of a single county court—coroner's reports, case files, docket books, jail rolls, judgment books—not to mention a state's prison records and a county's newspapers, vital records, census records, tax lists, genealogies, broadsides, pamphlets, histories based on oral testimony or tradition, and letters and diaries from personal records. To ask future historians to work through such records would be an overwhelming burden. That is why we have taken thorough research notes, even on matters not of immediate concern to our studies, in the hope that future scholars might find them useful. We have photographed (where permitted) or typed verbatim the testimony or depositions of witnesses so that future scholars can see the evidence firsthand. And many of us have taken notes not only on homicides but also on a range of violent crimes and deaths—suicides, accidents, sexual assaults, aggravated assaults, robberies—on the assumption that each form of violence may shed light on others.

We also want the HVD to be a repository for datasets that could be augmented, corrected, recoded, and reinterpreted by future scholars. We have left a record of the sources consulted and inferences drawn so that historians can search for additional sources and know our reasoning when we consid-

ered relationships, motives, or whether a controversial death was from homicide, suicide, accident, or natural causes. We hope that future historians
will supplement our research, fix our mistakes, find new patterns, and develop new interpretations.

We have created templates and codebooks we hope will work for a broad
range of historians, criminologists, and sociologists.[4] But because the vast
majority of historians are humanists who work with widely differing sources, our templates are free form to a degree so that all evidence of potential
interest can find a place.

The first page of our worksheet describes the incident and its legal outcome. It includes the narrative as well as details of the scene (description,
location, activity, witnesses, bystanders), the cause of death (weapons, injuries, medical assistance, time between injury and death), the inquest (coroner,
verdict, cause of death, culpability), the circumstances of the death (relationships, precipitants, motive, aggressor, mental illness, alcohol or substance
abuse), criminal proceedings (charges, warrants, arrests, bonds, trials, sentences), and the researcher's interpretation.

The second page describes evidence for each incident with bibliograph-
ical references. It provides space to enter verbatim the contents of surviving
records, including those that provide personal information on victims or suspects (genealogies, census records). The third page describes victims and suspects (ethnicity, race, gender, age, physical characteristics, literacy, marital
status, children, occupation, residence, birthplace, religious affiliation). It provides room for personal histories of victims and suspects along with mem-
berships in voluntary associations, military service, and political officeholding.

As scholars who began our work before the advent of digital cameras and
laptop computers, we have spent much time transcribing typewritten, hand-
written, and xeroxed notes. That is how we archived Cornelia Dayton's data
on colonial and revolutionary Connecticut, Mike Denham's on territorial
and antebellum Florida, James Wilkinson's on nineteenth-century Virginia,
and Kenneth Wheeler's on nineteenth-century Ohio, as well as data I gathered for *American Homicide*. I should add that it was a fun process—not only
because we enjoyed working together but also because of the satisfaction of
giving new life to old notes. Gathering such data is easier today, especially
because of the advent of searchable newspaper archives. But when it comes
to working through legal and police records, it is still an old-fashioned slog—
a matter of taking careful notes, thinking critically about what has or has
not been found, and organizing the evidence in meaningful ways.

My colleagues Wendy Regoeczi, Rania Issa, and I are carrying the work
into more recent times with our National Homicide Data Improvement Project, for which we have undertaken a pilot study of homicides in Ohio, 1959
to present. We are gathering data from death certificates, mortality records

of the Ohio Department of Health and the National Center for Health Statistics, Supplementary Homicide Reports from the FBI, newspapers, coroner's records, and case files and logbooks of the police departments in Cleveland, Columbus, and Cincinnati. We have been gratified by support from law enforcement, medical examiners, and health officials. And we have discovered why such research is necessary. For example, of the 1,615 homicides and probable homicides we discovered of children ages fifteen and younger from 1959 through 1988, only 82 percent are classified correctly in the Ohio Department of Health records, 67 percent in the National Center for Health Statistics' compressed mortality files, and 62 percent in the FBI's Supplementary Homicide Reports. Each database not only misses a substantial number of homicides but also classifies a considerable number of accidental deaths as homicides. We have found an alarming number of probable homicides, judging from the severity and multiplicity of wounds, of preschool children classified as deaths due to "lack of care" in the seventh revision of the International Classification of Diseases (ICD) codes or as deaths from "violence of unknown intent" in subsequent revisions of the ICD codes. Several pathologists who performed autopsies for county coroners in Ohio in that era told us that the decision to classify a child's death as a homicide rested solely with the coroner—an elected official. And each pathologist told us of autopsies they performed on children they believed had died of intentional violence that were classified without their consent as nonhomicides or as deaths from violence of unknown intent. We did not find racial bias in the classification of child homicides in the data compiled by the Ohio Department of Health (ODH). The ODH data classify 82 percent of the homicides and probable homicides of both black and white children correctly and misclassify or misplace child homicides in other categories at nearly identical percentages. The FBI Supplementary Homicide Reports, however, show substantial bias. They classify 69 percent of the homicides of black children correctly but only 58 percent of homicides of white children (Roth, Regoeczi, and Issa 2019; Dror et al. 2021).[5]

My colleagues and I believe that comprehensive historical research has substantial benefits. It can help social scientists determine with a high degree of accuracy how rates of particular kinds of homicide have varied across time and space and give humanists an opportunity to understand homicides in social and cultural context. The problem is that it takes years of work to construct such narratives and spreadsheets. We feel that the payoff has been great and have been gratified by the reception of our work. But no one has followed our lead, and no historian has contributed data to our database in nearly a decade, because rigorous work on the history of homicide—pioneered by scholars like Eric Monkkonen and Roger Lane—has gone out of fashion among historians of the United States, except for studies of lynching and mob violence (Brundage 1993; Carrigan and Webb 2013; Gilje 1996; Pfeifer 2006, 2011, 2014; Tolnay and Beck 1995; Waldrep 2002; Williams 2012).[6]

I wish scholars could learn how fascinating it is to travel the country and study the history of violence. It is a chance to meet local historians, genealogists, and officials interested in our work and eager to share what they know about violence in their communities, past and present. We spend weeks in court houses, coroner's offices, and homicide squad rooms, learning about what is happening today as we study the past. We find odd things, like a stash of evidence from a 1950s pornography case that a former county clerk squirreled away where he thought no one would find it or a sawed-off shotgun that should have been destroyed decades ago. We learn things in confidence that we cannot share and work with confidential records the closer we get to the present. It is vital that we preserve a sense of trust. And we learn painful things about the challenges communities face due to the opioid epidemic, deindustrialization, loss of small farms, racial animosity, and the like. I believe that such experiences can only enrich our understanding of the past.

The decline of interest in homicide among historians may stem in part from the decline in public concern in the United States over violence because of the crime drop of the mid and late 1990s. Another obstacle is the turn away from quantification, which has left fewer scholars in the field with a love and appreciation for statistics, even though a solid year of freshman statistics would give historians the skills to tackle nearly every quantitative problem they may face. Yet another is the vibrancy of microhistories of violent events—studies that seek to recreate social and culture worlds of the past by focusing on a particular homicide, riot, or lynching. These histories have taught us much (see Cohen 1999; Gram 2017; McLaurin 1991), but they do not engage the history of homicide.

It may simply be that there are many fruitful, career-enhancing ways to be a historian that do not involve being a data drudge. As Homer Simpson taught his son Bart in one of our family's favorite episodes of the show, "If it's hard to do, it's not worth doing."

If we fail to do such work as historians of the United States, however, we will never link up with cutting-edge projects like the NVDRS, the reach of which extends only back to 2003 for a handful of states. The confidential version of the NVDRS is a wonderful achievement, particularly because of its inclusion of narratives from law enforcement and medical examiners. The NVDRS data still require polishing; the narratives contain data about relationships and motives that have not been coded or are coded inaccurately. I wish the NVDRS could secure funding to research cases with contradictory or incomplete data. That would give historians a true gold standard from which to work back in time, because homicide reveals its deepest secrets only if we study it across great stretches of time and space.

There is perhaps greater hope for historians of homicide on the European front thanks to the work of historians in Scandinavia, who in recent years have produced the most impressive studies in the field (Lindström 2008; Österberg and Lindström 1988; Österberg 1991, 1995; Savolainen, Lehti, and Kivivuori 2008; Ylikangas, Karonen, and Lehti 2001). They are fortunate to work with the foremost collection of surviving inquisitions and court records, dating back to the fifteenth century. They have developed the best long-term time series in the field. But they too have felt the need to develop common templates for conducting and sharing violence research so that contemporary and historical researchers can engage one another productively.

Colleagues in Scandinavia have created the Historical Homicide Monitor (HHM), a social scientific effort to standardize the coding of historical homicide data in a way that is compatible with the European Homicide Monitor (EHM), which has been gathering standardized data on contemporary homicides in the Eurozone since 2003.[7] The HHM, unlike the HVD, relies solely on spreadsheets, but it contains fields for identifying sources and giving one-sentence narratives of each homicide. The HHM seeks to transform information "from qualitative-textual sources into a standardized and mostly quantitative format" (Kivivuori, Rautelin, et al. 2020).[8]

The HHM is an ambitious effort to gather data that speak to each of the major contemporary theories in criminology so that those theories can be tested rigorously. The theories of interest to the HHM include the following:

Civilizing and control theory
Self-control theory
Routine activity theory
Structural strain theory
General strain theory
Learning theory
Deterrence and rational choice
Evolutionary perspectives
Social interactionism
Gender perspectives
Forensic and public health perspectives
Desistance perspective

The HHM speaks not only to theoretical perspectives of interest to the EHM but also to perspectives of interest to historians, especially to the civilization and social control theses. The hope is that the EHM will someday be made retroactively compatible with the HHM so that the databases can fit together seamlessly. Helpfully, the HHM codebook specifies the relationship of each HHM variable to variables in the EHM: whether the variables are identical, particular to the HHM, or coded differently.

The HHM focuses on the basics of each incident (place, time, weapons and wounds, persons involved, motives, detection, sanctions). Many fields remain empty, of course, given the limitations of historical sources. But as the HHM's pilot project on homicides Denmark, Sweden, and Finland has shown, rich historical data are available and nearly complete in some fields. The first essay from the collaborators, for instance, finds that routine activity theory is a powerful tool for understanding cycles of past homicides—daily, weekly, and seasonal—even though past cycles differ from today's cycles. For instance, in eastern Finland—one of the most violent rural areas in Europe then and now—homicides cluster in May and September, on the days surrounding the biannual sessions of the circuit court. The homicide victims were witnesses about to testify—evidence of the sometimes counterproductive impact of the law in a region where self-help justice was the norm. In the seventeenth century, as today, people were more likely to be killed during leisure activities than at work, especially if alcohol was involved. And it is good to see routine activity theory confirmed with the finding that one of the deadliest places in early modern Scandinavia was the sauna (Kivivuori, Lehti, et al. 2020).

The HHM spreadsheets contain 127 fields. Like the HVD, the HHM is designed to wring every bit of information it can from historical sources so that future historians can spend their time augmenting the HHM with data from new sources rather than reanalyzing sources that have already been studied. Given the labor involved, I fear that the project may have as much trouble as the HVD in enlisting future scholars. The HHM is nonetheless worth the effort.

The EHM, which involves many of the same scholars as HVD, has published findings from its pilot project on homicides in Denmark, Finland, Iceland, Norway, and Sweden, 2007–2016. As with the HVD and NVDRS, the EHM, by consulting multiple sources, has arrived at homicide totals that differ, sometimes substantially, from those in police and health statistics. The EHM has also produced interesting results about the impact of immigration on homicide rates. Homicide rates for native residents are nearly uniform across the five nations, ranging from 0.41 per 100,000 persons per year in Denmark to 0.57 in Iceland. The sole, long-standing exception is Finland, with a rate of 1.90. The rates are uniformly higher for immigrants, from 1.42 in Denmark to 2.08 in Norway. Surprisingly, native residents are more likely than immigrants to be homicide victims in Finland (Lehti et al. 2019).[9]

As the authors note, it is difficult to press the analysis further with the EHM because of the small number of homicides in these five nations over the ten years in the study and because of missing data. In the two nations where data are available on homicide rates for the children of immigrants, their victimization rates are lower than their parents' rates, even though immigrant children in Finland live in a far more violent society than those in Denmark. The rate for immigrant children in Finland is slightly lower than the rate for their parents' generation—1.23 versus 1.48—but dramatically lower in Denmark, 0.78 versus 1.42. What might we make of that difference? It is possible that assimilation has lowered the homicide rate of immigrants and that the drop was greater in societies with lower overall homicide rates. But absent data from the other three nations, we cannot know if we have found a general pattern.

The EHM data already reveal intriguing, robust patterns. For instance, why are Asian immigrants three times more likely to be homicide victims in Norway than in three other nations with data (3.05 per hundred thousand versus 1.02 to 1.42)? That difference—statistically as well as substantively significant—accounts for the entire difference in the homicide rate between immigrants in Norway (2.08) and the three other nations (1.42 to 1.58). Without the EHM, that difference would be invisible.

The EHM also reveals the need for HHM data. Urban homicide rates are higher than rural rates in four nations in the current EHM database, but not in Finland, where rates are higher in small towns and in the countryside in northern and eastern provinces. That pattern is long standing. Why it has survived to this day is a matter for contemporary research, but its origins lie deep in Finland's past. Until historians gather data of the same character and quality as the EHM—a task that is quite possible, given the quality of the surviving records for northern Europe—it will be impossible to know how much has changed and how much has stayed the same when looking at the motives and circumstances of various kinds of homicide among different social groups over time.

Fortunately, the EHM is expanding its reach. Estonia and Switzerland have joined, and France, Poland, and Scotland are considering membership. The data will grow richer as the EHM's time series lengthens. But without complementary data from the HHM, the EHM series will remain far too short to explain many patterns visible today.

Conclusion

I hope that this brief tour of the work of the historical profession's data drudges will inspire others to join the effort. Gathering data of this quality and complexity is a daunting task. Few have volunteered to carry the work forward. If each scholar of crime and violence were to work up the data for a particular local jurisdiction, we would have magnificent data across time and space. The data, of course, would generate more questions than answers. Indeed, they could not answer any questions without a deep understanding of the history of the times and places from which the data come. They would be mute. But with such data, gathered with the interests of both humanists and social scientists in mind, we would be well on our way to recognizing the patterns we need to explain—and the human experiences that lie behind those patterns.

NOTES

1. The Crime, Justice, and Law Network of the Social Science History Association is at https://ssha.org/networks/crime/. The Criminal Justice Network of the European Social Science History Conference is at https://esshc.iisg.amsterdam/en/criminal-justice-call-papers.

2. The NVDRS is at https://www.cdc.gov/violenceprevention/datasources/nvdrs/index.html. Accessed February 25, 2021.

3. The HVD is at https://cjrc.osu.edu/research/interdisciplinary/hvd. Accessed February 25, 2021.

4. The templates and codebooks for the HVD worksheets and spreadsheets are at https://cjrc.osu.edu/research/interdisciplinary/hvd/worksheets. Accessed February 25, 2021.

5. Dror et al., 2021, "Cognitive Bias in Forensic Pathology Decisions," *Journal of Forensic Sciences* 66, https://doi.org/10.1111/1556-4029.14697, argues that forensic pathologists are prone to cognitive racial bias, but the experiment was flawed. When it asked 133 pathologists to decide from several scenarios whether a child had died from homicide, accident, or violence of unknown intent, it assigned the pathologists randomly to two groups. One group was told that the child in the scenario was a black child in the care of the mother's boyfriend. The other was told that the child was a white child in the care of the child's grandmother. Forensic pathologists are well aware that children are more likely to be killed by a nonrelative than a relative, especially by a mother's boyfriend who is not the biological father. Race and the identity of the caregiver should not be conflated in a study of cognitive bias.
We have not worked through reams of death certificates for accidental deaths of children in Ohio, 1959–1988. We have, however, worked through every death classified as a homicide or death from violence of unknown intent. A future study of accidents may reveal racial bias.

6. Exceptions include Jeff Forret, 2015, *Slave against Slave: Plantation Violence in the Old South* (Baton Rouge: Louisiana State University Press); and Jeffrey S. Adler, 2019, *Murder in New Orleans: The Creation of Jim Crow Policing* (Chicago: University of Chicago Press). Forret and Adler continue to conduct rigorous research on the history of homicide.

7. The HHM is at https://helda.helsinki.fi/handle/10138/313437. The EHM is at https://www.universiteitleiden.nl/en/research/research-projects/governance-and-global-affairs/european-homicide-monitor#tab-1. Accessed February 26, 2021.

8. Available at https://helda.helsinki.fi/bitstream/handle/10138/313437/Research_Briefs_40_Kivivuori_etal_2020.pdf?sequence=7&isAllowed=y. Accessed February 27, 2021.

9. Available at https://helda.helsinki.fi/bitstream/handle/10138/306217/Katsauksia_37_Lehti_etal_2019.pdf?sequence=5&isAllowed=y. Accessed February 27, 2021.

REFERENCES

Bretschneider, Falk, Anja Johansen, René Levy, and Xavier Rousseaux. 2017. "Twenty Years of Crime, History, and Societies." *Crime, History, and Societies* 21 (2): 17–30.

Brundage, W. Fitzhugh. 1993. *Lynching in the New South: Georgia and Virginia, 1880–1930*. Urbana: University of Illinois Press.

Carrigan, William D., and Clive Webb. 2013. *Forgotten Dead: Mob Violence against Mexicans in the United States, 1848–1928*. New York: Oxford University Press.

Cohen, Patricia Cline. 1999. *The Murder of Helen Jewett: The Life and Death of a Prostitute in Nineteenth-Century New York*. New York: Knopf.

Eckberg, Douglas L. 2001. "Stalking the Elusive Homicide: A Capture-Recapture Approach to the Estimation of Post-Reconstruction South Carolina Killings." *Social Science History* 25:67–91.

Eisner, Manuel. 2001. "Modernization, Self-Control, and Lethal Violence: The Long-Term Dynamics of European Homicide Rates in Theoretical Perspective." *British Journal of Criminology* 41:618–38.

Elias, Norbert. 1982. *The Civilizing Process*. Translated by Edmund Jephcott. New York: Pantheon.

Fyson, Donald. 2009. "Men Killing Men: Homicide in Quebec, 1760–1860." Paper delivered at the Social Science History Association, Long Beach, CA, November 14, 2009.

Gilje, Paul A. 1996. *Rioting in America*. Bloomington: Indiana University Press.

Gould, Roger V. 2003. *Collision of Wills: How Ambiguity about Social Rank Breeds Conflict*. Chicago: University of Chicago Press.

Gram, David. 2017. *Killers of the Flower Moon: The Osage Murders and the Birth of the FBI*. New York: Vintage.

Grimsted, David. 1998. *American Mobbing, 1828–1861: Toward Civil War*. New York: Oxford University Press.

Gurr, Ted Robert. 1981. "Historical Trends in Violent Crime: A Critical Review of the Evidence." *Crime and Justice: An Annual Review of Research* 3:295–353.

Kivivuori, Janne, Martti Lehti, Mona Rautelin, Dag Lindström, and Jeppe Büchert Netterström. 2020. "Time Cycles of Homicide in the Early Modern Nordic Area." *Nordic Journal of Criminology* 21:152–69.

Kivivuori, Janne, Mona Rautelin, Guðbjörg Sigrûn Bergsdóttir, Sven Granath, Jónas Orri Jónasson, Petri Karonen, Anu Koskivirta, Martti Lehti, Dag Lindström, Jeppe Büchert Netterström, and Mikkel Møller Okholm. 2020. *Historical Homicide Monitor 2.0: General Instructions and Coding Manual*. Research Briefs 40/2020 Institute of Criminology and Legal Policy, University of Helsinki (1) 20–21.

LaFree, Gary. 1998. *Losing Legitimacy: Street Crime and the Decline of Social Institutions*. Boulder, CO: Westview.

Lane, Roger. 1979. *Violent Death in the City: Suicide, Accident, and Murder in Nineteenth-Century Philadelphia*. Cambridge, MA: Harvard University Press.

Lehti, Martti, Janne Kivivuori, Guðbjörg S. Bergsdóttir, Heidi Engvold, Sven Granath, Jónas O. Jónasson, Marieke Liem, Mikkel M. Okholm, Mona Rautelin, Karoliina Suonpää, and Vibeke S. Syversen. 2019. *Nordic Homicide Report: Homicide in Denmark, Finland, Iceland, Norway, and Sweden, 2007–2016*. Research Briefs 37/2019.

Lindström, Dag. 2008. "Homicide in Scandinavia: Long-Term Trends and Their Interpretation." In *Violence in Europe: Historical and Comparative Perspectives*, edited by Sophie Body-Gendrot and Pieter Spierenburg, 43–64. New York: Springer Verlag.

McLaurin, Melton A. 1991. *Celia: A Slave*. Athens: University of Georgia Press.

McMahon, Richard. 2013. *Homicide in Pre-famine and Famine Ireland*. Liverpool: Liverpool University Press.

Mitchell, Linda E., Mark Micale, and Philip Dwyer. 2018. "History, Violence, and Steven Pinker." *Historical Reflections* 44:1.

Monkkonen, Eric. H. 2001. *Murder in New York City*. Berkeley: University of California Press.

Österberg, Eva. 1991. "Social Arena or Theatre of Power? The Courts, Crime and the Early Modern State in Sweden." In *Theatres of Power: Social Control and Criminality in Historical Perspective*, edited by Heikki Pihlajamäki, 8–24. Helsinki: Matthias Calonius Society.

———. 1995. "Gender, Class, and the Courts: Scandinavia." In *Crime History and Histories of Crime: Studies in the Historiography of Crime and Criminal Justice in Modern History*, edited by Clive Emsley and Louis A. Knafla, 47–65. Westport: Greenwood Press.

Österberg, Eva, and Dag Lindström. 1988. *Crime and Social Control in Medieval and Early Modern Swedish Towns*. Studia Historica Upsaliensia. Uppsala: Acta Universitatis Upsaliensis.

Pfeifer, Michael J. 2006. *Rough Justice: Lynching in America, 1874–1947*. Urbana: University of Illinois Press.

———. 2011. *The Roots of Rough Justice: Origins of American Lynching*. Urbana: University of Illinois Press.

———. 2014. "At the Hands of Parties Unknown? The State of the Field of Lynching Scholarship." *Journal of American History* 101 (3): 832–46.

Pinker, Steven. 2011. *The Better Angels of Our Nature: Why Violence Has Declined*. New York: Viking.

Rogers, John D. 1987. *Crime, Justice, and Society in Colonial Sri Lanka*. London Studies on South Asia 5. London: Curzon Press.

Roth, Randolph. 2001. "Child Murder in New England." *Social Science History* 25:101–47.

———. 2012a. *American Homicide*. Cambridge, MA: Belknap Press of Harvard University Press.

———. 2012b. "Measuring Feelings and Beliefs That May Facilitate (or Deter) Homicide." *Homicide Studies* 16:196–217.

———. 2017. "Criminologists and Historians of Crime: A Partnership Well Worth Pursuing." *Crime, History, and Societies* 21 (2): 387–400.

Roth, Randolph, Cornelia Hughes Dayton, Kenneth Wheeler, James Watkinson, Robb Haberman, James M. Denham, and Douglas L. Eckberg. 2008. "The Historical Violence Database: A Collaborative Research Project on the History of Violent Crime and Violent Death." *Historical Methods* 41:81–98.

Roth, Randolph, Wendy Regoeczi, and Rania Issa. 2019. "The Difficulty of Counting the Number of Children Killed in Homicides in the United States, 1959–1988." Paper presented at the annual meeting of the American Society of Criminology in San Francisco, CA.

Savolainen, Jukka, Martti Lehti, and Janne Kivivuori. 2008. "Historical Origins of a Cross-National Puzzle: Homicide in Finland, 1750 to 2000." *Homicide Studies* 12:67–89.

Spierenburg, Pieter. 2008. *A History of Murder: Personal Violence in the Middle Ages to the Present*. New York: Polity.

Stone, Lawrence. 2008. "Interpersonal Violence in English Society, 1300–1800." *Past and Present* 101 (1983): 22–23

Tolnay, Stewart E., and E. M. Beck. 1995. *A Festival of Violence: An Analysis of Southern Lynchings, 1882–1930*. Urbana: University of Illinois Press.

Waldrep, Christopher. 2002. *The Many Faces of Judge Lynch: Extralegal Violence and Punishment in America*. 2nd ed. New York: Palgrave Macmillan.

Williams, Kidada E. 2012. *They Left Great Marks on Me: African American Testimonies of Racial Violence from Emancipation to World War I*. New York: New York University Press.

Wood, Arthur Lewis. 1961. *Crime and Aggression in Changing Ceylon: A Sociological Analysis of Homicide, Suicide, and Economic Crime*. Transactions of the American Philosophical Society, n.s., 51, pt. 8. Philadelphia: Literary Licensing, LLC.

Ylikangas, Heikki, Petri Karonen, and Martti Lehti. 2001. *Five Centuries of Violence in Finland and the Baltic Area*. Columbus: Ohio State University Press.

2

Thirty Years of Homicide in America

A Postmortem of 1990–2019

Mark T. Berg and Ethan M. Rogers

Introduction

Over the past two decades, much has been written about the contours of American crime trends. This body of scholarship has offered compelling stories about the factors responsible for the Great American Crime Decline in the 1990s (Zimring 2007). The recent unforeseen surge in homicide rates across American cities is a direct reminder that crime trends remain an enduring puzzle. Similar to other macrolevel social indicators, such as unemployment or consumer prices, crime rates must be subject to constant scientific monitoring. As far back as Durkheim (1895), scholars have held the belief that the form and frequency of crime varies according to the conditions of the social system (Rosenfeld and Messner 2010). Crime is a product of social change. A sudden rise in homicides among young adult males, for instance, may indicate something crucial about emerging shifts in the unique social fabric of that population. Perhaps a crucial lesson of the Great American Crime Decline is that temporal differences in crime rates are a type of barometer through which to gauge the performance of social institutions. Reflecting on that era, "many are now convinced that something fundamental changed in America during the early 1990s" (Baumer and Wolff 2014, 5). There has always been a great deal of policy interest in patterns of homicide and "the practitioner . . . almost always turns to the question of change" (Rosenfeld 2018, 5). Accurate and timely information on the nature of crime trends is thus essential to evaluations of crime control policy.

The study of crime trends is built on basic descriptive evidence of stability and change. Description is a cornerstone of the scientific enterprise. As it goes, explanations for contemporary crime trends must be developed around basic facts about the nature of the problem. These facts are needed to propose and evaluate theoretically derived hypotheses about the forces responsible for crime trends. Disaggregation proves to be a valuable device; there is no singular homicide trend but rather one of many attributes. Aggregate homicide rates, indeed, tend to mask sharp differences among demographic subgroups, weapon type, and circumstance—each of which deserves analytical attention. Research has shown, for instance, that a disproportionate fraction of the homicide increase in the late 1980s and early 1990s was concentrated among young African American males (Blumstein, Rivara, and Rosenfeld 2000). Relying solely on the total homicide rate can thus lead to misleading conclusions about causes of temporal variation in rates.

To advance ongoing scientific efforts to monitor and explain contemporary crime trends, this chapter provides a descriptive portrait of trends in homicide victimization in the United States over the thirty-year period from 1990 through 2019. We focus on this period because patterns of homicide in the era preceding—the 1970s and 80s—are well-documented elsewhere (e.g., Blumstein, Rivara, and Rosenfeld 2000; National Research Council 2008). To ascertain detailed information about components of the aggregate homicide trend, we partition rates by gender, race, age, and weapon type. The chapter briefly describes how changes in the lethality of crime might inform our understanding of homicide trends (Berg 2019); it then turns to a discussion of the recent 2020 uptick in murder rates across American cities.

Documenting Homicide Trends

Data

For the purpose of exploring homicide victimization trends from 1990 through 2019, we use a multiply imputed national database of murder and nonnegligent manslaughter with information dating back to 1976 derived from the Supplemental Homicide Reports (SHR) (Fox 2020). As part of the Uniform Crime Reporting (UCR) program, the SHR contains information pertaining to circumstances of each homicide incident known to law enforcement, including demographic indicators of victim and offender, relationship between victim and offender, and type of weapon used. Even though the SHR provides the most comprehensive public account of the nation's homicide burden, the data system is not without limitations. A substantial amount of data is missing from the SHR owing to incomplete cases (i.e., item missingness) and agency nonreporting (i.e., unit missingness). Fox (2020) implemented a two-stage multivariate strategy to add incomplete case information on homicide incidents and adjust for cases not recorded in the SHR (see Fox and Swatt 2009). To compute homicide rates per capita, we divided the SHR victimization counts for each year by population data obtained from the National Center for Health Statistics (NCHS) and multiplied that fraction by a constant of 100,000.

Aggregate Trends

Sizable and unforeseen changes in levels of violent crime arouse a great deal of interest among academics and policymakers alike in social factors responsible for the movements in trends. Periods of stability, however, are also noteworthy and meaningful. As described in detail elsewhere, the steep but short-lived increase in homicides beginning in the mid-1980s and followed by a sustained fall in the 1990s defines an important period in the contemporary history of lethal violence (Rosenfeld 2018). The past thirty years have also witnessed fluctuations in homicide rates, but the period is mostly defined by a continuation of the long-term decline from the rate's peak, which occasionally has been interrupted by episodic departures.

Figure 2.1 displays homicide victimization and offending rates from 1990 to 2019 in the United States. As shown, the homicide victimization rate declined by about 47 percent from 1990 (9.39 per 100,000) to 2019 (5.00 per 100,000). This drop was driven, in large part, by the forces of the Great American Crime Decline. From its peak in 1991 until around 2000, the rate of victimization fell by about 43 percent, with no clear indication of a sharp reversal. Further inspection of SHR data indicates that from 1993 through 1999, year-to-year declines were in the range of 6 to 10 percent. After 2000, homicide victimization rates remained largely stable, nearing 5.5 to 6 per capita until another albeit slower decline unfolded from 2006 to 2011—an era corresponding with the onset of the Great Recession (see Parker, Mancik, and Stansfield 2017). This period saw an unforeseen spike in homicide victimizations in 2015 and 2016 (Rosenfeld and Fox 2019), the largest year-to-year increases since 1991. Specifically, homicide victimization rates increased by 21 percent from 2014 (4.45 per 100,000) to 2016 (5.39 per 100,000), returning rates to levels last seen in 2008. The recent trends in homicide victimization are noteworthy when placed in the context of the era immediately preceding the 1990s: rates of homicide victimization have hovered around 4 and 6 over the past twenty years, whereas they varied between 8 and 10 during the twenty-five years prior to the Great American Crime Decline. Despite some growth in homicide victimization rates in the past several years, they remain far below rates of the 1970s, 80s, and early 90s. The current chapter focuses on patterns of homicide *victimization*; it is worth stressing that homicide

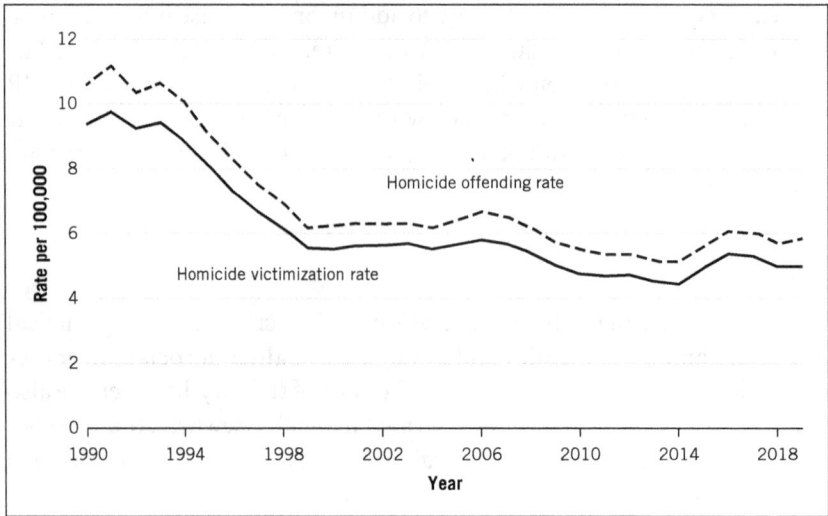

Figure 2.1 U.S. Homicide Victimization and Offending Rates, 1990–2019

offending and *victimization* trends move in tandem despite relatively elevated levels of offending. Of course, this pattern largely results from the fact that victimization and offending counts are generated in the same incidents.

Trends by Sex

Disaggregating homicide victimization trends by the sex of the victim reveals the extent to which males disproportionately die because of homicide relative to women (see Fox and Fridel 2017). As shown in figure 2.2, both men and women experienced a general decline in homicide rate from the early 1990s onward. From 1990 to 2019 specifically, the homicide rate for males and females declined by about 47 percent (14.81 to 7.92) and 49 percent (4.23 to 2.17), respectively. Much of the narrowing of the gender gap is due to the substantial decline in male victimizations through approximately 2000. The *absolute* difference between men and women in homicide victimization decreased from 10.58 to 5.75—a decline of roughly 47 percent. However, the *relative* difference in homicide victimization rates between men and women persist. The shaded columns in the background of figure 2.2 show a slight reduction in the male-to-female rate ratio in the late 1990s followed by a quick return to the male-to-female differences identified in the early 90s. In the past decade, the male-to-female rate ratio has remained above 3.5, meaning that, after adjusting for population levels, there were approximately three hundred and fifty male victims of homicide for every hundred female victims of homicide.

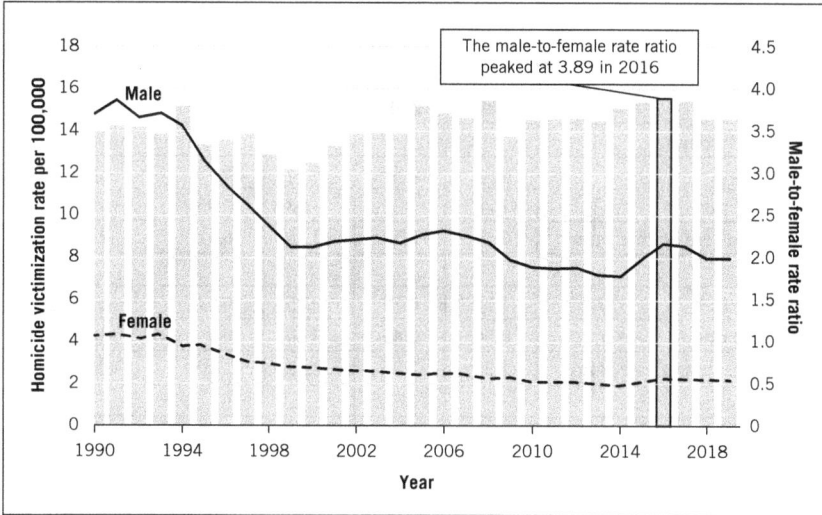

Figure 2.2 U.S. Homicide Victimization Rates by Sex and Male-to-Female Rate Ratios, 1990–2019

Sex differences in homicide victimization vary considerably across the victim-offender relationship (see table 2.1). First, while the rates of victimization by family members, acquaintances, and strangers are higher among men than women, the rate of victimization by an intimate partner is higher among women. In 2019, for instance, nearly one woman (0.95) per 100,000 women in the United States was killed by an intimate partner. By contrast, men were killed by an intimate partner less than half that rate (0.40 per 100,000 men). Second, women are most often killed by their intimate partners, while intimate partners are the least common offender against male victims. Third, male-to-female rate ratios are much larger among stranger and acquaintance homicides than intimate partner homicides. Most notably, in 2019, approximately one thousand men were killed by a stranger per hundred women. In contrast, among intimate partner homicides, approximately fifty men were killed per hundred women. There is notable variation in the trends in male-to-female rate ratios. Male-to-female rate ratios of stranger homicides, for instance, have increased by more than 50 percent over the past three decades. The gender gap in family killings has declined. Note that the declining male-to-female rate ratios of intimate partner homicides suggest that the gap is *increasing*—not decreasing—meaning that female rates are increasingly exceeding male rates. These patterns underscore the importance of disaggregating sex-specific violence trends by victim-offender relationship (see also Fox and Fridel 2017; Lauritsen and Heimer 2008). Efforts to understand sex differences in homicide fall short without a consideration

TABLE 2.1 U.S. HOMICIDE VICTIMIZATION RATES PER 100,000 BY SEX
AND MALE-TO-FEMALE RATE RATIOS BY RELATIONSHIP TO OFFENDER

	1990	2000	2010	2019	1990 to 2019 % Change
Intimate Partner					
Male rate	0.96	0.46	0.38	0.40	−58.3%
Female rate	1.70	1.23	0.98	0.95	−44.3%
Male-to-female rate ratio	0.57	0.37	0.38	0.42	−25.1%
Family					
Male rate	1.26	0.88	0.85	0.94	−25.3%
Female rate	0.50	0.43	0.40	0.45	−10.1%
Male-to-female rate ratio	2.53	2.06	2.12	2.10	−17.0%
Acquaintance					
Male rate	8.64	4.62	4.16	4.42	−48.8%
Female rate	1.45	0.75	0.51	0.57	−60.7%
Male-to-female rate ratio	5.95	6.15	8.11	7.75	+30.3%
Stranger					
Male rate	3.95	2.50	2.15	2.16	−45.3%
Female rate	0.58	0.30	0.18	0.21	−64.4%
Male-to-female rate ratio	6.77	8.32	11.99	10.40	+53.6%

of variation across intimate partner, family member, acquaintance, and stranger relationships.

Trends by Race

Black individuals experience levels of homicide victimization risk many times those of other racial groups—a pattern evident in decades of homicide data. The racial gap in homicide widened by a large degree during the mid-to-late 1980s, largely due to rising rates among young Black males (Blumstein, Rivara, and Rosenfeld 2000). Although the racial gap has narrowed since, it remains pronounced—Black homicide victimization rates far exceed those of other population groups on a yearly basis. The graphs in figure 2.3 illustrate the nature of these disparities over the past thirty years. The scale of the racial differences in homicide victimization between Black, white, and other groups is evident in the graph on the left-hand side. In 1990, the Black homicide victimization rate was 35.7 per 100,000, while the white rate neared 5.6 per 100,000. Racial comparisons in homicide trends, however, are more readily grasped by multiplying the victimization rates for the racial groups by four (displayed on the right-hand side). This adjusts the rates upward. Despite the sizable gap between Black homicide victimization rates and the other two groups, each similarly benefited from a considerable decrease in killings during the era beginning in the mid-to-late 1990s. For instance, Black

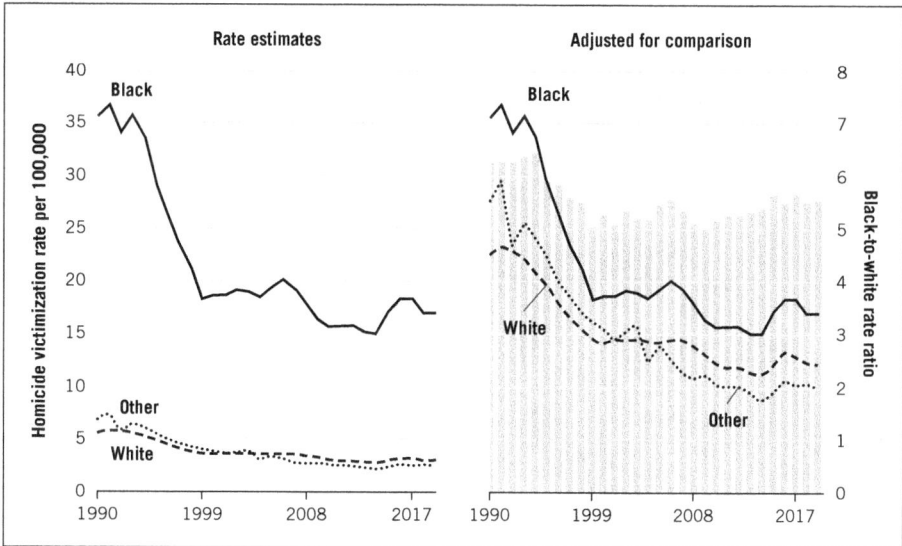

Figure 2.3 U.S. Homicide Victimization Rates by Race and Black-to-White Rate Ratios, 1990–2019 (*Note: In right panel, victimization rates for white and other racial groups are multiplied by four for comparison purposes. Shaded columns represent Black-to-white rate ratios.*)

rates fell by about 52 percent from their peak levels in 1990 to around 17.1 in 2019. White rates plummeted more than 46 percent during the same thirty-year period.

The Black-to-white rate ratios are plotted behind the trend lines as shaded columns. The rate ratios for 1990 indicate that there were more than six Black homicide victims for every incident involving a white victim. The Black-to-white rate ratio declined through the 1990s and has since hovered between 5.1 and 5.7 in most years, meaning the number of Black individuals killed for every white victim has not exhibited significant variation in the past two decades. Aside from a brief period in the mid-2000s, when Black rates of homicide victimization trended upward or downward, the white and other category rates generally followed a similar pattern.

Just how much Black men are disproportionately burdened by homicide is brought into sharp focus when rates are measured relative to their proportional representation in the United States population. Figure 2.4 displays the percentage of homicide victimizations experienced by white and Black men across different age groupings in 1990 and 2019 indexed against their representation in the population. White twenty-five-to-forty-nine-year-old men in 1990 accounted for approximately 20 percent of all killings that year and about 17 percent of the total U.S. population. Black men in the same age

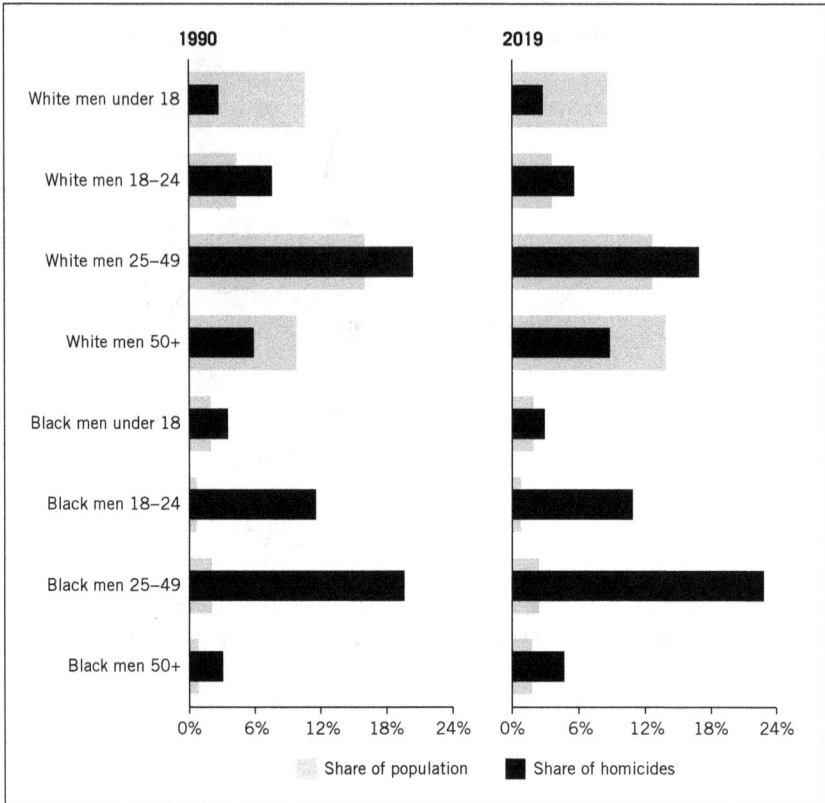

Figure 2.4 Share of U.S. Population and Homicide Victimization among White and Black Men by Age Group, 1990 and 2019

bracket suffered about 19 percent of homicide victimizations that year, but their representation accounted for only about 4 percent of the total population. These observations make clear that the burden of homicide remains excessively felt by young Black men relative to other groups. Any credible explanation of homicide victimization patterns over the past thirty years must account for this demographic fact.

Trends by Age

Nearly everywhere it is studied, serious violence is highly concentrated among younger segments of the population. Homicide is no different. Young adults are the most vulnerable to deadly violence both as victims and offenders. The trends shown in figure 2.5 illustrate the age-graded nature of homicide victimization over the past thirty years in the United States. Across the time

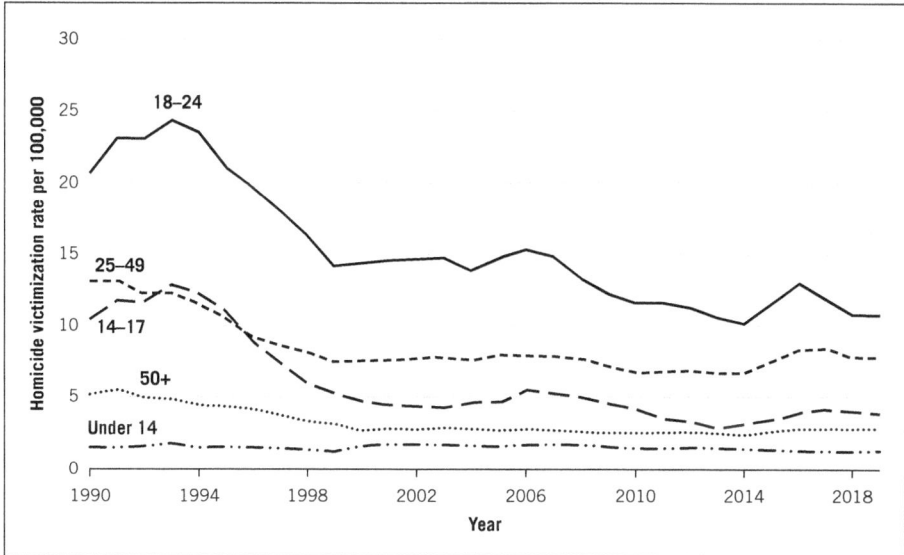

Figure 2.5 U.S. Homicide Victimization Rates by Age Group, 1990–2019

series, individuals under the age of fourteen have suffered the lowest levels of homicide, followed by those fifty and older. Eighteen-to-twenty-four-year-olds have been killed at the highest rates. In 1993, the rate of victimization among eighteen-to-twenty-four-year-old adults was over 24 per 100,000 and then fell more than 41 percent by 2000 to 14.3. By 2019, the rate was roughly 56 percent below its peak in the 1990s.

Some scholars have claimed that the late 1990s marked the end of an era that began in the 1980s in which the United States was besieged by an "epidemic of youth violence" (Cook and Laub 1998). One observation from figure 2.5 is somewhat consistent with this position: levels of homicide among fourteen-to-seventeen-year-old youth steadily climbed into the early 1990s to a series high of 12.9 in 1993. For this group of youth, rates of homicide victimization remained elevated through the mid-1990s and dropped thereafter to levels like those for much older adults. Generally, despite large differences in the burden of homicides across different age groups, the trends for each follow a common trajectory marked by comparable peaks and valleys.

Figure 2.6 illustrates different age-homicide victimization curves for three periods of the thirty-year series. Comparing the three curves, it is apparent that 1990 was the deadliest year for individuals of all ages—that is, regardless of whether someone was fifteen, thirty, or forty-five, rates of homicide victimization were far higher in 1990 than in 2000 and 2019. The 2000 and 2019 trends are typical of the general age-homicide curve (Blumstein 2017). It

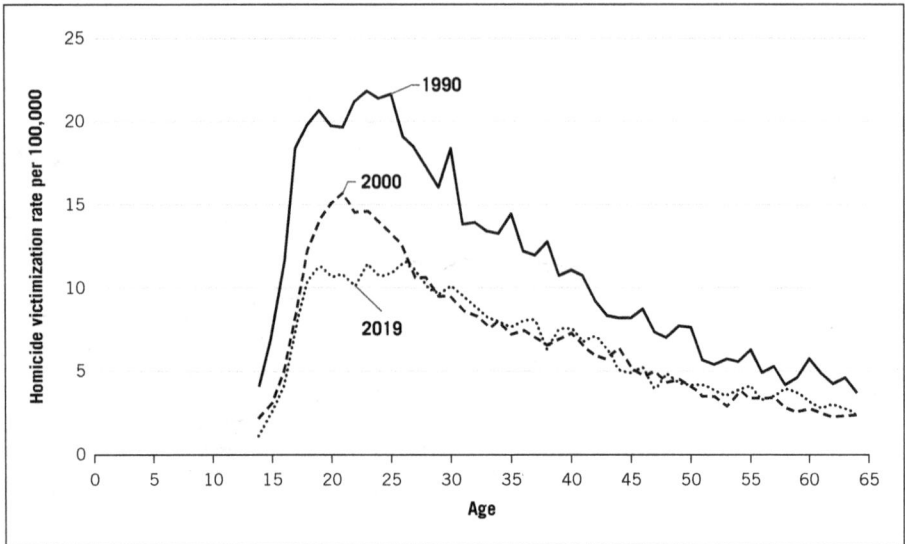

Figure 2.6 U.S. Age Homicide Victimization Curve, 1990, 2000, and 2019

appears that individuals roughly between ages eighteen and twenty-six have benefited the most from the decline in homicide rates from 1990 through 2019.

Figure 2.6 also shows how, in most years, victimization risk rises through adolescence, reaching its highest point in the young adult years. Risk levels then gradually decline throughout the life course. Homicide victimization risk does not fall back to its levels preceding the peak risk period in emerging adulthood until individuals reach their early forties. The figure shows that since 1990, the peak age of homicide risk has shifted to younger ages, perhaps because of the overall shrinking levels of homicide among older individuals. There are some noteworthy departures in the 2019 curve from the earlier curves: not only is its peak victimization age younger but also the duration of peak risk years is flatter and longer than before. Given the modest variation in the peak and shape of the different age curves, it does not appear that homicide victimization rates are defined by strict invariance. These basic descriptive patterns suggest that birth cohort replacement might hold clues to the puzzle of modern violence trends (see also O'Brien and Stockard 2009, 97). For instance, a longitudinal analysis of the Pittsburgh Youth Study found that cohorts of adolescents who came of age in the years following the peak crime era of the early 1990s reported a significantly lower prevalence of violence involvement relative to same-age youth from earlier cohorts (Berg et al. 2016).

It is instructive to consider the degree of age homogamy between offenders and victims to determine whether younger people kill younger people or whether younger people are targeted disproportionately by offenders of all ages. This information casts critical light on the role of age in the convergence of homicide victims and offenders, especially the ages of those responsible for the deaths of the group most at risk in the present analysis: eighteen-to-twenty-four-year-olds. Table 2.2 arrays information pertaining to the ages of offender and victim in homicide incidents in 2019. Note that the offender and victimization age groupings are not perfectly aligned. Nevertheless, the table provides evidence of age homogamy. For instance, the column of eighteen-to-twenty-four-year-old victims reveals that most of their offenders are from the same age group, followed by offenders who are slightly older—in the twenty-five-to-thirty-four-year-old bracket. By comparison, most victims under the age of fourteen are killed by much older individuals, with nearly 35 percent of offenders between the ages of twenty-five and thirty-four.

Trends by Weaponry

Firearms are of central importance to scholarly debates regarding the nature of deadly violence in America. Trends in homicide victimization must be disaggregated by weapon type to understand how weaponry governs year-to-year variation in the burden of killings. The left-hand graph in figure 2.7 clearly illustrates how, each year, most homicides are committed with a gun. Only a fraction of homicide victimizations involve a knife or other type of weapon. As was the case throughout much of the 1970s and 80s (Blumstein, Rivara, and Rosenfeld 2000), all of the increase in homicide victimizations during the early 1990s resulted from rising firearm homicides. The number of incidents involving knives and other weaponry remained mostly stable. The rate of firearm homicide victimizations peaked at 6.7 per 100,000 in 1993 and fell by more than 40 percent by the next decade. Similarly, incidents involving knives reached their high mark of 1.67 per 100,000 slightly earlier, in 1991, and declined by nearly 43 percent by 2000. Homicide incidents in which the

TABLE 2.2 PERCENT OF HOMICIDE VICTIMIZATIONS INVOLVING OFFENDERS ACROSS AGE GROUPS BY VICTIM AGE, 2019

Offender Age Group	All Victimizations	by Victim Age Group				
		Under 14	14–17	18–24	25–49	50+
Under 18	5.9%	4.3%	32.5%	9.0%	3.7%	3.3%
18–24	28.9%	27.9%	42.1%	55.7%	23.0%	15.2%
25–34	31.0%	35.4%	11.6%	24.8%	37.8%	22.8%
35–49	22.8%	27.5%	9.8%	8.0%	27.2%	27.5%
50+	11.5%	4.9%	4.0%	2.5%	8.3%	31.2%
Total	100.0%	100.0%	100.0%	100.0%	100.0%	100.0%

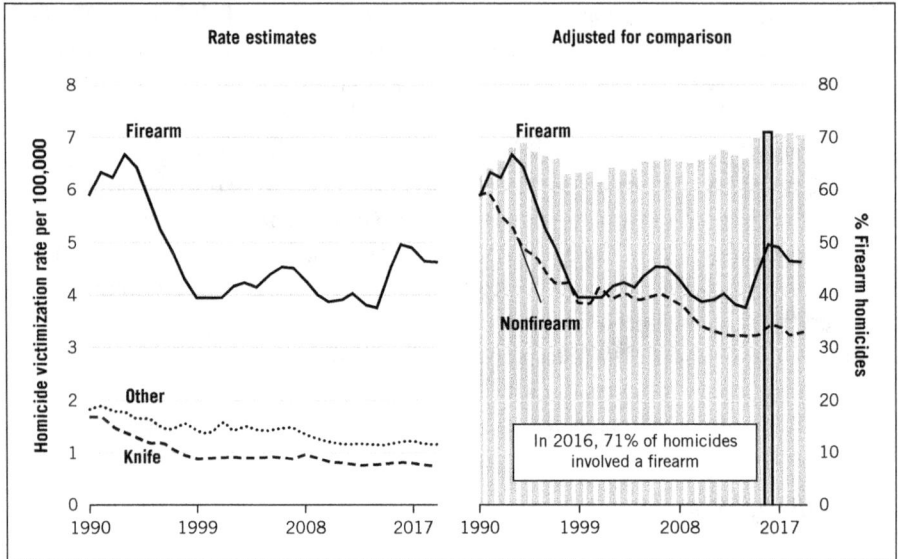

Figure 2.7 U.S. Homicide Victimization Rates by Weapon Type and Percentage of Homicides That Involve Firearms, 1990–2019 (*Note: In right panel, nonfirearm victimization rates are multiplied by 1.68 to adjust the rates to the levels of firearm homicide in 1990. Shaded columns represent the percentage of homicides that involved firearms.*)

assailant used some other type of weapon fell by about 30 percent over the same window of years.

The panel on the right-hand side of figure 2.7 combines knives and other types of weaponry into a single category: nonfirearm incidents. For ease of comparison, this omnibus category is multiplied by a constant of 1.68, adjusting the rates to the levels of firearm homicide in 1990. Combined, the two graphs in figure 2.7 convey that firearm and nonfirearm homicide have often fallen in a similar fashion; however, increases tend to be especially dramatic among firearm homicides. For instance, following the large decrease of the mid-1990s, firearm homicides began to gradually climb until they crested around 2006—a 15 percent increase. Nonfirearm homicides remained more or less stable during that period—a 4 percent decrease. Additionally, from 2014 to 2016, the firearm homicide rate increased by 32 percent, but a similar change was not evident in the nonfirearm rates.

The columns in the graph on the right side of figure 2.7 correspond to the percentage of total homicide victimizations each year committed with a firearm. The share of firearm homicides does not vary significantly from year to year—in the thirty-year era examined here, the percentage shifted between 61 and 69 percent until the past few years. Since 2015, approximately 70 percent of victims die by gunfire each year, a level not previously recorded for such a stretch of consecutive years. This increase in the share of firearm homicides appears driven by the unexpected rise in the firearm homicide rate in 2015 and 2016 rather than any decreases in nonfirearm homicide.

The weapon trends are further disaggregated by demographic group in table 2.3, which reveals a few noteworthy patterns. First, the disproportionate killing of Black men appears driven by firearm-related victimizations. In 1990, the firearm victimization rate among Black men (45.4 per 100,000) was nearly 1.23 times the firearm victimization rate among white men (36.9 per 100,000). The nonfirearm rate, however, was lower among Black men than white men. This pattern has been exacerbated over the past thirty years. In 2019, 85.3 percent of Black male victims were killed by gunfire—a share much higher than white males (63.9 percent), Black females (66.5 percent), and white females (48.9 percent). Furthermore, the figure shows that across the board, *no group* has experienced a decrease in the proportion of its homicides committed with firearms. Among Black women, for instance, the proportion of gun homicide victimizations has grown appreciably with each decade to the point where the share in 2019 is 43 percent higher than in 1990.

Altogether, these disaggregated trends suggest that gun homicides contribute enormously to the total homicide victimization burden. This fact was obvious thirty years ago and remains in the present era—perhaps more so than before. Whatever policy choice expands access to firearms in the population will likely contribute to rising homicide rates.

TABLE 2.3 U.S. HOMICIDE VICTIMIZATION RATES BY WEAPON AND FIREARM SHARE ACROSS RACE AND SEX

	1990	2000	2010	2019	1990 to 2019 % Change
Black Male					
Firearm rate	45.4	40.0	32.6	39.8	−12.3%
Nonfirearm rate	16.0	7.8	7.1	6.9	−57.0%
% Firearms	74.0%	80.0%	82.1%	85.3%	+15.3%
White Male					
Firearm rate	36.9	23.4	22.4	24.4	−33.7%
Nonfirearm rate	22.6	15.5	14.3	13.8	−38.8%
% Firearms	62.0%	60.2%	61.0%	63.9%	+3.1%
Black Female					
Firearm rate	6.5	4.1	3.3	5.4	−16.8%
Nonfirearm rate	7.5	4.5	3.0	2.7	−63.6%
% Firearms	46.5%	47.7%	52.4%	66.5%	+43.0%
White Female					
Firearm rate	10.3	7.6	7.0	7.7	−25.5%
Nonfirearm rate	11.9	9.7	8.2	8.0	−32.7%
% Firearms	46.4%	44.1%	46.1%	48.9%	+5.5%

Other Considerations

Lethality of Crime

Research on homicide could benefit from a shift in focus to temporal variation in dispute escalation or lethality. A singular focus on homicide ignores the prospect that the frequency of homicide changes relative to the volume of interpersonal conflicts (see Berg 2019). The volume of interpersonal disputes in a society and the proportion of those that result in deadly violence can vary independently (Felson, Berg, and Rogers 2014). Researchers must account for the fact that killings often result from the escalation of nonlethal disputes—which tend to be frequent but minor. For instance, a country's homicide rate, in many ways, reflects both the tendency of its citizens to become involved in hostile disputes *and* the tendency of the aggrieved to use lethal means to resolve those disputes. To understand aggregate trends in lethal violence, researchers must study the nature of violent incidents rather than the mere frequency of incident outcomes (Berg 2019). Crime and deadly violence are not synonymous social indicators. The approach to studying the nature of incidents, indeed, conceives of homicide, typically the culmination of moralistic conflicts, as a numerator and minor acts of aggression and predation (i.e., property crime) as denominators. Lethality thus differs across time and among groups because of changes in either of these constituent pieces.

The literature on violence and the social psychology of aggression provides a general framework to understand temporal and spatial variation in lethality (e.g., Courtwright 2009; Tedeschi 1997). According to this research, individuals seldom express their grievances; most injustices fade away with memory. Few disputes lead to verbal aggression, and a smaller number result in physical violence. Only a fraction result in deadly altercations. Furthermore, disputants are not necessarily motivated to engage in violence at the beginning of a dispute and are instead motivated by the actions of the adversary. Variation in the frequency of lethality results from an expansion in opportunity structures that encourage grievances and thus the formation of disputes, particularly in activities beyond the usual reach of legal protections. Another important source of trends in lethal escalation may be cultural mechanisms related to honor and the collective authority granted to the state to punish law violators (Baumer, Vélez, and Rosenfeld 2018). Moreover, the frequency by which disputes escalate to killings rise when lethal weaponry becomes increasingly accessible. The accessibility of firearms depends, to some extent, on the structure of various legal restrictions. Over the past twenty years or so, several states have passed permissive gun laws, including some that allow so-called constitutional carry of concealed firearms (Cook and Goss 2020).

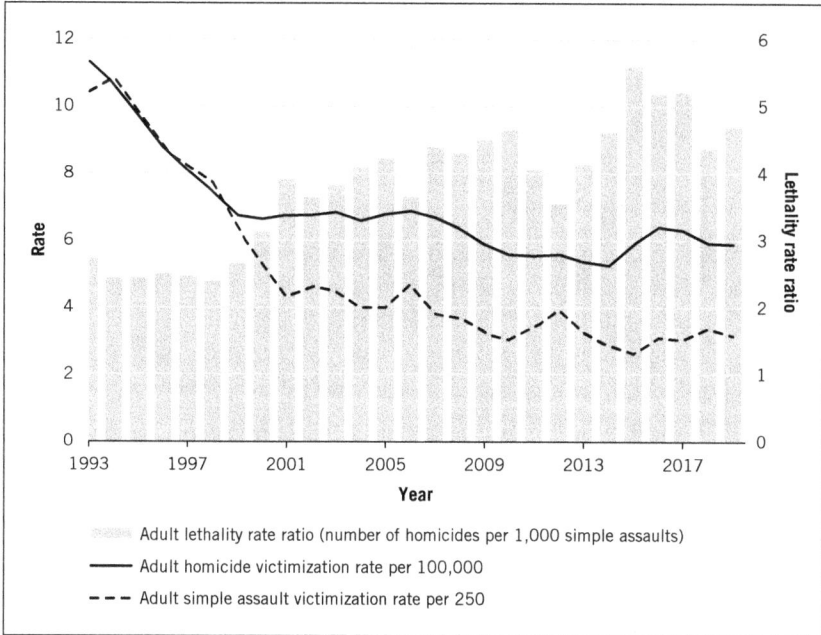

Figure 2.8 U.S. Homicide and Simple Assault Victimization Rates and Lethality Rate Ratios (Aged 18 and Older), 1993–2019

Figure 2.8 illustrates trends in the rate of homicide and simple assault victimization from 1993 through 2019 for persons aged eighteen and older in the United States. Simple assault victimizations per year were calculated using the NCVS Victimization Analysis Tool (NVAT) at www.bjs.gov. Note that trends are expressed in different per capita rates for comparison purposes. Additionally, the lethality rate ratios (the number of homicides per thousand simple assaults) are represented by shaded columns. The lethality ratio indicates the number of killings for every thousand simple assaults reported in the NCVS.

A few patterns deserve attention. First, the 1990 decline in simple assault follows a similar pattern to the 1990 decline in homicide. The rates of both homicide and simple assault declined by about 40 percent from 1993 to 1999 (40.3 percent and 38.9 percent, respectively). Second, while the decline in homicide rates began to slow in the 2000s, assault rates continued to trend downward. From 2000 to 2019, homicide rates declined by 11.2 percent, and simple assault rates declined by 41 percent. As is obvious in the figure, one cannot make claims about trends in violence from either assault or homicide rates alone. Third, due to divergence between homicide and simple assault rates in the early 2000s, lethality has risen over the past two decades—de-

spite the decline in homicide. Lethality rate ratios increased by about 50 percent, from 3.1 murders for every thousand simple assaults in 2000 to 4.7 murders for every thousand simple assaults in 2019. Conflict in America has
become deadlier with time.

The 2020 Homicide Spike

Preliminary reporting indicates a sharp rise in homicide in the first year of
the 2020s. While a full panel of official statistics has not yet been released,
even conservative estimates suggest that the 2020 rise in homicide will exceed
the previous largest year-to-year increase of 12.7 percent in 1968 (Rosenfeld,
Abt, and Lopez 2021). For instance, data that the FBI received from 12,974 law
enforcement agencies show that homicide rates were up 24.7 percent from
2019 (FBI Crime Data Explorer 2020). A 25 percent spike would bring the
U.S. homicide victimization rate to a level higher than any year in the twenty-first century, though still far lower than the peak rates of the late 80s and
early 90s (see fig. 2.9, column with dashed outline).

In figure 2.9, we display the homicide victimization trend for a sample
of 177 U.S. cities with populations over one hundred thousand (black line).
The 2019 and 2020 data were downloaded from the FBI's preliminary quarterly report—agencies were excluded if they did not follow reporting guidelines, had incomplete or inconsistent data, or had changes in reporting practices. The homicide victimization trends were then extended back to 1990
using data from the UCR program (Kaplan 2020). As shown, the trend for
this sample of cities closely parallels the U.S. homicide victimization trend.
For instance, homicide victimization rates from 1991 to 2000 among the city
sample and the U.S. total declined by 47 and 43 percent, respectively. In both
samples, homicide rates increased by about 20 percent from 2014 to 2016.
However, the 2020 spike appears to have been slightly larger among the city
sample than estimates for the U.S. total. Specifically, in the 177 U.S. cities
with populations over one hundred thousand, homicide victimization rates
increased by almost 37 percent from the previous year (see also Arthur and
Asher 2021; Rosenfeld, Abt, and Lopez 2021). Some of the country's biggest
cities—not included in these data owing to nonreporting—document even
greater spikes, with New York up 43 percent and Chicago up 55 percent
(Rosenfeld, Abt, and Lopez 2021). These preliminary data indicate that the
burden of the recent homicide surge has been widespread, albeit stronger in
larger cities.

Dissecting the sharp rise in 2020 by characteristics of the victims and
weapons involved will reveal important facts about the nature of the problem
and allow for a consideration of the forces responsible. For instance, whether the spike was more pronounced among a specific demographic group or

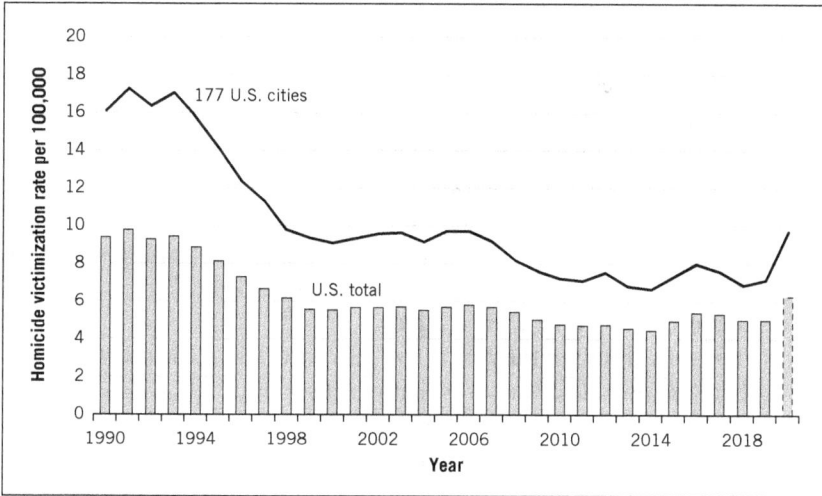

Figure 2.9 Homicide Victimization Rates for United States and 177 Large U.S. Cities, 1990–2020 (*Note: 2020 homicide victimization rates for the United States are based on preliminary estimates of a 24.9 percent increase. The 177 U.S. cities have populations over one hundred thousand.*)

whether it was widespread—as in 2015 and 2016 (Rosenfeld and Fox 2019)—remains a question to be explored by future research. Additionally, scholars must consider changes in lethality during this period. Preliminary FBI data show that, while homicide has increased, reported property crime is down 8 percent from the previous year. These diverging trends indicate possible growth in the lethality of predatory acts. Among the sample of 177 U.S. cities, for instance, the property lethality rate ratio rose by 47.8 percent from 2019 to 2020—from 2.3 to 3.5 homicides per thousand reported property crimes. Any convincing explanation for the recent spike in homicide victimization must account for what appears to be a sharp increase in lethality.

Conclusion

Descriptive investigation of homicide trends from 1990 to 2019 provides a postmortem of lethal violence in the wake of the Great American Crime Decline. The disaggregated rates suggest that, in many ways, the past is prologue. There is limited indication of substantial, sustained volatility in the thirty-year period of the data series. The total volume of killings has declined considerably relative to the early 1990s. However, relative differences in homicide victimization across demographic subgroups have remained stable—the downturns and upswings tend to move in tandem despite marked difference in levels. The burden of lethal violence continues to be disproportionally felt by young Black men year after year. And women continue to experience higher levels of homicide at the hands of intimate partners. As has been true for decades, firearms are the weapon of choice in most homicide victimization incidents. Thirty years of data confirm that firearms are implicated in most killings across demographic subgroups but are especially common in cases when Black men are targeted. The sustained stability of these known patterns is as fascinating and worthy of explanation as phases of instability. Perhaps this long-term persistence has greater meaning when one considers the numerous policy transformations and social changes that have occurred since 1990 in the United States.

While many trends of the past thirty years are defined by enduring patterns, there are notable departures that merit serious inquiry. For one, the evidence we present suggests the lethality of disputes is climbing despite the drop in homicide (Berg 2019). America has become increasingly peaceful with time, but its crime has become deadlier. The data also indicate that the peak of the age-homicide curve has flattened over successive years. Whether this changing form reflects cohort effects or something fundamental about shifts in the age-graded distribution of homicide risk should be the focus of future work. The first year of the new decade offers yet another puzzle for criminologists. Given the available evidence, albeit incomplete, it appears that 2020 will stand as one of the deadliest years in the United States in decades. Is the country at the beginning stages of a sustained increase in the rate of murder? Are we on the cusp of a new era of rising crime rates? Theory can offer a useful guide to predict where trends may be headed. None of this work, however, can be satisfactory or complete without the practice of data disaggregation in the series. Altogether, the descriptive patterns presented here should be inform existing hypotheses about the conditions responsible for changes in homicide victimization patterns and inspire new and compelling questions about the nature of American crime trends.

REFERENCES

Arthur, Rob, and Jeff Asher. 2021. "What Drove the Historically Large Murder Spike in 2020? The Pandemic, Police Violence, and More Guns All Contributed to an Unprecedented Rise in Murders across the United States." *Intercept*, February 21, 2021. Accessed March 14, 2021. https://theintercept.com/2021/02/21/2020-murder-homicide-rate-causes/.

Baumer, Eric P., María B. Vélez, and Richard Rosenfeld. 2018. "Bringing Crime Trends Back into Criminology: A Critical Assessment of the Literature and a Blueprint for Future Inquiry." *Annual Review of Criminology* 1 (1): 39–61. https://doi.org/10.1146/annurev-criminol-032317-092339.

Baumer, Eric P., and Kevin T. Wolff. 2014. "Evaluating Contemporary Crime Drop(s) in America, New York City, and Many Other Places." *Justice Quarterly* 31 (1): 5–38. https://doi.org/10.1080/07418825.2012.742127.

Berg, Mark T. 2019. "Trends in the Lethality of American Violence." *Homicide Studies* 23 (3): 262–84. https://doi.org/10.1177/1088767919849643.

Berg, Mark T., Eric Baumer, Richard Rosenfeld, and Rolf Loeber. 2016. "Dissecting the Prevalence and Incidence of Offending during the Crime Drop of the 1990s." *Journal of Quantitative Criminology* 32 (3): 377–96.

Blumstein, Alfred. 2017. "Some Trends in Homicide and Its Age-Crime Curves." In *The Handbook of Homicide*, edited by Fiona Brookman, Edward R. Maguire, and Mike Maguire, 44–53. Hoboken, NJ: John Wiley. https://doi.org/10.1002/9781118924501.ch3.

Blumstein, Alfred, Frederick P. Rivara, and Richard Rosenfeld. 2000. "The Rise and Decline of Homicide—and Why." *Annual Review of Public Health* 21 (1): 505–41. https://doi.org/10.1146/annurev.publhealth.21.1.505.

Cook, Philip J., and Kristin A. Goss. 2020. *The Gun Debate: What Everyone Needs to Know.* Oxford: Oxford University Press.

Cook, Philip J., and John H. Laub. 1998. "The Unprecedented Epidemic in Youth Violence." *Crime and Justice* 24 (January): 27–64. https://doi.org/10.1086/449277.

Courtwright, David T. 2009. *Violent Land: Single Men and Social Disorder from the Frontier to the Inner City.* Cambridge, MA: Harvard University Press.

Durkheim, Emile. 1895. *The Rules of Sociological Method.* Chicago: Alcan Press.

FBI Crime Data Explorer. 2020. "Preliminary Quarterly Uniform Crime Report." March 14, 2019. https://crime-data-explorer.app.cloud.gov/explorer/national/united-states/prelim-quarter.

Felson, Richard B., Mark T. Berg, and Meghan L. Rogers. 2014. "Bring a Gun to a Gunfight: Armed Adversaries and Violence across Nations." *Social Science Research* 47: 79–90.

Fox, James Alan. 2020. *Imputed Supplementary Homicide Reports, 1976–2019.* Boston, Northeastern University.

Fox, James Alan, and Emma E. Fridel. 2017. "Gender Differences in Patterns and Trends in U.S. Homicide, 1976–2015." *Violence and Gender* 4 (2): 37–43. https://doi.org/10.1089/vio.2017.0016.

Fox, James Alan, and Marc L. Swatt. 2009. "Multiple Imputation of the Supplementary Homicide Reports, 1976–2005." *Journal of Quantitative Criminology* 25 (1): 51–77. https://doi.org/10.1007/s10940-008-9058-2.

Kaplan, Jacob. 2021. Jacob Kaplan's Concatenated Files: Uniform Crime Reporting Program Data: Offenses Known and Clearances by Arrest, 1960-2019:ucr_offenses_known_yearly_1960_2019_csv.zip. Ann Arbor, MI: Inter-university Consortium for Political and Social Research [distributor], 2021-01-16. https://doi.org/10.3886/E100707V16-74013.

Lauritsen, Janet, and Karen Heimer. 2008. "The Gender Gap in Violent Victimization, 1973–2004." *Journal of Quantitative Criminology* 24:124–47.

National Research Council (NRC). 2008. *Understanding Crime Trends: Workshop Report.* Washington, DC: National Academies Press. https://doi.org/10.17226/12472.

O'Brien, Robert M., and Jean Stockard. 2009. "Can Cohort Replacement Explain Changes in the Relationship Between Age and Homicide Offending?" *Journal of Quantitative Criminology* 25:79–101.

Parker, Karen F., Ashley Mancik, and Richard Stansfield. 2017. "American Crime Drops: Investigating the Breaks, Dips and Drops in Temporal Homicide." *Social Science Research* 64:154–70. https://doi.org/10.1016/j.ssresearch.2016.09.029.

Rosenfeld, Richard. 2018. "Studying Crime Trends: Normal Science and Exogenous Shocks." *Criminology* 56 (1): 5–26. https://doi.org/10.1111/1745-9125.12170.

Rosenfeld, Richard, and James Alan Fox. 2019. "Anatomy of the Homicide Rise." *Homicide Studies* 23 (3): 202–24. https://doi.org/10.1177/1088767919848821.

Rosenfeld, Richard, and Ernesto Lopez. 2020. "Pandemic, Social Unrest, and Crime in U.S. Cities." *Federal Sentencing Reporter* 33 (1–2): 72–82.

Rosenfeld, Richard, and Steven F. Messner. 2010. "The Normal Crime Rate, the Economy, and Mass Incarceration: An Institutional Anomie Perspective of Crime Control Policy." In *Criminology and Public Policy: Putting Theory to Work*, edited by Hugh Barlow and Scott Decker, 45–65. Philadelphia: Temple University Press.

Tedeschi, James T. 1997. "A Social Interactionist Interpretation of the Motives for Youth Violence." *Nebraska Symposium on Motivation* 44:179–222.

Zimring, Franklin E. 2007. *The Great American Crime Decline*. New York: Oxford University Press.

3

Data Sources for Studying Homicide

WENDY REGOECZI AND JOHN JARVIS

Introduction

A number of data sources and analytical techniques exist for studying homicide. The most prominent of these are official records maintained by governmental agencies such as the police, hospitals, medical examiners/coroners, courts, and similar institutions. A growing source of information includes data compiled by individuals and organizations that are not necessarily linked to governmental functions, including newspaper accounts, social media sites, and other crowdsourced data collections. Prior to about 1930, court records and newspaper accounts were perhaps the most significant source of information on homicide trends and patterns. Starting around 1930 and continuing to this day, police data and vital statistics records have formed the basis of most studies of homicide and lethal violence. In more recent years, crowdsourced and social media inspired data collections have emerged, purporting to illuminate what other data sources appear to lack. The trends, emerging themes, and challenges posed by each of these data sources are the focus of the discussion here.

Official Records Data for Studying Homicide

The Federal Bureau of Investigation's Uniform Crime Reports (UCR)

In 1929, the Federal Bureau of Investigation (FBI) commenced an effort to collect information about crimes known to police by compiling uniform crime reports submitted by law enforcement agencies across the country. The goal was to produce annual crime counts that shed light on the offenses and arrests that police across the country confront while exercising their public safety duties. These statistics are published yearly as the Uniform Crime Reports (UCR). The UCR divides crimes into Part I and Part II offenses. Murder and nonnegligent manslaughter are included in the Part I offenses that make up the nation's crime index, a grouping of the eight most serious offenses: homicide, forcible rape, robbery, aggravated assault, burglary, motor vehicle theft, larceny-theft, and arson. Individual police agencies complete what is known as a Return A report every month, which includes these categories, and submit that report to the FBI for inclusion in the FBI's annual *Crime in the United States* publication. From this data source, annual rates of murder and nonnegligent manslaughter as well as similar counts for the other seven crimes considered Part I offenses can and have been derived, along with additional information such as the number of unfounded and founded offenses and the number of offenses cleared. Some agencies do not report their information to the FBI. Consequently, the FBI employs strategies for accounting for missing reports via a complex imputation procedure. This imputation leads to fairly accurate estimates for crimes at the national level of aggregation but is less viable for regional, state, or local estimates (see Barnett-Ryan and Griffith 2016; Lynch and Jarvis 2008).

Beginning in 1977, UCR data on homicide were complimented by the advent of the Supplementary Homicide Reports (SHR). The SHR is an additional report law enforcement agencies fill out for each murder, nonnegligent manslaughter, and justifiable homicide occurring in their jurisdiction. There is a separate section for reporting negligent manslaughter (i.e., death caused by the negligent but unintentional behavior of another individual). The SHR allows for the collection of data on the sex, race, age, and ethnicity of each victim and offender involved in the offense, the relationship between victim and offender, the weapon used, the circumstances surrounding the offense, and whether one or multiple victims and/or offenders were involved. Consequently, these additional details have afforded a great many studies focusing on the demographics of homicide and varying patterns now detectable in the available data. Within the FBI UCR, homicide, regarded as the most serious crime, is the only type of criminal offense for which detailed information is collected for each incident. Only aggregate-level counts as afforded by the Return A are collected for other types of offenses included in the traditional UCR program.

The FBI's National Incident-Based Reporting System (NIBRS)

By the late 1980s, desire for a more detailed understanding of crime and concern regarding lack of detail in the UCR system (sometimes referred to as the Summary system) led to the development of a committee to evaluate the UCR with an eye to modernizing crime data collection. The committee's final report, *Blueprint for the Future of the Uniform Crime Reporting Program*, recommended moving to an incident-based data collection system. The redesigned UCR system, called the National Incident-Based Reporting System (NIBRS), was designed to address the traditional UCR system limitations, and it has been in large measure successful. This success was fostered by providing multiple opportunities for feedback on the new reporting system and running a pilot demonstration in a group of law enforcement agencies in South Carolina. Test data were received in NIBRS format as early as 1989. Multiple agencies began reporting in NIBRS formats as early as 1990, and usable data for larger aggregates of agencies emerged in about 1996.

One of the chief advantages of NIBRS is the additional detail provided by the collection of fifty-eight elements on forty-nine Group A offenses captured in six different data segments: administrative, offense, property, victim, offender, and arrestee. The least change occurred with respect to the offense of homicide. The definition of homicide stayed the same, and the SHR inspired the level of detail collected on the other crimes. NIBRS has resulted in some improvements in homicide data collection. For example, NIBRS permits the collection of information on multiple offenders (up to 99) and multiple victims (up to 999). NIBRS also includes more variables than the SHR, such date of offense and date of arrest of offender(s), among other variables. Such information affords research into both the factors that impact whether a homicide is cleared by arrest or some other means and whether the characteristics of offender, victim, and offense influence how long it takes to solve a crime. Unlike the SHR, NIBRS collects information on the location of the offense using forty-five detailed location codes as well as the time of the incident. Thus, the implementation of NIBRS has increased not only the amount of information collected on homicide incidents but also some details that illuminate the context within which incidents take place. NIBRS homicide count data is commensurate with prior reporting in UCR and SHR, affording continuity in long term trends but subject to reporting variations, as was the case in traditional UCR reporting efforts.

Unfortunately, the implementation of NIBRS capabilities by law enforcement agencies around the country has been slow. While agencies could start submitting data in NIBRS format in 1989, as of 2021, only 11,794 out of 18,806 police agencies (62.7 percent) submit data to the FBI in NIBRS format. This represents law enforcement agencies covering approximately 65 percent of the U.S. population (see www.fbi.gov/cde for more specifics relative to individual states and localities). Furthermore, small and medium-sized law enforcement agencies have been most likely to adopt the NIBRS system, although that may change as NIBRS became the sole reporting mechanism for crime data in January 2021. Nevertheless, NIBRS data provide an effective means for studying a number of aspects of homicide, including the time it takes for homicides to be cleared, Hispanic homicide victimization, homicide among the elderly, mass murder, lethal intimate partner violence, and variation in race-specific homicide offending and victimization rates across U.S. cities.

National Center for Health Statistics' National Vital Statistics System (NVSS)

The National Center for Health Statistics (NCHS) at the Centers for Disease Control and Prevention (CDC) operates the National Vital Statistics System (NVSS). In existence since 1933, NVSS data are generated by vital systems responsible for registrations such as births and deaths. The NVSS mortality data are derived from standardized death certificates filed across the country. As required by state law, medical examiners or coroners investigate all homicides and complete the medical aspects of death certificates. Death certificates are forwarded to the state vital statistics offices and then to the NCHS, where the death is classified on the basis of the International Classification of Diseases (ICD).

NVSS death certificate data include decedent sex, age, race, ethnicity, marital status, level of education, resident status, residence, cause of death, and nature of injuries sustained. Deaths are coded by the victim's place of residence as opposed to the location of the incident. NVSS data have been used to study homicide victimization. As death certificates do not include information on the suspected perpetrator of a homicide, the NVSS provides no data on homicide offending or subtypes of victim/offender relationships such as intimate partner homicides.

NVSS data are available to the public through the Centers for Disease Control's WONDER (Wide-ranging ONline Data for Epidemiologic Research) and WISQARS (Web-Based Injury Statistics Query and Reporting System) systems. The WONDER system provides county-level national mortality data for the years 1968 through 2016 that can be broken down by age, race, ethnicity, gender, year, urbanization, and underlying cause of death. Underlying cause of death data are also available online from 1999 forward; researchers can run analyses on the homicide data as a whole or by specific injury mechanism (e.g., firearm, suffocation, etc.).

Individual Police Agency Records and Files

The police are typically first responders for incidents believed to be suspicious deaths and have a legal responsibility to record information relative to such calls for service. As such, the information retained by police agencies and the case files reflecting these incidents are a primary source of data for the study of homicide. However, there is great variability in the quantity and quality of such data. Records management systems, if used, are often structured and managed to suit the needs of particular police agencies and criminal justice mechanisms at work in those jurisdictions rather than any particular research interest. Data quantity and quality vary widely, but the details of incident, victims, witnesses, and a myriad of other contextual information about the police and criminal justice response to the homicide can be garnered. Unfortunately, not only are such data painstaking to collect and use for research purposes but getting access to police data for research purposes rather than official investigative purpose is also difficult. Nonetheless, several police agencies have partnered with researchers in an effort to better understand responses to cases of murder and other forms of violence. Such efforts have led to insights of these dynamics in cities such as Cleveland, New York City, Rochester, Atlanta, and Phoenix, among others.

National Violent Death Reporting System (NVDRS)

The National Violent Death Reporting System is an important effort to integrate data on violence from multiple sources, including law enforcement agencies, medical examiners/coroners, and death certificates. Part of the CDC's National Center for Injury Prevention and Control, the NVDRS is a state-based system that includes data on homicide, suicide, firearm-related deaths, deaths from legal intervention, and violent deaths from other causes. It began in 2002 with the participation of six states (Massachusetts, Maryland, New Jersey, Oregon, South Carolina, and Virginia). Additional states were added from 2002 through 2018, by which point all fifty states, the District of Columbia, and Puerto Rico were included. The dataset includes over six hundred data elements and thus provides far more detail about individual incidents than other national-level datasets, including details about the injury, circumstances, and extensive demographic information. The NVDRS is one of few datasets where homicides can be linked with suicides to identify cases of homicide-suicide and where multiple victims of the same perpetrator killed at different points in time can be connected. It can also be used to study homicide victimization of the homeless, current or former military members, and pregnant women. The publicly available NVDRS data can be analyzed through CDC's WISQARS. A restricted access case-level version of the dataset includes short narratives. Investigators must apply to the CDC and meet eligibility requirements to gain access to this version of the dataset.

As with NIBRS, it has taken many years for all states to become part of the NVDRS; thus, for some states, only a couple of years of data are available.

Like other official datasets on homicide, it suffers from underreporting, although to a lesser extent than the SHR and NVSS. Narratives are missing for a significant number of homicide cases (Barber et al. 2016). The data can also require considerable cleaning before use to identify coding errors.

The National Homicide Data Improvement Project is modeled after the NVDRS and being pilot tested in Ohio with extensive detail on all homicides in a cluster sample of forty-seven counties in Ohio from 1959 through 2010 (Roth et al. 2015). It integrates data from the SHR, NCHS, Ohio Department of Health, local police department case files, death certificates, and newspapers. Preliminary analyses of the Ohio pilot data have provided further evidence of the significant number of homicides missing from official national databases.

Other Sources of Data for Studying Homicide

Newspaper Accounts

Media coverage of deaths in communities predate most organized efforts to research and study homicide. In fact, newspaper accounts of homicides are prevalent in historical examinations of homicide patterns and trends. In studies preceding the implementation of national data collection systems on homicide, newspaper articles were used to construct estimates of homicide rates and trends and provide a picture of the extent and patterns of violence in a number of areas across the United States. Newspaper accounts have also been used to supplement official homicide data. More recently, they have formed the basis of studies seeking to examine subtypes of homicides that are difficult to research using official data sources, such as serial killing, school shootings, homicides by police, and mass murder.

Social Media and Data Scraping

Closely related to newspaper reports are recent data collection efforts that attempt to harvest information from various internet media sources to construct data reflecting occurrences of homicide and other types of violence. Efforts in this arena include the Murder Accountability Project, among others. Observers or commentators who focus on trends in violence have employed sophisticated data scraping tools to extract information from various and sometimes disparate websites to assemble such sources of information. Some efforts have illuminated facets of these incidents that other data collection efforts have been unable to uncover, and others have created grey literature or grey data with unknown reliability and integrity.

Comparing and Linking Data Sources

A handful of studies exist comparing counts, trends, and patterns across some of the aforementioned sources of homicide data. Several of these studies emerged in the 1990s when different sources of data seemed to be indicating disparate trends. However, on closer inspection and accounting for variances in methodology, more correspondence than discordance has been found. For example, a 1998 analysis of trends in 1993 NIBRS data compared to UCR data from the same time frame found correspondence between the two datasets for estimating characteristics of arrestees (Chilton and Jarvis 1998).

A more common comparison is of the SHR/UCR and the NVSS. A 2014 publication from the Bureau of Justice Statistics indicates that homicide rates in the NVSS and SHR from 1981 through 2011 follow very similar trends at the national level, although the NVSS shows a slightly higher rate and count of homicides than the SHR. Other research has found higher numbers of homicides reported through the NVSS than the FBI (Rokaw, Mercy, and Smith 1990). This pattern generally holds at the state level, although there are a few states where SHR homicide counts exceed those reported through the NVSS. A similar study by Riedel (1999) comparing UCR Return A reports, SHR rates, and NCHS rates shows very close agreement between UCR Return A rates and NCHS rates, with the NCHS reporting an average of 4 percent more homicides than the UCR Return A and 17 percent more than the SHR.

Two other national studies have compared vital statistics data to either SHR or Return A data from the UCR. Rokaw, Mercy, and Smith (1990) reported 7 percent more homicides in the vital statistics records than the SHR but found that the discrepancy could be as high as 42 percent. Cantor and Cohen's comparison of vital statistics and UCR records from 1933 through 1975 found that agreement between the two series varies depending on time period examined.

Comparisons at the county level show even greater variability, although it is common for counties to have more homicides reported through vital statistics than the SHR. In most counties, the differences in counts between the two data sources are not extremely large, but in a few counties, they number in the thousands (Wiersema, Loftin, and McDowall 2000). An assessment of the accuracy of homicide rates for large U.S. cities calculated from SHR data demonstrated the rates are very reliable, particularly when the sample is limited to cities that consistently report SHR records to the FBI (Loftin et al. 2015). The authors recommend either not including inconsistently reporting cities or using vital statistics or other data to impute missing values for those cities; they suggest limiting the calculation of subgroup-specific rates to those that have large populations at risk.

As previously noted, variations in the total counts from many of these data sources are more prolific at lower levels of aggregation, as the dynamics of how these reports are populated by various actors are less transparent at regional and national levels than at state, local, or even neighborhood levels of precision. Nonetheless, explanations for variations in total homicides reported remain sought and merit understanding. For example, there are several reasons why NVSS-reported homicide numbers are higher than numbers from other sources. The fact that state vital registrars are required to report deaths due to homicide to the NCHS, whereas reporting homicides to the FBI through the UCR and NIBRS is voluntary, is one source of variation. There are also differences with respect to the definitions used and therefore the types of deaths counted as homicides through each system. The NVSS, for example, includes assaults from motor vehicle crashes, while the SHR does not, even though comparable data could be extracted from NIBRS. Additionally, the SHR data do not include homicides occurring in federal prisons, military bases, or on Indian reservations. While the NIBRS program does cover federal law enforcement agencies, their participation in reporting data has been low, and federal data may be excluded from crime estimates calculated using NIBRS data.

Attempts to extract or identify individual cases from different homicide data sources to determine whether a case reported in multiple records system is, in fact, the same case have also proven difficult. The Bureau of Justice Statistics attempted to match 1,783 SHR records with 1,855 vital statistics records for July 1986 for all but a couple U.S. states. They only succeeded in matching 1,191 cases (Rand 1993). Similarly, a case-by-case comparison of law enforcement and vital statistics data on homicides in California from 1990 to 1999 found that 93 percent of law enforcement records could be matched to a vital statistics record (Van Court and Trent 2004). This left 2,421 unmatched cases for which only SHR data existed. Cases were least likely to have a match of SHR and vital statistics records when involving Hispanic victims, family members other than intimate partners, weapons other than handguns, felony homicides, negligent manslaughters, and cases investigated by medical examiners (as opposed to coroners). For cases that could be matched, records from the two data systems were most likely to report the same information about the victim's gender and race and were least likely to agree on the victim's age (Riedel and Regoeczi 2006). All of these disparities pose challenges for research when conducting analyses involving these types of variables.

Units of Analysis in Homicide Data and Research

Individual Level

A wide range of studies focus on individual-level variables and covariates. A number of these involve analyses of the publicly available datasets discussed previously, particularly the SHR. Using victim, offender, and offense data from the SHR and NIBRS, researchers have examined demographic patterns of homicides in general and of homicide subtypes including intimate partner killings, familicide, child homicides, parricide, gang homicides, and lethal gun violence. Other researchers have drawn on richer contextual data with greater detail relative to the dynamics of homicide by examining data from local police departments in cities such as Chicago, Illinois; Cleveland, Ohio; New York City; Miami, Florida; Philadelphia, Pennsylvania; and St. Louis, Missouri. These localized studies have contributed important findings to the homicide literature on such diverse topics as deviant homicides, gang-motivated versus gang-affiliated homicides, elderly versus nonelderly homicide victims, as well as qualitative analyses of homicide narratives to explore the presence of such concepts as face saving and the code of the street. While these efforts also draw on official records that reside in police agencies or other institutions, their level of detail and narratives exceed the summary overviews and overall tallies that national, regional, and state databases contain.

Neighborhood Level

Neighborhood-level studies of homicide are the least common, largely due to the challenges of collecting data at this unit of analysis. These types of studies typically require access to data from one or more local police departments that can be linked to neighborhood-level census data or some other unique identifier. Combined analysis of individual and neighborhood-level variables is relatively uncommon, but when carried out, it typically employs methods for conducting multilevel analyses. This type of research has addressed such questions as racial variations in neighborhood-level homicide rates, the impact of neighborhood structural conditions on homicides across place and time, and the effect of neighborhood context on media coverage of homicides. Other areas inspired by these types of data and analysis include examinations of immigration on local homicide rates as well as whether neighborhood characteristics influence homicide solvability. Of particular importance are multilevel analyses of data from the Project on Human Development in Chicago Neighborhoods, which has been critical to demonstrating variation in collective efficacy across neighborhoods. Such effects have been shown to mediate the impact of concentrated disadvantage on homicide counts across Chicago neighborhoods.

City, County, State Level

A large body of aggregate-level research exists assessing structural correlates of city, county, and state homicide rates. Most studies of this kind employ UCR data for the dependent variable and assess the impacts of a range of structural predictors including poverty, racial composition, segregation, immigration, divorce rates, season, and regional variation in homicide rates. As the field increasingly recognizes the importance of disaggregating homicide rates, a smaller group of studies examine predictors of specific types of homicide rates, including sex, race, or age-specific homicide rates and gun-related, gang-related, drug-related, and felony homicides. Studies using rates derived from the UCR Return A form and the SHR typically use three-year averages to address potential year-to-year fluctuations in local homicide rates. Studies also examine changes over time in city-specific homicide rates from local police department data or, less frequently, local medical examiner data.

Inherent Methodological Challenges

No matter which source of data is used to examine homicide, inherent challenges exist in leveraging the information data provide. Stated more precisely, limitations in each data source must be overcome or addressed.

Uniform Crime Reports

Although considered one of the most accurate measures of homicide, UCR data in general and SHR data in particular suffer a number of limitations. The most significant and recurring of these limitations is the fact that the entire reporting system is voluntary in nature, so not all law enforcement agencies submit reports for all months or all years. In fact, some agencies do not report for many years. Even though an SHR form is supposed to be filled out monthly for all murders and nonnegligent manslaughters reported through the UCR, the number of homicides enumerated through the SHR is always less than the number of homicides reported through UCR Return A reports. In some cases, these differences are in the thousands.

Additional analytical challenges are encountered relative to items missing for some information collected on SHR forms. As a result of declining rates of homicide clearance in the United States, information on offenders is missing for one-third of cases or more. Data on victim/offender relationships are sometimes problematic as a result of confusion over whether to code the relationship of the victim to the offender or the offender to the victim and from incidents of multiple victims and/or multiple offenders receiving the same code for all relationships (Maltz 1999). The SHR lacks categories for ex-boyfriend and ex-girlfriend. The coding of circumstances can be problematic as well. While the SHR form provides for descriptions of events leading up to the homicide, the limited amount of space discourages lengthy descriptions. The complex set of events that culminate in homicide are ultimately summarized with the selection of a single circumstance code, which may obscure other contributing circumstances. A large proportion of homicide circumstances are classified as unknown, and this proportion varies considerably across cities (Maxfield 1989). Fortunately, SHR datasets containing imputations for missing values are widely available. A commonly used version produced by James Alan Fox and Marc Swatt can be accessed through the Inter-university Consortium for Political and Social Research.

Another area that poses challenges is ethnicity data. In spite of the SHR form allowing for the collection of ethnicity data through codes for Hispanic and non-Hispanic victims and offenders, these codes are infrequently filled in by law enforcement agencies and are missing in upward of 48 percent of cases. Questions have been raised with respect to the reliability of ethnicity data as collected by law enforcement agencies. Classification on the basis of ethnicity is largely done on the basis of a person's appearance and/or last name rather than self-reported by the person. As a result, the SHR may not provide an effective means to study differences in patterns of Hispanic and non-Hispanic offending and victimization.

NIBRS

The availability of NIBRS creates significant advantages for examining not only homicide but also forms of violence resulting in less than lethal outcomes. Particularly relevant to the study of homicide are reports of aggravated assaults accompanied by serious injuries, which are reported and available in the NIBRS. It is feasible that many of these cases could and would have been homicides if not for life-saving efforts by others. Nonetheless, while more data for understanding homicide and comparing it with other crimes are afforded by NIBRS, many of the limitations of the UCR persist in NIBRS. The nonreporting or partial reporting of crimes as well as the potential for items to be missing in the variables reported that plague UCR also impact NIBRS. Additional challenges include the accuracy of variables such as time and day of incident, location codes, and (as in the SHR) circumstance coding. Lastly, while NIBRS affords many advantages, the complexity of the data reported and the complexities of file structures in the available data often pose challenges for researchers. One example of these difficulties specific to NIBRS is tabulating crime counts. Since NIBRS provides for multiple victims, offenders, and offenses to be enumerated where UCR only provides for summary counts of the most serious offenses, NIBRS crime counts are usually higher than UCR counts. While less germane to homicide counts, this change in enumeration methodology within NIBRS as compared to UCR creates burdens for some to explain. Of course, the variation is due to changes in counting rules within two similar yet distinct systems of crime reporting and not necessarily due to changes in the frequency of crimes occurring. This ambiguity, along with a complicated structure for accessing NIBRS data as stored in publicly available data, likely has contributed to many researchers seeking homicide data that pose fewer complexities for analysis. It can be very difficult to correctly link victim and offender segments in cases where there are multiple victims and/or multiple offenders and to ensure that appropriate demographic characteristics are connected to the correct individual. This had led some researchers to limit analyses to offenses involving only one victim and one offender. So while NIBRS affords significant advantages for studying homicides and violence (and numerous other crimes), the inherent limitations of voluntarily reported data reflecting crimes known to the police persist, along with myriad other computational dilemmas. That said, NIBRS still represents a step forward in data quality and quantity for furthering our understanding of what police encounter when homicides come to their attention.

Police Agency–Specific Data

Individual agency records, while generally contextually superior to other sources of homicide data, often require varying forms of data storage and retrieval efforts for research purposes. Another limitation that these data pose is the wide variation in content commonly found, as investigative processes vary enormously. Case file data are often not electronic; data must be collected by hand, which can take months and sometimes years to complete. Lastly, and again perhaps most importantly, access to such data for general research efforts is limited.

Newspapers and News Media–Sourced Data

The use of newspaper accounts to study homicide has a long history. Generally, newspapers are a good source for indications of overall enumerations of incidents that occurred. In other words, if someone dies, the newspapers are generally reliable in reporting that a death occurred. Beyond this high-level reporting, details are often either not available or misreported due to incorrect witness reporting, conflicting accounts, or misinterpretations of statements overheard or prematurely reported. Using this source of homicide data requires methods of examining adjacent days of reporting to minimize some of these reporting errors. Even then, the facts reported in newspapers, like on social media, are often different from what the police have actually been able to collect and use for the investigation of such incidents.

Social Media–Sourced Data

While social media–sourced data collections are increasingly common, these data, similar to newspapers, also present limitations that must be addressed if used to study homicide. First, as with many other homicide data sources, the validity and reliability of data as compiled is often dubious or unknown. Validation efforts or processes must be attended to for these data and their quality and authenticity to survive scientific scrutiny. Second, and related to the initial limitation, is the difficulty of assuring objectivity and identifying suspected or known biases in the source site used to extract such data. Social media sites often are value laden in their content and by their very nature are for social commentary rather than objective reporting of the facts of a given incident. As such, some attention to triangulating this sort of data for concurrent validity on the details of the case is needed but often not employed or documented.

Analytical Hurdles

External to the data sources reviewed here, analytical complexities of many exogenous variables commonly examined in connection to homicides are prevalent. Studies examining structural predictors of homicide rate often use a number of measures, including but not limited to economic disadvantage, poverty, median family income, income inequality, education level, unemployment, and family structure (especially percent of female-headed households with children under eighteen years of age), which overlap considerably. This overlap poses two difficulties: (1) the quality of data for these variables is impacted by many of the same limitations in collecting homicide data detailed here, so the validity and reliability of these measures may require similar scrutiny for awareness of limitations if used for research proposes; and (2) analytically, many of these measures will be found to be collinear, requiring statistical procedures to eliminate or minimize multicollinearity. Failing this, regression analyses can result in misattribution of the explained variance. Fortunately, analytical procedures such as principal components analysis can be employed to address such difficulties.

Another hurdle somewhat related to aggregation issues emerges when examining place-specific homicides. In spite of public perception, homicide continues to be infrequent in most geographical locations, creating analytical challenges with respect to infrequent occurrences in small geographic locales. Particularly at lower levels of aggregation, many locations will have no homicides reported for one or more years of data. This type of data structure is not suitable for widely used statistical techniques such as ordinary least squares regression. Instead, these data are more likely to follow a Poisson distribution. Consequently, negative binomial regression models have been increasingly applied to studying counts of homicides for smaller units of analysis to account for both frequent zero counts and overdispersion in data due to the resulting skewed distribution.

Conclusion

For decades, homicide researchers have relied on the UCR and SHR for data on lethal violence. A shift away from these data sources has begun and is likely to increase in the years to come. The UCR and SHR have been phased out and replaced with NIBRS. With the FBI's recent shift to a NIBRS-only data collection system, researchers reluctant to use NIBRS due to its slow adoption by larger police agencies may become more willing to do so. Furthermore, NIBRS employs a more robust methodology to handle missing data than the UCR did. At the same time, the NVDRS has been expanded to incorporate all fifty states, the District of Columbia, and Puerto Rico. The extensive details on homicide in the NVDRS will open the field to a number of interesting and important questions for homicide researchers. We hope to see continued efforts by groups of individual researchers to build their own homicide datasets through original data collection. The culmination of these changes and an ongoing commitment to developing the highest quality homicide data possible will help position those studying lethal violence to identify the most effective strategies for reducing and preventing homicide.

REFERENCES

Barber, Catherine, Deborah Azrael, Amy Cohen, Matthew Miller, Deonza Thymes, David Enze Wang, and David Hemenway. 2016. "Homicides by Police: Comparing Counts from the National Violent Death Reporting System, Vital Statistics, and Supplementary Homicide Reports." *American Journal of Public Health* 106:922–27.

Barnett-Ryan, Cynthia, and Emily H. Griffith. 2016. "The Dynamic Nature of Crime Statistics." In *The Wiley Handbook on the Psychology of Violence*, edited by C. A. Cuevas and C. M. Rennison. https://doi.org/10.1002/9781118303092.ch1.

Bureau of Justice Statistics. 2014. *The Nation's Two Measures of Homicide*. U.S. Department of Justice, Office of Justice Programs. NCJ 247060.

Cantor, David, and Lawrence E. Cohen. 1980. "Comparing Measures of Homicide Trends: Methodological and Substantive Differences in the Vital Statistics and Uniform Crime Report Time Series (1933–1975)." *Social Science Research* 9:121–45.

Chilton, Roland, and John Jarvis. 1998. "Victims and Offenders in Two Crime Statistics Programs: A Comparison of the National Incident-Based Reporting System (NIBRS) and the National Crime Victimization Survey." *Journal of Quantitative Criminology* 15 (2): 193–205.

Fox, James Alan, and Swatt, Marc L. Uniform Crime Reports [United States]: Supplementary Homicide Reports With Multiple Imputation, Cumulative Files 1976–2007. Inter-university Consortium for Political and Social Research [distributor], 2009-02-24. https://doi.org/10.3886/ICPSR24801.v1.

Loftin, Colin, David McDowall, Karise Curtis, and Matthew D. Fetzer. 2015. "The Accuracy of Supplementary Homicide Report Rates for Large U.S. Cities." *Homicide Studies* 19:6–27.

Lynch, James P., and John P. Jarvis. 2008. "Missing Data and Imputation in the Uniform Crime Reports and the Effects on National Estimates." *Journal of Contemporary Criminal Justice* 24 (1): 69–85. https://doi.org/10.1177/1043986207313028.

Maltz, Michael D. 1999. *Bridging Gaps in Police Crime Data (NCJ 176365)*. Washington, DC: Bureau of Justice Statistics. http://www.bjs.gov/content/pub/pdf/bgpcd.pdf.

Maxfield, Michael G. 1989. "Circumstances in Supplementary Homicide Reports: Variety and Validity." *Criminology* 27:671–95.

Rand, Michael R. 1993. "The Study of Homicide Caseflow: Creating a Comprehensive Homicide Dataset." In *Questions and Answers in Lethal and Non-lethal Violence: Proceedings of the Second Annual Workshop of the Homicide Research Working Group*, 103–18. Washington, DC: Government Printing Office.

Riedel, Marc. 1999. "Sources of Homicide Data: A Review and Comparison." In *Homicide: A Sourcebook of Social Research*, edited by M. Dwayne Smith and Margaret A. Zahn, 75–95. Thousand Oaks, CA: Sage.

Riedel, Marc, and Wendy C. Regoeczi. 2006. "A Case-By-Case Comparison of the Classification of Law Enforcement and Vital Statistics Data on Homicide." *Criminal Justice Policy Review* 17:61–82.

Rokaw, W. M., J. A. Mercy, and J. C. Smith. 1990. "Comparing Death Certificate Data with FBI Crime Reporting Statistics on U.S. Homicides." *Public Health Reports* 105:447–55.

Roth, Randolph, Wendy C. Regoeczi, Michael Maltz, and Douglas Eckberg. 2015. *Quality Data Is the First Step: The National Homicide Data Improvement Project*. Report Submitted to the National Science Foundation. Criminal Justice Research Center, Columbus OH.

Van Court, Jason, and Roger B. Trent. 2004. "Why Didn't We Get Them All?: Analyzing Unlinked Records in California's Linked Homicide File." *Homicide Studies* 8:311–21.

Wiersema, Brian, Colin Loftin, and David McDowall. 2000. "A Comparison of SHR and Vital Statistics Estimates for U.S. Counties." *Homicide Studies* 4:317–40.

4

Cross-National Homicide

Meghan Rogers and William Alex Pridemore

Introduction

In this chapter, we take stock of cross-national homicide research. In 1999, LaFree published a foundational review of this literature in Smith and Zahn's *Homicide: A Sourcebook of Social Research*. Over the last two decades, scholars have cited his review nearly three hundred times, and many still refer to it. We draw on the structure and succinct presentation style of LaFree's review to shape our chapter, updating it with new information and trends in the literature. We summarize data sources and their limitations, major research themes, empirical results, and potential avenues for new research. Our goal is to provide a starting point and basic toolkit for current and future scholars of cross-national homicide.

National homicide rates vary remarkably, from less than 1 per 100,000 residents in Japan, South Korea, and several European nations to over 30 and even 40 per 100,000 residents in South Africa and several Latin and South American nations. Homicide rates of many nations and world regions also exhibit substantial temporal variation. Likewise, nations vary widely on structural and cultural characteristics such as history, economic resources, state legitimacy, and level of social protection provided to citizens. It is likely these characteristics covary with homicide rates in both direct and nuanced ways. Yet national homicide reporting systems differ in their definition of homicide and their reliability in measuring or recording homicides; operationalizing theoretical concepts and sociocultural characteristics with existing data gathered for other purposes is complicated, so assessing associations is challenging. These complexities mean scholars tend to revisit common, safe themes rather than offering new testable theories or meaningful innovations. Homicide rates reveal something deep about nations and cultures, so we must continually improve our understanding by accurately measuring them, detecting their patterns, and discovering their causes and consequences.

Sources of Cross-National Homicide Data

There were four available sources of national homicide data when LaFree (1999) wrote his review: INTERPOL, World Health Organization (WHO), United Nations, and Archer and Gartner's (1984) dataset collected from multiple sources. There are currently four interrelated sources of homicide data across nations: WHO mortality database, WHO Global Health Observatory Data, United Nations Office of Drugs and Crime (UNODC), and World Bank World Development Indicators.

The WHO mortality database is now available only in raw data format. While the data are typically updated annually, the source requires researchers to build a bridge across updates. This includes knowing International Classification of Disease (ICD) codes back to the seventh revision. In raw data format, WHO mortality data are available from 1950 to 2021. However, key limitations include a sample of mostly Western nations and large temporal gaps in homicide data for many nations.

WHO has replaced its mortality database with the Global Health Observatory, which collects data utilizing the same method as the Global Status on Homicide report (World Health Organization 2020). These data are updated annually and available from 2000 to 2019. Homicide data from this source are a mixture of mortality data from national vital statistics registration systems, criminal justice data from the UNODC, and homicide counts from WHO's imputation model. A critical limitation of the WHO Global Health Observatory data for cross-national homicide scholars is that its imputation model includes national characteristics in which researchers are often interested as independent variables (Kanis et al. 2017): gender inequality, alcohol consumption, proportion of the population living in urban areas, proportion of the population male aged fifteen to thirty years old, infant mortality, and religious fractionalization (World Health Organization 2021). Thus, using data from nations for which homicide counts are imputed introduces the major flaw of including the same variables on both sides of the statistical equation.

The next source of national homicide data is the UNODC. These data are gathered from the United Nations Crime Trends Survey, with supplemental data derived from several sources. The latter sources vary significantly across nations, and most overlap with the WHO Global Health Observatory data.

However, the UNODC raw data do not differentiate between WHO Global Health Observatory and WHO mortality data. Due to the different data sources employed from each nation, there is little uniformity guaranteed across nations (Smit, de Jong, and Bijleveld 2012). Because the definition of what is considered homicide varies across nations and even within nations among data sources, scholars are likely not always measuring precisely what they think they are measuring when utilizing UNODC data (Smit, de Jong, and Bijleveld 2012).

The World Bank World Development Indictors database uses data from the UNODC. There is nearly perfect overlap between the two sources. Figure 4.1 provides average annual homicide rates for the four homicide data sources. The UNODC and World Bank World Development Indicators are the same except for 1991, 1995, and 2014–2016, in which there are slight deviations between the two. The precise cause of these small differences is unclear, but they are not due to sample size differences, as the rates in the figure are limited to the sample of fifty-three nations for which homicide data are available across all sources.

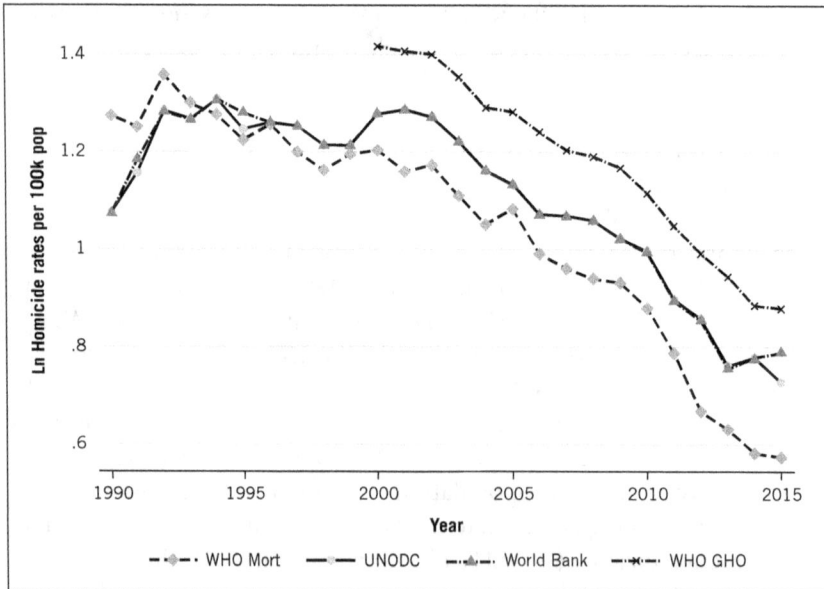

Figure 4.1 Average Yearly Homicide Rates across the Four Homicide Data Sources (*Data source: World Health Mortality Database [WHO Mort], United Nations Office on Drugs and Crime [UNODC], World Bank World Development Indicators [World Bank], World Health Organization Global Health Observatory [WHO GHO], https://www.who.int/data/data-collection -tools/who-mortality-database.)*

The trade-off for cross-national homicide scholars is that they can either have data on a larger and more representative sample (UNODC) or data that provide some comfort in the consistency of what is being measured (WHO). Both data sources possess elemental flaws if not employed carefully. In recent years, the trend has been toward maximizing sample size; the question is at what cost, because this practice appears to sacrifice validity.

Theoretical Perspectives on Cross-National Homicide

There have been no significant theoretical developments in cross-national homicide research in the twenty-first century (LaFree 2021). Research often derives from earlier theories on economic stress, modernization, and institutional anomie, though in recent years the literature appears to be more variable than theory driven.

Economic Stress Theories and Conflict Theories

Economic explanations of crime are centuries old, but modern explanations of the effects of economic stress on national homicide rates are rooted in Wallerstein's (1974) world systems theory (LaFree 1999). This theory proposes that a nation's status in the world hierarchy has a direct impact on its economic welfare. Core nations have the highest income levels and are often the strongest capitalist societies (Chase-Dunn 1980); semiperipheral nations are in a transitional state of development, and peripheral nations are typically the most underdeveloped economically and politically. World systems theory, itself rooted in conflict theories, argues that core nations often exploit peripheral nations.

Since LaFree's review, there has been little advancement in conflict-oriented economic stress theories as they relate to homicide, with only a handful of studies exploring the theory's core tenets. General tests of its efficacy have not provided substantial support (LaFree 2005; LaFree, Curtis, and McDowall 2015; Rogers and Pridemore 2018). "Economic stress" appears to be a catch-all term for studies employing some measure of a nation's economic standing such as unemployment or gross domestic product (GDP). Many include inequality and poverty, though like unemployment and GDP, explanations of exactly how they affect national homicide rates are often vague and do not necessarily adhere to underlying conflict arguments found within economic stress or world systems theory. Authors argue that these economic indicators influence homicide rates, but the origins of these conditions are considered exogenous to the model, with little or no systematic explanation of how or whether they might otherwise affect violence.

Modernization

Like conflict theories, modernization theories now receive substantially less attention in cross-national homicide literature. Modernization theory originates from Durkheim's (1933) discussion of societal transition from mechanical to organic solidarity. Shelley (1981) elaborated on Durkheim's ideas, arguing that crime in societies undergoing modernization is fueled by population movement into urban areas and the potential weakening of formal and informal social control this creates. Shelley's arguments follow Thomas and Znaniecki's (1927) discussion of the breakdown of formal and informal social control mechanisms among Polish peasants who migrated to the United States. Shelley maintained that the more rapid the transition, the greater the increase in crime rates.

There has been little development in applying modernization theory to national homicide rates since LaFree's (1999) review. One key reason is a set of limitations resulting from long-running misinterpretations of Durkheim's expectations for homicide as a result of social change (DiCristina 2004; Pridemore and Kim 2006). For many years in this early literature, criminologists argued that development is generally anomic, and thus more developed societies have higher homicide rates. This is an empirical question, but it is not consistent with Durkheim's ideas. Durkheim argued that evolutionary change allows societies time to adjust norms to fit changing appetites. Nonrapid development, with its transition to social bonds based on interdependence and complementary differences, should create a "religion of humanity" that values the individual, with a concomitant decline in homicide rates. If this transition occurs too quickly, the revolutionary change creates an anomic division of labor and social deregulation because norms and values cannot keep pace, leaving unchecked appetites. These ideas have often been confused in the cross-national criminological literature, with many hypothesizing that modernization more generally, regardless of the pace of change, creates anomic conditions and thus higher crime rates. Durkheim also argued that homicide rates decrease with development because the "sentiments about collective things" associated with mechanical societies—which are more likely to incite people to violence—weaken and diminish in number over time. This part of the argument is largely ignored in the homicide literature.

While there are fewer references to modernization theory in the literature now, there are clearer discussions and illustrations of the idea that interpersonal violence tends to decline with development (Eisner 2001; Pinker 2011). Still, studies that examine national homicide rate trends find weak or little support for the theory (LaFree 2005; LaFree, Curtis, and McDowall 2015; Rogers and Pridemore 2018), as national trends do not converge as much as modernization would have us expect. Consistent with these findings, Nivette's (2011) meta-analysis of cross-national studies of crime showed little support for modernization-related concepts. However, all these tests use data from the last several decades, so it could be that historical convergence occurred before more complete data were available to test the theory.

Institutional Anomie Theory

While institutional anomie theory (IAT) was developed in the 1990s, its application to cross-national homicide research came largely after LaFree's review in 1999. IAT proposes that cultural values can generate institutional imbalances within a nation, leading to more crime. Originally, IAT sought to explain why the United States has significantly higher pecuniary crime rates (Messner and Rosenfeld 1997; 2007). The theory proposes that the American dream comprises four core cultural values: individualism, universalism, fetishism for money, and achievement. Individuals are expected to succeed (achievement), measured by economic gain (fetishism for money), by themselves (individualism), with the assumption that everyone can achieve success no matter their start in life or the conditions they experience (universalism). When this economic achievement–based orientation is allowed to dominate, institutions like the family, education, polity, and religion are weakened. The original goals of these institutions may even be corrupted by the runaway achievement orientation, and institutions become less capable of fulfilling their aims, including controlling members' behaviors.

Although IAT is theoretically rich and dense and thus difficult to test in its entirety, Messner and Rosenfeld and other scholars distilled it into key propositions that seem especially relevant to the cross-national context (Chamlin and Cochran 1995). More than a decade ago, Bjerregaard and Cochran (2008, 42) provided a concise description of empirical evidence for IAT, stating that it is "consistently inconsistent." The same appears true today. As can be seen from our brief discussion of other theories, however, while support is mixed for IAT in cross-national homicide research, it is one of the few theories receiving some attention today, as conflict and modernization theories have fallen out of favor and much cross-national research is more variable driven than theory driven.

Summary of Findings from Cross-National Homicide Studies

Economic Inequality and Poverty

At the time of LaFree's review, one of the most consistent predictors of national homicide rates was income inequality, as measured by the Gini coefficient (LaFree 1999; Nivette 2011). In cross-national research, however, scholars failed to control for poverty, the most consistent predictor in the much larger literature on subnational U.S. homicide rates and typically strongly statistically confounded with the Gini coefficient. This omission was likely the result of the scarcity of comparable measures of poverty across nations with widely diverging income levels. Working independently but at the same time, Paré and Felson (2014) and Pridemore (2008; 2011) addressed this by drawing on international literature in other fields and on earlier work by Loftin and Parker (1985) on the same problem in the United States, which employed infant mortality as a proxy for poverty. Both Paré and Felson and Pridemore found an association between poverty and national homicide rates; the inequality-homicide association disappeared when they controlled for poverty.

These contrary findings have renewed interest in the topic and generated further cross-national homicide research. In several studies of other structural covariates of national homicide rates that controlled for poverty and inequality, Rogers and Pridemore (e.g., 2017b; 2013) found a positive association for the former and a null association for the latter. Santos, Testa, and Weiss (2018), on the other hand, argued that poverty only matters in low homicide nations. They found that poverty is not—and inequality is—significantly associated with homicide across its entire distribution of rates. This indirectly supports the results of Messner, Raffalovich, and Sutton (2010), who found an inequality-homicide association in a very limited set of developed nations that mostly exhibit low homicide rates.

Rogers and Pridemore (2020) outlined limitations of inequality-homicide research, mainly the reductionist theoretical mechanism that links income inequality and national homicide rates and its operationalization in macro-level studies. They suggested alternative measures for assessing the impact of perceived inequality on national homicide rates. Based largely on the arguments of Blau and Blau (1982), the main explanation for an inequality-homicide association is that individuals on the lower end of the income distribution feel resentment due to inequality. This perception increases the likelihood that some will express their anger in different ways, including violence. But this frustration-aggression hypothesis is an individual-level explanation of a structural or population-level phenomenon of homicide rates. Moreover, the most often utilized measure of inequality, the Gini coefficient, does not meet construct validity because it does not measure the level of inequality perceived by citizens within a nation, which research in other fields has shown is not closely associated with income inequality as measured by economic indicators. Rogers and Pridemore (2020) use the International Social Survey Programme (2012) and the World Values Survey (WVS) to measure income inequality as perceived by citizens, which is more consistent with theory and creates a macrolevel analogue of social sentiment. None of the measures of perceived inequality correlate with the Gini coefficient, nor do any have a significant association with national homicide rates.

Regardless of the final answer to questions about associations between national homicide rates and poverty and inequality, renewed attention has been given to the topic since LaFree's (1999) review. We are now somewhat uncertain about what has been the most consistent predictor of national homicide rates at the time, and poverty—the most consistent predictor of U.S. homicide rates but absent from cross-national studies—appears to be associated with national homicide rates.

Population Structure and Percent Young

For decades, scholars have argued that the percent of the population that is young should be positively associated with national homicide rates. The argument is based mainly on the age-crime curve hypothesis, which states that the young are the most criminogenic population (Fiala and LaFree 1988; Hirschi and Gottfredson 1983; Cohen and Land 1987; Chilton and Spielberger 1971). Thus, due to compositional effects, we should expect higher national homicide rates in nations where the share of the population that is young is larger.

Within recent cross-national homicide literature, both the age-crime curve and the compositional effect have come into question. To test the age-crime curve, scholars must obtain data nation by nation because there is no centralized source of age-specific crime data. Steffensmeier and colleagues explored the hypothesis in South Korea, Taiwan, and India (Steffensmeier, Lu, and Na 2020; Steffensmeier, Lu, and Kumar 2019; Steffensmeier, Zhong, and Lu 2017). In none of their findings from these nations did they observe the expected age-crime curve.

In extensive exploratory data analyses, Rogers (2014) found that the young do not consistently exhibit the highest age-specific homicide rates across nations or within nations over time. Further, Rogers and Pridemore (2017a; 2016) conducted a large review of cross-national homicide findings and carried out their own analyses, systematically testing whether the percent of the population that is young had a significant association with total and gender-specific homicide rates. They observed that 87 percent of published models over decades of research do not show a significant positive association between percent young and homicide rates, and in none of their own analyses was there a significant association between percent young and either total or gender-specific homicide rates.

Culture

The role of culture has been largely ignored in cross-national homicide research (Stamatel 2016), mainly because of the limitations of operationalizing it with quantitative measures. It is typically easier to quantify social structural factors than characteristics of prevailing culture and values, and LaFree's (1999) review contains little discussion of culture because of lack of research on it. Understanding the role of culture in explaining national differences in violence is crucial, however, and in the period since LaFree's review, we have seen the creation of new measures, greater and more creative use of existing measures, and a small but growing empirical literature on the cultural covariates of national homicide rates.

Hofstede's (1998; 2001) cultural measures are a promising avenue for criminological research exploring homicide across nations. Karstedt (2015) employed his measures of power-distance and individualism-collectivism to explore whether democratic values are associated with national homicide rates. She employed measures of authoritarianism and egalitarianism (Hofstede's power-distance measures) that address "power, domination and subordination" between different status groups (Karstedt 2015, 463). In addition, she explored the relationship between individualism and collectivism, measuring "detachment from traditional family bonds" (Karstedt 2015, 463). Her results show that nations with individualistic and egalitarian values tend to have lower violence rates as long as there are some egalitarian social structures in place. Using Hofstede's measures, Stamatel (2016) found that scores on the combined individualism-egalitarianism continuum have significant direct negative effects on homicide rates and operate indirectly via their impact on a democracy index combining the political and civil liberties scales from Freedom House.

There are other examples of tests of culture and cross-national homicide rates. Scholars are increasingly using the WVS to operationalize culture, for example with IAT (Chamlin and Cochran 2007). Lin and Mancik (2020) employed the WVS, the Inglehart-Welzel indices specifically, to test the Durkheimian perspective that homicide rates are higher where traditional values are stronger. These indices capture traditional-religious versus secular-rational values and survival versus self-expression (Inglehart and Baker 2000). In this case, Lin and Mancik (2020) did not discover any direct effects of traditional-religious versus rational-secular values or survival versus self-expressive values on national homicide rates. Another example is a study by Altheimer (2013) testing Nisbett and Cohen's (1996) culture of honor hypothesis. The latter argued that a culture of honor drives higher violence rates in places where herding economies are or were historically prevalent. Herders are economically vulnerable because their flocks are constantly at risk; they must be ferocious in the flock's defense when anything remotely threatening arises, including threats or insults from others. Altheimer did not measure cultural values directly, but he did use economic data to measure per capita

presence of herding animals, including cattle, pigs, sheep, and goats. He found no support for the Nisbett and Cohen hypothesis.

There are an increasing number of ways to measure cultural characteristics cross-nationally. These include ready-made indices like Hofstede (2001) and Inglehart and Welzel (2005) and surveys like the WVS, European Barometer, Latinobarometer, and International Social Survey Programme from which scholars can construct their own measures and indices. While social structure has dominated the cross-national homicide literature, it is almost certain that cultural characteristics influence national homicide rates, so this is fertile ground for future research. Given the small number of studies and the growing ability to operationalize cultural concepts, we expect this area of research to increase.

Political Structure and State Legitimacy

A growing empirical literature addresses the effects of political structure and state legitimacy on national homicide rates. Generally, Stamatel (2006), Karstedt (2015; 2006), and Pridemore (2005) all highlighted the effects of the unique historical, cultural, and political background of eastern European nations on their homicide rates. Rogers and Pridemore (2018) found that these nations have some of the strongest similarities in homicide trends relative to any other region. Democratic values (Stamatel 2016; Karstedt 2006) and freedom from government market restraint (Messner and Rosenfeld 1997) are just some factors of political economy and legitimacy that may account for differences in national homicide rates.

The role of political legitimacy and perception of the government's right to govern have been explored in the cross-national homicide literature. While there remains debate about how to operationalize political legitimacy across nations (Beetham 2013; Gilley 2006), there is evidence that it can affect national homicide rates. Nivette and Eisner (2013) described three mechanisms through which political legitimacy might account for differences in violence: social control, self-help, and inequality. If citizens perceive the government as legitimate, they are more likely to allow it to control their behaviors. If citizens do not perceive their government as legitimate, they may be more likely to utilize self-help methods including violence, taking justice into their own hands to right perceived wrongs. Finally, when governments fail to appropriately restrain inequality, citizens might perceive that the social contract has been broken, making them less likely to abide by the contract and resulting in higher violence rates. Nivette and Eisner (2013) found direct negative effects of political legitimacy on national homicide rates, though their measures did not allow them to determine through which mechanism the association was operating. Their findings are consistent with Chamlin and Cochran (2006), who drew similar conclusions based on cross-national analyses. Paré and Felson (2014) and Dawson (2018) examined the effects of legitimacy of the police on national homicide rates. Using a range of measures, Paré found that police performance is negatively and significantly associated with national homicide rates. Similarly, using the WVS and the European Values Survey, Dawson found a significant negative association between police legitimacy and national homicide rates as measured by WHO and UNODC. Finally, a recent study by Escaño (2021) employing fixed effects models for sixteen nations in Latin America between 2000 and 2017 shows a significant negative association between state legitimacy and homicide rates. This covariate seems particularly relevant in the region, which has the highest regional homicide rate in the world and where many governments have struggled with legitimacy.

These studies provide excellent foundations for future research. With the expectation that political legitimacy affects national homicide rates, scholars can explore various mechanisms—including those described by Nivette and Eisner—that create an association. Political legitimacy and political structure may have more complex mediating and moderating effects on national homicide rates. Like culture, the impact on national homicide rates of political structure, political legitimacy, and specific social control agencies like the police present fruitful opportunities for theoretical and empirical advancement.

Roadmap for Future Research

It has been more than twenty years since LaFree published the review we refer to and emulate throughout our chapter. Cross-national homicide scholars must address significant challenges for this research area to flourish over the next twenty years and beyond; we mention a few general ones here.

First, we must better understand the homicide measures available to us. The content of each measure is nuanced, and there are fundamental tradeoffs to using each source that scholars must appreciate. We must work with agencies like WHO and UNODC, which centralize data, and with individual governments to expand the number of nations for which reliable homicide data are available. Many nations do not report, report questionable homicide counts, or report erratically, and there are regions (like much of Africa) from which we have little data at all.

Second, the current literature is largely atheoretical and variable driven, so our theoretical explanations must become more sophisticated. This includes expanding beyond the usual suspects, especially the hyperfocus on economic factors, in the structural and cultural factors we consider. Even for often-used explanatory factors like inequality and poverty, we lack adequately precise and sophisticated macrolevel explanations. We must use what we already know from this literature, be more creative in our thinking about explanations, and integrate ideas from other disciplines—all to consider and test more meaningful explanations about why national homicide rates vary so remarkably.

Third, we must be more creative in operationalizing theoretical concepts by better understanding the array of available data. In the past, scholars relied almost solely on information gathered by national governments. An increasing amount of information available from nongovernment resources measuring a wide range of structural and cultural characteristics of nations should be of interest to us; in the last several years, cross-national homicide scholars have begun employing these sources more effectively.

Finally, we suggest that the research area move toward using an open science framework. Replication is one of several aspects of this framework. In criminology generally (McNeeley and Warner 2015; Pridemore, Makel, and Plucker 2018) and in cross-national homicide research specifically (Pridemore 2011), there are very few replications. One important reason for this is lack of data sharing. In the spirit of collaborating to best understand the causes and consequences of national homicide rates, we encourage scholars to practice open science methods and make their data and research process publicly available to the extent that doing so is possible for any particular study. Over the last several years, we have posted a mix of data, code, supplemental results, and other information from many of our own cross-national studies here: https://sites.google.com/site/homicidedata/.

Cross-national homicide research has expanded since LaFree's (1999) review. He found thirty-four quantitative cross-national homicide studies published before 1999. Nivette (2011) referenced fifty-four studies in her meta-analysis of cross-national homicide. Koeppel, Rheinberger-Dunn, and Mack (2015) referenced eighty-four cross-national homicide studies in their literature review. We found forty-one studies of homicide published between 2015 and May 2021 that included at least two nations. Figure 4.2 provides a graph of published English-language studies with homicide as the outcome variable and more than one nation in the sample. Cross-national homicide research is experiencing a renaissance in the criminological literature. While we are happy to see the growth of cross-national homicide literature, advancements remain slow on central issues like theory development and exploration of structural covariates beyond the usual suspects. Understanding the causes of the wide variation in national homicide rates is a noble mission, and we look forward to improvements in theory, data, method, and knowledge from creative and sophisticated cross-national scholars and their research.

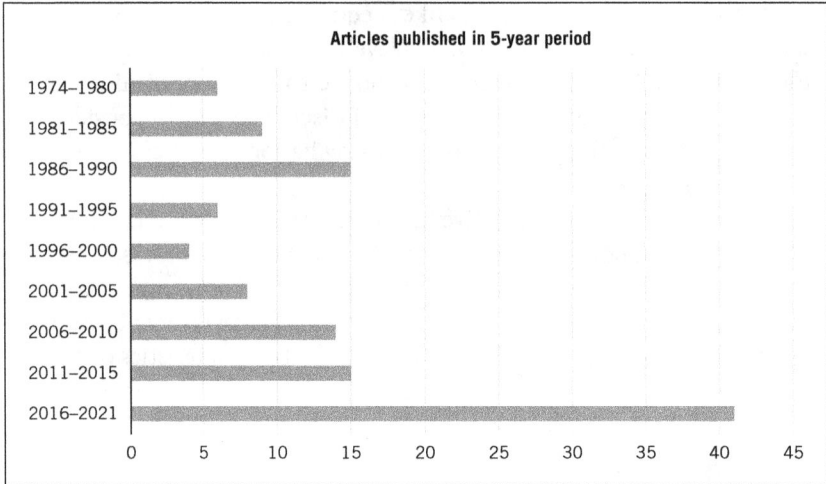

Figure 4.2 English-Language Studies Published before May 2021 with Homicide as Main Outcome and More Than One Nation in Sample (*Data source: World Health Mortality Database [WHO Mort], United Nations Office on Drugs and Crime [UNODC], World Bank World Development Indicators [World Bank], World Health Organization Global Health Observatory [WHO GHO].*)

REFERENCES

Altheimer, Irshad. 2013. "Herding and Homicide across Nations." *Homicide Studies* 17 (1): 27–58.

Archer, David, and Rosemary Gartner. 1984. *Violence and Crime in Cross-National Perspective*. New Haven, CT: Yale University Press.

Beetham, David. 2013. *The Legitimation of Power*. New York: Palgrave Macmillan.

Bjerregaard, Beth, and John K. Cochran. 2008. "A Cross-National Test of Institutional Anomie Theory: Do the Strength of Other Social Institutions Mediate or Moderate the Effects of the Economy on the Rate of Crime?" *Western Criminology Review* 9 (1): 31–48. http://search.ebscohost.com/login.aspx?direct=true&db=sih&AN=34156708&site=ehost-live.

Blau, Judith R., and Peter M. Blau. 1982. "The Cost of Inequality: Metropolitan Structure and Violent Crime." *American Sociological Review* 47 (1): 114. https://doi.org/10.2307/2095046.

Chamlin, Mitchell B., and John K. Cochran. 1995. "Assessing Messner and Rosenfeld's Institutional Anomie Theory: A Partial Test." *Criminology* 33 (3): 411–29. https://doi.org/10.1111/j.1745-9125.1995.tb01184.x.

———. 2006. "Economic Inequality, Legitimacy, and Cross-National Homicide Rates." *Homicide Studies* 10 (4): 231–52. https://doi.org/10.1177/1088767906292642.

———. 2007. "An Evaluation of the Assumptions That Underlie Institutional Anomie Theory." *Theoretical Criminology* 11 (1): 39–61. https://doi.org/10.1177/1362480607072734.

Chase-Dunn, Christopher. 1980. "Socialist States in the Capitalist World-Economy." *Social Problems* 27 (5): 505–25. https://doi.org/10.3868/s050-004-015-0003-8.

Chilton, Roland, and Adele Spielberger. 1971. "Is Delinquency Increasing? Age Structure and the Crime Rate." *Social Forces* 49 (3): 487–93. http://sf.oxfordjournals.org/content /49/3/487.short.

Cohen, Lawrence E., and Kenneth C. Land. 1987. "Age Structure and Crime: Symmetry versus Asymmetry and the Project of Crime Rates through the 1990s." *American Sociological Review* 52 (2): 170–83.

Dawson, Andrew. 2018. "Police Legitimacy and Homicide: A Macro-comparative Analysis." *Social Forces* 97 (2): 841–66. https://doi.org/10.1093/sf/soy043.

Dicristina, Bruce. 2004. "Durkheim's Theory of Homicide and the Confusion of the Empirical Literature." *Theoretical Criminology* 8 (1): 57–91. https://doi.org/10.1177 /1362480604039741.

Durkheim, Emile. 1933. *The Division of Labor in Society*. Glencoe, IL: Macmillan.

Eisner, M. 2001. "Modernization, Self-Control and Lethal Violence: The Long-Term Dynamics of European Homicide Rates in Theoretical Perspective." *British Journal of Criminology* 41 (4): 618–38. https://doi.org/10.1093/bjc/41.4.618.

Elias, Norbert. 2000. *The Civilizing Process: Socoiogenic and Psychogenetic Investigations*. Oxford edition. Oxford: Blackwell.

Escaño, Guillermo J. 2021. "A Test of Latin America-Specific Structural Covariates of Homicide Rates." Paper presented at the Annual Meeting of the American Society of Criminology, Chicago.

Fiala, Robert, and Gary LaFree. 1988. "Cross-National Determinants of Child Homicides." *American Sociological Review* 53 (3): 432–45.

Gilley, Bruce. 2006. "The Determinants of State Legitimacy: Results for 72 Countries." *International Political Science Review* 27 (1): 47–71. https://doi.org/10.1177/01925121 06058634.

Hartnagel, Timothy F. 1982. "Modernization, Female Social Roles, and Female Crime: A Cross-National Investigation." *Sociological Quarterly* 23 (4): 447–90.

Hirschi, Travis, and Michael R. Gottfredson. 1983. "Age and the Explanation of Crime." *American Journal of Sociology* 89 (3): 552–84. http://www.jstor.org/stable/10.2307/27 79005.

Hofstede, Geert H. 1998. "Attitudes, Values and Organizational Culture: Disentangling the Concepts." *Organization Studies* 19 (3): 477–93.

———. 2001. *Culture's Consequences: Comparing Values, Behaviors, Institutions, and Organization across Nations*. Thousand Oaks, CA: Sage.

Inglehart, Ronald, and Wayne E. Baker. 2000. "Modernization, Cultural Change, and the Persistence of Traditional Values." *American Sociological Review* 65 (1): 19–51. https:// doi.org/10.2307/2657288.

Inglehart, Ronald, and Christian Welzel. 2005. *Modernization, Cultural Change, and Democracy: The Human Development Sequence*. Cambridge: Cambridge University Press.

International Social Survey Programme. 2012. "Social Inequality IV." https://www.gesis .org/en/issp/modules/issp-modules-by-topic/social-inequality/2009.

Kanis, Stefan, Steven F. Messner, Manuel P. Eisner, and Wilhelm Heitmeyer. 2017. "A Cautionary Note about the Use of Estimated Homicide Data for Cross-National Research." *Homicide Studies* 21 (4): 312–24. https://doi.org/10.1177/108876791771 5670.

Karstedt, Susanne. 2006. "Democracy, Values, and Violence: Paradoxes, Tensions, and Comparative Advantages of Liberal Inclusion." *Annals of the American Academy of Political and Social Science* 605 (1): 50–81. https://doi.org/10.1177/0002716206288248.

————. 2015. "Does Democracy Matter? Comparative Perspectives on Violence and Democratic Institutions." *European Journal of Criminology* 12 (4): 457–81. https://doi.org/10.1177/1477370815584499.

Koeppel, Maria D.H., Gayle M. Rhineberer-Dunn, and Kristin Mack. 2015. "Cross-National Homicide: A Review of the Current Literature." *International Journal of Comparative and Applied Criminal Justice* 39 (1): 47–85.

LaFree, Gary. 1999. "A Summary and Review of Cross-National Comparative Studies of Homicide." In *Homicide: A Sourcebook of Social Research*, edited by M. Dwayne Smith and Margaret A. Zahn, 125–45. Thousand Oaks, CA: Sage.

————. 2005. "Evidence for Elite Convergence in Cross-National Homicide Victimization Trends, 1956 to 2000." *Sociological Quarterly* 46 (1): 191–211. https://doi.org/10.1111/j.1533-8525.2005.00009.x.

————. 2021. "Progress and Obstacles in the Internationalization of Criminology." *International Criminology* 1:58–69. https://doi.org/10.1007/s43576-021-00005-2.

LaFree, Gary, Karise Curtis, and David McDowall. 2015. "How Effective Are Our 'Better Angels'? Assessing Country-Level Declines in Homicide since 1950." *European Journal of Criminology* 12 (4): 482–504. https://doi.org/10.1177/1477370815584261.

Lin, Kai, and Ashley M. Mancik. 2020. "National Culture on the Cross-National Variation of Homicide: An Empirical Application of the Inglehart–Welzel Cultural Map." *Sociological Forum* 35 (4): 1114–134. https://doi.org/10.1111/socf.12640.

Loftin, Colin, and Robert Nash Parker. 1985. "An Errors-in-Variable Model of the Effect of Poverty on Urban Homicide Rates." *Criminology* 23 (2): 269–87.

McNeeley, Susan, and Jessica J. Warner. 2015. "Replication in Criminology: A Necessary Practice." *European Journal of Criminology* 12 (5): 581–97.

Messner, Steven F. 1986. "Modernization, Structural Characteristics, and Societal Rates of Crime: An Application of Blau's Macrosociological Theory." *Sociological Quarterly* 27 (1): 27–41. https://doi.org/10.1111/j.1533-8525.1986.tb00247.x.

Messner, Steven F., Lawrence E. Raffalovich, and Gretchen M. Sutton. 2010. "Poverty, Infant Mortality, and Homicide Rates in Cross-National Perspective: Assessments of Criterion and Construct Validity." *Criminology* 48 (2): 509–37. doi:10.1111/j.1745-9125.2010.00194.x.

Messner, Steven F., and Richard Rosenfeld. 1997. "Political Restraint of the Market and Levels of Criminal Homicide: A Cross-National Application of Institutional-Anomie Theory." *Social Forces* 75 (4): 1393–416. https://doi.org/10.1093/sf/75.4.1393.

————. 2007. *Crime and the American Dream*. 4th ed. Belmont, CA: Wadsworth.

Neuman, W. Lawrence, and Ronald J. Berger. 1988. "Competing Perspectives on Cross-National Crime: An Evaluation of Theory and Evidence." *Sociological Quarterly* 29 (2): 281–313. https://doi.org/10.1111/j.1533-8525.1988.tb01255.x.

Nisbett, Richard E., and Dov Cohen. 1996. *Culture of Honor: The Psychology of Violence in the South*. Boulder, CO: Westview Press.

Nivette, Amy E. 2011. "Cross-National Predictors of Crime: A Meta-Analysis." *Homicide Studies* 15 (2): 103–31. https://doi.org/10.1177/1088767911406397.

Nivette, Amy E., and Manuel Eisner. 2013. "Do Legitimate Polities Have Fewer Homicides? A Cross-National Analysis." *Homicide Studies* 17 (1): 3–26. https://doi.org/10.1177/1088767912452131.

Paré, Paul-Philippe, and Richard B. Felson. 2014. "Income Inequality, Poverty, and Crime across Nations." *British Journal of Sociology* 65 (3): 434–58. https://doi.org/10.1111/1468-4446.12083.

Pinker, S. 2011. *The Better Angels of Our Nature: Why Violence Has Declined.* New York: Viking.

Pridemore, William Alex. 2005. "Social Structure and Homicide in Post-Soviet Russia." *Social Science Research* 34 (4): 732–56. https://doi.org/10.1016/j.ssresearch.2004.12.005.

———. 2008. "A Methodological Addition to the Cross-National Empirical Literature on Social Structure and Homicide: A First Test of the Poverty-Homicide Thesis." *Criminology* 46 (1): 133–54.

———. 2011. "Poverty Matters: A Reassessment of the Inequality-Homicide Relationship in Cross-National Studies." *British Journal of Criminology* 51 (5): 739–72. https://doi.org/10.1093/bjc/azr019.

Pridemore, William Alex, and Sang-Weon Kim. 2006. "Democratization and Political Change as Threats to Collective Sentiments: Testing Durkheim in Russia." *Annals of the American Academy of Political and Social Science* 605 (82): 82–103.

Pridemore, William Alex, Matthew C. Makel, and Jonathan A. Plucker. 2018. "Replication in Criminology and the Social Sciences." *Annual Review of Criminology* 1:19–38.

Rogers, Meghan L. 2014. "A Descriptive and Graphical Analysis of the (Lack of) Association Between Age and Homicide Cross-Nationally." *International Criminal Justice Review* 24 (3): 235–53.

Rogers, Meghan L., and William Alex Pridemore. 2013. "The Effect of Poverty and Social Protection on National Homicide Rates: Direct and Moderating Effects." *Social Science Research* 42 (3): 584–95. https://doi.org/http://dx.doi.org/10.1016/j.ssresearch.2012.12.005.

———. 2016. "The (Null) Effects of Percent Young on 15 to 24 Age-Specific and Male- and Female-Specific Cross-National Homicide Rates." *Homicide Studies* 20 (3): 257–92. https://doi.org/10.1177/1088767915613105.

———. 2017a. "A Comprehensive Evaluation of the Association between Percent Young and Cross-National Homicide Rates." *British Journal of Criminology* 57 (5): 1080–100. https://doi.org/10.1093/bjc/azw039.

———. 2017b. "How Does Social Protection Influence Cross-National Homicide Rates in OECD Nations?" *Sociological Quarterly* 58 (4): 576–94. https://doi.org/10.1080/00380253.2017.1367265.

———. 2018. "Do National Homicide Rates Follow Supranational Trends?" *Journal of Research in Crime and Delinquency* 55 (6): 691–727. https://doi.org/10.1177/0022427818785210.

———. 2020. "Perceived Inequality and Cross-National Homicide Rates." *Justice Quarterly* 39 (2): 225–51. https://doi.org/10.1080/07418825.2020.1729392.

Santos, Mateus Rennó, Alexander Testa, and Douglas B. Weiss. 2018. "Where Poverty Matters: Examining the Cross-National Relationship between Economic Deprivation and Homicide." *British Journal of Criminology* 372 (2): 1–22. https://doi.org/10.1093/bjc/azx013.

Shelley, Louise I. 1981. *Crime and Modernization: The Impacts of Industrialization and Urbanization on Crime.* Carbondale: Southern Illinois University Press.

Smit, Paul R., Rinke R. de Jong, and Catrien J. H. Bijleveld. 2012. "Homicide Data in Europe: Definitions, Sources, and Statistics." In *Handbook of European Homicide Research: Patterns, Explanations, and Country Studies,* edited by M. C. A. Liem and William Alex Pridemore, 5–23. New York: Springer.

Smith, M. Dwayne, and Margaret A. Zahn. 1999. *Homicide: A Sourcebook of Social Research.* Thousand Oaks, CA: Sage.

Stamatel, Janet P. 2006. "Incorporating Socio-historical Context into Quantitative Cross-National Criminology." *International Journal of Comparative and Applied Criminal Justice* 30 (2): 177–207. https://doi.org/10.1080/01924036.2006.9678752.

———. 2016. "Democratic Cultural Values as Predictors of Cross-National Homicide Variation in Europe." *Homicide Studies* 20 (3): 239–56. https://doi.org/10.1177/1088 767915611178.

Steffensmeier, Darrell, Yunmei Lu, and Sumit Kumar. 2019. "Age-Crime Relation in India: Similarity or Divergence vs. Hirschi/Gottfredson Inverted j-Shaped Projection?" *British Journal of Criminology* 59 (1): 144–65. https://doi.org/10.1093/bjc/azy011.

Steffensmeier, Darrell, Yunmei Lu, and Chongmin Na. 2020. "Age and Crime in South Korea: Cross-National Challenge to Invariance Thesis." *Justice Quarterly* 37 (3): 410–35. https://doi.org/10.1080/07418825.2018.1550208.

Steffensmeier, Darrell, Hua Zhong, and Yunmei Lu. 2017. "Age and Its Relation to Crime in Taiwan and the United States: Invariant, or Does Cultural Context Matter?" *Criminology* 55 (2): 377–404. https://doi.org/10.1111/1745-9125.12139.

Thomas, William I., and Florian Znaniecki. 1927. *The Polish Peasant in Europe and America*. New York: Alfred A. Knopf.

Tonry, Michael. 2014. "Why Crime Rates Are Falling throughout the Western World." *Crime and Justice: A Review of Research* 43:1–63.

Trent, Carol L. S., and William Alex Pridemore. 2012. "A Review of the Cross-National Empirical Literature on Social Structure and Homicide." In *Handbook of European Homicide Research: Patterns, Explanations, and Country Studies*, edited by M. C. A. Liem and William Alex Pridemore, 111–35. New York: Springer.

United Nations Office on Drugs and Crime. 2021. "DATAUNODC. Victims of Intentional Homicide, 1990–2018." https://dataunodc.un.org/content/data/homicide/homicide -rate.

Wallerstein, Immanuel. 1974. "The Rise and Future Demise of the World Capitalist System: Concepts for Comparative Analysis." *Comparative Studies in Society and History* 16 (4): 387–415. https://doi.org/10.1017/S0010417500007520.

World Health Organization. 2020. "Global Status Report on Preventing Violence against Children 2020." https://www.who.int/violence_injury_prevention/violence/status _report/2014/report/Method_for_data_collection.pdf?ua=1.

———. 2021. "Estimating Global Homicide Deaths." https://www.who.int/violence_in jury_prevention/violence/status_report/2014/report/Estimating_global_homicide _deaths.pdf?ua=1.

II

The Scope

5

Social Structure and Homicide

JAMES TUTTLE, PATRICIA L. McCALL, AND KENNETH C. LAND

Introduction

Research exploring structural correlates of homicide rates provides a unique opportunity to understand the causes of crime. Criminologists have long recognized that criminal behavior cannot be reduced simply to individual characteristics or inherent attributes of offenders; research must examine the characteristics and social dynamics of groups and communities (Shaw and McKay 1942). While individual-level theory and causality is often the focus of American criminology, several criminogenic social processes are best understood at the macrolevel (Rosenfeld 2011). By addressing the context under which crime is more (or less) likely to occur, macrolevel research provides an opportunity to address the ultimate causes of patterns of criminal behavior across communities and geographic locales. Additionally, analyses of aggregate crime rates can inform public policy (McCall and Brauer 2014; Tuttle 2018). The ability to explain or even predict trends in aggregate crime rates can lend credence to criminologists, providing the opportunity to shape public debates on the causes of crime (Baumer, Vélez, and Rosenfeld 2018; Land and McCall 2001).

Macrolevel homicide research presents a unique set of challenges. Beyond the difficulties of comprehending the complex dynamics of large social groups, macrolevel researchers are confronted with issues related to data availability, model specification, and statistical inference. Because macrolevel research on crime rates is reliant on secondary data, the operationalization and measurement of theoretical concepts tend to be less precise. There are many instances in the literature where data are unavailable for precise conceptual operationalization, contributing to issues related to inconsistent model specification and dramatically different findings across studies (see Trent and Pridemore 2012). Even when quality data are available, aggregate-level research is often plagued by issues of multicollinearity (Gordon 1968). Because of these issues, macrolevel homicide research has not always produced consistent and/or replicable results.

In a now classic study of structural predictors of homicide, Land, McCall, and Cohen (1990) addressed the challenges of conducting macrolevel research. Land and colleagues found that the previous literature was inconsistent, as statistically significant findings varied from study to study. Inconsistencies in regression model specification and apparent collinearity bias among the regressors plagued previous research. To address these issues, Land and colleagues (1990) applied principal components analysis to the matrix of correlations among eleven structural predictors used as explanatory variables in one or more prior studies of homicide. This approach facilitated the specification and estimation of a consistent baseline model that incorporated composite indices of highly correlated explanatory variables as regressors. The authors addressed the impact of the correlates of homicide rates during different time periods and across different levels of aggregation (city, metropolitan area, and state), uncovering largely consistent correlates/structural covariates of homicide. Since its publication, Land and colleagues (1990) has become one of the foundational works regarding methodological considerations of macrolevel homicide research.

Using Land and colleagues (1990) as a point of departure, this chapter summarizes major developments within the literature on macrolevel homicide research. Specifically, we address methodological concerns raised by Land and colleagues (1990) as well as their initial question: Are there any consistent correlates of aggregate homicide rates? While more comprehensive reviews and meta-analyses of the literature can be located elsewhere (LaFree 1999; Nivette 2011; Pratt and Cullen 2005; Trent and Pridemore 2012), this chapter focuses on methodological concerns, including collinearity, measurement, and model specification. While this chapter addresses methodological issues in macrolevel homicide research, researchers should be cognizant of the specific theoretical and practical considerations of conducting research at different levels of aggregation not addressed in this chapter. To begin this discussion, we address the issue of collinearity in aggregate-level homicide research.

Collinearity Issues in Homicide Research

One assumption for reliable and substantively meaningful statistical estimates of multivariate regression analyses is that the model is properly specified, including no multicollinearity among explanatory/independent variables. Multicollinearity is a type of collinearity bias that refers to the occurrence of relatively strong correlations among explanatory variables within a regression model. Multicollinearity produces biased or inaccurate results for estimated regression coefficients. Typically, a correlation coefficient of 0.7 or greater between explanatory variables in preliminary bivariate analyses is considered indicative of multicollinearity concerns. While the assumption of no multicollinearity applies equally to individual-level and aggregate-level data, it is more pertinent to aggregate-level research as bivariate correlations tend to be inflated at higher levels of aggregation (Clark and Avery 1976). As a result, macrolevel research is much more likely to present issues of multicollinearity, especially when similar social processes produce multiple related outcomes. Because economic and social deprivation tend to cluster together across social space (Sampson 2012), differentiating the impact of distinct but related concepts and their measures is often fraught with collinearity problems in regression analyses of aggregate-level phenomena. Therefore, careful attention must be paid to bivariate associations between explanatory variables in preliminary analyses as well as other measures such as variance inflation factors when estimating regression models.

An additional but often overlooked collinearity issue is the *partialing fallacy*. This type of bias can occur even when covariates do not share a strong bivariate correlation (e.g., $r < 0.7$). A typical manifestation of the partialing fallacy is when two covariates share a moderate-to-strong bivariate correlation while simultaneously displaying relatively weak bivariate correlations with the dependent variable. The partialing fallacy often causes explanatory variables to appear as *not* statistically significant predictors of the dependent variable in regression analyses, even when a true relationship exists (Gordon 1968). When this type of collinearity bias is present, researchers often make a Type II error—when one accepts the null hypothesis that a variable does not contribute explained variation in the dependent variable when, in fact, it does. Variance inflation factors and traditional multicollinearity indicators will not necessarily detect such partialing problems, so it is necessary to examine the nature of relationships between even moderately correlated covariates relative to each individual covariate's correlation with the dependent variable and to scrutinize a series of nested models in preliminary analysis to determine if the partialing fallacy is present. If a model omitting one of the two suspect covariates shows a statistically significant coefficient but both variables fail to achieve statistical significance when included in the model together, the partialing fallacy is likely at play. When this occurs, the researcher needs to consider remedies for this model misspecification, such as omitting one of the impacted covariates or combining the suspect covariates into an index (if they are related measures of a theoretical concept).

When researchers fail to eliminate collinearity problems, models produce erroneous results. As Land and colleagues (1990) demonstrate, one of the major reasons for inconsistent findings across ecological studies of homicide is failure to adequately address collinearity issues. Regression models plagued by excessive collinearity often appear unstable, with dramatically different results across model specifications. In some cases, associations appear in the opposite of their true direction (for example, a positive association flipping its sign to a negative association).

Since Land and colleagues' (1990) publication, macrolevel homicide researchers have been much more cognizant of issues of collinearity—though often, multicollinearity is addressed while potential partialing fallacy issues are overlooked. Researchers usually provide some indication that multicollinearity is not an issue by creating an index combining highly correlated covariates (Krivo and Peterson 1996), examining variance inflation factors (Ouimet 2012), or exploring nested models to check the stability of coefficients (Tuttle 2019). These strategies should be pursued to determine whether collinearity is a potential problem.

Measurement and Model Specification in Homicide Research

Another issue that contributes to discrepancies in identifying factors predicting homicide rates in the macrolevel research literature is inconsistent model specification. Without including a set of factors consistently across different studies of macrolevel variation in homicide rates, consistent findings may be elusive, and some models may even be misspecified. Land and colleagues (1990) propose a model that accounts for six structural predictors of homicide rate: resource deprivation/affluence, population structure, family disruption, age structure, unemployment rate, and region. While the precise set of predictors of homicide is subject to debate, the lack of consistent model specification across studies prevents direct comparison of results. A few studies feature a model specification similar to that of Land and colleagues (1990). For example, McCall, Land, and Parker (2010) update the original analyses to include more recent decades (1970, 1980, 1990, and 2000) and confirm the continued importance of four factors—resource deprivation, population structure, family disruption, and southern region—that exerted a significant and positive impact in their sample of U.S. cities. Two other covariates were somewhat less consistently associated with homicide: age structure often failed to achieve statistical significance (there was even a *negative* association with percentage aged fifteen to twenty-nine in 1980), and unemployment only achieved a statistically significantly association during the 1990 and 2000 time periods. Some researchers (Baller et al. 2001; Tcherni 2011) have emulated this model specification, including measurement of factors similar to both Land et al. (1990) and McCall et al. (2010). However, much of the research on structural correlates of homicide does not include a standard or consistent model specification. This lack of consistency in the cross-national homicide literature has been outlined elsewhere (i.e., Trent and Pridemore 2012), but we briefly address inconsistencies in covariates accounted for in previous macrolevel homicide research.

While it is not clear whether Land and colleagues (1990) identified the "correct" structural model specification to be used as the standard, it is clear that model specification varies significantly from study to study. Certainly, studies exploring more recent time periods or geographic locales may discover that some covariates are no longer important predictors of homicide rate. The following discussion focuses on the six factors identified by Land and colleagues (1990) as relevant covariates of homicide, addressing to what degree these factors are included in structural homicide analyses and associated with homicide in the current literature. The factor that is nearly universally assessed in macrolevel homicide research is economic deprivation (or affluence). But the precise measurement and/or number of variables utilized to operationalize economic deprivation differs across studies.

Economic Deprivation/Affluence

The association between economic deprivation and crime is nearly incontrovertible. A measure of economic deprivation/affluence is universally accounted for in macrolevel research on homicide, and there is almost always a positive and significant association between economic deprivation and homicide rates. However, the precise measure of deprivation varies considerably across studies. Researchers often employ a deprivation index, combining some elements of absolute deprivation (poverty), relative deprivation (inequality), and prevalence of other social disadvantages (Baller et al. 2001; McCall et al. 2010; McCall, Parker, and MacDonald 2008; Ousey and Lee 2010). Some studies consider multiple measures of socioeconomic deprivation (Lee et al. 2003), while others include separate measures of poverty and inequality within the same model (Burraston, McCutcheon, and Watts 2018; Burraston et al. 2019; Kovandzic, Vieraitis, and Yeisley 1998; Pridemore 2005).

Researchers have begun to parse different specifications of the economic deprivation and homicide association. Neighborhood-level research has addressed theoretical claims that economic (and social) disadvantage has a nonlinear accelerating effect on crime at greater concentrations of poverty. Wilson (1987) argues that in neighborhoods with high degrees of economic and social disadvantage, communities become effectively isolated from the rest of society. In addition to economic motivations to commit crime produced by poverty, social control and cultural adaptations to isolation (see

Sampson and Wilson 1995) cause crime rates to exceed the expectation of a simple linear association after a certain threshold. Evidence for this theoretical prediction has been mixed. For example, Hannon (2005) finds an accelerating impact of higher levels of disadvantage index on homicide in New York City census tracts, supporting Wilson's (1987) proposition. However, other researchers have noted a decelerating impact of disadvantage on homicide, as the impact of additional poverty concentration on homicide seems to diminish in the most disadvantaged neighborhoods (McNulty 2001). While there is agreement that economic deprivation contributes to higher rates of homicide, the precise functional form of this association remains unclear (Hipp and Yates 2011).

In cross-national homicide research literature, there is a burgeoning debate concerning the impact of absolute deprivation (poverty) versus relative deprivation (inequality). In previous cross-national research, income inequality has been one of the most consistent predictors of homicide rates (LaFree 1999; Nivette 2011). However, recent criticism of this apparent consensus has focused on the lack of consideration of poverty within this literature (Paré and Felson 2014; Pridemore 2008). The debate concerning the relative impact of poverty and inequality could lead to a productive refinement of cross-national theories of crime, but it is unlikely to be resolved with current available evidence. Instead of using a direct measure of poverty, cross-national poverty and homicide literature often relies on the indirect proxy measure of infant mortality, which is strongly associated with income inequality (Messner, Raffalovich, and Sutton 2010). Further multilevel analyses are required to truly resolve this debate (Tuttle 2021), as there is overlap between poverty and inequality both theoretically and empirically in macrolevel research. For now, the jury is still out on the relative importance of absolute versus relative deprivation in macrolevel studies of homicide.

Population Composition

No other factor exerts an impact on homicide as consistently as economic deprivation, but population composition is often accounted for in some way in structural analyses of homicide. In the analysis by Land and colleagues (1990), the measure of population composition was constructed by combining data on population size and density due to collinearity between these two measures. Some subsequent researchers have explicitly followed this strategy for an index of population composition (McCall et al. 2010; Ousey and Lee 2010). Others have employed a stand-alone measure of population size (Krivo and Peterson 2000; Parker 2001) or population density (MacDonald and Gover 2005). Overall, meta-analyses suggest that degree of urbanization/

density as a stand-alone measure exerts a relatively modest impact on aggregate crime rates (Pratt and Cullen 2005).

Population indicators are often associated with homicide rates at lower levels of aggregation in U.S. samples (Land et al. 1990; Lee et al. 2003; McCall et al. 2010), but there is no consistent association in the cross-national literature (Nivette 2011; Trent and Pridemore 2012). This may be indicative of processes operating at different levels of analysis. At the neighborhood level, greater population density is indicative of lack of interpersonal social relations (Wirth 1938) and lack of social control (Sampson and Groves 1989). However, when comparing nations as a whole, the degree of urbanization and/or population density within a country may be indicative of other social processes, such as increased economic development and modernization. Accordingly, inconsistent findings may be expected at different levels of analysis.

Age Structure

Surprisingly, despite fairly consistent evidence that young people tend to commit a disproportionate number of crimes (Hirschi and Gottfredson 1983), age structure is inconsistently associated with homicide in macrolevel homicide research. During some eras, the percentage of population of peak crime-offending age (approximately fifteen to twenty-nine) is strongly associated with crime rates, allowing for fairly accurate forecasts (Blumstein, Cohen, and Miller 1980; Cohen and Land 1987; Land and McCall 2001). However, researchers using age structure to predict crime trends forecasted an increase in crime during the 1990s (Bennett, Dilulio, and Walters 1996), an era that corresponded with the largest *decrease* in homicide rates in the post–World War II era. Lack of consistent findings on the impact of percentage of young people in the population is common within the homicide literature (McCall et al. 2013; Rogers and Pridemore 2017).

These inconsistent findings have been clarified, to some degree, in recent research. In subnational aggregates, such as city-level level variations in homicide, the null findings between age structure and homicide are likely due to differential institutional engagement. Drawing on the influential theory of age-graded differential institutional engagement by Sampson and Laub (1993), McCall and colleagues (2013) argue that juveniles and young adults engaged in conventional institutions, such as college or occupational training/employment, are less likely to commit crime. Conversely, disengaged youth are more likely to be involved in crime. The null and inconsistent findings may be explicated by accounting for the institutional engagement of youth within a local community (Dollar et al. 2017). Additionally, a recent cross-national study by Santos, Testa, Porter, and Lynch (2019) suggests that the impact of age structure on homicide is dependent on national context. In regions with relatively high rates of homicide, such as Latin America, there may be little impact of percent young on homicide. Conversely, in regions with relatively low rates of homicide, such as western Europe, there is a strong correlation between percent young and homicide. Overall, while age structure is not consistently associated with homicide as expected based on crime-prone age arguments, in certain contexts it is an import factor shaping homicide rates.

Family Disruption

Often operationalized as the percentage of divorced males (i.e., Land et al. 1990), measures of family disruption or family structure are often significantly associated with homicide rates (Pratt and Cullen 2005). Typically, researchers assess the impact of a stand-alone divorce rate on homicide rates (Hannon 2005; MacDonald and Gover 2005; McCall et al. 2010; Ousey and Lee 2010; Tcherni 2011). However, family disruption can manifest in other ways. For example, the prevalence of single-parent households can be indicative of family disruption. This measure is less often employed as a stand-alone measure in regression analyses on homicide rates and is instead combined with other measures of family disruption (Beaulieu and Messner 2010).

Family disruption/structure measures are sometimes combined with economic deprivation measures. Land and colleagues (1990) among others (Krivo and Peterson 2000; McCall et al. 2010; Sampson and Groves 1989) have combined measures of single parenthood ("female-headed households") with other variables into an economic deprivation index. This combination of economic deprivation and family disruption measures is the result, in part, of methodological and theoretical considerations. Methodologically, collinearity issues operating between single parenthood and economic deprivation necessitate combining these measures into an index. Theoretically, single parenthood reduces the supervision of juveniles and neighborhood capacity to exert social control, a feature of neighborhoods with concentrated disadvantage and lack of collective efficacy (Sampson 2012). Overall, whether included as a separate measure or a combined measure of concentrated disadvantage, family disruption is consistently associated with higher rates of homicide.

Unemployment

Despite being featured in Land and colleague's (1990) analysis, unemployment is often *not* included in structural models of homicide rates. The absence of unemployment in homicide models is likely due to null and inconsistent findings. Unemployment sometimes exerts a negative impact on homicide (Land et al. 1990), no significant impact on homicide (McCall et al. 2010), or a positive impact on homicide (Tcherni 2011). Employing an annual time series analysis, Cantor and Land (1985) demonstrated opposite effects of unemployment on aggregate-level crime rates vis-à-vis short-term versus long-term influences, explained by criminal opportunity and criminal motivation respectively, illuminating mixed findings in the literature (Chiricos 1987). Other efforts have been made to explicate these inconsistent findings, focusing either on historical era (i.e., Carlson and Michalowski 1997) or cross-sectional and longitudinal variation separately (i.e., South and Cohen 1985). However, many scholars have not included unemployment in studies of structural covariates of homicide, possibly due to limited and inconsistent impact.

For alternative measures of economic distress, researchers have turned to other potential indicators. Consumer inflation (McCall and Brauer 2014; Tuttle 2018) and consumer sentiment (Rosenfeld 2009) have been used as indicators of economic conditions, which are significantly and positively associated with homicide rates. Going forward, scholars may need to examine types of economic distress other than unemployment that impact aggregate homicide rates.

Region

Finally, regional differences have commonly been accounted for in analyses of homicide rates (Land et al. 1990). Controls for region were originally conceptualized as an indicator of a difficult-to-measure subculture of southern violence in the United States (Gastil 1971). The distinctness of southern homicide rates has diminished in more recent decades but still exerts a significant impact (McCall et al. 2010). Increasingly, researchers have included multiple or different regional controls within models, accounting for western states as well (Beaulieu and Messner 2010; Tcherni 2011). In addition to the substantive considerations of a regional control variable, accounting for region assists in reducing omitted variable bias.

Cross-national homicide researchers have followed this example, including statistical controls to account for cultural distinctions within global regions that have exceptionally high homicide rates even after accounting for standard structural variables. For example, Neapolitan (1994) suggests that high rates of homicide in Latin America are due to machismo cultural values. While some scholars have questioned whether it is culture or other structural factors that contribute to high homicide rates in Latin America (Chon 2011), these regional controls are among the strongest predictors of cross-national variation in homicide (Nivette 2011). Overall, geographical region appears to be a robust predictor of homicide rates.

Additional Factors: Race and Ethnicity

Additional factors addressed in homicide research are racial inequality, composition, and segregation. Land and colleagues (1990) include racial composition (measured as percent black) in their economic deprivation index due to the high degree of collinearity between race and economic deprivation measures. Subsequent research has tried to parse these influences to examine the direct impact of racial inequality and segregation. Stemming from the work of Massey and Denton (1993), researchers have addressed the impact of racial segregation on homicide rates. Theoretically, racial segregation is hypothesized to operate through social isolation from mainstream institutions, contributing to higher rates of homicide (Lee and Ousey 2005). Racial segregation has a robust impact on homicide rates, contributing to significantly higher rates of homicide victimization among black people (Light and Thomas 2019; Peterson and Krivo 1993). However, the impact of racial and ethnic segregation is mediated, in part, by conventional measures of concentrated economic disadvantage (Feldmeyer 2010), suggesting the strong association between economic and social disadvantage.

An additional line of inquiry addressing the impact of race and ethnicity on homicide is the so-called Latino paradox. During the 1990s, homicide rates declined dramatically in the United States, corresponding with a dramatic increase in immigration from Latin American countries. This apparent paradox suggests that increasing Latino immigration actually contributed to a decline in homicide rates (Sampson 2008), despite immigrants, as a group, experiencing high rates of economic and social marginalization. The precise mechanism behind this paradox is disputed; it could be due to migrants disproportionately aspiring to upward mobility and refraining from crime or being a group that assists in the revitalization of distressed communities. Subsequent reviews of this research suggest that there is a negative association between immigration and crime, yet a comprehensive review of this literature demonstrates that this effect is inconsistent and fairly weak (Ousey and Kubrin 2018).

At the center of the theoretical link between race/ethnicity and homicide is the implicit racial invariance hypothesis, which assumes that the impact of structural predictors of homicide is the same across racial/ethnic groups. Usually, tests of the racial invariance hypothesis focus on whether economic deprivation exerts a similar impact on racially disaggregated crime rates. While it appears that economic deprivation contributes to higher rates of homicide among all racial/ethnic groups (Peterson and Krivo 2005), some research suggests differences across racial groups. For example, Ousey (1999) finds that different forms of deprivation have a stronger impact on white homicide rates than black homicide rates. Additionally, Parker and McCall (1999) demonstrate that the correlates of white and black interracial and intraracial homicide rates differ. The potential differences in the correlates of homicide across racial groups as well as the independent effect of racial segregation on homicide suggest that the independent impact of race needs to be included in research on homicide, especially in U.S. samples, although researchers must be cognizant of collinearity issues operating among measures of racial composition, inequality, and economic deprivation.

Are There Any Consistencies in Macrolevel Homicide Research?

Structural analysis of homicide has progressed significantly since the seminal analysis of Land and colleagues (1990), but concerns about our knowledge of structural determinants of homicide remain. The baseline model employed by Land and colleagues (1990) provides a solid starting point for homicide researchers. Without a baseline model, it is difficult to make direct comparisons across studies to build on our knowledge base of the forces driving homicide rates and trends. Data limitations may make estimation of the exact same model specifications, with consistent measurement and inclusion of control variables, difficult. However, to the extent possible, macrolevel homicide researchers must strive to be consistent in estimating comparable baseline regression models.

Accumulated knowledge of the social and economic factors that contribute to variation in homicide rates substantiates the importance of some of the factors outlined by Land and colleagues (1990). However, subsequent research has indicated other relevant factors and different regression model configurations. This is unsurprising because theoretical explanations may dictate different causal models depending on the unit of analysis; historical changes and the period effects of social and economic forces result in varying impacts on homicidal behavior over time. Researchers should be cognizant of the factors that emerge as consistent predictors of homicide rates and ensure their inclusion in future research.

Substantively, a few conclusions can be drawn about the structural predictors of homicide. The most consistent finding in this literature is the impact of economic and social deprivation on homicide rates. The precise measurement of deprivation varies, but concentrated poverty/disadvantage, income inequality, and racial/ethnic marginalization are consistently linked to higher rates of homicide. Additionally, family disruption often exerts a significant impact on homicide rates, although this finding is not as universal as the association between homicide and deprivation measures. Finally, there is a consistent impact of geographical region on homicide rates in both the United States and in cross-national research. Other factors that impact homicide rate are more dependent on social and historical context and level of analysis, such as population structure, age structure, and unemployment.

Methodologically, the structural analysis of homicide has made progress in some areas but fallen short in others. Researchers appear much more aware of the issues posed by multicollinearity and have heeded the advice of Land and colleagues (1990) to create indices of highly correlated and conceptually consistent explanatory variables. However, the awareness of and correction for partialing fallacy measurement problems still plague homicide research, thereby putting into question the inferences drawn in certain studies. The structural analysis of homicide remains fraught with methodological issues. Inconsistent measurement and model specification are problems among aggregate-level homicide studies.

To continue to refine our understanding of the structural correlates of homicide, more attention needs to be directed to differences across levels of analysis. Careful attention should be paid to important theoretical and empirical comparisons across different levels of aggregation, as the conceptualization, causal modeling, and factors influencing homicide rates may not be invariant at different levels of analysis (i.e., Trent and Pridemore 2010). Whereas this chapter highlights methodological issues crucial to sound homicide research, theoretical arguments and research questions should drive model specification. The article by Land and colleagues (1990) serves as a solid starting point for addressing the structural correlates of homicide, but future research needs to continue to refine our understanding of how the impact of classical covariates differs systematically across samples at different levels of aggregation.

REFERENCES

Baller, Robert D., Luc Anselin, Steven F. Messner, Glenn Deane, and Darnell F. Dawkins. 2001. "Structural Covariates of U.S. County Homicide Rates: Incorporating Spatial Effects." *Criminology* 39 (3): 561–88. https://doi.org/10.1111/j.1745-9125.2001.tb00933.x.

Baumer, Eric P, María B. Vélez, and Richard Rosenfeld. 2018. "Bringing Crime Trends Back into Criminology: A Critical Assessment of the Literature and a Blueprint for Future Inquiry." *Annual Review of Criminology* 1:39–61. https://doi.org/10.1146/annurev-criminol-032317-092339.

Beaulieu, Mark, and Steven F. Messner. 2010. "Assessing Changes in the Effect of Divorce Rate on Homicide Rates across Large U.S. Cities, 1960–2000: Revisiting the Chicago School." *Homicide Studies* 14 (1): 24–51. https://doi.org/10.1177/1088767909353020.

Bennett, William J., John J. Dilulio, and John P. Walters. 1996. *Body Count: Moral Poverty—And How to Win America's War Against Crime and Drugs.* New York: Simon & Schuster.

Blumstein, Alfred, Jacqueline Cohen, and Harold D. Miller. 1980. "Demographically Disaggregated Projections of Prison Populations." *Journal of Criminal Justice* 8 (1): 1–26. https://doi.org/10.1016/0047-2352(80)90056-2.

Burraston, Bert, James C. McCutcheon, and Stephen J. Watts. 2018. "Relative and Absolute Deprivation's Relationship with Violent Crime in the United States: Testing an Interaction Effect between Income Inequality and Disadvantage." *Crime & Delinquency* 64 (4): 542–60. https://doi.org/10.1177/0011128717709246.

Burraston, Bert, Stephen J. Watts, James C. McCutcheon, and Karli Province. 2019. "Relative Deprivation, Absolute Deprivation, and Homicide: Testing an Interaction between Income Inequality and Disadvantage." *Homicide Studies* 23 (1): 3–19. https://doi.org/10.1177/1088767918782938.

Cantor, David, and Kenneth C. Land. 1985. "Unemployment and Crime Rates in the Post–World War II United States: A Theoretical and Empirical Analysis." *American Sociological Review* 50 (3): 317–32. https://doi.org/10.2307/2095542.

Carlson, Susan M., and Raymond J. Michalowski. 1997. "Crime, Unemployment, and Social Structures of Accumulations: An Inquiry into Historical Contingency." *Justice Quarterly* 14 (2): 209–41. https://doi.org/10.1080/07418829700093311.

Chiricos, Theodore G. 1987. "Rates of Crime and Unemployment: An Analysis of Aggregate Research Evidence." *Social Problems* 34 (2): 187–212. https://doi.org/10.2307/800715.

Chon, Don Soo. 2011. "Contributing Factors for High Homicide Rates in Latin America: A Critical Test of Neapolitan's Regional Subculture of Violence Thesis." *Journal of Family Violence* 26:299–307. https://doi.org/10.1007/s10896-011-9365-5.

Clark, W. A. V., and Karen L. Avery. 1976. "The Effects of Data Aggregation in Statistical Analysis." *Geographical Analysis* 8 (4): 428–38. https://doi.org/10.1111/j.1538-4632.1976.tb00549.x.

Cohen, Lawrence E., and Kenneth C. Land. 1987. "Age Structure and Crime: Symmetry versus Asymmetry and the Projection of Crime Rates through the 1990s." *American Sociological Review* 52 (2): 170–83. https://www.jstor.org/stable/2095446.

Dollar, Cindy B., Patricia L. McCall, Kenneth C. Land, and Joshua Fink. 2017. "Age Structure and Neighborhood Homicide: Testing and Extending the Differential Institutional Engagement Hypothesis." *Homicide Studies* 21 (4): 243–66. https://doi.org/10.1177/1088767917702474.

Feldmeyer, Ben. 2010. "The Effects of Racial/Ethnic Segregation on Latino and Black Homicide." *Sociological Quarterly* 51 (4): 600–623. https://doi.org/10.1111/j.1533-8525.2010.01185.x.

Gastil, Raymond D. 1971. "Homicide and a Regional Culture of Violence." *American Sociological Review* 36 (3): 412–27. https://doi.org/10.2307/2093082.

Gordon, Robert A. 1968. "Issues in Multiple Regression." *American Journal of Sociology* 73:592–616. https://doi.org/10.1086/224533.

Hannon, Lance E. 2005. "Extremely Poor Neighborhoods and Homicide." *Social Science Quarterly* 86 (s1): 1418–34. https://doi.org/10.1111/j.0038-4941.2005.00353.x.

Hipp, John R., and Daniel K. Yates. 2011. "Ghettos, Thresholds, and Crime: Does Concentrated Poverty Really Have an Accelerating Increasing Effect on Crime?" *Criminology* 49 (4): 955–90. https://doi.org/10.1111/j.1745-9125.2011.00249.x.

Hirschi, Travis, and Michael Gottfredson. 1983. "Age and the Explanation of Crime." *American Journal of Sociology* 89 (3): 552–84. https://www.jstor.org/stable/2779005.

Kovandzic, Tomislav V., Lynne M. Vieraitis, and Mark R. Yeisley. 1998. "The Structural Covariates of Urban Homicide: Reassessing the Impact of Income Inequality and Poverty in the Post-Reagan Era." *Criminology* 36 (3): 569–600. https://doi.org/10.1111/j.1745-9125.1998.tb01259.x.

Krivo, Lauren J., and Ruth D. Peterson. 1996. "Extremely Disadvantaged Neighborhoods and Urban Crime." *Social Forces* 75 (2): 619–48. https://doi.org/10.1093/sf/75.2.619.

———. 2000. "The Structural Context of Homicide: Accounting for Racial Differences in Process." *American Sociological Review* 65 (4): 547–59. https://www.jstor.org/stable/2657382.

LaFree, Gary. 1999. "Summary and Review of Cross-National Comparative Studies of Homicide." In *Homicide: A Sourcebook of Social Research*, edited by M. Dwayne Smith and Margaret A. Zahn, 125–45. Thousand Oaks, CA: Sage.

Land, Kenneth C., and Patricia L. McCall. 2001. "The Indeterminacy of Forecasts of Crime Rates and Juvenile Offenses." In *Juvenile Crime, Juvenile Justice*, edited by Joan McCord, Cathy Spatz Wisdom, and Nancy A. Crowell, appendix B. Washington, DC: National Academy Press.

Land, Kenneth C., Patricia L. McCall, and Lawrence E. Cohen. 1990. "Structural Covariates of Homicide Rates: Are There Any Invariances across Time and Social Space?" *American Journal of Sociology* 95 (4): 922–63. https://www.jstor.org/stable/2780646.

Lee, Matthew, Michael Maume, and Graham Ousey. 2003. "Social Isolation and Lethal Violence Across the Metro/Nonmetro Divide: The Effects of Socioeconomic Disadvantage and Poverty Concentration on Homicide." *Rural Sociology* 68 (1): 107–31.

Lee, Matthew, and Graham Ousey. 2005. "Institutional Access, Residential Segregation, and Urban Black Homicide." *Sociological Inquiry* 75 (10): 31–54.

Light, Michael T., and Julia T. Thomas. 2019. "Segregation and Violence Reconsidered: Do Whites Benefit from Residential Segregation?" *American Sociological Review* 84 (4): 690–725. https://doi.org/10.1177/0003122419858731.

MacDonald, John M., and Angela R. Gover. 2005. "Concentrated Disadvantage and Youth-on-Youth Homicide: Assessing the Structural Covariates over Time." *Homicide Studies* 9 (1): 30–54. https://doi.org/10.1177/1088767904271433.

Massey, Douglas S., and Nancy A. Denton. 1993. *American Apartheid: Segregation and the Making of the Underclass*. Boston: Harvard University Press.

McCall, Patricia L., and Jonathan R. Brauer. 2014. "Social Welfare Support and Homicide: Longitudinal Analyses of European Countries from 1994 to 2010." *Social Science Research* 48:90–107. https://doi.org/10.1016/j.ssresearch.2014.05.009.

McCall, Patricia L., Kenneth C. Land, Cindy Brooks Dollar, and Karen F. Parker. 2013. "The Age Structure-Crime Rate Relationship: Solving a Long-Standing Puzzle." *Journal of Quantitative Criminology* 29:167–90. https://doi.org/10.1007/s10940-012-9175-9.

McCall, Patricia L., Kenneth C. Land, and Karen F. Parker. 2010. "An Empirical Assessment of What We Know about Structural Covariates of Homicide Rates: A Return to a Classic 20 Years Later." *Homicide Studies* 14 (3): 219–43. https://doi.org/10.1177/10 88767910371166.

McCall, Patricia L., Karen F. Parker, and John M. MacDonald. 2008. "The Dynamic Relationship between Homicide Rates and Social, Economic, and Political Factors from 1970 to 2000." *Social Science Research* 37 (3): 721–35. https://doi.org/10.1016/j.ssre search.2007.09.007.

McNulty, Thomas L. 2001. "Assessing the Race-Violence Relationship at the Macro Level: The Assumption of Racial Invariance and the Problem of Restricted Distributions." *Criminology* 39 (2): 467–90. https://doi.org/10.1111/j.1745-9125.2001.tb00930.x.

Messner, Steven F., Lawrence E. Raffalovich, and Gretchen M. Sutton. 2010. "Poverty, Infant Mortality, and Homicide Rates in Cross-National Perspective: Assessments of Criterion and Construct Validity." *Criminology* 48 (2): 509–37. https://doi.org/10.1111/j .1745-9125.2010.00194.x.

Neapolitan, Jerome L. 1994. "Cross-National Variation in Homicide: The Case of Latin America." *International Criminal Justice Review* 4 (1): 4–22. https://doi.org/10.1177 /105756779400400102.

Nivette, Amy E. 2011. "Cross-National Predictors of Crime: A Meta-Analysis." *Homicide Studies* 15 (2): 103–31. https://doi.org/10.1177/1088767911406397.

Ouimet, Marc. 2012. "A World of Homicides: The Effect of Economic Development, Income Inequality, and Excess Infant Mortality on the Homicide Rates for 165 Countries in 2010." *Homicide Studies* 16 (3): 238–58. https://doi.org/10.1177/1088767912442500.

Ousey, Graham C. 1999. "Homicide, Structural Factors, and the Racial Invariance Assumption." *Criminology* 37 (2): 405–26. https://doi.org/10.1111/j.1745-9125.1999.tb 00491.x.

Ousey, Graham C., and Charis E. Kubrin. 2018. "Immigration and Crime: Assessing a Contentious Issue." *Annual Review of Criminology* 1:63–84. https://doi.org/10.1146/annurev-criminol-032317-092026.

Ousey, Graham C., and Matthew R. Lee. 2010. "The Southern Culture of Violence and Homicide-Type Differentiation: An Analysis across Cities and Time Points." *Homicide Studies* 14 (3): 268–95. https://doi.org/10.1177/1088767910371182.

Paré, Paul-Phillippe, and Richard Felson. 2014. "Income Inequality, Poverty and Crime across Nations." *British Journal of Sociology* 65 (3): 434–58. https://doi.org/10.1111/1468-4446.12083.

Parker, Karen F. 2001. "A Move toward Specificity: Examining Urban Disadvantage and Race-and Relationship-Specific Homicide Rates." *Journal of Quantitative Criminology* 17:89–110. https://doi.org/10.1023/A:1007578516197.

Parker, Karen F., and Patricia L. McCall. 1999. "Structural Conditions and Racial Homicide Patterns: A Look at the Multiple Disadvantages in Urban Areas." *Criminology* 37 (3): 447–78. https://doi.org/10.1111/j.1745-9125.1999.tb00493.x.

Peterson, Ruth D., and Lauren J. Krivo. 1993. "Racial Segregation and Black Urban Homicide." *Social Forces* 71 (4): 1001–26. https://doi.org/10.1093/sf/71/4/1001.

———. 2005. "Macrostructural Analysis of Race, Ethnicity, and Violent Crime: Recent Lessons and New Directions for Research." *Annual Review of Sociology* 31:331–56. https://doi.org/10.1146/annurev.soc.31.041304.122308.

Pratt, Travis C., and Francis T. Cullen. 2005. "Assessing Macro-level Predictors and Theories of Crime: A Meta-Analysis." *Crime and Justice* 32:373–450. https://www.jstor.org/stable/3488363.

Pridemore, William A. 2005. "Social Structure and Homicide in Post-Soviet Russia." *Social Science Research* 34 (4): 732–56. https://doi.org/10.1016/j.ssresearch.2004.12.005.

———. 2008. "A Methodological Addition to the Cross-National Empirical Literature on Social Structure and Homicide: A First Test of the Poverty-Homicide Thesis." *Criminology* 46 (1): 133–54. https://doi.org/10.1111/j.1745-9125.2008.00106.x.

Rogers, Meghan L., and William A. Pridemore. 2017. "Percent Young and Cross-National Homicide Rates." *British Journal of Criminology* 57 (5): 1080–100. https://doi.org/10.1093/bjc/azw039.

Rosenfeld, Richard. 2009. "Crime Is the Problem: Homicide, Acquisitive Crime, and Economic Conditions." *Journal of Quantitative Criminology* 25:287–306. https://doi.org/10.1007/s10940-009-9067-9.

———. 2011. "The Big Picture: 2010 Presidential Address to the American Society of Criminology." *Criminology* 49 (1): 1–26. https://doi.org/10.1111/j.1745-9125.2010.00216.x.

Sampson, Robert J. 2008. "Rethinking Crime and Immigration." *Contexts* 7 (1): 28–33. https://doi.org/10.1525/ctx.2008.7.1.28.

———. 2012. *Great American City: Chicago and the Enduring Neighborhood Effect.* Chicago: University of Chicago Press.

Sampson, Robert J., and W. Byron Groves. 1989. "Community Structure and Crime: Testing Social-Disorganization Theory." *American Journal of Sociology* 94 (4): 774–802. https://www.jstor.org/stable/2780858.

Sampson, Robert J., and John H. Laub. 1993. *Crime in the Making: Pathways and Turning Points through Life*. Boston: Harvard University Press.

Sampson, Robert J., and William J. Wilson. 1995. "Toward a Theory of Race, Crime, and Urban Inequality." In *Crime and Inequality*, edited by John Hagan and Ruth D. Peterson, 37–56. Stanford, CA: Stanford University Press.

Santos, Mateus R., Alexander Testa, Lauren C. Porter, and James P. Lynch. 2019. "The Contribution of Age Structure to the International Homicide Decline." *PLOS ONE* 14 (10): e0222996. https://doi.org/10.1371/journal.pone.0222996.

Shaw, Clifford R., and Henry D. McKay. 1942. *Juvenile Delinquency and Urban Areas*. Chicago: University of Chicago Press.

South, Scott J., and Lawrence E. Cohen. 1985. "Unemployment and the Homicide Rate: A Paradox Resolved?" *Social Indicators Research* 17:325–43. https://doi.org/10.1007/BF00290320.

Tcherni, Maria. 2011. "Structural Determinants of Homicide: The Big Three." *Journal of Quantitative Criminology* 27:475–96. https://link.springer.com/article/10.1007%2Fs10940-011-9134-x.

Trent, Carol L. S., and William A. Pridemore. 2010. "Do the Invariant Findings of Land, McCall, and Cohen Generalize to Cross-National Studies of Social Structure and Homicide?" *Homicide Studies* 14 (3): 296–335. https://doi.org/10.1177/1088767910371184.

———. 2012. "A Review of the Cross-National Empirical Literature on Social Structure and Homicide." In *Handbook of European Homicide Research: Patterns, Explanations, and Country Studies*, edited by Marieke C. A. Liem and William A. Pridemore, 111–35. New York: Springer. https://doi.org/10.1007/978-1-4614-0466-8_7.

Tuttle, James. 2018. "Specifying the Effect of Social Welfare Expenditures on Homicide and Suicide: A Cross-National, Longitudinal Examination of the Stream Analogy of Lethal Violence." *Justice Quarterly* 35 (1): 87–113. https://doi.org/10.1080/07418825.2017.1293711.

———. 2019. "Murder in the Shadows: Evidence for an Institutional Legitimacy Theory of Crime." *International Journal of Comparative and Applied Criminal Justice* 43 (1): 13–27. https://doi.org/10.1080/01924036.2017.1397037.

———. 2021. "Inequality, Concentrated Disadvantage, and Homicide: Towards a Multilevel Theory of Economic Inequality and Crime." *International Journal of Comparative and Applied Criminal Justice* 46 (3): 215–32. https://doi.org/10.1080/01924036.2021.1942103.

Wilson, William J. 1987. *The Truly Disadvantaged: The Inner City, the Underclass, and Public Policy*. Chicago: University of Chicago Press.

Wirth, Louis. 1938. "Urbanism as a Way of Life." *American Journal of Sociology* 44 (1): 1–24. https://www.jstor.org/stable/2768119.

6

Neighborhoods and Homicide

Egohoods as a Solution to Methodological Challenges

John R. Hipp and Xiaoshuang Iris Luo

Introduction

Homicides are a function of persons interacting within a particular social and physical environment, where environmental context is presumed important for explaining the occurrence of homicide. Indeed, a large body of literature has explored the question of which environmental characteristics are associated with higher homicide rates. A large proportion of this literature has used macro-units of analysis to address this question—that is, asking whether certain characteristics of cities or counties explain why some have more homicides than others (Baller et al. 2001; Land, McCall, and Cohen 1990; McCall, Land, and Parker 2011). This literature has yielded some rich insights. Nonetheless, many existing theories—such as social disorganization or routine activity theories—posit mechanisms that play out over much smaller geographic scales, such as neighborhoods or even smaller micro-units (Browning, Feinberg, and Dietz 2004; Morenoff, Sampson, and Raudenbush 2001; Sampson and Raudenbush 1999). Accounting for smaller-scale processes requires the study of homicides in neighborhoods, and a smaller body of literature has explored these questions.

Although existing research on homicides in neighborhoods has provided important insights, considering the context of smaller geographic scales involves some methodological challenges. One methodological challenge is defining proper geographic units. Specifically, what is an appropriate neighborhood unit? There have been numerous studies exploring this question more generally, as defining neighborhoods is quite contentious (Talen 2019). A takeaway from this literature is that researchers should measure features of the environment at the scale at which they are expected to impact the outcome measure (Hipp 2007). Although most existing studies exploring the spatial distribution of homicides have used census-defined tracts or combinations of tracts (Mears and Bhati 2006; Sampson, Raudenbush, and Earls 1997) to measure neighborhoods (Arnio and Baumer 2012; Hannon 2005), it is not clear whether tracts clearly define specific neighborhoods. It is also questionable whether they accurately capture the spatial patterns of residents salient for impacting the location of homicides.

A second methodological challenge is the small number of homicide events. Although it is certainly good that homicides do not occur often, their infrequency is a statistical challenge for studies wishing to measure them at smaller geographic scales. As a consequence, although there is a growing literature of studies focusing on various types of crime at very small geographic units such as blocks or street segments, this is challenging when studying homicide. The rarity of homicides implies that aggregating homicides to small units results in considerable measurement error due to the infrequency of homicide events. This in turn results in considerably weakened statistical power, which can yield untrustworthy results.

A third challenge for studies of homicides in neighborhoods is the difficulty of obtaining longitudinal data. As a consequence, there exist a limited number of longitudinal studies. Whereas cross-sectional studies can show the characteristics of neighborhoods with more homicides, they provide limited causal evidence. There is a danger in extrapolating too much information from the evidence of cross-sectional studies. It is therefore important that researchers bring additional longitudinal evidence to the question of which neighborhoods experience more homicides to better assess the robustness of existing cross-sectional evidence and test existing theories.

We therefore propose a strategy in this chapter that addresses these challenges by using neighborhood units that have an explicit spatial component to them. Specifically, we utilize the egohood, a geographic unit introduced by Hipp and Boessen (2013), in our analysis. Egohoods move away from the nonoverlapping unit strategy common to nearly all neighborhood definitions (such as block groups, tracts, zip codes, etc.) and instead construct units that overlap. As a result, they explicitly account for the spatial movement of offenders, targets, and potential guardians. Furthermore, because egohoods are constructed to include a census block and all blocks within a particular radius (a half mile in this study), they are large enough to better address the statistical problem of the rarity of homicides compared to micro–geographic units. We propose using egohoods to combat methodological challenges, but remember, studies on how environmental features affect homicide changes over time are deficient empirically, especially concerning longitudinal studies of homicide in smaller geographic units. In this chapter, we move beyond studies viewing the cross-sectional relationship of neighborhood features and homicides by constructing data for the city of Los Angeles at two time points (2000 and 2010) and estimating models capturing change over this time period.

Literature Review

Measuring Neighborhoods

A body of literature has focused on the location of crime within micro–geographic units such as blocks or street segments, but these studies have largely excluded homicides, presumably because of the rarity and nonspecific spatial location of homicides. Only a few studies have focused on homicide. For example, one study focused on how homicide locations moved spatially and temporally in Newark, New Jersey, over a twenty-six-year period (Zeoli et al. 2012). However, this study was focused on the movement of homicides over time in small locations, not on explaining why homicide occurred in particular locations. Homicide studies tend to focus on neighborhood units rather than micro-units and most often use census tracts to define neighborhood boundaries. Thus, studies have used cross-sectional data to assess whether homicides are more likely to occur in commercial districts (Browning et al. 2010), immigrant-concentrated neighborhoods (Chenane and Wright 2018), or neighborhoods with more economic inequality (Messner and Tardiff 1986; Morenoff, Sampson, and Raudenbush 2001), more racial inequality (Torres 2019), or more active streets (Browning and Jackson 2013). A limitation of using census tracts as neighborhood units is that both offenders and targets can move about the spatial landscape (Hipp 2016). Indeed, one study developed a typology of such mobility patterns (Tita and Griffiths 2005). Given this spatial mobility, there are limitations to existing studies that rely on non-overlapping units such as census tracts, raising the need to consider an alternative measure of neighborhoods, as we discuss next.

Egohoods as Neighborhood Units

We use egohoods as our measure of neighborhoods. Egohoods are built on the insight that the spatial patterns of individuals tend to exhibit a spatial decay function. Thus, rather than confining their social lives to their own census tract, residents tend to engage in activities in a radius around their home with a distance decay function. Although there are, of course, exceptions, studies consistently find this pattern, on average, for activity spaces

(Lee and Kwan 2010; Moudon et al. 2006; Ren and Kwan 2009; Sastry, Pebley, and Zonta 2002). Studies measuring residents' social networks likewise find that they exhibit a distance decay function and are not constrained to neighborhood, however defined (Caplow and Forman 1950; Festinger, Schachter, and Back 1950; Hipp and Perrin 2009). Studies from the mental mapping literature that ask residents to draw the boundaries of their own neighborhood find that residents tend to place themselves in the center of their perceived neighborhood (Coulton et al. 2001, 375; Grannis 2009, 99–101). And the rich body of literature on the journey to crime finds that offenders tend to travel in a distance decay pattern in which they are more likely to offend closer to home and less likely to offend further away (Bernasco and Block 2009; Rengert, Piquero, and Jones 1999; Rossmo 2000). All of these insights provide justification for our approach of egohoods rather than defined neighborhoods.

In the egohoods approach, there is no presumption that egohoods are a "real" neighborhood unit or that residents perceive this unit as their neighborhood.[1] Instead, the approach intends to capture the spatial patterns of persons—offenders, targets, and guardians—and how these patterns can give rise to crime. Furthermore, this approach captures the social environment around a small geographic unit. For example, although Hipp and Boessen (2013) did not include homicides in their study, they found that whereas inequality and racial/ethnic heterogeneity sometimes have weak or null relationships with crime in traditional neighborhoods, they exhibit quite strong relationships in egohoods (particularly inequality). As they explained, the typical strategy of constructing neighborhoods minimizes differences *within* neighborhoods on various dimensions, including socioeconomic status (SES), and maximizes differences across neighborhoods; typical neighborhoods are therefore constructed such that they minimize the measured amount of inequality within them.

Egohoods more appropriately capture inequality that exists across the spatial environment. For example, if a higher income neighborhood (based on traditional definitions such as tracts) is next to a lower income one, they each have relatively low inequality. However, we might expect that the adjacent inequality between these two neighborhoods affects the amount of crime (as offenders can easily cross neighborhood boundaries); egohoods directly account for this. In their study, Hipp and Boessen (2013) found that this was indeed the case, as income inequality had a very strong relationship with crime in egohoods but almost no relationship in units such as block groups or tracts. Thus, when measuring distributional variables (such as racial heterogeneity or inequality), it is particularly important to appropriately define neighborhood boundaries. Egohoods pick up expected spatial patterns of residents.

Longitudinal Studies

Another challenge in assessing homicides in neighborhoods is that most studies are cross-sectional. Capturing the relationship between various structural measures and homicide rates at a point in time is informative, but a better understanding of whether these relationships hold in longitudinal designs is needed. A body of literature has studied homicides in cities over time and thus has better assessed the relationship between changes in structural measures and in homicide rates in cities. For example, a study assessed how changing divorce rates impact homicides across large cities over time (Beaulieu and Messner 2009), and another assessed how demographic changes impact homicide rates (Parker, Mancik, and Stansfield 2017). A study of 404 U.S. counties demonstrated the different results that can be obtained for cross-sectional versus longitudinal analyses of the same measures (Phillips 2006), highlighting the need for longitudinal studies to assess possible distinctions. It is possible that measures at a point in time, or stock measures, can have different implications from change measures, or flow measures, and there is a need for neighborhood level studies to test this.

Fewer studies have examined homicide in neighborhoods over time. For example, one study tested and found no relationship between immigration flows and homicide rates in Chicago census tracts from 1980 to 1995 (Chavez and Griffiths 2009). Research in San Diego actually found that tracts with an increasing foreign-born population experienced *reductions* in homicides from 1980 to 2000 (Martinez, Stowell, and Lee 2010). Other research of Chicago neighborhoods in the 1990s found evidence that the legal cynicism of neighborhoods explained the persistence of high homicide rates (Kirk and Papachristos 2011). A study of census tracts in St. Louis from 1980 to 1994 was able to explain levels of homicide in 1980 but had limited ability to explain the changes across these neighborhoods over the subsequent period (Kubrin and Herting 2003), whereas another study with the same data showed important differences in predictors of homicide trajectories based on type of homicide (Kubrin 2003). Recent research has focused on how gentrification in Chicago neighborhoods can impact homicides (Papachristos et al. 2011).

Among studies exploring how homicides change over time in neighborhoods, a handful of research employs exploratory techniques. For example, one study used life-course methods to study how change in neighborhood disadvantage was related to changes in homicide in New York City neighborhoods from 1985 to 2000 using latent trajectory models (Fagan and Davies 2004). Another strategy is to utilize growth mixture models. Two studies in Chicago utilized this approach, with one studying latent trajectory groups of different homicide types among Chicago tracts from 1980 to 1995

(Griffiths and Chavez 2004). Another found different neighborhood patterns of change over a particularly long time period, 1965 to 1995 (Stults 2010). Finally, exploratory spatial techniques were used for Chicago neighborhoods to study the spatial diffusion of youth-gang homicides across neighborhoods in Chicago (Cohen and Tita 1999).

Our goal in this chapter is to address both the methodological challenges and the dearth of longitudinal studies concerning homicides in neighborhoods, proposing the utilization of egohoods to estimate both cross-sectional and longitudinal models using crime data from Los Angeles City in 2000 and 2010. We next turn to our description of the data and methods.

Data and Methods

Data

Our study site is Los Angeles City. We used crime data obtained from the Los Angeles Police Department covering the years 2000–2002 and 2008–2010. Crime events were geocoded to latitude–longitude point locations using a geographic information system (ArcGIS 10.2) and placed in the appropriate census block. The geocoding match rate was over 96 percent. We constructed several sociodemographic variables based on the 2000 U.S. Census, the 2010 U.S. Census, and American Community Survey five-year estimates for 2008–2012. Land use data were obtained from the Southern California Association of Governments (SCAG) dataset that provides information on land use characteristics of all parcels in the city. The units of analysis are all egohoods in the city: here, an egohood is a census block and all blocks surrounding it within a half mile radius. We constructed similar variables aggregated to tracts, allowing us to compare the results of the two strategies of neighborhood units.

Dependent Variables

We computed the number of homicides in each egohood and tract for each year. To account for the rarity of homicides, we constructed three-year averages by using the count of homicides from 2000 to 2002 for the first time point, and from 2008 to 2010 for the second time point.

Independent Variables

We created measures that capture our constructs of interest in egohoods and tracts in 2000, 2010, and the change over the decade. Some census variables are not reported in units smaller than block groups or tracts, so for these variables we imputed values to blocks before aggregating to egohoods. We used synthetic estimation for ecological inference (Cohen and Zhang 1988; Steinberg 1979) to assign values to blocks within the block group; this approach combines information about the larger unit and the smaller unit when making the imputation (Boessen and Hipp 2015).[2]

To capture the economic environment, we constructed measures of average logged household income and income inequality. Income inequality was measured by assigning household incomes to the midpoint of their reported range (the census-reported household incomes in ranges of values), log transforming these values, multiplying them by the number of observations in each income bin, computing the average logged household income, and then computing the standard deviation of logged income based on these values.[3] We followed the approach of Hipp and Kubrin (2017); we used information on the racial/ethnic composition of each block and imputed the binned income values based on the particular race/ethnicity to match block racial composition to improve the precision of imputed values to blocks before constructing buffer values.

We constructed measures of the racial/ethnic composition as the percent Black, percent Latino, percent Asian, and percent other race (with percent White as the remainder). We accounted for racial/ethnic mixing by computing racial/ethnic heterogeneity as a Herfindahl index based on the five racial categories mentioned previously—this was computed as one minus a sum of squares of the proportion of each group. Larger values indicated more heterogeneous areas. We constructed a measure of percent immigrants given evidence that neighborhoods with more immigrants often have lower crime rates (Ousey and Kubrin 2018).

Residential instability was captured as the percent homeowners. We accounted for changes in the local population by constructing a measure of population (logged).[4] Changing population can impact crime by creating more vacant units, which we captured with the percent vacant units. We included a measure of the percent aged sixteen to twenty-nine to capture those at the prime offending ages. Another set of measures captured the built environment with variables of the proportion land use of different features: (1) offices; (2) industrial; (3) retail; (4) residential; and (5) vacant lots, with all other land uses as the remainder. The summary statistics for the variables used in the analyses are displayed in table 6.1. We see that the average egohood population is about sixty-five hundred persons (after exponentiating the logged population), about 50 percent larger than the population of a typical census tract (the tracts here have an average population of about thirty-six hundred persons).

TABLE 6.1 SUMMARY STATISTICS FOR VARIABLES USED IN ANALYSES

| | Half-Mile Egohoods | | | | | | Tracts | | | | | |
| | 2000 | | 2010 | | Change | | 2000 | | 2010 | | Change | |
	Mean	S.D.	Mean	S.D.	Mean	S.D.	Mean	S.D.	Mean	S.D.	Mean	S.D.
Outcome variable												
Homicides	1.44	1.97	0.85	1.18	-0.60	1.26	0.56	0.77	0.32	0.48	-0.24	0.63
1/2 mile egohood variables												
Average household income (logged)	3.57	0.47	3.85	0.45	0.28	0.22	10.79	0.49	11.06	0.51	0.27	0.21
Income inequality	0.93	0.08	0.92	0.11	0.00	0.10	43.95	5.59	38.75	8.76	-5.20	8.80
Percent home owners	45.2	25.5	44.7	24.5	-0.5	4.7	38.8	26.0	38.3	26.5	-0.5	8.7
Percent vacant units	4.7	3.1	6.4	3.2	1.7	3.0	4.7	3.2	6.9	4.6	2.3	4.7
Percent Black	10.5	16.6	9.0	13.8	-1.5	3.8	10.4	16.1	8.8	13.8	-1.5	4.9
Percent Latino	40.9	27.9	43.3	27.9	2.4	6.1	46.2	28.7	48.0	29.2	1.8	9.3
Percent Asian	9.6	9.3	10.6	9.8	1.0	2.5	10.2	10.8	11.5	11.9	1.3	4.7
Percent other race	2.9	1.5	2.7	1.3	-0.3	1.0	3.0	2.1	2.3	2.3	-0.7	2.5
Racial/ethnic heterogeneity	0.48	0.16	0.49	0.16	0.01	0.06	0.47	0.16	0.47	0.17	0.00	0.09
Percent immigrants	37.6	14.4	37.7	12.5	0.1	6.0	41.1	15.4	40.3	14.0	-0.8	7.1
Percent aged sixteen to twenty-nine	22.4	6.8	22.6	6.8	0.3	2.7	23.7	8.0	23.8	8.8	0.1	5.1
Crime population (logged)	8.77	0.98	8.83	0.89	0.06	0.35	8.17	0.36	8.20	0.38	0.02	0.16
Percent office land use	1.2	3.2	3.9	7.3	2.8	6.4	1.4	4.4	2.8	4.3	1.5	6.2
Percent industrial land use	7.2	14.3	6.4	13.5	-0.8	7.9	5.6	12.8	4.3	9.6	-1.3	16.2
Percent retail land use	4.0	4.3	7.8	10.3	3.8	9.7	4.6	6.5	6.6	7.1	2.0	9.5
Percent residential land use	53.1	27.1	31.9	12.7	-21.3	20.7	51.9	30.2	64.9	24.7	13.0	40.0
Percent vacant land use	4.6	10.9	3.1	9.0	-1.6	6.7	4.5	12.8	5.9	14.3	1.4	19.5

Note: N = 29,159 egohoods

Methods

We estimated three models with our egohoods variables.[5] Two cross-sectional models are based on 2000 and 2010 data, and the third model captures change in the measures over the decade, explaining the change in homicide. Since the outcome measure is a count variable, and it did not exhibit over-dispersion, we estimated the two cross-sectional models as Poisson regression models. The longitudinal model was estimated as a generalized structural equation model in Stata with a Poisson link function to capture the count nature of the outcome variable. In the longitudinal model, the outcome variable was the count of homicides in 2010, and we included the log transformed count of homicides in 2000 (after adding one to account for egohoods with no homicides) with its coefficient constrained to one; this specification was equivalent to a change model given the Poisson function of the 2010 homicides. We included the difference version of the other variables and thus captured whether change in these variables is related to change in homicides over the decade. We estimated three analogous models with data aggregated to tracts to compare the results with our egohood models. Given that we included logged population in all models, the results can be interpreted as homicide rates.

Results

We begin with the results for the cross-sectional egohood models in 2000 and 2010 in table 6.2 and compare the results over these two decadal points to assess the stability of the estimates. We compare the egohood results to those estimated using the more traditional neighborhood definition of census tracts. Beginning with SES measures, we see in models 1 and 2 of table 2 that the presence of higher average income of households in the egohood is associated with fewer homicides in both 2000 and 2010. A one–standard deviation increase in average household income is associated with 12 percent fewer homicides in 2000 (exp(-.2461*.5) = .884) and 28 percent fewer in 2010 (exp (-.6474*.5) = .723). In the two cross-sectional models using tracts as the geographic units of analysis (models 4 and 5), the average household income variable has somewhat smaller coefficients that are not statistically significant. Thus, it appears that the egohoods approach better captures the spatial pattern of the relationship of SES and homicides while addressing the limited statistical power of homicides. We see evidence that income inequality is related to the level of homicides in egohoods. A 0.1-point increase in income inequality (about one standard deviation) is associated with 9 percent and 6 percent more homicides in 2000 and 2010, respectively. This sharply contrasts with the results in the tract models, in which the coefficients are essentially zero.

TABLE 6.2 MODELS PREDICTING HOMICIDE IN HALF-MILE EGOHOODS AND TRACTS IN LOS ANGELES

	Half-Mile Egohoods Models			Tract Models		
	2000 (1)	2010 (2)	Change (3)	2000 (4)	2010 (5)	Change (6)
Average household income (logged)	-0.246 **	-0.647 **	0.588 **	-0.059	-0.574 †	-0.306
	-(6.16)	-(16.73)	(9.68)	-(0.26)	-(1.92)	-(1.01)
Income inequality	0.886 **	0.574 **	-0.094	0.014	0.011	0.004
	(8.26)	(5.84)	-(1.01)	(1.43)	(1.08)	(0.46)
Percent owners	-0.004 **	0.000	-0.002	0.000	0.002	-0.006
	-(6.98)	-(0.33)	-(1.05)	-(0.01)	(0.51)	-(0.74)
Percent vacant units	0.042 **	0.055 **	-0.035 **	0.035 *	0.040 **	0.004
	(16.48)	(20.04)	-(15.59)	(2.42)	(2.88)	(0.33)
Percent Black	0.025 **	0.021 **	-0.044 **	0.030 **	0.026 **	-0.036 **
	(45.53)	(29.38)	-(19.82)	(7.44)	(4.89)	-(2.95)
Percent Latino	0.015 **	0.016 **	0.001	0.020 **	0.024 **	-0.009
	(19.82)	(18.05)	(0.25)	(3.74)	(3.99)	-(0.89)
Percent Asian	-0.006 **	-0.011 **	-0.024 **	-0.001	0.006	-0.019
	-(4.95)	-(8.21)	-(6.91)	-(0.06)	(0.66)	-(1.12)
Percent other race	-0.124 **	-0.254 **	-0.074 **	-0.073 *	-0.023	0.002
	-(14.26)	-(17.62)	-(8.18)	-(1.98)	-(0.54)	(0.06)
Racial/ethnic heterogeneity	0.619 **	0.980 **	0.131	0.795 *	0.439	-0.242
	(11.72)	(13.71)	(0.86)	(2.07)	(0.83)	-(0.30)
Percent immigrants	0.002 *	-0.009 **	-0.021 **	-0.005	-0.013	-0.004
	(2.29)	-(7.66)	-(12.23)	-(0.65)	-(1.44)	-(0.34)

	Model 1		Model 2		Model 3		Model 4		Model 5		Model 6	
Percent aged sixteen to twenty–nine	−0.013	**	−0.011	**	−0.028	**	−0.003		−0.015		−0.008	
	−(9.23)		−(6.37)		−(9.12)		−(0.26)		−(1.38)		−(0.64)	
Crime population (logged)	0.701	**	0.812	**	0.192	**	0.802	**	0.600	**	0.380	**
	(42.39)		(37.39)		(11.27)		(5.07)		(3.09)		(0.99)	
Percent office land use	0.009	**	0.001		0.001		0.013		−0.007		0.012	
	(5.54)		(0.96)		(0.43)		(1.30)		−(0.44)		(1.11)	
Percent industrial land use	−0.002	**	0.004	**	−0.002	*	0.007	*	−0.001		−0.005	
	−(3.31)		(6.33)		−(2.34)		(2.52)		−(0.09)		−(1.43)	
Percent retail land use	0.003	**	0.000		0.004	**	0.005		−0.010		−0.002	
	(2.73)		(0.41)		(5.82)		(0.77)		−(1.00)		−(0.23)	
Percent residential land use	−0.004	**	0.000		0.005	**	−0.004	*	−0.002		0.004	*
	−(12.23)		−(0.01)		(14.56)		−(2.32)		−(0.60)		(2.02)	
Percent vacant land use	−0.004	**	−0.011	**	0.010	**	0.005		0.000		0.010	**
	−(3.21)		−(5.94)		(7.79)		(0.86)		(0.04)		(2.96)	
Intercept	−6.847	**	−6.440	**	−1.366	**	−8.733	**	−1.443		−1.748	**
	−(25.52)		−(23.31)		−(59.93)		−(2.99)		−(0.39)		−(12.80)	
R square	0.455		0.370		0.605		0.230		0.161		0.471	

** p < .01, * p < .05, † p < .10 (two-tail test). T-values in parentheses. N = 29,159 egohoods.
Note: For change models 3 and 6, the variables are the difference in the measures from 2000 to 2010.

Turning to housing measures, the presence of more homeowners in the egohood is associated with fewer homicides in 2000, although there is no relationship in 2010. This measure has no relationship with homicides in the tract models. In both sets of models at both time points, the presence of more vacant units is associated with a higher number of homicides. For this measure, we find that the magnitude of effect is similar in the egohood and tract models. A one–standard deviation increase in vacant units is associated with 14 to 19 percent more homicides in egohoods and 12 to 20 percent more in tracts.

There are also differences for measures capturing the racial composition of the area. The presence of more Black people or Latinos is associated with more homicides in both sets of models at both time points. The coefficients are somewhat stronger for percent Black compared to percent Latino. Interestingly, the coefficients are larger in the tract models than the egohood models, although this may reflect the fact that this approach does not capture SES and inequality effects as well as egohoods do. There is evidence in the egohood models that a greater composition of Asians or other race residents is associated with lower homicides (these effects tend to not be statistically significant in the tract models). There is also more consistent evidence across both time points in the egohood models that racial/ethnic heterogeneity is positively associated with homicide: a one–standard deviation increase in racial/ethnic heterogeneity is associated with 10 to 17 percent more homicides in egohoods.

There is mixed evidence for the presence of immigrants and homicide relationship. In 2000, egohoods with more immigrants have somewhat higher homicide rates, but in 2010 this flips to a negative relationship (with a coefficient more than four times larger). And the presence of more persons aged sixteen to twenty-nine is negatively associated with homicides in the egohood models, contrary to some expectations but consistent with the findings of many other ecological studies. In the tract models, neither variable is statistically significant.

We also account for the built environment of the area, although these measures exhibit inconsistent results over the two decadal points. Whereas a higher percentage of office or retail land use in the egohood is associated with more homicides in 2000, there are no such relationships in 2010. Likewise, the negative relationship between residential land use and homicides in 2000 evaporates to nonsignificance in 2010. And whereas egohoods with more industrial land use have fewer homicides in 2000, they have more homicides in 2010. Only vacant land use is consistent over both decades, as egohoods with more vacant land have lower homicides at both time points. Note that this result for vacant lots differs from the results for vacant units, which serve as a crime attractor for homicides. It appears that vacant lots do not attract homicides in the same way, at least in cross-sectional models. Most of these measures show nonsignificant relationships with homicides in the tract models.

Longitudinal Models

We describe the results for longitudinal models for egohoods in model 3 (and contrast them with the tracts results in model 6). Whereas higher average income is protective for homicides in egohoods in the cross-sectional models, the pattern is different in the change models: here, egohoods with increasing average income actually experience greater increases in homicides. A one–standard deviation greater increase in average household income over the decade is associated with a 14 percent greater homicide increase. This result contrasts with the findings of Papachristos and colleagues (Papachristos et al. 2011), who found that Chicago neighborhoods undergoing gentrification (based on a measure of coffee shops) experienced falling homicide rates. And whereas income inequality is strongly associated with more homicides at a point in time, there is no evidence that increasing inequality is associated with changes in number of homicides. Likewise, whereas egohoods with more vacant units at a point in time have more homicides, increasing vacant units over the decade is actually associated with falling homicides (10 percent fewer for a one–standard deviation change). Thus, the results from the longitudinal models differ considerably from the cross-sectional results.

Turning to the racial composition measures, we see differences in the cross-sectional models for the two most disadvantaged racial/ethnic minorities: Black people and Latinos. Whereas egohoods with more of these two groups at a point in time have more homicides, an increasing percentage of Latinos in the egohood has no relationship with change in homicides, and an increasing percentage of Black people is associated with falling homicides. A 3.8 percentage point increase in Black residents is associated with 15 percent fewer homicides in the egohood. The other two racial/ethnic measures—percent Asian and percent other race—exhibit results in the longitudinal model that are similar to the cross-sectional models, as increasing percentages of these two groups are associated with decreasing homicides. Whereas higher levels of racial/ethnic heterogeneity at a point in time are associated with more homicides, there is no evidence that increasing racial/ethnic heterogeneity is related to changes in homicides.

The patterns for percent immigrants and percent aged sixteen to twenty-nine are similar in the longitudinal models as in the cross-sectional models. An increasing percentage of people aged sixteen to twenty-nine or of immigrants in the egohood is associated with decreasing homicides. Whereas a one–standard deviation increase in immigrants in 2010 is associated with

12 percent fewer homicides, a one–standard deviation greater increase in immigrants during the decade is also associated with 12 percent fewer homicides. The analogous values for percentage aged sixteen to twenty-nine in 2010 or the change over the decade are 7 percent fewer homicides. It is interesting to observe very similar magnitudes for these two variables whether measured at a point in time (2010) or as they change over the decade. Also, one–standard deviation greater increasing egohood population is associated with 7 percent greater increasing homicides.

We again see the inconsistency of land use measures, which not only exhibit inconsistent patterns in the cross-sectional models but also different relationships in the longitudinal model compared to the cross-sectional models. Whereas increasing percentage of industrial land use in the egohood is associated with falling homicides, an increasing percentage of retail, residential, or vacant land use is associated with increasing homicides.

It is interesting to note that the change model using tracts has much weaker statistical power compared to the egohood model and therefore much less statistical significance. In the tract model, only the change in percent Black and percent residential or vacant land use are statistically significant measures. Thus, we argue that the combination of the spatial imprecision of using tracts as a neighborhood definition and the general rarity of homicides limits the statistical power of models using traditional, nonoverlapping boundary definitions of neighborhoods. This is further accentuated in change models, which have even less statistical power than cross-sectional models.

Conclusion

This study has utilized a relatively novel geographic unit of neighborhoods—the egohood—to measure the relationship between various structural measures and homicides across neighborhoods in the city of Los Angeles. By using data across two decadal points, we are able to compare and contrast the results obtained in cross-sectional models to those from longitudinal models. We argue that the spatial precision of egohoods makes them preferable to more common measures of neighborhoods that typically are nonoverlapping. We highlight some key findings of this chapter here.

First, we find that the results from egohood models are much more robust than those from models using a more traditional definition of neighborhoods—census tracts. For most of the measures, coefficients are noticeably larger in the egohood models compared to the tract models, consistent with the idea that egohoods provide greater spatial precision for the theoretical construct of interest. In many cases, these larger coefficients are statistically significant in the egohoods models but not in the tract models, further evidence of the limited information available in the tract models. The egohood models better explain the spatial pattern of homicides, as the model fit (based on pseudo r-square) is often more than double that of the tract models. Furthermore, we find that distribution measures—such as racial/ethnic heterogeneity and income inequality—are much better measured in egohoods and therefore exhibit robust cross-sectional relationships with homicides that are not present in the tract models. This is consistent with the results of Hipp and Boessen's (2013) study of other types of crime. Based on the tract models alone, we would inappropriately conclude that inequality is unrelated to homicide levels. However, the egohood models demonstrate that they have a strong positive relationship; the pattern is similar for racial/ethnic heterogeneity. Thus, explicitly accounting for spatial patterns by using egohoods is a beneficial strategy for researchers measuring homicides in neighborhoods.

Second, there are striking differences in egohood results from our cross-sectional models and our longitudinal model, where many measures have coefficients of opposite signs in the longitudinal model compared to the cross-sectional models. And this is not because the processes change over these two time points, as we find that the coefficients for the cross-sectional models at the two time points are relatively similar. Instead, it appears that the relationships between changes in many of these measures and changes in homicides are distinctly different from the static relationships at a point in time. This has not been adequately demonstrated previously, in part due to the relatively few longitudinal studies of neighborhoods and homicides. It may also be because of the statistical unreliability of homicides in longitudinal models when using traditional units such as tracts: indeed, we demonstrate using our same dataset that the longitudinal model with tracts detects very few significant effects. Future studies in other geographic locales using egohoods would provide more information regarding this question.

Third, the reasons why the coefficients differ so sharply between cross-sectional and longitudinal models has not been adequately considered theoretically and will require much more consideration. Given that neighborhoods tend to exhibit considerable stability over time (Sampson 2006), it may be that the changes that do occur are actually out of the ordinary and therefore differentially impact the change in homicides. Another possibility is that some of our change measures indirectly capture gentrification; this change in neighborhood composition has a destabilizing effect and thus alters the level of crime (Papachristos et al. 2011). Yet another possibility is that the speed of change in neighborhoods is important, as was demonstrated in a study viewing Part I crimes other than homicides (Hipp and Branic 2017). Regardless of which process might be at work, much more theoretical thought is needed to explain what the change in these measures means compared to what they capture as stock measures at a point in time.

We acknowledge some limitations to this study. It focuses on egohoods within a single city, raising questions about generalizability to other cities. The study also focuses on a single decade—one that experienced a large economic recession—so it is a question for future research whether these patterns are similarly observed in other time periods. Finally, we focus on change over a ten-year period. However, more rapid change may be important—that is, year to year change—and the speed of the change may also be important (Hipp and Branic 2017).

In conclusion, this chapter demonstrates the utility of egohoods as a unit of analysis for studies on homicides in neighborhoods. Our cross-sectional models with egohoods provide robust evidence of associations between most structural measures and homicides at both time points compared to models using a more traditional definition of neighborhoods (census tracts), revealing the benefits of egohoods for addressing the methodological challenge of rarely occurring crime events such as homicides. We also see strikingly different results between cross-sectional models and longitudinal models using egohoods, where coefficients capturing homicide changes over a decade often exhibit opposite signs compared to stock measures at a point in time. This highlights the need for further research on how changes of structural measure may affect homicides and theoretical consideration of how these relationships might operate in longitudinal designs.

NOTES

1. In fact, whether they know it or not, residents are part of many overlapping egohoods, not just the one in which they are at the center. They are included in many other blocks' egohoods—in the egohoods of all the blocks within their own egohood.

2. In the synthetic estimation for ecological inference approach, an estimated model predicts the variable of interest at a larger geographic unit of analysis and then uses the parameter estimates from this model and the values of these variables in a smaller geographic unit to impute the missing variable in the smaller units. This strategy assumes that the relationship between variables at one unit of analysis is similar at a different level, rather than assuming that there is no relationship at all (as is the more typical strategy of uniform imputation). The variables included in these imputation models are percent owners, racial/ethnic composition, percent divorced households, percent households with children, percent vacant units, population density, and age structure (percent aged zero to four, five to fourteen, twenty to twenty-four, twenty-five to twenty-nine, thirty to forty-four, forty-five to sixty-four, and sixty-five and up, with percent aged fifteen to nineteen as the reference category).

3. For the highest, most open-ended range, we assigned the midpoint value as being 25 percent greater than the bottom value.

4. When constructing egohoods, we only included the population of the egohood containing crime information. For egohoods in the center of the city, this is the same as the population total. However, for egohoods near the boundary of the city, our measure only included the population in the part of the egohood within the city boundary (since we did not have crime data for the area outside the city boundary).

5. Note that the construction of egohood variables creates considerable spatial correlation among the measures. This can impact the standard errors. However, there are countervailing processes: whereas correlated measures artificially deflate the standard errors in our models, the overestimated residual term artificially inflates the standard errors. Hipp and Boessen (2013) found in their study that estimating spatial error models yielded standard errors very similar to models ignoring the spatial correlation, indicating that these two processes cancelled out in their study area.

REFERENCES

Arnio, Ashley N., and Eric P. Baumer. 2012. "Demography, Foreclosure, and Crime." *Demographic Research* 26:449–88.

Baller, Robert D., Luc Anselin, Steven F. Messner, Glenn Deane, and Darnell F. Hawkins. 2001. "Structural Covariates of US County Homicide Rates: Incorporating Spatial Effects." *Criminology* 39:561–90.

Beaulieu, Mark, and Steven F. Messner. 2009. "Assessing Changes in the Effect of Divorce Rates on Homicide Rates across Large U.S. Cities, 1960–2000: Revisiting the Chicago School." *Homicide Studies* 14:24–51.

Bernasco, Wim, and Richard L. Block. 2009. "Where Offenders Choose to Attack: A Discrete Choice Model of Robberies in Chicago." *Criminology* 47:93–130.

Boessen, Adam, and John R. Hipp. 2015. "Close-Ups and the Scale of Ecology: Land Uses and the Geography of Social Context and Crime." *Criminology* 53:399–426.

Browning, Christopher R., Reginald A. Byron, Catherine A. Calder, Lauren J. Krivo, Mei-Po Kwan, Jae Yong Lee, and Ruth D. Peterson. 2010. "Commercial Density, Residential Concentration, and Crime: Land Use Patterns and Violence in Neighborhood Context." *Journal of Research in Crime and Delinquency* 47:329–57.

Browning, Christopher R., Seth L. Feinberg, and Robert D. Dietz. 2004. "The Paradox of Social Organization: Networks, Collective Efficacy, and Violent Crime in Urban Neighborhoods." *Social Forces* 83:503–34.

Browning, Christopher R., and Aubrey L. Jackson. 2013. "The Social Ecology of Public Space: Active Streets and Violent Crime in Urban Neighborhoods." *Criminology* 51:1009–43.

Caplow, Theodore, and Robert Forman. 1950. "Neighborhood Interaction in a Homogeneous Community." *American Sociological Review* 15:357–66.

Chavez, Jorge M., and Elizabeth Griffiths. 2009. "Neighborhood Dynamics of Urban Violence: Understanding the Immigration Connection." *Homicide Studies* 13:261–73.

Chenane, Joselyne L., and Emily M. Wright. 2018. "The Role of Police Officer Race/Ethnicity on Crime Rates in Immigrant Communities." *Race and Justice*. 11 (1): 3–27.

Cohen, Jacqueline, and George Tita. 1999. "Diffusion in Homicide: Exploring a General Method for Detecting Spatial Diffusion Processes." *Journal of Quantitative Criminology* 15:451–93.

Cohen, Michael Lee, and Xiao Di Zhang. 1988. *The Difficulty of Improving Statistical Synthetic Estimation*. Washington, DC: Bureau of the Census.

Coulton, Claudia J., Jill Korbin, Tsui Chan, and Marilyn Su. 2001. "Mapping Residents' Perceptions of Neighborhood Boundaries: A Methodological Note." *American Journal of Community Psychology* 29:371–83.

Fagan, Jeffrey, and Garth Davies. 2004. "The Natural History of Neighborhood Violence." *Journal of Contemporary Criminal Justice* 20:127–47.

Festinger, Leon, Stanley Schachter, and Kurt Back. 1950. *Social Pressures in Informal Groups*. Stanford, CA: Stanford University Press.

Grannis, Rick. 2009. *From the Ground Up: Translating Geography into Community through Neighbor Networks*. Princeton, NJ: Princeton University Press.

Griffiths, Elizabeth, and Jorge M. Chavez. 2004. "Communities, Street Guns and Homicide Trajectories in Chicago, 1980–1995: Merging Methods for Examining Homicide Trends across Space and Time." *Criminology* 42:941–78.

Hannon, Lance. 2005. "Extremely Poor Neighborhoods and Homicide." *Social Science Quarterly* 86:1418–34.

Hipp, John R. 2007. "Block, Tract, and Levels of Aggregation: Neighborhood Structure and Crime and Disorder as a Case in Point." *American Sociological Review* 72:659–80.

———. 2016. "General Theory of Spatial Crime Patterns." *Criminology* 54:653–79.

Hipp, John R., and Adam Boessen. 2013. "Egohoods as Waves Washing across the City: A New Measure of 'Neighborhoods.'" *Criminology* 51:287–327.

Hipp, John R., and Nicholas Branic. 2017. "Fast and Slow Change in Neighborhoods: Characterization and Consequences in Southern California." *International Journal of Urban Sciences* 21:257–81.

Hipp, John R., and Charis E. Kubrin. 2017. "From Bad to Worse: How Changing Inequality in Nearby Areas Impacts Local Crime." *Russell Sage Foundation Journal* 3:129–51.

Hipp, John R., and Andrew J. Perrin. 2009. "The Simultaneous Effect of Social Distance and Physical Distance on the Formation of Neighborhood Ties." *City & Community* 8:5–25.

Kirk, David S., and Andrew V. Papachristos. 2011. "Cultural Mechanisms and the Persistence of Neighborhood Violence." *American Journal of Sociology* 116:1190–1233.

Kubrin, Charis E. 2003. "Structural Covariates of Homicide Rates: Does Type of Homicide Matter?" *Journal of Research in Crime and Delinquency* 40:139–70.

Kubrin, Charis E., and Jerald R. Herting. 2003. "Neighborhood Correlates of Homicide Trends: An Analysis Using Growth-Curve Modeling." *Sociological Quarterly* 44:329–50.

Land, Kenneth C., Patricia L. McCall, and Lawrence E. Cohen. 1990. "Structural Covariates of Homicide Rates: Are There Any Invariances across Time and Social Space?" *American Journal of Sociology* 95:922–63.

Lee, Jae Yong, and Mei-Po Kwan. 2010. "Visualisation of Socio-spatial Isolation Based on Human Activity Patterns and Social Networks in Space-Time." *Tijdschrift voor Economische en Sociale Geografie* 102:468–85.

Martinez, Ramiro, Jacob I. Stowell, and Matthew T. Lee. 2010. "Immigration and Crime in an Era of Transformation: A Longitudinal Analysis of Homicides in San Diego Neighborhoods, 1980–2000." *Criminology* 48:797–829.

McCall, Patricia L., Kenneth C. Land, and Karen F. Parker. 2011. "Heterogeneity in the Rise and Decline of City-Level Homicide Rates, 1976–2005: A Latent Trajectory Analysis." *Social Science Research* 40:363–78.

Mears, Daniel P., and Avinash S. Bhati. 2006. "No Community Is an Island: The Effects of Resource Deprivation on Urban Violence in Spatially and Socially Proximate Communities." *Criminology* 44:509–48.

Messner, Steven F., and Kenneth Tardiff. 1986. "Economic Inequality and Levels of Homicide: An Analysis of Urban Neighborhoods." *Criminology* 24:297–317.

Morenoff, Jeffrey D., Robert J. Sampson, and Stephen W. Raudenbush. 2001. "Neighborhood Inequality, Collective Efficacy, and the Spatial Dynamics of Urban Violence." *Criminology* 39:517–59.

Moudon, Anne Vernez, Chanam Lee, Allen D. Cheadle, Cheza Garvin, Donna Johnson, Thomas L. Schmid, Robert D. Weathers, and Lin Lin. 2006. "Operational Definitions of Walkable Neighborhood: Theoretical and Empirical Insights." *Journal of Physical Activity and Health* 3:S99–S117.

Ousey, Graham C., and Charis E. Kubrin. 2018. "Immigration and Crime: Assessing a Contentious Issue." *Annual Review of Criminology* 1:63–84.

Papachristos, Andrew V., Chris M. Smith, Mary L. Scherer, and Melissa A. Fugiero. 2011. "More Coffee, Less Crime? The Relationship between Gentrification and Neighborhood Crime Rates in Chicago, 1991 to 2005." *City & Community* 10:215–40.

Parker, Karen F., Ashley Mancik, and Richard Stansfield. 2017. "American Crime Drops: Investigating the Breaks, Dips and Drops in Temporal Homicide." *Social Science Research* 64:154–70.

Phillips, Julie A. 2006. "Explaining Discrepant Findings in Cross-Sectional and Longitudinal Analyses: An Application to U.S. Homicide Rates." *Social Science Research* 35:948–74.

Ren, Fang, and Mei-Po Kwan. 2009. "The Impact of the Internet on Human Activity–Travel Patterns: Analysis of Gender Differences Using Multi-group Structural Equation Models." *Journal of Transport Geography* 17:440–50.

Rengert, George F., Alex R. Piquero, and Peter R. Jones. 1999. "Distance Decay Reexamined." *Criminology* 37:427–45.

Rossmo, D. Kim. 2000. *Geographic Profiling.* Boca Raton: CRC Press.

Sampson, Robert J. 2006. "How Does Community Context Matter? Social Mechanisms, and the Explanation of Crime Rates." In *The Explanation of Crime: Context, Mechanisms, and Development*, edited by P. O. H. Wikstrom and R. J. Sampson, 31–60. New York: Cambridge University Press.

Sampson, Robert J., and Stephen W. Raudenbush. 1999. "Systematic Social Observation of Public Spaces: A New Look at Disorder in Urban Neighborhoods." *American Journal of Sociology* 105:603–51.

Sampson, Robert J., Stephen W. Raudenbush, and Felton Earls. 1997. "Neighborhoods and Violent Crime: A Multilevel Study of Collective Efficacy." *Science* 277:918–24.

Sastry, Narayan, Anne R. Pebley, and Michela Zonta. 2002. "Neighborhood Definitions and the Spatial Dimension of Daily Life in Los Angeles." California Center for Population Research: Working Paper Series. Santa Monica, CA.

Steinberg, Joseph. 1979. "Synthetic Estimates for Small Areas: Statistical Workshop Papers and Discussion." National Institute on Drug Abuse Research Monograph Series, 24:282. Washington, DC: National Institute on Drug Abuse.

Stults, Brian J. 2010. "Determinants of Chicago Neighborhood Homicide Trajectories: 1965–1995." *Homicide Studies* 14:244–67.

Talen, Emily. 2019. "Neighborhood." New York: Oxford University Press.

Tita, George, and Elizabeth Griffiths. 2005. "Traveling to Violence: The Case for a Mobility-Based Spatial Typology of Homicide." *Journal of Research in Crime and Delinquency* 42:275–308.

Torres, Samuel A. 2019. "Vulnerable to Disparity? The Imperfect Alignment of Neighborhood Relative Inequality with the Racial Invariance Thesis." *Justice Quarterly* 37:763–88.

Zeoli, April M., Jesenia M. Pizarro, Sue C. Grady, and Christopher Melde. 2012. "Homicide as Infectious Disease: Using Public Health Methods to Investigate the Diffusion of Homicide." *Justice Quarterly* 31:609–32.

7

Doing Fieldwork in Homicide Investigation

FIONA BROOKMAN AND HELEN JONES

Introduction

Criminological research into homicide has been, and remains, overwhelmingly quantitative in nature (Brookman 2015). Whether exploring causes of homicide or responses to it, research—particularly in the United States—is dominated by quantitative studies, many using multivariate statistical methodologies. As a result, less is known about the benefits and challenges of using qualitative methods to study homicide. For example, in the last decade, the journal *Homicide Studies* has published 181 articles on the topic of homicide, but only 21 of these (12 percent) adopt qualitative research techniques.[1] There are, of course, many benefits to quantitative research. It is particularly well suited to unraveling crime trends, patterns, and distributions and to studying cross-national comparisons and causal connections between sociodemographic variables and crime. In addition, it is often possible to test or duplicate quantitative studies, especially when researchers use existing statistics or datasets. Nevertheless, qualitative research permits unrivaled access to people's thoughts, motivations, behaviors, identity, and cultural practices. For these reasons, it is a particularly useful approach for understanding *how* and *why* individuals or groups behave in particular ways.

In this chapter, we document some of the challenges and benefits of qualitative research on homicide, focusing on our experiences of collaborative ethnographic fieldwork on homicide investigation. We draw on a four-year ethnographic study of British homicide investigations[2] that used interviews, observations, and documentary analysis to provide an in-depth understanding of how forensic sciences and technologies (FSTs)[3] contribute to contemporary police investigation of homicide (see Brookman et al. 2020a for fuller discussion of the study methodology). We focus on the most revealing aspect of the research in this chapter, namely our immersion into the world and work of homicide detectives. By recounting some of our experiences of multisite, collaborative ethnography, we hope to illuminate the challenges and value of ethnographic studies to the discipline of criminology and, specifically, homicide studies.

We begin by providing a brief flavor of different kinds of qualitative studies on homicide as well as some pertinent ethnographic studies of different parts of the criminal justice system (CJS). We then reflect on different approaches to collaborative ethnography and our own approach before recounting some of the challenges and benefits of fieldwork on homicide investigation.

Qualitative Research on Homicide: A Brief Overview

Qualitative research on homicide comes in a variety of guises (Brookman 2015). Perhaps the most prevalent approach involves interviewing offenders, most often while they are in custody. In-depth interviews have been conducted with men and women (and even children, see Shaw 2000) in many parts of the world who have killed in various contexts. These include, for example, Dobash et al.'s interviews in Britain of men who killed men, women, and children (e.g., see Dobash and Dobash 2020); Brookman's (2003) interviews of men in Britain who killed other men; Lindegaard's (2017) interviews of men in South Africa who killed other men; Sollund's (2008) interviews with male refugees in Norway convicted of the rape and murder of women; and Presser's (2012) interviews with a mass murderer in Tennessee. Other studies have interviewed women imprisoned for killing their children (Oberman and Meyer 2008) or their intimate partners (Schneider 2014). More unusually, some researchers have interviewed murderers outside custody—for example, Parker's (1990) interviews with life sentence prisoners included some who had been released on license.[4] Interviews have also been conducted with family members of homicide victims (Armour 2002) and those bereaved by homicide (Rock 1998). In different ways, these qualitative studies provide valuable insights into why people kill and the impact of killings.

Other qualitative approaches include the analysis of official documentary sources, "true crime" biographies, and autobiographies. They also include the qualitative analysis of the written manifesto of a terrorist (Berntzen and Sandberg 2014) and the confessions of (former) mafiosos (Gambetta 1996). Finally, some researchers have adopted ethnographic methods to study homicide.

Ethnographic research is, as Atkinson et al. (2001, 4) aptly note, "grounded in a commitment to the first-hand experience and exploration of a particular social or cultural setting on the basis of (though not exclusively by) participant observation." Ethnographic methods are particularly useful because they enable the researcher "to become immersed in the formal and informal activities of a given community" (Wyatt and Wilson-Kovacs 2019, 2). While observation and participation are core features of the ethnographic approach, in many cases fieldwork also includes use of other research methods such as interviews, conversations, and the analysis of documents.

Unsurprisingly, there are, to our knowledge, no participant observation studies by social scientists of the act of unlawful homicide (such research would be unethical). Numerous ethnographic studies of street violence and gang life, however, include accounts from, and sometimes observations of, young people's participation in serious violence (Decker and Van Winkle 1996; Densley 2013; Harding 2014), as do several memoirs from former violent offenders, including Islamic terrorists (e.g., Saleem 2017) and gang members (e.g., Goh 2008; Smith 2019). In various ways, these accounts provide important insights into the nature and etiology of violence and homicide. In contrast to the understandable paucity of observational studies of homicide, ethnographic methods have, for many decades, been used to study organizations that respond to it, to which we now turn.

Ethnographies of Criminal Justice Organizations

Early police ethnographies date back to the 1960s (see Bacon, Loftus, and Rowe 2020 for an overview) and focus predominately on the experiences and practices of uniformed police officers in various countries, including Britain (Rowe 2007), the United States (Van Maanen 1973), the Netherlands (Punch 1979; Van Hulst 2013), and France (Fassin 2013). Other researchers have observed the work of detectives (Hobbs 1989) or specialist police units, including ethnographic studies of detectives investigating illegal employment and illegal residence (Loyens 2014); covert police investigators (Mac Giollabhuí, Goold, and Loftus 2016); "drug detectives" (Bacon 2016); detectives investigating domestic violence and high-volume crime (Hällgren, Lindberg, and Rantatalo 2021); and detectives involved in policing transnational crime (Sausdal 2020).

A small but significant number of studies have employed ethnographic methodologies to examine homicide investigation. These include Innes's (2003) study of homicide investigations in an English constabulary; Westmarland's (2013) observations of homicide detectives in a large U.S. city; Brookman's observations of homicide detectives in both Britain and the United States (see Brookman, Maguire, and Maguire 2019); Dabney's (2019) ethnographic study of a metropolitan police department in the southeastern region of the United States; and Allsop's (2018) observations of an English major crime review team reviewing cold case murders.

Finally, numerous ethnographic studies of other parts of the CJS or different groups of professionals working within it are of relevance to our knowledge and understanding of homicide investigation. These include ethnographic studies of how crime scene investigators make sense of crime scenes (Wyatt 2014); the role of Swedish crime scene technicians in the production of forensic evidence (Kruse 2020); the work of digital media investigators in collecting and interpreting digital evidence (Wilson-Kovacs 2021); and the analytical work of forensic laboratories (Lynch et al. 2008). Further along the CJS process, there are rich ethnographic studies of prosecution and courtroom processes, including Scheffer's (2010) observations of a law firm, barristers' chamber, and two crown courts; Offit's (2017) participant observation in three U.S. attorneys' offices; Wettergren and Bergman Blix's (2016) study of Swedish prosecutors' preparations for trial; studies by Van Oorschot (2014) of clerks and judges in a Dutch criminal court; and studies by Bennett and Feldman (2014) of storytelling in trials.

The aforementioned studies focus on the complex interactions and practices that take place at particular moments of the criminal justice process or among particular criminal justice actors. By contrast, ethnographic studies of the whole process—from crime scene to court—are rare. Notable exceptions include Kruse's (2016) ethnographic study of the Swedish CJS tracing the movement of forensic evidence between crime scene and court and Brookman et al.'s (2020b) British ethnographic study of how homicide cases are investigated, constructed, and travel through the CJS.

In the remainder of this chapter, we share some of our experiences of observing the police and other criminal justice actors as they work together to investigate homicide. We pick out key moments at different stages of the investigative trajectory, foregrounding challenges (and whether and how we overcame them) while drawing on the experiences of other ethnographers. We begin by setting out various approaches to collaborative ethnography and the strategy we adopted.

Approaches to Collaborative Ethnography

Numerous accounts now exist of the experiences of lone policing ethnographers (Dabney and Brookman 2018; Fassin 2013; Loftus 2009; Punch 1979; Souhami 2020). There are, however, very few discussions of the realities of collaborative or multiresearcher ethnography, even for research that involved more than one fieldworker (e.g., Mac Giollabhuí, Goold, and Loftus 2016). One notable exception is the illuminating paper by Buford May and Pattillo-McCoy (2000, 66), which distinguishes two approaches to collaborative ethnography: one in which "two or more ethnographers coordinate their field-work efforts to gather data from a single setting," and one in which several researchers gather data concerning the same social phenomenon but from different social settings.

Our Study of Homicide Investigations

Our study included both of the collaborative ethnography approaches. Specifically, ours was a coordinated effort to gather data on one social phenomenon—homicide investigation. It sometimes involved us being in a single setting (i.e., the same homicide unit), observing the same moments of the investigation together. More often, we observed investigations in different police services or at different moments of the same investigation. In the latter, we would decide what parts of the investigation to shadow and divide our time accordingly. Of the seven hundred hours we spent observing different moments of eleven live homicide investigations, one hundred twenty hours (17 percent) involved joint observations.

Our fieldwork took us from homicide (or major crime) units to crime scenes, where we observed discussion and debate among crime scene managers, senior investigating officers (SIOs), detectives, forensic scientists, and other experts. We accompanied detectives to the streets where they identified and pursued leads (including house-to-house and CCTV inquiries) and shadowed detectives as they tracked suspects using various digital technologies. We attended team briefings led by SIOs[5] and observed recorded interviews with suspects, forensic strategy meetings, barristers' case conferences, and crown court trials, where we came face-to-face with defendants, their families, and the family members of the victims. In summary, our ethnographic research was multisited (Marcus 1995) and multitimed (see Lynch et al. 2008), involving researching many sites over an extended period (thirty-two months total).

Reflections from the Field: Observing Homicide Investigation

Ethnographic research with criminal justice agencies is generally planned months, sometimes years, before the project begins. This is in part because such intensive and intrusive research often requires negotiating protracted access at different levels of an organization, putting research agreements in place, and considering a host of ethical and practical issues. All of these matters can be complicated when one is dealing with sensitive information of the kind that arises during homicide investigation. Space does not permit a discussion of the ethical challenges of conducting research on the police or the complexities of access negotiations (see Bacon, Loftus, and Rowe 2020;

Dabney and Brookman 2018; Rowe 2007; Van Maanen 2003). Instead, we focus on some of the challenges and opportunities that emerge after fieldwork commences: (i) maintaining efforts to access people, places, and events; (ii) dealing with feelings of discomfort during observational research; (iii) creating and sharing field notes; (iv) facing challenges to note-taking; and (v) seizing unanticipated fieldwork opportunities. All research sites and data related to research participants and homicide cases have been given pseudonyms or otherwise disguised to protect the identities of those involved.

Access All Areas: The Rhetoric and Reality

Our research agreements (formal and informal) with the police services had very few exclusionary clauses and were broad ranging in terms of the kinds of activities, people, and documents we could theoretically access during investigations. Nevertheless, we anticipated that accessing some places, spaces, people, and documents might prove difficult, especially during live homicide investigations, and this was our experience. Scheffer's (2010) reflections on legal ethnography resonated with us as we attempted to access many different investigative spaces. As he aptly notes, "legal ethnography is typically not about penetrating a group only. It is also about accessing a number of discursive artefacts such as files, documents, arenas, meetings, archives, etc. These various sites complicate the task of access, since there is no single test to pass" (xxiii).

For example, we never managed to observe a postmortem or speak with a pathologist despite our best efforts and, in one case, the efforts of police to broker our access. Our research agreements were with the police services, so our entry to sites not controlled by police was always more precarious. On some occasions, detectives deflected us from observing parts of the investigation, as illustrated in the following field note extract:

> I suggest [observing] phone work but he [the SIO] is a little wary as he says there is some sensitive work happening and they are in a tiny room at the end of the corridor with no extra room for me. I mention house-to-house but he says this is "boring." And so I suggest CCTV (Lewis is heading this and I know he will be helpful). So I head back into the room as Lewis is still in there briefing officers. He welcomes me. I have missed most of the meeting by now but he kindly updates me. (Extract from Brookman's field notes, Operation C02)

Several hours later, Brookman accompanied detectives onto the streets and into various commercial and private premises to try and recover useful CCTV of the murder suspects. This aspect of the research emerged as an important focal point of our findings, highly illustrative of the tensions between what SIOs assume detectives can do and what they actually can do (see Brookman and Jones 2021).

At other times, homicides happened, but the police forgot to call us. On these occasions, we missed the start of the investigation and either chose not to observe the case at all (if we felt we had missed too much) or, in a few cases, felt able to fill in the gaps sufficiently by arranging one-on-one briefings with the SIO, reading the SIO policy file or current situation report, speaking to other officers about what had happened, viewing scene photographs, and attending the scene at a later date.

On other occasions, we were actively engaged in observations but found ourselves sidelined. For example, in one police service, a young male detective inspector (DI) seemed reluctant to include us fully in his interactions at the crime scene, as the following field note extract illustrates:

> We follow Kamal [DI] and Luke [Detective Sergeant] into the cordoned area as they meet with other specialist officers and receive an update. It is difficult to hear it due to the traffic noise and Kamal does not exactly invite us into the fold [I am struck with how different it is from observing in the USA where I was always invited into the 'inner circle']. (Extract from Brookman's field notes, Operation W11)

The same DI tended to exclude us from key moments of investigations, though we became more adept at overcoming these challenges. For example, on one occasion, Jones bypassed Kamal (who was about to start a briefing and had not invited her to attend) by asking the SIO if she could attend. He happily agreed. In short, in this police service, one detective seemed a little reticent about our research, so we had to navigate our interactions with him and our observations carefully, without jeopardizing our relationships with the investigative team.

In contrast to occasions when we were excluded and/or felt that we had to be pushy, we also experienced individual officers and police services that went above and beyond to accommodate our research. One police service, for example, gave us lifts to and from the airport, our accommodation, and the homicide unit and was open and welcoming throughout our fieldwork.

We experienced a good deal of police input in terms of what kinds of homicide they felt would be most useful for us to observe, as the following field note extract illustrates:

> Julian [detective superintendent] called giving me "the heads up" that there has been a stabbing overnight in XXX and that the victim is alive at the moment but if he dies, this will be a very interesting murder

investigation as it appears to be drug related and the offenders are at large and it will be "a proper whodunit." (Extract from Brookman's field notes, Operation C01)

Noticeably, detectives were often of the view that the most useful cases for us to observe were those where offenders were "at large" with a "manhunt" underway or that were "proper whodunits" with no obvious suspects. By contrast, detectives tried to steer us away from what they perceived to be more mundane aspects of investigations (such as CCTV inquiries), easy-to-solve cases, or those that might involve little forensic input—including a one-punch manslaughter and a "straightforward" fight. On some occasions we took the advice offered by detectives, while on others we chose to observe the investigation despite their reservations. We made these decisions based on our aim of covering a diverse range of cases and investigations. While it is not unusual for researchers to want to be at the center of the action (see for example Parker 1990), we were also interested in observing routine and mundane aspects of investigations (see Van Hulst 2020; Van Oorschot 2014).

In summary, there were occasions when we were purposely or accidentally excluded from seeing and hearing things and others when we were steered toward particular kinds of cases, investigations, or investigative activity. Our responses varied depending on how important we felt it was to observe the event and our feelings and perceptions in the moment.

The Uncomfortable Observer

Much has been written about researchers' roles as observers, participants, or both and how these roles can change during research (see Brookman 2015). During our research, we found ourselves crossing the line from observer to participant observer. For example, we numbered jury bundles, wrapped and moved exhibits, and helped download CCTV footage (see also Mac Giollabhuí, Goold, and Loftus 2016; Rowe 2007; Westmarland 2013). Here, we focus on one aspect of the researcher role that has received relatively little scholarly attention—what we term the "uncomfortable observer" (see for exceptions Javaid 2019; Koning and Ooi 2013; Pettit 2020; Sløk-Andersen and Persson 2021; Souhami 2020).[6]

We use the term "uncomfortable observer" to refer to occasions when the researcher feels particularly out of place, like an intruder or imposter, or uneasy. These feelings can arise for many different reasons and in varying contexts and can impact, negatively or positively, the ability to collect data and the overall research experience (see later section on challenges to note-taking). On some occasions, simply finding the right place to sit or stand can be important—giving, for example, a good vantage point for data collection

(Scheffer 2010). On others, physical positioning can enable one to blend in and feel comfortable, as illustrated in the following field note:

> To begin with I felt a bit lost. The office was a lot busier and there weren't enough chairs / desks for everyone. I managed to sit at a computer in the middle of the second bank of desks but I felt more comfortable sitting at the edge of the room as I felt a bit exposed there when writing notes. As it turned out, after the briefing I managed to move to the window seat where I had sat the previous day, opposite Henry again, and felt more comfortable. (Extract from Jones's field notes, Operation E12)

Often, these kinds of uncomfortable moments occur early in fieldwork, in new and unfamiliar environments, but they can also arise when the ordinary changes or routines are disrupted.

On other occasions, when we met members of the public or other professionals, we became uncomfortable if we were not introduced properly or honestly. For example, during a barrister's conference at the police station, Brookman was not introduced to the QC (Queen's Counsel) leading the event:

> Everyone is now sat in the meeting room. . . . No one has explained who I am and I am not sure if Dawn [SIO] has informed the CPS [Crown Prosecution Service]. The QC arrives last and says hello to us all before starting the meeting. . . . As things wrap up the QC looks directly at me and asks if we have met and who I am. It felt a little awkward as we ought to have been introduced and ideally permission sought for me to be there but Dawn is pretty laid back. (Extract from Brookman's field notes, Operation E12)

Sometimes, our role was not explained by detectives to third parties. For example, Fiona was introduced to a family during house-to-house inquiries as the officer's "colleague," and Jones was even described to court staff as a police officer. There were times when it seemed easier for us to assume the role of detective to ensure our smooth access into private or official spaces not controlled by police. Nevertheless, we questioned the truthfulness of our access, generally experiencing unease in these situations and, sometimes, fear that our "cover could be blown," with negative consequences.

Finally, there were occasions when we were treated as proxy detectives and asked for our opinions, recommendations about working practices, or input about investigations (see also Mason-Bish 2019, 264). While this could be taken as a positive sign that one is trusted or has been accepted or embraced by the group (Westmarland 2013, 316), we often felt put on the spot and were guarded in our responses. We were concerned about overstating our knowledge and inadvertently offending our research participants. We generally managed these situations by declining to comment, although sometimes we offered reassuring words if it felt appropriate.

> Just before I left Dawn [SIO] asked to have a chat with me. We went and sat on a bank of desks near to the balcony. She said that she would value any critique I had of her and how it was a learning experience for her. I explained that I wasn't there to critique her but to observe. . . . I commented that she had acknowledged the contribution from others, and had rationalised and justified her decision. (Extract from Jones's field note, Operation E11)

In the following example, Brookman sat with a female detective inside the home of a family who lived next door to the residence of a suspected domestic homicide. The detective asked family members a series of questions, trying to establish evidence of prior domestic violence or controlling behavior by the suspect toward the victim. As her questioning came to a close, she invited Brookman's input.

> Tanya asked me if there was anything else to ask. I quietly said, "shall we check if he's seen her [the victim] on her own?" Tanya asked and he confirmed that he had never seen her on her own. (Extract from Brookman's field notes, Operation C01)

Brookman instinctively gave input on this occasion despite feeling awkward, as she had become curious about the extent of the suspect's controlling behavior toward the victim and wondered whether he had prevented her leaving the house alone. Nevertheless, whether the officer ought to have asked for Brookman's input and whether she ought to have answered is debatable—further examples of how one must carefully manage fieldwork encounters. Sløk-Andersen and Persson (2021, 73) argue that "awkward encounters in ethnographic work can be of great methodological value when studying organizational phenomena." Moreover, they suggest that these experiences "should be placed front and center" of analysis rather than marginalized as "exceptions or failures" (73). We certainly intend to return to our field notes and examine more carefully our own awkward moments in future analysis.

Collaborative Fieldwork and Field Notes

There are various approaches to gathering field notes during team fieldwork. In Buford May and Pattillo-McCoy's (2000) study, for example, one pair of researchers took turns recording and writing up field notes. Another pair discussed their observations, then one took responsibility for writing the collective observations. Buford May and Pattillo-McCoy, by contrast, elected to each record their observations separately, with little conversation about what they had observed. They wrote their field notes at separate residences, and their perceptions of the research site were shared with each other "by writing those perceptions directly into the fieldnotes" (68).

As ours was a collaborative ethnography, we had to decide how to record our observations. To begin with, we agreed that we would write down "everything" (Becker 1998, 76) or as much detail as possible of what we observed (Paik and Harris 2015), including the seemingly mundane (see Van Hulst 2020, 107; Van Oorschot 2014, 443). On occasion, we included sketches of environments we found ourselves in (e.g., crime scenes, the layout of the courtrooms or major investigation rooms) or added images of streets where murders had occurred extracted from Google Street View. We also described the weather, sounds, smells, and sometimes emotions we experienced.

Naturally, we recorded our independent observations separately. We shared and discussed our field notes once typed up with the research team, two of whom who were not involved in data collection. The field notes sometimes contained our impressions, reflections, thoughts, and questions, routinely recorded in squared brackets or boxes to demarcate from the recordings of what we saw and heard.

On occasions when we jointly observed the same activities, we decided to record our observations separately. There were a few instances when one of us or other briefly took a lead or solo role in recording field notes as the observations took place, but these were rare. Again, we shared our field notes as soon as they had been typed. Naturally, we sometimes shared our reflections and thoughts about what we had observed over coffee or during lunch breaks or evening meals. We were not precious about producing sterile field notes uncontaminated by discussion.

We always endeavored to individually interrogate our field notes at the end of each day, tidy up particularly messy scrawl while our memories were fresh, fill in gaps, and add further impressions and thoughts. We tended to our field notes in these ways at opportune downtime or quiet moments during fieldwork. Unlike some other researchers, we were rarely able to type up our field notes on the same day (see Paik and Harris 2015). Our observations were often so lengthy and intense that we were simply too tired and needed to sleep before resuming observations early the next morning. We generally managed to type our field notes in full within the same week.

Our field notes enabled us to compare practices across four different police services. We were also able to compare our field notes of joint observations. Undoubtedly, our different experiences and backgrounds impacted how we received information, stories, and worldviews of the detectives (Brookman et al. 2020a). We have since concluded that there are definite benefits to having four eyes instead of two, as our different note-taking styles were somewhat complementary. We were relieved to discover that we seemed to record key events, moments, decisions, disagreements, and utterances in much the same way, but the meanings we each ascribed to our observations quite often differed.

Challenges to Note-taking

Depending on the setting being observed, ethnographers may choose to take written field notes inconspicuously, utilizing private spaces (see Loftus 2009). In fact, numerous police ethnographers recount how they chose to keep open note-taking to a minimum in order to ensure that officers spoke freely (see Quinton 2020; Rowe 2007). Bacon (2016, 85–86), for example, rarely put pen to paper, opting for "eavesdropping," "mental notes," and regular excursions to the "toilet cubicle to scribble down notes." Nevertheless, he subsequently discovered that "note taking abstinence was not always possible or preferable" (86) and that research participants often expected him to write down what they were saying.

For ease, completeness, and transparency (see Souhami 2020 on the latter), we tried to enter every setting with our notebook in hand, openly ready to make notes. By doing so, our note-taking became an accepted and expected part of our roles as researchers (Emerson, Fretz, and Shaw 2011, 37). Most of the time this approach worked well; given that police officers often engage in note-taking themselves (e.g., during briefings and when engaged in outside inquiries), our note-taking was part of normal organizational practice, was never questioned, and did not appear to inhibit conversations. Nevertheless, there were certain spaces and places where our note-taking led to unanticipated problems. For example, during one observation of a murder trial, Jones was prevented from taking notes by an employee of Witness Services who escorted her into the courtroom at the crown court.

> Just as we were about to leave Witness Services, Gail saw my notebook and asked whether I had got permission to take notes. I explained that I never knew we needed permission and that both Brookman and I had taken notes yesterday. We had just got to the main door to leave Witness Services and there is a sign that says no mobile phones and no notetaking. Gail explained that although it's a public gallery it is the judge's decision whether they allow notes to be taken. We returned to the office so that Gail could ask permission. (Extract from Jones's field notes, W12)

Although this encounter happened in early 2017, a crown court hearing (*Ewing v. Cardiff Crown Court*) had ruled in February 2016 that note-taking does not require judicial permission and that anyone can take notes without consent (although in certain circumstances, with good reason, note-taking can be prohibited). Our ignorance of this ruling meant that we were unable to defend our note-taking and was an important lesson to us to be better informed about where and when it is permitted (see also Scheffer 2010).

Note-taking raises other challenges. On occasion, we did not understand everything we heard during briefings. We were not familiar with all of the acronyms or jargon used by the police and did not always comprehend fully the detail of technical or medical information discussed. In these instances, we recorded what we thought we had heard or seen and endeavored to fill the gaps in our notes and understanding as soon as practically possible. Sometimes we asked detectives to clarify what we thought we had heard; on other occasions our analysis of documents relating to the investigation revealed what we needed to know.

As many ethnographers will attest, typing up field notes is a time-consuming activity that takes at least as long as the fieldwork itself (Emerson, Fretz, and Shaw 2011; Norris 1993). Some ethnographers choose not to type up their field notes at all. For example, Manning (2018, 239), recounting his observations of the Metropolitan Police in the early 1970s, reveals that he did not use a tape recorder or shorthand and did not type up the notes from the spiral notebooks he still has. He suggests that "detailed, organized, systematic and lengthy field notes are rare, perhaps a mythical idea." We are inclined to disagree, given our painstaking attempts to produce such notes! However, he is correct in reminding us of the work of Jackson (1990) and other colleagues (see Sanjek 1990) who have illuminated the complex relationship between field observations, written notes, analyses, and writing up—and in his assertion that the extent to which field notes "reflect, interpret, distort, or omit some aspects of social reality, continues to be an issue for many sociologists" (239). Nevertheless, we are of the view that it is important to amass detailed field notes, particularly on collaborative projects, and type these up into accounts that can be shared and discussed as soon as practically possible.

Finally, Brookman's past fieldwork experiences taught her that always having a recording device handy is an invaluable way of gathering verbatim data without needing to take detailed field notes. We always had a digital recording device close by and asked to turn it on at opportune moments in the field. For instance, we recorded informal conversations with detectives while driving to and from crime scenes (see also Brookman 2015) and found these recordings to be an important substitute to field notes—especially in situations with multiple people engaged in dialogue. We also recorded our conversations during informal tours of forensic science facilities and digital forensic units.

Following Cases and Seizing Opportunities

Many ethnographers discover that "ethnographic work is not always orderly" (Fetterman 1989, 12), and it often transpires that the most interesting or informative observations result from chance encounters combined with a willingness and flexibility to seize unanticipated research opportunities (Dabney and Brookman 2018). Such was our experience. For example, while observing the reinvestigation of a cold case in which the suspect had been identified through a familial DNA search, we became aware that the prosecution barrister would be heavily involved in deciding which forensic opportunities to pursue. Although not part of our proposed methodology, we approached the SIO and asked if it would be possible to attend the barrister's case conferences (similar to meetings between attorneys and police in the United States). The SIO made a request to the barrister, who gave her approval. From these conferences, we gathered many new insights about how evidence is selected and shaped by prosecutors. During two conferences, we sat with detectives, the female barrister, and each forensic scientist (in turn) around a large oak table in Barristers' Chambers and observed the barrister questioning the scientists about their DNA work and how they might present their findings. As the conversations unfolded, it became clear that the barrister wished to inflate, if possible, the significance of the results. Both scientists stuck firmly to recommended ways of reporting findings from DNA analysis. We found the whole encounter fascinating, and our serendipitous glimpse into a rarely seen backstage (Goffman 1959) arena of the CJS led us to actively pursue other opportunities to observe barristers' conferences.

Conclusions

Qualitative research on homicide comes in numerous guises. In this chapter, we have paid particular attention to some of the challenges of undertaking collaborative ethnography on homicide investigation. In so doing, we hope to have provided a flavor of the realities, promises, and pitfalls of fieldwork with police and other criminal justice agencies. We have, of course, just scratched the surface of the many challenges that accompany ethnographic research. We have not discussed the challenge of analyzing the large volumes of data produced or the significant demands of anonymizing data. We have not tackled the ethical dilemmas that often accompany ethnographic research, nor have we discussed the risks of fieldwork (see Urbanik 2018). We have also not talked about different ways of ending fieldwork, whether or how to keep the door open to return (see Manning 2015; Dabney and Brookman 2018), or the inevitable exploration and accounting of the self that emerges during the practice and writing of ethnography (e.g., Ferrell 2018 on autoethnography).

Nonetheless, we hope that by sharing some of our experiences with a relatively neglected research technique in homicide studies, we will inspire further research of this kind. Ethnographic research is demanding and at times daunting but also exhilarating and rewarding. It requires patience, tenacity, flexibility, and curiosity without judgment. It permits unrivaled exploration of events as they unfold and of people as they cocreate these events. There is often no (or limited) training in the techniques of ethnography in our discipline and various (sometimes contested) ways of doing ethnographic research, including recent calls to think afresh about what the future holds for ethnography (e.g., see Fraser 2018 on moving ethnography). If any of this sounds attractive, we invite you to give it a go.

NOTES

1. As of July 24, 2021. Determined by searching for "homicide OR murder" anywhere in all 201 articles published between 2011 and 2020. Book reviews, introductions to special issues, and articles in honor of Margo Wilson were removed, leaving 181 articles. Articles were then searched and checked to identify those that used qualitative methods. Search terms including "qualitative," "ethnography," "ethnographic," and "NVivo" were used to identify the 21 articles that adopt some kind of qualitative research methods.

2. The HIFS Project was funded by the Leverhulme Trust and involved a collaboration across three universities: USW (Professor Fiona Brookman, principal investigator, and Dr. Helen Jones, research fellow), Northumbria University (Professor Robin Williams), and University of Strathclyde (Professor Jim Fraser). It ran between January 2015 and December 2018. Brookman and Jones gathered all of the data.

3. We adopt a broad definition of FSTs including DNA profiling, fingerprint examination, blood pattern and trace evidence analysis, ballistics interpretation, and analysis of digital data and devices.

4. Released "on licence" means that for the rest of their sentence the released prisoner must abide by certain conditions.

5. The SIO leads and oversees the investigation, acting as both an investigator and manager. The SIO develops and implements the investigative strategy and manages resources (see Brookman, forthcoming). The role is similar to lead detective in the United States but with some overlaps with the role of lieutenant.

6. See also Jackson (1990) on field notes and emotion.

REFERENCES

Allsop, Cheryl. 2018. *Cold Case Reviews: DNA, Detective Work and Unsolved Major Crimes.* Oxford: Oxford University Press.

Armour, Marilyn Peterson. 2002. "Journey of Family Members of Homicide Victims: A Qualitative Study of Their Post Homicide Experience." *American Journal of Orthopsychiatry* 72:372–82. https://doi.org/10.1037/0002-9432.72.3.372.

Atkinson, Paul, Amanda Coffey, Sara Delamont, John Lofland, and Lyn H. Lofland. 2001. *Handbook of Ethnography*. London: SAGE.

Bacon, Matthew. 2016. *Taking Care of Business: Police Detectives, Drug Law Enforcement and Proactive Investigation*. Oxford: Oxford University Press.

Bacon, Matthew, Bethan Loftus, and Mike Rowe. 2020. "Ethnography and the Evocative World of Policing (Part 1)." *Policing and Society* 30 (1): 1–10. https://doi.org/10.1080/104 39463.2019.1701453.

Becker, Howard. 1998. *Tricks of the Trade: How to Think about Your Research While You're Doing It*. Chicago: University of Chicago Press.

Bennett, W. Lance, and Martha S. Feldman. 2014. *Reconstructing Reality in the Courtroom*. 2nd ed. New Orleans: Quid Pro Books.

Berntzen, Lars Erik, and Sveinung Sandberg. 2014. "The Collective Nature of Lone-Wolf Terrorism: Anders Behring Breivik and the Anti-Islamic Movement." *Terrorism and Political Violence* 26 (5): 759–79. https://doi.org/10.1080/09546553.2013.767245.

Brookman, Fiona. 2003. "Confrontational and Grudge Revenge Homicides in England and Wales." *Australian and New Zealand Journal of Criminology* 36 (1): 34–59. https://doi.org/10.1375/acri.36.1.34.

———. 2015. "Researching Homicide Offenders, Offenses and Detectives Using Qualitative Methods." In *The Handbook of Qualitative Criminology*, edited by Heith Copes and J. Mitchell Miller, 236–52. New York: Routledge.

———. Forthcoming. *Understanding Homicide*. 2nd ed. London: SAGE.

Brookman, Fiona, and Helen Jones. 2021. "Capturing Killers: The Construction of CCTV Evidence during Homicide Investigations." *Policing and Society* 32 (2): 125–44. https://doi.org/10.1080/10439463.2021.1879075.

Brookman, Fiona, Helen Jones, Robin Williams, and Jim Fraser. 2020a. "Crafting Credible Homicide Narratives: Forensic Technoscience in Contemporary Criminal Investigations." *Deviant Behavior* 43 (3): 340–66. https://doi.org/10.1080/01639625.2020.1 837692.

———. 2020b. "Dead Reckoning: Unravelling How 'Homicide' Cases Travel from Crime Scene to Court Using Qualitative Research Methods." *Homicide Studies* 24 (3): 283–306. https://doi.org/10.1177/1088767920907374.

Brookman, Fiona, Edward R. Maguire, and Mike Maguire. 2019. "What Factors Influence Whether Homicide Cases Are Solved? Insights from Qualitative Research with Detectives in Great Britain and the United States." *Homicide Studies* 23 (2): 145–74. https://doi.org/10.1177/1088767918793678.

Buford May, Reuben A., and Mary Pattillo-McCoy. 2000. "Do You See What I See? Examining a Collaborative Ethnography." *Qualitative Inquiry* 6 (1): 65–87. https://doi.org/10.1177/107780040000600105.

Dabney, Dean. 2019. "Doing Death Work: A Typology of How Homicide Detectives Orient to Their Work." *Policing and Society* 30 (7): 777–94. https://doi.org/10.1080/10439463.2019.1593981.

Dabney, Dean, and Fiona Brookman. 2018. "Fieldwork with Homicide Detectives: 60 Minutes of Reflections from a British and American Criminologist." In *Doing Ethnography in Criminology: Discovery through Fieldwork*, edited by Stephen K. Rice and Michael D. Maltz, 91–113. New York: Springer International.

Decker, Scott H., and Barrik Van Winkle. 1996. *Life in the Gang*. Cambridge: Cambridge University Press.

Densley, James A. 2013. *How Gangs Work: An Ethnography of Youth Violence*. London: Palgrave Macmillan.

Dobash, Russell P., and R. Emerson Dobash. 2020. *Male-Male Murder*. London: Routledge.

Emerson, Robert M., Rachel I. Fretz, and Linda L. Shaw. 2011. *Writing Ethnographic Fieldnotes*. 2nd ed. Chicago: University of Chicago Press.

EWHC 183 (Admin). 2016. "Ewing v Crown Court Sitting at Cardiff and Newport." England and Wales High Court (Administrative Court) Decisions. http://www.bailii.org/ew/cases/EWHC/Admin/2016/183.html.

Fassin, Didier. 2013. *Enforcing Order: An Ethnography of Urban Policing*. Cambridge: Polity.

Ferrell, Jeff. 2018. "Criminological Ethnography: Living and Knowing." In *Doing Ethnography in Criminology: Discovery through Fieldwork*, edited by Stephen K. Rice and Michael D. Maltz, 147–61. New York: Springer International.

Fetterman, David. 1989. *Ethnography Step by Step*. Newbury Park: SAGE.

Fraser, Alistair. 2018. "The Ghost of Ethnography Future." In *Doing Ethnography in Criminology: Discovery through Fieldwork*, edited by Stephen K. Rice and Michael D. Maltz, 179–85. New York: Springer International.

Gambetta, Diego. 1996. *The Sicilian Mafia: The Business of Private Protection*. Cambridge, MA: Harvard University Press.

Goffman, Erving. 1959. *The Presentation of Self in Everyday Life*. London: Penguin Books.

Goh, Kim. 2008. *Conquering the Dragon: The True Life Story of a Former Triad Gang Member*. Milton Keynes: Authentic Media.

Hällgren, Markus, Ola Lindberg, and Oscar Rantatalo. 2021. "Sensemaking in Detective Work: The Social Nature of Crime Investigation." *International Journal of Police Science & Management* 23 (2): 119–32. https://doi.org/10.1177/1461355720980759.

Harding, Simon. 2014. *The Street Casino: Survival in the Violent Street Gang*. Bristol: Polity Press.

Hobbs, Dick. 1989. *Doing the Business: Entrepreneurship, the Working Class, and Detectives in the East End of London*. Oxford: Oxford University Press.

Innes, Martin. 2003. *Investigating Murder: Detective Work and the Police Response to Criminal Homicide*. Oxford: Oxford University Press.

Jackson, Jean E. 1990. *Fieldnotes*. Ithaca, NY: Cornell University Press.

Javaid, Aliraza. 2019. "Hear My Screams: An Auto-ethnographic Account of the Police." *Methodological Innovations* 12 (3): 205979911988427. https://doi.org/10.1177/2059799119884279.

Koning, Juliette, and Can-Seng Ooi. 2013. "Awkward Encounters and Ethnography." *Qualitative Research in Organizations and Management: An International Journal* 8 (1): 16–32. https://doi.org/10.1108/17465641311327496.

Kruse, Corinna. 2016. *The Social Life of Forensic Evidence*. Oakland: University of California Press.

———. 2020. "Swedish Crime Scene Technicians: Facilitations, Epistemic Frictions and Professionalization from the Outside." *Nordic Journal of Criminology* 21 (1): 67–83. https://doi.org/10.1080/2578983X.2019.1627808.

Lindegaard, Marie Rosenkrantz. 2017. "Homicide in South Africa: Offender Perspectives on Dispute-Related Killings of Men." In *Handbook of Homicide*, edited by Fiona Brookman, Edward R. Maguire, and Mike Maguire, 499–514. Chichester: Wiley-Blackwell.

Loftus, Bethan. 2009. *Police Culture in a Changing World*. Oxford: Oxford University Press.

Loyens, Kim. 2014. "Rule Bending by Morally Disengaged Detectives: An Ethnographic Study." *Police Practice and Research* 15 (1): 62–74. https://doi.org/10.1080/15614263.2013.770941.

Lynch, Michael, Simon A. Cole, Ruth McNally, and Kathleen Jordan. 2008. *Truth Machine: The Contentious History of DNA Fingerprinting*. Chicago: University of Chicago Press.

Mac Giollabhuí, Shane, Benjamin Goold, and Bethan Loftus. 2016. "Watching the Watchers: Conducting Ethnographic Research on Covert Police Investigation in the United Kingdom." *Qualitative Research* 16 (6): 630–45. https://doi.org/10.1177/1468794115622529.

Manning, Peter. 2015. "Researching Police Using Qualitative Methods." In *The Handbook of Qualitative Criminology*, edited by Heith Copes and J. Mitchell Miller, 265–82. New York: Routledge.

———. 2018. "A Taste of Ethnography." In *Doing Ethnography in Criminology: Discovery through Fieldwork*, edited by Stephen K. Rice and Michael D. Maltz, 237–45. New York: Springer International.

Marcus, George E. 1995. "Ethnography in/of the World System: The Emergence of Multi-sited Ethnography." *Annual Review of Anthropology* 24:95–117.

Mason-Bish, Hannah. 2019. "The Elite Delusion: Reflexivity, Identity and Positionality in Qualitative Research." *Qualitative Research* 19 (3): 263–76. https://doi.org/10.1177/1468794118770078.

Norris, Clive. 1993. "Some Ethical Considerations on Field-Work with the Police." In *Interpreting the Field: Accounts of Ethnography*, edited by Dick Hobbs and Tim May, 123–43. Oxford: Oxford University Press.

Oberman, Michelle, and Cheryl L. Meyer. 2008. *When Mothers Kill: Interviews from Prison*. New York: New York University Press.

Offit, Anna. 2017. "With Jurors in Mind: An Ethnographic Study of Prosecutors' Narratives." *Law, Culture and the Humanities* 17 (3): 462–84. https://doi.org/10.1177/1743872117717426.

Paik, Leslie, and Alexes Harris. 2015. "Court Ethnographies." In *The Handbook of Qualitative Criminology*, edited by Heith Copes and J. Mitchell Miller, 283–95. New York: Routledge.

Parker, Tony. 1990. *Life after Life: Interviews with Twelve Murderers*. London: Harper Collins.

Pettit, Harry. 2020. "Uncomfortable Ethnography: Navigating Friendship and 'Cruel Hope' with Egypt's Disconnected Middle-Class." *Emotion, Space and Society* 36:100714. https://doi.org/10.1016/j.emospa.2020.100714.

Presser, Lois. 2012. "Getting on Top through Mass Murder: Narrative, Metaphor, and Violence." *Crime, Media, Culture* 8:3–21. https://doi.org/10.1177/1741659011430443.

Punch, Maurice. 1979. *Policing the Inner City: A Study of Amsterdam's Warmoesstraat*. London: Macmillan.

Quinton, Paul. 2020. "Officer Strategies for Managing Interactions during Police Stops." *Policing and Society* 30 (1): 11–27. https://doi.org/10.1080/10439463.2019.1606220.

Rock, Paul. 1998. *After Homicide: Practical and Political Responses to Bereavement*. Oxford: Clarendon Press.

Rowe, Mike. 2007. "Tripping over Molehills: Ethics and the Ethnography of Police Work." *International Journal of Social Research Methodology* 10 (1): 37–48. https://doi.org/10.1080/13645570600652792.

Saleem, Kamal. 2017. *The Blood of Lambs: A Former Terrorist's Memoir of Death and Redemption*. Brentwood: Howard Books.

Sanjek, Roger, ed. 1990. *Fieldnotes: The Makings of Anthropology*. Ithaca, NY: Cornell University Press.

Sausdal, David. 2020. "Everyday Policing: Toward a Greater Analytical Appreciation of the Ordinary in Police Research." *Policing and Society* 31 (7): 1–14. https://doi.org/10.1080/10439463.2020.1798955.

Scheffer, Thomas. 2010. *Adversarial Case-Making: An Ethnography of English Crown Court Procedure*. Boston: BRILL.

Schneider, Rachel Zimmer. 2014. *Battered Women Doing Time: Injustice in the Criminal Justice System*. Boulder, CO: First Forum Press.

Shaw, James E. 2000. *Jack and Jill and Why They Kill: Saving Our Children, Saving Ourselves*. Seattle: Onjinjinkta.

Sløk-Andersen, Beate, and Alma Persson. 2021. "Awkward Ethnography: An Untapped Resource in Organizational Studies." *Journal of Organizational Ethnography* 10 (1): 65–78. https://doi.org/10.1108/joe-09-2020-0036.

Smith, Richard E. 2019. *God Don't Lie: A Memoir by a Former Racist Gang Member and All-Round Miscreant*. Meadville: Christian Faith.

Sollund, Ragnhild. 2008. "Tested Neutrality: Emotional Challenges in Qualitative Interviews on Homicide and Rape." *Journal of Scandinavian Studies in Criminology and Crime Prevention* 9:181–201. https://doi.org/10.1080/14043850802450138.

Souhami, Anna. 2020. "Constructing Tales of the Field: Uncovering the Culture of Fieldwork in Police Ethnography." *Policing and Society* 30 (2): 206–23. https://doi.org/10.1080/10439463.2019.1628230.

Urbanik, Marta-Marika. 2018. "Shots Fired: Navigating Gun Violence and a University's Intervention While in the Field." In *Doing Ethnography in Criminology: Discovery through Fieldwork*, edited by Stephen K. Rice and Michael D. Maltz, 303–24. New York: Springer International.

Van Hulst, Merlijn. 2013. "Storytelling at the Police Station: The Canteen Culture Revisited." *British Journal of Criminology* 53 (4): 624–42. https://doi.org/10.1093/bjc/azt014.

———. 2020. "Ethnography and Narrative." *Policing and Society* 30 (1): 98–115. https://doi.org/10.1080/10439463.2019.1646259.

Van Maanen, John. 1973. "Observations on the Making of Policemen." *Human Organization* 32 (4): 407–18. https://doi.org/10.17730/humo.32.4.13h7x81187mh8km8.

———. 2003. "The Moral Fix: On the Ethics of Fieldwork." In *Qualitative Approaches to Criminal Justice Perspectives from the Field*, edited by Mark R. Pogrebin, 363–76. London: SAGE.

Van Oorschot, Irene. 2014. "Seeing the Case Clearly: File-Work, Material Mediation, and Visualizing Practices in a Dutch Criminal Court." *Symbolic Interaction* 37:439–57. https://doi.org/10.1002/symb.126.

Westmarland, Louise. 2013. "'Snitches Get Stitches': US Homicide Detectives' Ethics and Morals in Action." *Policing and Society* 23 (3): 311–27. https://doi.org/10.1080/10439463.2013.784313.

Wettergren, Asa, and Stina Bergman Blix. 2016. "Empathy and Objectivity in the Legal Procedure: The Case of Swedish Prosecutors." *Journal of Scandinavian Studies in Criminology and Crime Prevention* 17 (1): 19–35. https://doi.org/10.1080/14043858.2015.1136501.

Wilson-Kovacs, Dana. 2021. "Digital Media Investigators: Challenges and Opportunities in the Use of Digital Forensics in Police Investigations in England and Wales." *Policing: An International Journal* 44 (4): 669–82. https://doi.org/10.1108/pijpsm-02-2021-0019.

Wyatt, David. 2014. "Practising Crime Scene Investigation: Trace and Contamination in Routine Work." *Policing and Society* 24 (4): 443–58. https://doi.org/10.1080/10439463.2013.868460.

Wyatt, David, and Dana Wilson-Kovacs. 2019. "Understanding Crime Scene Examination Through an Ethnographic Lens." *Wiley Interdisciplinary Reviews: Forensic Science* 1 (6). https://doi.org/10.1002/wfs2.1357.

8

Examining Black Homicide through Lenses of Epidemiology

SHARON D. JONES-EVERSLEY, JACQUELINE RHODEN-TRADER, AND JOHNNY RICE II

Introduction

The 2020 Census shows that Black[1] people comprise 12.1 percent of the U.S. population. Yet according to homicide data from the Federal Bureau of Investigation (FBI) Uniform Crime Reporting, in 2019, 54.7 percent of homicide victims and 55.9 percent of homicide offenders were Black (FBI Uniform Crime Reporting Program 2019a, 2019b). The excessive homicide deaths that impact Black people and their communities require a focus of study incorporating the structural determinants of Black homicide, the detrimental health consequences that feed a reciprocal cycle of disadvantage and homicide risk, and prevention and policy. Researchers, practitioners, policymakers, and learners can expand the public health lens of epidemiology to delve deeper into the factors contributing to high homicide deaths among Black people specifically and their impact on Black community health.

Epidemiology is a subsector of public health that studies the distribution and determinants of health-related states or events (health, disease, injury, and death) in specified populations. Epidemiological analysis of homicide encompasses multiple sources of data and societal intel from a specified geographic population (Whitman, Benbow, and Good 1996). Exploring homicides through the lenses of spatial, criminological, social, and legal epidemiological methodologies offers promising pathways to assess intersecting structural determinants like racism, poverty, or mass incarceration, which also contribute to excessive homicide deaths among Black people (Hinton and Cook

2021; Link and Phelan 1995; Miller 2015). More importantly, diverse epidemiological methodologies may lead to primordial homicide prevention efforts that aid in dismantling the inequalities and disparities in the U.S. criminal justice system.

Primordial prevention alters inequitable societal and economic structures with the precise aim of (1) locating and identifying underlying risks and (2) addressing and dismantling health and death determinants of risk factors (Jones-Eversley et al. 2020). Unlike traditional prevention strategies that reactively treat and minimize risk factors, primordial prevention proactively targets mediating risk factors in a specified geographic population with the sole intent of dismantling and avoiding the reemergence of said factors (Giampaioli 2007). Through targeted health education and health promotion policies, laws, and practices, primordial prevention normalizes healthy living in a specified geographic population. Including spatial, criminological, social, and legal epidemiological methodologies in primordial homicide prevention efforts strengthens homicide prevention research, policies, and practice. Figure 8.1 defines the epidemiological methodologies and demonstrates their intersecting capacities individually and collectively to heighten primordial homicide prevention.

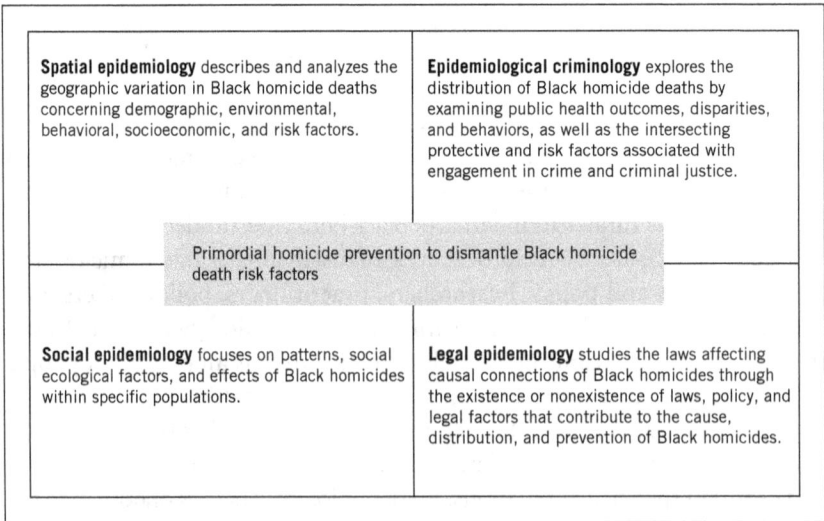

Spatial epidemiology describes and analyzes the geographic variation in Black homicide deaths concerning demographic, environmental, behavioral, socioeconomic, and risk factors.	**Epidemiological criminology** explores the distribution of Black homicide deaths by examining public health outcomes, disparities, and behaviors, as well as the intersecting protective and risk factors associated with engagement in crime and criminal justice.
Primordial homicide prevention to dismantle Black homicide death risk factors	
Social epidemiology focuses on patterns, social ecological factors, and effects of Black homicides within specific populations.	**Legal epidemiology** studies the laws affecting causal connections of Black homicides through the existence or nonexistence of laws, policy, and legal factors that contribute to the cause, distribution, and prevention of Black homicides.

Figure 8.1 Diverse Epidemiological Methodologies with Primordial Prevention to Address Black Homicides (*Note: This figure visualizes the potential of including spatial, criminological, social, and legal epidemiological methodologies in primordial homicide prevention efforts. Source: Adapted from S. Jones-Eversley, A.C. Adedoyin, L. James-Townes, and J. Rice, 2022, "Due Process and Justice in Black Communities," in* Why the Police Should Be Trained by Black People, *edited by Natasha C. Pratt-Harris, 1st ed., 34. New York: Routledge.*)

Traditional Theories of Inequality and Homicide

The United States is a stratified society plagued by social inequities; 1 to 2 percent of its population controls wealth, power, and privilege (Beckert 2022; Volscho and Kelly 2012). Americans identify the lower class, poor people, and disadvantaged urban areas as the primary cause of crime, perhaps because drugs, murder, and gangs are more prevalent in inner-city areas in America (Houghton et al. 2021). Lack of economic opportunities, unemployment, lack of educational opportunities, poor health outcomes, and the loss of community leaders are also highly prevalent in inner-city areas. Social structure theorists believe that people may choose to use crime to survive under such conditions because environment influences behavior. Thus, disadvantaged economic conditions and resulting destructive behavior are the primary causes of crime and violence. Poverty, income inequality, hopelessness, and despair all feature as key drivers of homicide.

As discussed in chapter 5 of this volume (Tuttle et al. 2023), social structure theories include several subtheories: social disorganization, strain, and cultural deviance. Social disorganization theory posits that residential turnover, heterogeneity, and impoverished conditions within the urban environment affect crime rates. Such factors facilitate the breakdown of institutions of social control, resulting in deteriorated housing, large numbers of single-parent households, and school dropout rates. Strain theory hypothesizes that crime is partly a function of conflict between people's goals and the means they can legally use to obtain them, resulting in feelings of anger and despair that can concentrate spatially to create more combustible situations (Agnew 1992). Cultural deviance theory, a combination of social disorganization and strain theories, posits that independent subcultures maintain unique values and beliefs driven by circumstances that conflict with conventional social norms, making them more likely to experience crime-producing social forces. Cultural norms are passed down through cultural transmission. Scholars, practitioners, and policymakers must investigate the potential impact of social structure on social control policies and practices in American society from a structural racism perspective.

Social Structure Theory, Structural Racism, and African Americans

Since the era of slavery, the criminal justice system has had a strained and dehumanizing relationship with Black people in America (Morris 2022). Its history is inundated with both racism and hierarchal justification of injustices toward Black people. And despite the heightened injustices of the 1960s, current social-psychological factors contributing to the racially stratified U.S. criminal justice system are seemingly worse. Comparatively, "unlike the present period, inner-city communities prior to 1960 exhibited the features of social organization—including a sense of community, positive neighborhood identification, and explicit norms and sanctions against aberrant behavior" (Wilson 1987, 3). "Lower-class, working-class, and middle-class black families all lived more or less in the same communities (albeit in different neighborhoods), sent their children to the same schools, availed themselves of the same recreational facilities and shopped at the same stores," (Wilson 1987, 7) most of which were Black owned. These types of Black communities were due largely to the racist segregation policies of the South.

After segregation, the Black middle class amassed more wealth and was no longer confined to certain neighborhoods. As a result, they fled urban areas for more affluent parts of cities and suburbs. Segregated communities left unskilled and minimally skilled working classes struggling amid growing unemployment rates that gripped urban communities during the 1970s. The loss of stability created the social disorganization found in America's inner cities today, as they are exclusively comprised of the most disadvantaged segments of the Black urban community. Accordingly, this population views itself as being outside the mainstream of American society. It is plagued with a myriad of problems, including high unemployment, low skills, inadequate schooling, transitional neighborhoods, and high crime rates.

Although African Americans have made significant economic gains over the last fifty years, a large segment of the population, particularly those concentrated in the ghettos of American cities, have regressed economically and socially. Chicago School sociologists Clifford Shaw and Henry McKay's (1942) depiction of social disorganization theory aptly explains this schism among Black people. Their depiction ascribes that African Americans have improved their social and economic positions through professional employment, higher education, and homeownership, significantly widening the bridge between the haves and have nots. With their newfound wealth and status, middle-class African Americans moved to the suburbs for a more comfortable and prestigious lifestyle, not looking back to the communities from whence they came. Even though middle-class Black people move to suburban and affluent areas, racial inequality and injustice prevail (Cashin 2000). Their newfound status in the social strata allows them to naively differentiate themselves from "those Blacks." In doing so, they falsely validate mainstream America's views and support for policies that deal with those deemed indigent, uneducated, and underclass. Spatial analysis from 1960 to 2020 confirms that Shaw and McKay's portrayals of African Americans who live in disadvantaged communities in Chicago and the United States more broadly remain disproportionately represented in classifications of homicide in the criminal justice system (De Biasi and Circo 2021; Sharkey and Marsteller 2022).

An Example of Homicides in Baltimore City

Baltimore, Maryland, is consistently ranked among the cities with the highest homicide rates in the United States. With rising homicide rates in predominantly Black neighborhoods of Baltimore, community residents face considerable trauma and growing racial health disparities with middle-class Black people and residents of predominantly white neighborhoods. From the late 1970s to the early 1980s, Baltimore City boasted a population of over one million. In 2020, it had a population of 529,000—half its size after forty years—the result of significant population exit and reductions in local investment. Once an economic power engine, it has become a hub for nonprofits, small businesses, urban blight, and homicide. Catchment areas with high drug distribution, addiction, vacant parcels, liquor stores, and poverty concentration show higher rates of homicide than those that do not have these poverty and violence-inducing qualities (Smith et al. 2022). In addition to high Black homicide rates, West Baltimore was the epicenter of the 2015 riots after the death of Freddie Gray, who died while in the custody of the Baltimore police. The community outrage revealed deeply embedded distrust of police and high legal cynicism.

Epidemiological Criminology Lens

The intersecting health and safety issues regarding premature Black deaths in Baltimore and other cities with rising crime rates and widening homicide disparities warrant a broader understanding (Conrick et al. 2022). The epidemiological criminology framework provides recognition of the criminal nature of violence and of public health implications resulting from harm and premature death. The framework interconnects criminal justice and public health with an emphasis on identifying and addressing health risks and preventing violence and crime (Akers et al. 2010). On a community level, the framework considers crime a social disease. Akers and Lanier (2009, 39), originators of the term "epidemiological criminology" and early proponents of this framework, note that "the intersections between criminal justice and public health theories, methods, and approaches can help to explain the dynamic relations between these two fields of study." The framework views health and criminal behavior and biomedical and behavioral disparities. Individual (micro), familial/community (meso), and societal and global environments (macro/structural) provide a process by which to understand surveillance data.

Examining the influence of psychological, biological, sociological, and environmental factors allows a broad framework to better understand how to select variables that influence health risk and crime. In explaining the framework, Potter and Akers (2010) deem law a social product that formalizes criminal behavior. According to Potter and Akers (2010), the confluence of criminal behavior and health issues fit within the epidemiological criminology framework. Historically, criminal justice and public health have coexisted and operated in separate silos regarding the prevention of violence. A collaborative approach that considers sharing information and leveraging resources across disciplines affords a broader lens for antiviolence and antiracism organizations to understand intersecting factors and various levels of prevention. When using primordial prevention to dismantle meditating risk factors, organizations can play a significant role in (1) addressing health disparities; (2) decreasing health inequities across the lifespan; and (3) impacting the intergenerational health and wellness of Black people. The epidemiological criminology framework for the prevention of Black homicides seeks to understand and respond to increased homicides in Black communities (see fig. 8.2).

The adapted model builds on the epidemiological framework presented by Potter and Akers and provides prevention-based, practice-centered pathways to address priority issues such as homicide, suicide, and premature Black death associated with negative health outcomes of racism and interpersonal and community violence. Such an applied framework is warranted in examining homicide trends, particularly for young Black males in Baltimore City. Unfortunately, the high frequency of premature death (before twenty-five years of age) for young Black males has been socially normalized and justified in the United States (Jones-Eversley et al. 2020). Allied stakeholders and building coalitions that are willing to understand the cultural contexts of Black homicides are essential to addressing homicide disparities (Wang et al. 2016). Safe Streets and the National Association for the Advancement of Colored People (NAACP) are examples of community-based antiviolence and antiracism organizations aimed at addressing community-level homicide, structural racism, and other health disparities (Buggs et al. 2022).

The NAACP, a historic civil rights organization, was established in 1909 with the primary aim of advancing justice for Black people subjected to racism, discrimination, and violence (NAACP 2021). The NAACP's introduction of antilynching legislation starting in the 1920s and advocacy pre– and post–civil rights era increased societal awareness regarding horrific targeted acts, such as mob violence leading to lynchings, to which Black people were subjected from their white counterparts (Zangrado 1965). The NAACP ac-

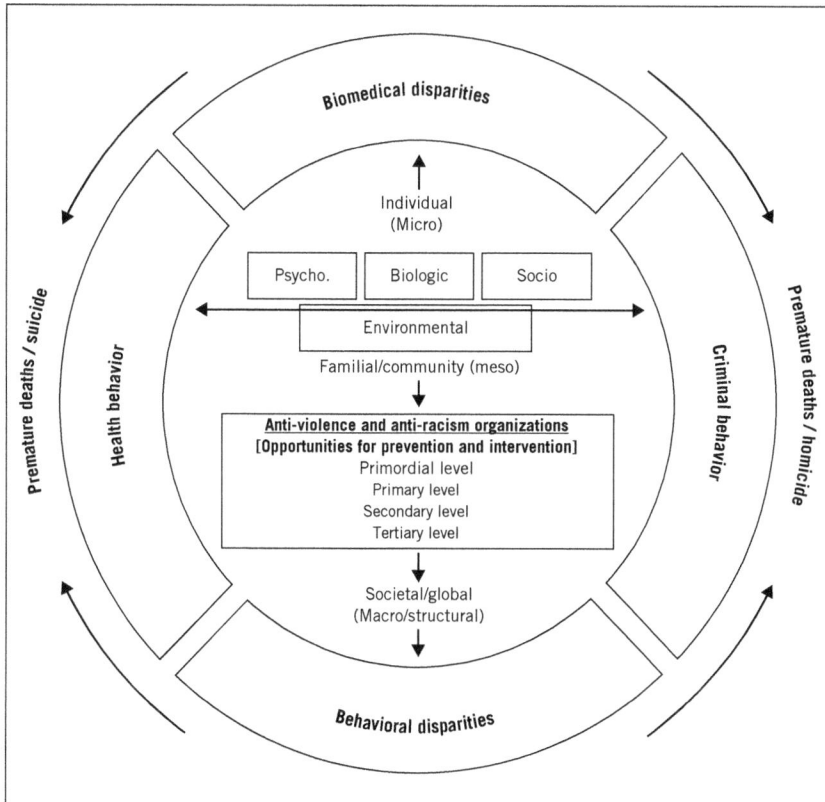

Figure 8.2 Applied Epidemiological Criminology Framework for Prevention and Response to Black Homicides (*Source: Adapted from Potter and Aker's* Epidemiological Criminology Framework, *edited by Eve Waltermaurer and Timothy Akers [New York: Routledge, 1999], 598.*)

tively confronted and exposed disturbing incidents of interracial violence and homicides led by white perpetrators with Black victims.

Thanks to the foundational work of the NAACP and other invested allies, President Joe Biden signed the first federal antilynching legislation, the Emmett Till Antilynching Act, providing penalties of up to thirty years in prison for those who defy the law and carry out lynchings (Rush 2022). The NAACP is also working to address intraracial violence, such as acts carried out by Black perpetrators toward Black victims. The NAACP recognizes that homicide in the Black community, particularly death by firearm, is a significant criminal justice and public health problem that needs addressing and has offered recommendations such as enhancing penalties for gun traffickers (NAACP 2018). The Baltimore chapter of the NAACP and civil rights leaders such as the late U.S. congressman Parren J. Mitchell and Supreme Court justice Thurgood Marshall have invested in improving the plight of Black people nationwide as well as in their native Baltimore.

Complementary to the advocacy of the NAACP, emerging community-based violence intervention initiatives have shown promise in addressing Black homicide. For instance, Safe Streets Baltimore was established in 2007 with the aim of reducing gun violence by using violence interrupters to identify and prevent conflicts through intentional mediation consisting of anti-violence messages and activities that promote positive change (Mayor's Office of Neighborhood Safety and Engagement 2021).

The Safe Streets program was adopted based on the success of the Cease Fire model, developed in 2007 in Chicago by epidemiologist Dr. Gary Slutkin. The model emphasizes treating violence as a disease, reflecting a public health approach to violence prevention and reduction. It was adopted in Baltimore City based on its proven success in reducing violence in Chicago neighborhoods affected by violence (Ritter 2009). An early evaluation of the Baltimore Safe Streets program found evidence of reduced gun violence in communities targeted for intervention. Currently, efforts are underway to conduct an extensive internal program evaluation, as the initiative has expanded. Sites have been added to neighborhoods affected by high gun violence to acquire insight to support program improvement (Mayor's Office of Neighborhood Safety and Engagement 2021). More recently, an internal review identified key areas for improvement based on gaps (Skene 2022). Stakeholders have acknowledged the high levels of risk for cease violence workers carrying out duties in communities plagued by violence. They argue that additional support and investment in Safe Streets are needed and justified (Rice II 2021).

Former Baltimore City mayor Kurt L. Schmoke was an early proponent of using a public health approach to address the issue of violence in Baltimore in the 1980s. Mayor Schmoke broadened the lens and systemic dialogue of crime and violence as public health matters rather than law enforcement responses after a crime of violence such as homicide. He viewed crime as an epidemic and attributed high crime rates to weak firearm laws and a lack of treatment for those who suffer from substance misuse. In 1992, Mayor Schmoke wrote, "Crime shatters families; it raises the cost of doing business; it erodes the tax base by driving the middle class to the suburbs; it disrupts learning; it takes resources away from other essential services; and all too often it steals our future by ending the lives of our children."

Fast forward thirty years, and Baltimore City's failure to develop primordial crime prevention to address inherent risk factors contributing to high crime and homicide rates has only continued Brandon Scott, the current mayor of Baltimore City, introduced a five-year comprehensive violence prevention plan in 2021, focusing on three specific pillars: (1) a public health approach to violence; (2) community engagement and interagency collaboration; and (3) evaluation and accountability, showing his commitment to a broader framework for tackling these issues (Scott 2021). While there is debate regarding the plan's immediate impact as homicide incidents continue to rise in Baltimore City, the plan considers gun violence prevention, victim services, services toward trauma, and other critical areas connected to Baltimore residents' health and safety. The epidemiological criminology framework and geospatial analysis visualization tools could leverage the plan to examine root causes, hot spots, expected multiyear trends, and intersecting factors influencing Black homicide in Baltimore City.

Black homicide in Baltimore City is not just a local law enforcement, criminal justice system, or Black community problem. Black homicide is a Baltimore City, Maryland, America, and global matter. Thus, developing solutions and garnering diverse yet conscientious insights will further leverage primordial homicide prevention efforts (Jones-Eversley et al. 2022). The concentration of crime in Baltimore City and the minimization of disparate health outcomes for the Black community reflect the dysfunction noted in the *New York Times'* seminal piece dissecting the city's troubled history (MacGillis 2019). It will take transformative leaders, residents, and public and private organizations with committed stamina to bring positive change to Baltimore City. Social and legal epidemiology methodologies may aid in obtaining the transformative reversal Baltimore needs to address its disturbing Black homicide trends.

Social Epidemiology Lens

Traditional systematic reviews and meta-analyses quantify the prevalence and characteristics of homicide. But social epidemiology of homicide additionally acknowledges individual, social, social structural, and population factors that contribute to the loss of Black lives to homicide. Social-ecological data and information gathered from the social epidemiology lens can humanize Black homicide primordial prevention efforts. The 338 Baltimoreans who died from homicide in 2021 are viewed as more than numbers in statistical analysis. Instead, the prevalence of their personal, interpersonal, and neighborhood-level homicide incident factors are assessed to capture and contextualize the intersecting factors of their untimely deaths (Kennedy et al. 2021).

Scholars, practitioners, policymakers, and learners can benefit greatly from equitable and eco-social approaches that humanize descriptive and analytic social epidemiological processes (Petteway et al. 2019). When geospatial analysis intersects occurrences of protective and meditating risk factors and eco-social structural factors associated with homicide are completed, legal epidemiology would be the ideal step toward structurally establishing equitable policies, laws, and practices in Baltimore City.

Legal Epidemiology Lens

Legal epidemiology is not a single, legal approach to health equity. Legal epidemiology's surveillance, legal data, and outcome monitoring fortify primordial prevention efforts within the specified geographic population. In the case of Baltimore City's homicide trends, evidence-based legal surveillance would be used to investigate resident participation, law enforcement records, enacted laws, homicide prevention efforts, and safety controls. Empirical homicide data would be collected and analyzed, and legal evaluation outcomes would be reported, communicated, and publicized. Legal surveillance and evaluations would determine if policy changes, new public health laws, or litigation are needed to ensure Baltimore City has structural factors and legal pathways to decrease Black homicide trends (Ramanathan et al. 2017; Thomas et al. 2020).

Once policy changes through new public health laws or litigation, longitudinal legal epidemiological studies could monitor Baltimore City's population-level primordial prevention efforts. Studies could access legal effectiveness, compliance, and inferences that may benefit other municipalities challenged by increasing homicide trends. With policy enactments and successful litigations, legal epidemiology has the potential to mirror the groundbreaking legal successes of the civil rights movement. Leveraging social science and social justice with diverse epidemiological (social and legal) methodologies may lead to promising outcomes for primordial homicide prevention efforts in Baltimore City.

Implications

As promising as all epidemiological (criminological, social, and legal) methodologies are, without structural stability in the local government, the success of any primordial prevention effort in Baltimore City will be compromised. Structural shifts in key leadership roles (mayor and police chief) may contribute to Baltimore's disturbing homicide rates. In 2015, Stephanie Rawlings Blake was elected, and she hired a new police chief amid increasing crime rates. Shortly after that, in 2016, newly appointed mayor Catherine Pugh removed and replaced Rawling's police chief. That chief soon resigned amid charges of tax violations. An interim chief of police was named that same year, and by the next year, a new chief had been hired. Two years later, Mayor Catherine Pugh was charged and found guilty of conspiracy to com-

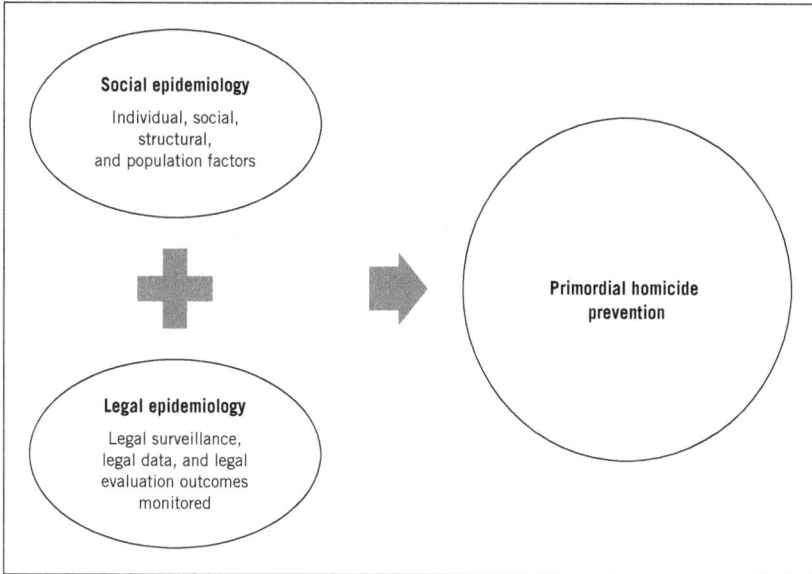

Figure 8.3 Joint Use of Social Epidemiology and Legal Epidemiology to Address Black Homicides (*Note: This figure reflects the complementary attributes of social epidemiology and legal epidemiology in leveraging sustainable, health-equity-driven primordial homicide prevention efforts.*)

mit wire fraud, among other federal charges. Baltimore was then placed in consent decree status amid gross violation findings by the Department of Justice.

Baltimore City's Black homicide trends appear near or at epidemic proportions. Schools are performing poorly, employment opportunities that provide a living wage require high skills many do not possess, and a shrinking tax base and vacant parcels make the city ripe for violent crime and homicide. Many members of Baltimore's socioeconomically disadvantaged population have lost hope. Youth have become desensitized to the violence that plagues their communities, and those with the wherewithal exit the city at the first chance they get. Living in Baltimore, often depicted as "one of the most dangerous cities in America," may have psychological and physical effects on its residents. Knowing that these depictions of Baltimore City are accurate causes additional stress and anxiety among Baltimoreans (Bloom 2022). Social structural and differential association theorists are spot on in their views that multiple factors influence crime rates. Baltimore has too many of those factors, regrettably dimming its charm. Baltimore's homicides reveal a concentration of hot spots.

Conclusion

There must be recognition from policymakers, researchers, practitioners, and learners that racism, discrimination, white supremacy, and differential treatment have fostered criminal justice and health disparities. Thus, Baltimore's current dilemma is not new; it is a crisis resulting from adverse policy and practices toward its Black community spanning generations and decades. Historic disinvestment in and distrust of mainstream criminal justice, healthcare, and social welfare systems by Black residents manifest in heightened distrust toward key systems agents and actors such as the police. The distrust between the police and community, even more present post–Freddie Gray and coupled with continued unarmed shootings of Black persons and mass shootings locally and nationwide, make transformative change difficult.

As noted in the Consent Decree report findings of the United States Department of Justice (USDOJ) after it reviewed the Baltimore City Police Department (BCPD), the USDOJ found that Black persons in low-income communities were subject to unconstitutional policing. The BCPD agreed to implement cultural awareness and sensitivity training centered on the culture of the Black community and strategies aimed at reducing complaints due to perceived bias and discrimination (Consent Decree 2017).

It is important that the Black community and its residents most at risk to poor health outcomes and homicide not be viewed as the primary source of these problems. Unfortunately, mischaracterizations of Black residents often ensue, generating racialized conspiracies that blame homicides as victim-precipitated events and assume Black homicide victims share responsibility for their violent deaths. Shared responsibility encompasses perceived accountability for victimization based on victim actions, system actions, or potentially both. Increasing diversity and equity in the criminal justice and public health systems can allow for the influx of culturally sensitive leaders willing to humanize Black homicides and not racialize them. Baltimore City needs transformative leaders who understand the Black community; bold leaders with the audacity of hope for a better Baltimore City; competent leaders to leverage primordial homicide prevention efforts with diverse epidemiological methodologies to dismantle a racially stratified law enforcement and criminal justice system; and competent and ethical leaders who are not afraid to confront Black homicide trends while transparently engaging the Black community and its allies to create humane, equitable, and sustainable pathways toward justice, health, and safety.

NOTE

1. The terms "Black" and "African American" or "African Americans" are used interchangeably throughout the chapter. Agyemang, C., R. Bhopal, and M. Bruijnzeels. 2005.

"Negro, Black, Black African, African Caribbean, African American, or What? Labelling African Origin Populations in the Health Arena in the 21st Century." *Journal of Epidemiology & Community Health*, 59 (12): 1014–8. http://dx.doi.org/10.1136/jech.2005.035964.

REFERENCES

Agnew, Robert. 1992. "Foundation for a General Strain Theory of Crime and Delinquency." *Criminology* 30 (1): 47–88

Akers, R. L., and G. F. Jensen. 2010. "Social Learning Theory: Process and Structure in Criminal and Deviant Behavior." In *The SAGE Handbook of Criminological Theory*, edited by Eugene McLaughlin and Tim Newburn, 56–72. Los Angeles: Sage.

Akers, Timothy A., and Mark M. Lanier. 2009. "'Epidemiological Criminology': Coming Full Circle." *American Journal of Public Health* 99 (3): 397–402.

Armstrong-Moore, Roxanne, Martin White, and Thomas Burgoine. 2021. "Stakeholder Experiences of Using Online Spatial Data Visualization Tools for Local Public Health Decision Support: A Qualitative Study." *Health & Place* 71:102648.

Beckert, Jens. 2022. "Durable Wealth: Institutions, Mechanisms, and Practices of Wealth Perpetuation." *Annual Review of Sociology* 48.

Bloom, Laura. 2022. "Crime in America: Study Reveals the 10 Most Unsafe Cities (It's Not Where You Think)." *Forbes*. https://www.forbes.com/sites/laurabegleybloom/2022 /02/23/crime-in-america-study-reveals-the-10-most-dangerous-cities-its-not-where -you-think/?sh=7495848f7710.

Buggs, S. A., D. W. Webster, and C. K. Crifasi. 2022. "Using Synthetic Control Methodology to Estimate Effects of a Cure Violence Intervention in Baltimore, Maryland." *Injury Prevention* 28 (1): 61–67.

Cashin, Sheryll D. 2000. "Middle-Class Black Suburbs and the State of Integration: A Post-integrationist Vision for Metropolitan America." *Cornell L. Rev.* 86:729.

Conrick, Kelsey, Avanti Adhia, Alice Ellyson, Miriam Haviland, Vivian Lyons, Brianna Mills, and Ali Rowhani-Rahbar. 2022. "067 Modeling the Association of Structural Racism with Disparities in Firearm Homicide Victimization." *Injury Prevention* 28:A23.

Consent Decree. 2017. *United States of America v. Police Department of Baltimore City* (17-cv-0099-JKB). https://www.mdd.uscourts.gov/sites/mdd/files/ConsentDecree_1.pdf.

De Biasi, Alaina, and Giovanni Circo. 2021. "Capturing Crime at the Micro-place: A Spatial Approach to Inform Buffer Size." *Journal of Quantitative Criminology* 37 (2): 393–418.

Elliott, Paul, and Daniel Wartenberg. 2004. "Spatial Epidemiology: Current Approaches and Future Challenges." *Environmental Health Perspectives* 112:998–1006.

Federal Bureau of Investigation Uniform Crime Reporting Program. 2019a. "Criminal Justice Information Services Division: Expanded Homicide Data Table 2." https://ucr .fbi.gov/crime-in-the-u.s/2019/crime-in-the-u.s.-2019/tables/expanded-homicide-data -table-2.xls.

———. 2019b. "Criminal Justice Information Services Division: Expanded Homicide Data Table 3." https://ucr.fbi.gov/crime-in-the-u.s/2019/crime-in-the-u.s.-2019/tables/ex panded-homicide-data-table-3.xls.

Gaylord-Harden, Noni K., Suzanna So, Grace J. Bai, David B. Henry, and Patrick H. Tolan. 2017. "Examining the Pathologic Adaptation Model of Community Violence Exposure in Male Adolescents of Color." *Journal of Clinical Child & Adolescent Psychology* 46:125–35.

Giampaoli, Simona. 2007. "Primordial Prevention of Cardiovascular Disease—The Role of Blood Pressure." *European Cardiovascular Disease* 3 (2): 20–21.

Hinton, Elizabeth, and DeAnza Cook. 2021. "The Mass Criminalization of Black Americans: A Historical Overview." *Annual Review of Criminology* 4:261–86.

Houghton, August, Olan Jackson-Weaver, Eman Toraih, Nicholas Burley, Terence Byrne, Patrick McGrew, Juan Duchesne, Danielle Tatum, and Sharven Taghavi. 2021. "Firearm Homicide Mortality Is Influenced by Structural Racism in US Metropolitan Areas." *Journal of Trauma and Acute Care Surgery* 91 (1): 64–71.

Jones-Eversley, Sharon D., Christon Adedoyin, Lori James-Townes, and J. Johnny Rice. 2022. "Due Process and Justice in Black Communities." In *Why the Police Should Be Trained by Black People: In the Midst of Pandemics and Beyond*, edited by N. C. Pratt-Harris. 1st ed. New York: Routledge Press.

Jones-Eversley, Sharon D., Johnny Rice, A. Christson Adedoyin, and Lori James-Townes. 2020. "Premature Deaths of Young Black Males in the United States." *Journal of Black Studies* 51 (3): 251–72.

Kennedy, Briohny, Lyndal Bugeja, Jake Olivier, Marilyn Johnson, Phuong Hua, Sjaan Koppel, and Joseph E. Ibrahim. 2021. "Epidemiology of Homicide in Community-Dwelling Older Adults: A Systematic Review and Meta-analysis." *Trauma, Violence, & Abuse*: 15248380211030250.

Lanfear, Charles C. 2022. "Collective Efficacy and the Built Environment." *Criminology* 60:370–96.

Link, Bruce G., and Jo Phelan. 1995. "Social Conditions as Fundamental Causes of Disease." *Journal of Health and Social Behavior* (extra issue): 80–94. https://doi.org/10.2307/2626958.

MacGillis, Alec. 2019. "The Tragedy of Baltimore." *New York Times Magazine.*

Mayor's Office of Neighborhood Safety and Engagement. 2021. "Safe Streets." City of Baltimore. https://monse.baltimorecity.gov/safe-streets-0.

Miller, Lisa L. 2015. "What's Violence Got to Do with It? Inequality, Punishment, and State Failure in US Politics." *Punishment & Society* 17:184–210.

Morris, Ronald L. 2022. *The Dark Side of the Criminal Justice System: War Crimes & the Black Community, 1960–1990.* Lanham, MD: Rowman & Littlefield.

National Association for the Advancement of Colored People (NAACP). 2018. "Gun Violence Prevention Issue Brief." https://naacp.org/resources/gun-violence-prevention-issue-brief.

———. 2021. "Our History." https://naacp.org/about/our-history.

Petteway, Ryan, Mahasin Mujahid, Amani Allen, and Rachel Morello-Frosch. 2019. "Towards a People's Social Epidemiology: Envisioning a More Inclusive and Equitable Future for Social Epi Research and Practice in the 21st Century." *International Journal of Environmental Research and Public Health* 16:3983.

Potter, Roberto Hugh, and Timothy A. Akers. 2010. "Improving the Health of Minority Communities through Probation-Public Health Collaborations: An Application of the Epidemiological Criminology Framework." *Journal of Offender Rehabilitation* 49 (8): 595–609.

Ramanathan, Tara, Rachel Hulkower, Joseph Holbrook, and Matthew Penn. 2017. "Legal Epidemiology: The Science of Law." *Journal of Law, Medicine & Ethics* 45:69–72.

Rice II, Johnny. 2021. "When the 'Peacemakers' Become Victims." Crime Report. https://thecrimereport.org/2021/08/10/when-the-peacemakers-become-victims/.

Ritter, Nancy. 2009. "CeaseFire: A Public Health Approach to Reduce Shootings and Killings." National Institute of Justice. https://nij.ojp.gov/topics/articles/ceasefire-public-health-approach-reduce-shootings-and-killings.

Rucker, Julian M., and Jennifer A. Richeson. 2021. "Toward an Understanding of Structural Racism: Implications for Criminal Justice." *Science* 374 (6565): 286–90.

Rush, B. L. 2022. "H.R.55 - 117th Congress (2021–2022): Emmett Till Antilynching Act." Congress.gov. https://www.congress.gov/bill/117th-congress/house-bill/55.

Schmoke, Kurt. L. 1992. "A Public Health Solution to Violent Crime." *Archives of Otolaryngology–Head & Neck Surgery* 118 (6): 575–76.

Scott, Brandon M. 2021. *Baltimore City Comprehensive Violence Prevention Plan, Effective: July 1, 2021–June 30, 2026*. Baltimore City Government, Mayor Brandon M. Scott Office. https://mayor.baltimorecity.gov/sites/default/files/MayorScott-Comprehensive ViolencePreventionPlan-1.pdf.

Sharkey, Patrick, and Alisabeth Marsteller. 2022. "Neighborhood Inequality and Violence in Chicago, 1965–2020." *University of Chicago Law Review* 89 (2): 3.

Shaw, C. R., and H. D. McKay. 1942. *Juvenile Delinquency in Urban Areas*. Chicago: University of Chicago Press.

Skene, Lea. 2022. "Review Finds Baltimore Safe Streets Program Lacks Oversight: Baltimore Mayor Pledges $10 Million to Expand 'Violence Intervention Ecosystem.'" *Baltimore Sun*. https://www.baltimoresun.com/news/crime/bs-md-ci-cr-safe-streets -announcement-20220413-u3mfq543xva3fcmvs7vkm26uyi-story.html.

Smiley, Calvin John, and David Fakunle. 2016. "From 'Brute' to 'Thug': The Demonization and Criminalization of Unarmed Black Male Victims in America." *Journal of Human Behavior in the Social Environment* 26 (3–4): 350–66.

Smith, Bianca D., Quiana Lewis, Asari Offiong, Kalai Willis, Morgan Prioleau, and Terrinieka W. Powell. 2022. "'It's on Every Corner': Assessing Risk Environments in Baltimore, MD Using a Racialized Risk Environment Model." *Journal of Ethnicity in Substance Abuse*: 21: 1–15.

Taylor, Jeremy J., Kathryn E. Grant, Courtney A. Zulauf, Patrick J. Fowler, David A. Meyerson, and Sireen Irsheid. 2018. "Exposure to Community Violence and the Trajectory of Internalizing and Externalizing Symptoms in a Sample of Low-Income Urban Youth." *Journal of Clinical Child & Adolescent Psychology* 47 (3): 421–35.

Thompson, Betsy L., Lindsay K. Cloud, and Lance Gable. 2020. "Advancing Legal Epidemiology: An Introduction." *Journal of Public Health Management and Practice: JPHMP* 26:S1.

Trencher, Gregory. 2019. "Towards the Smart City 2.0: Empirical Evidence of Using Smartness as a Tool for Tackling Social Challenges." *Technological Forecasting and Social Change* 142:117–28.

Volscho, Thomas W., and Nathan J. Kelly. 2012. "The Rise of the Super-Rich: Power Resources, Taxes, Financial Markets, and the Dynamics of the Top 1 Percent, 1949 to 2008." *American Sociological Review* 77 (5): 679–99.

Wang, Haidong, Mohsen Naghavi, Christine Allen, Ryan M. Barber, Zulfiqar A. Bhutta, Austin Carter, Daniel C. Casey, et al. 2016. "Global, Regional, and National Life Expectancy, All-Cause Mortality, and Cause-Specific Mortality for 249 Causes of Death, 1980–2015: A Systematic Analysis for the Global Burden of Disease Study 2015." *Lancet* 388:1459–544.

Webster, Daniel W., Jennifer Mendel Whitehill, Jon S. Vernick, and Frank C. Curriero. 2013. "Effects of Baltimore's Safe Streets Program on Gun Violence: A Replication of Chicago's CeaseFire Program." *Journal of Urban Health* 90:27–40.

Webster, Daniel, Jennifer M. Whitehill, Jon S. Vernick, and Elizabth Parker. 2012. "Evaluation of Baltimore's safe street program: effects on attitudes, participant's experiences and gun violence." U.S. Department of Justice: Office of Justice Programs Report. No. 238604.

Whitman, Steven, Nanette Benbow, and Glenn Good. 1996. "The Epidemiology of Homicide in Chicago." *Journal of the National Medical Association* 88:781.

Wilson, William J. 1987. *The Truly Disadvantaged: The Inner City, the Underclass, and Public Policy.* Chicago: University of Chicago Press.

Wright, James E., Dongfang Gaozhao, Kenneth Dukes, and Da'Shay Templeton. 2022. "The Power of Protest on Policing: Black Lives Matter Protest and Civilians Evaluation of the Police." *Public Administration Review* 83 (1): 130–43. https://doi.org/10.1111/puar.13498.

Zangrando, Robert L. 1965. "The NAACP and a Federal Antilynching Bill, 1934–1940." *Journal of Negro History* 50 (2): 106–17.

III

The Nature of Homicide

9

Death under Review

Differentiating Lethal and Nonlethal Intimate Partner Violence

Kirk R. Williams, Kasey Ragan, Amy Magnus,
and Veronica Valencia Gonzalez

Introduction

Stories of domestic violence and intimate partner homicide often captivate and horrify the public, raising questions about how those in intimate partnerships could intentionally seek to control, hurt, or kill those they love. It is a startling social problem not only for the public but also for criminal justice professionals and advocates. To address this problem, domestic violence death review teams were assembled in the 1990s with the goal of enhancing how the criminal justice system, advocacy, and medical professionals "understand and respond to domestic violence" through multipartner collaborations (Websdale, Ferraro, and Barger 2019). Ideally, death review teams provide information to officials and practitioners to identify ways family violence may lead to homicide. They also provide families with appropriate services to prevent fatalities. Aligned with this ideal, the present study is the result of a collaboration between the investigators and a California death review team to develop a comprehensive and systematic method of analyzing domestic violence homicide cases. The focus here is on lethal violence involving intimate partners.

Two premises form the foundation of the present study. First, intimate partner homicide (IPH) is widespread throughout the world, with women at considerably higher risk of IPH than men. Based on data from sixty-six countries, conservative estimates show that among all women killed, approximately 38.6 percent suffer death at the hands of their intimate partners. More generous estimates increase that percentage to 47.4 percent. For men, approximately 6.3 percent to 6.5 percent are killed by their intimate partners (Stockl et al. 2013). A similar pattern persists in the United States. Homicide data reported to the National Violent Death Reporting System (NVDRS) over a ten-year period (2008–2017) demonstrate that when women are killed, approximately 40 percent of their deaths constitute IPH. The percentage for men is sharply lower at 4 percent (Williams, Stansfield, and Campbell 2021).

Second, efforts to prevent or reduce IPH are more effective with assessment instruments that identify people at risk of life-threatening violence from their intimate partners. Identification is the first step in effective case management and safety planning. It requires, of course, the development and implementation of risk assessment instruments with defensible predictive validity. The research literature is increasingly rich with predictive validation studies (see Hilton and Harris 2005; Messing and Thaller 2013; Messing et al. 2017 for reviews), but the emphasis tends to be on estimating the risk of persistent intimate partner violence (IPV), not IPH.

The present study contributes to existing literature and community-based conversations about the distinction between serious IPV and IPV that escalates to lethal levels. It builds on the two premises described by focusing on women killed by their male partners and using previously validated risk assessment instruments designed to predict persistent nonlethal IPV (Domestic Violence Screening Instrument, Revised, DVSI-R) and lethal IPV (Danger Assessment, DA). These two instruments were empirically applied to samples of lethal and nonlethal IPV cases. The analysis yielded a reduced set of risk factors that significantly and strongly differentiate lethal and nonlethal cases. However, the implications of this research suggest that systematic reviews of IPH should include additional data sources to have greater confidence in predictions of potential lethality.

Research on the Risk of IPH

Several empirical studies estimate the prevalence of IPH and identify risk factors associated with this form of lethality. A review of that literature is beyond the scope of this paper and would be redundant, as narrative and meta-analytic reviews are available (e.g., Campbell et al. 2007; Devries et al. 2013; Garcia, Soria, and Hurwitz 2007; Matias et al. 2020; Spencer 2018; Stockl et al. 2013). The most recent meta-analytic review analyzes twenty-eight quantitative studies. The vast majority were published in the past two decades and focus on femicide, the killing of women. The studies implemented retrospective and case-control research designs; most obtained data from official court, forensic, or medical records, although a small subset conducted interviews with proxies (survivors of the IPH victims).

Risk factors identified for IPH vary depending on the comparison made, such as IPH victims or perpetrators compared to IPV victims or perpetrators, IPH victims or perpetrators compared to other types of homicide victims or perpetrators, and IPH dyads versus IPV dyads. Regardless of the comparison, the general findings as summarized by Matias et al. (2020, 8)

> showed that the factors with the greatest predictive power of a lethal outcome are those related to a previous history of abusive relational dynamics. . . , for instance, the probability of IPH increases 18.5 times when a victim is threatened with a weapon, 11.36 times with any kind of threat, 10.57 times with a death threat, 6.7 times with a previous strangulation attempt, 5.83 times in the presence of controlling behaviors, 3.74 times if the victim is abused during pregnancy, 3.14 times in the cases of physical violence, and 2.79 times in the presence of stalking.

Since these factors differentiate IPH from IPV, the findings challenge the notion that IPH is the inevitable outcome of IPV—particularly persistent physical violence. Some IPV researchers support this notion (e.g., Sheehan et al. 2015; Campbell et al. 2007; Garcia, Soria, and Hurwitz 2007), while others contend that risk factors that differentiate IPH from persistent physical IPV can be identified (e.g., Dobash et al. 2007; Dutton and Kerry 1999; Goussinsky and Yassour-Borochowitz 2012). One important implication of these findings is that risk assessments should incorporate distinguishing risk factors to guide efforts to prevent or reduce IPH, particularly femicide.

Research on IPH Risk Assessments

As previously noted, several researchers have developed risk assessment instruments to predict persistent IPV and prevent IPV from resulting in death (see Hilton and Harris 2005; Messing and Thaller 2013; Messing et al. 2017 for reviews). The two instruments central to the present study are the DVSI-R and the DA. The DVSI-R is designed to predict persistence in IPV. The DA is designed to predict the likelihood of IPH. These assessments are based on empirically supported predictors of IPV and IPH, with studies supporting their predictive validity (Campbell, Webster, and Glass 2009; Gerstenberger, Stansfield, and Williams 2019; Williams and Grant 2006; Williams 2012; Stansfield and Williams 2014; Williams and Stansfield 2017).

The present research builds on pioneering research by Campbell and associates, who conducted an eleven-city study of risk factors associated with femicide (Campbell et al. 2003). Incorporating risk factors in the DA (see Campbell, Messing, and Williams 2017 for review), Campbell and associates compared IPH victims to a control group of women who had survived violent incidents. They found that the DA showed predictive validity with regard to intimate partner femicide (Campbell, Webster, and Glass 2009). A reduced version of the DA, the Lethality Screen, is now part of a lethality assessment program for first responders. It includes eleven of the original twenty DA items and is used by field practitioners and first responders to identify victim-survivors as being in "high danger" or "not high danger" for serious or lethal IPV. The Lethality Screen was evaluated using a prospective research design (six-month follow-up from baseline assessment) and found to have strong predictive validity (Messing et al. 2017).

A key empirical issue here is whether factors in a risk assessment instrument designed to predict persistence in IPV would overlap with those in a risk assessment instrument designed to predict lethality. Substantial overlap would result in both instruments predicting lethal and nonlethal outcomes similarly. However, if distinct risk factors predict IPH independently from persistent IPV (nonoverlapping risk factors), then identifying risk factors for lethality becomes a critical issue for preventing or reducing IPV from becoming lethal. This empirical issue guides our research effort and distinguishes our research from previous empirical studies. Specifically, those studies (see reviews cited previously) tend to use a compilation of risk factors identified in the empirical literature on IPV to differentiate lethal and nonlethal perpetration or victimization.

The Present Study

Our research used the two previously validated risk assessment instruments, the DVSI-R and DA, to empirically differentiate lethal IPV from nonlethal IPV. This objective is critical because the research findings could inform future efforts to identify red flags signaling risk of IPV becoming lethal. The findings could also identify targets (i.e., the risk factors linked to IPH) for interventions designed to prevent such lethal violence. As such, this study is pertinent to scholars and practitioners alike, serving as an opportunity to build knowledge about IPV and IPH for practitioners to leverage to prevent IPV from escalating to IPH.

We compared data on lethal IPV cases drawn primarily from coroner's reports from a California county between 2006 and 2017 (N = 68) to data on nonlethal cases supplied by a city's police department within that county during the same time period (N = 100). The data on nonlethal cases came from police reports, which could have been informed by interviews with perpetrators, victims, and/or other witnesses. The city is a large and demographically diverse urban area, and it is the only jurisdiction at this point willing to provide nonlethal felony cases for comparative analysis. We do not identify the California county, the specific coroner's office, or the city to protect the confidentiality of the data. Maintaining confidentiality was a condition for obtaining the data and a required component of the IRB review at the University of California, Irvine.

Comparing factors that differentiate lethal and nonlethal IPV using two different samples is not without precedent. Dobash et al. (2007) used the "Violent Men Study," which included a sample of 122 men convicted of a nonlethal domestic violence offense drawn from IPV cases in British court jurisdictions, and the "Murder in Britain Study," which included 106 men convicted of murdering an intimate female partner. Like the present study, data on the men who murdered their female partners were drawn from existing case files. However, unlike the present study, data on the nonlethal cases were obtained from in-depth interviews with the men convicted of IPV. The present study extracted data on nonlethal cases from police reports, as described here.

Data Collection Procedures

We limited the nonlethal cases to those with felony charges to ensure the sixty-eight lethal and one hundred nonlethal samples were comparable in that all include serious IPV incidents. Since nonlethal cases were limited to a single city in the California county, it is unknown whether those cases are comparable to nonlethal cases in other parts of the county. Determining comparability would require county-level data on such cases—which are currently unavailable—as well as an analysis that compares the city to the remainder of the county on the risk factors analyzed in the present research.

To approximate this type of analysis, we compared the lethal cases in the city with lethal cases in the remainder of the county. Specifically, we estimated a logistic regression model that included the risk factors used in the present research, with the dummy dependent variable being the city (scored 1) compared to the remainder of the county (scored 0). None of the risk factors had statistically significant estimated effects, suggesting lethal cases in the city do not differ significantly from those in the remainder of the county. Although speculative, we had some empirical basis for assuming that nonlethal cases in the city are comparable to those elsewhere in the county. The important comparison was whether nonlethal and lethal cases differ significantly across the risk assessment instruments analyzed here, a key question for our study and for practitioners aiming to mitigate and prevent IPH.

Table 9.1 presents the demographic comparison between the lethal and nonlethal samples. Both samples had low and insignificantly different percentages of African American perpetrators. The samples had high percentages of male perpetrators, with statistically insignificant differences between

TABLE 9.1 DEMOGRAPHIC CHARACTERISTICS OF THE LETHAL SAMPLE (N = 48) AND NONLETHAL SAMPLE (N = 98)[1]			
Demographic Characteristics	OC Lethal Sample	Anaheim Nonlethal Sample	t-value
% African-American	4.2	11.2	−1.41
% Latino	27.1	59.2	−3.80*
% Non-Latino White	58.3	17.3	5.51*
% Male	86.2	81.0	0.86

[1] Reduced sample size because of missing data on race or ethnicity.
*$p \geq 0.05$

the percent male in the two samples. Significant differences surfaced when comparing the two samples by ethnicity. The nonlethal sample had a significantly higher percentage of Latinx perpetrators, and the lethal sample had a significantly higher percentage of non-Latinx white perpetrators.

The IPH data were collected from coroner and police documents using the DVSI-R and the DA between November 2017 and August 2018. The city police department provided the nonlethal IPV data. Specifically, it provided a complete list of serious, felony (but nonlethal) IPV cases for each year in the 2006 to 2017 time period. Only closed felony cases were included in the sample, as opposed to cases where investigations or court proceedings were ongoing. Cases were then selected randomly for each year in the 2006 to 2017 time period. The number of nonlethal cases selected by year was comparable to the proportional representation of lethal cases by year. For example, if 5 percent of the total lethal cases occurred in 2011, then 5 percent of the non-lethal cases were allocated in 2011.

Analysis Plan

The initial analysis was designed to identify the individual risk factors in each risk assessment instrument that showed evidence of increasing the likelihood of lethal compared to nonlethal outcomes. That analysis involved specifying two multivariate models: one model included the risk factors drawn from the DVSI-R, and the second included the risk factors drawn from the DA (the list of these risk factors is available on request from the authors). Prior family violence intervention and treatment, an item in the DVSI-R, was omitted because no evidence of this risk factor was found in the police reports for the nonlethal sample, an issue discussed at the close of this chapter. The dependent variable in both models was a dummy variable coded 1 for lethal outcomes and 0 for nonlethal outcomes. Given this dichotomous dependent variable, logistic regression was used to estimate the two models. Once the statistically significant and positive individual risk factors were identified, the next analytical step involved distilling a reduced set of risk factors most predictive of lethal outcomes. Doing so required estimating a logistic regression model that included risk factors found to be statistically significant and positive in the initial analyses. The outcome measure in this equation again was the lethal versus nonlethal IPV dummy variable.

Empirical Findings

The results of estimating the multivariate model for the DVSI-R risk factors can be summarized in three key points. First, using the significance level of $p \geq 0.05$, no significant estimate effects were found for six of the nine DVSI-R risk factors: prior family violence, prior violation of court orders, prior or current substance abuse, employment status, verbal or emotional abuse, and violence escalation in the past six months. Second, the other three risk factors—prior nonfamily violence, children present during a prior and/or current IPV incident, and objects used as weapons—showed significant estimate effects, but the estimated effect was negative for children present. Specifically, the lethal sample was significantly lower than the nonlethal sample for evidence of children present during a prior and/or current IPV incident. Third, the lethal sample was significantly higher for the other two risk factors: objects used as weapons and prior nonfamily violence.

Concerning the analysis of risk factors drawn from the DA, two additional risk factors were included: evidence the perpetrator had mental health disorders and evidence of formal criminal justice or government agency involvement with the family prior to the current incident. These two items were found to be statistically significant predictors in the Campbell et al. (2003) eleven-city study.

Logistic regression yielded six statistically significant and positive estimates for potential lethality: threats or use of a deadly weapon, firearm possession, beliefs that the perpetrator was capable of killing the victim, evidence the perpetrator had mental health issues, previous criminal justice or government agency involvement, and prior or current sexual assault of the victim. None of the other estimated effects were statistically significant and positive in direction (lethality sample greater than nonlethal sample).

Synthesizing the Results

As noted previously, statistically significant risk factors were included in a final model and estimated using logistic regression. The results of the estimation are reported in table 9.2. As it shows, estimation yielded five risk factors that maintained independent, statistically significant, and positive effects: previous criminal justice or government agency involvement, prior

TABLE 9.2 RISK FACTORS SIGNIFICANTLY DIFFERENTIATING LETHAL AND NONLETHAL CASES		
Risk Factors	Bivariate *Gamma* Coefficient	Cumulative *AUC* Coefficient
Previous Agency Involvement	0.41	0.57
Prior Nonfamily Violence	0.53	0.59
Perpetrator Capable of Killing	0.85	0.63
Perpetrator Possesses Firearm	0.95	0.89
Prior/Current Threats/Use of Deadly Weapon	0.97	0.96

nonfamily violence, beliefs that the perpetrator was capable of killing the victim, perpetrator firearm possession, and prior and/or current threats or use of a deadly weapon.

The strength of the bivariate associations between each of these risk factors and the lethal/nonlethal outcome measure is shown in table 9.2. The Gamma coefficients range from a low of 0.41 for previous criminal justice or government agency involvement to a high of 0.97 for prior or current threats or use of a deadly weapon. These coefficients are moderate to very strong in magnitude.

To delineate empirically the independent contribution of each risk factor in predicting lethal outcomes, cumulative Area Under the Curve (AUC) coefficients were calculated. This calculation was performed by sequentially adding each risk factor to a logistic regression equation (i.e., five equations for the five risk factors), saving the predicted probabilities of lethality for each equation, and using the predicted probabilities to calculate the AUC coefficients reported in table 9.2. For example, the first logistic regression equation included only previous criminal justice or government agency involvement. The second included this risk factor and prior nonfamily violence involvement. The third included these two risk factors plus beliefs that the perpetrator was capable of killing the victim (see Heckert and Gondolf 2004; Hilton et al. 2004; Williams and Grant 2006 for previous usages of this analytical procedure in risk assessment research to generate propensity scores).

The results of this sequential analysis are shown in table 9.2. The AUC coefficients begin at 0.57 with previous criminal justice or government agency involvement alone in the logistic regression equation and ends with AUC = 0.96 with all five risk factors included in the analysis. These coefficients range from somewhat weak to very strong in magnitude. The most striking finding is the large increase in AUC coefficient when firearm possession and threats or use of deadly weapons are added—from 0.63 when beliefs the perpetrator was capable of killing the victim was included to 0.89 and 0.96, respectively.

Discussion

IPH is a serious and prevalent social problem that impacts communities world-wide. Considering our focus on differentiating lethal and nonlethal IPV, it is unsurprising that the lethal sample in our study had a significantly great-er percentage of cases scoring on firearm possession and threatened or at-tempted use of a deadly weapon, especially given that the sample consisted of victims killed by their intimate partners. It is surprising that the majority of risk factors analyzed in the present study were not significantly related to lethal compared to nonlethal outcomes despite previous research having consistently found significant relations between these factors and either IPV persistence or IPV becoming lethal.

Nonetheless, the present study empirically identifies a set of risk factors that demonstrate strong predictive capability. No doubt, these risk factors are connected to previous abusive dynamics or the construction of a "cage" of domination and coercive control (see Stansfield and Williams 2018; Stark 2009). Yet this set suggests that IPH is not the inevitable outcome of persis-tent IPV, particularly enduring physical violence. Further, these factors align with those reported in previous research on lethality. For example, the recent meta-analytic review by Matias et al. (2020) found that the strongest predic-tor of lethality was threats with a weapon. This risk factor was the strongest predictor in our analysis as well, along with possession of a firearm. As an-other example, Dobash et al. (2007), whose research is similar to our own, found that previous convictions for violent offenses was significantly higher in their lethality sample. We too found that previous arrests or convictions for nonfamily violence was significantly higher in the lethal compared to the nonlethal sample. Further, like the femicide research conducted by Camp-bell et al. (2003), we found that beliefs that the perpetrator was capable of kill-ing the victim and previous criminal justice involvement were significantly higher in the lethality sample.

What do these findings mean for criminal justice practitioners and social service providers conducting risk assessments? Stated simply, if the assess-ment portrays a man (men were the overwhelming percentage of both sam-ples) having the key characteristics identified in our study, professionals can confidently consider that they are dealing with a person who is "dangerous," capable of perpetrating lethal violence. He commonly uses violence in con-flicts with others, including those beyond his household, possesses firearms, and threatens or uses deadly weapons to intimidate others, so much so that his friends and family believe he is fully capable of killing his intimate partner.

Despite the strength of the associations supporting the predictive valid-ity of this set of risk factors, confidence in the "dangerous person" assump-tion should be tempered by a caveat. Whether a risk factor was present or absent in an individual case was determined by reviewing coroner's reports and/or police reports. These reports are limited sources of information. They shed light on some dimensions of perpetrators' lives, but many more dimensions remain in the dark. For example, police reports in the nonlethal sample yielded absolutely no evidence that any of the hundred cases had previously attended or been ordered to attend some form of family violence intervention or treatment. Given the relatively high prevalence of previous IPV in this sample (63 percent), the absence of any previous intervention or treatment strains credulity. Obtaining data on such factors requires a more comprehensive and in-depth review than is possible by relying solely on coroner's or police reports. Interviews with perpetrators, victims, or their friends and family may be required to measure risk factors more accurately.

Future research on risk factors associated with IPH should address two methodological issues. First, previous research comparing lethal and nonlethal cases has been primarily based on cases resulting in the arrest or conviction of a perpetrator. These official data are subject to identification and reporting bias. This bias is especially acute for nonlethal cases of IPV. Accordingly, future research should explore the "dark figure" of IPV that remains unknown when relying on official statistics (e.g., Brady and Nobles 2017). Surveys and/or interviews will be required to accomplish this task. Such data collection efforts are challenging because they are expensive and require participation of vulnerable persons who may be difficult to find and successfully recruit into surveys. These data collection efforts also raise research ethics concerns, such as retraumatization for the victim and their family and friends and risk to victims if their involvement in a survey becomes known.

Second, future research should expand collaborations with criminal justice and other institutions as well as sources of information on nonlethal and lethal cases. It is critical to review documents beyond coroner's or police reports (e.g., criminal history reviews) and include direct input from the parties involved in IPV (e.g., perpetrators, victims, and witnesses) to generate greater contextual knowledge and help prevent IPV escalation and IPH. As such, future research should explore obtaining direct input from those knowledgeable about violent relationships, such as close friends, coworkers, or family members. Such data collection efforts should follow a general principle: the completeness and accuracy of data informing the scoring of risk assessment instruments is likely to increase by expanding the diversity of information sources used to collect such data.

Conclusion

We offer three recommendations based on the findings of the present study. First, possession and use of deadly weapons is a critical issue for IPH, and thus, limiting access to these weapons is a critical preventive measure. Within the lethal sample, we found 72.1 percent of perpetrators possessed firearms and 92.6 percent threatened or used them against their partners. Intensifying enforcement of laws pertaining to firearm possession in IPV cases may be one avenue for preventing IPH. As Campbell et al. (2003, 1094) contend, "under federal law, individuals who have been convicted of domestic violence or who are subject to a restraining order are barred from owning firearms. Judges issuing orders of protection in cases of IPV should consider the heightened risk of lethal violence associated with abusers' access to firearms." Greater control over perpetrators' access to firearms must be enforced to prevent IPV from escalating to IPH.

Second, as noted previously, a more comprehensive, revealing, and defensible review of lethal IPV cases requires sources of information beyond coroner's and police reports. At a minimum, criminal history searches across all cases should be made available. Greater collaboration between researchers and death review teams can garner access to important data sources in addition to critical research that can help death review teams do their work. Any documentation about the history of intimate relationships ending in the death of a partner should be reviewed for systematic and comprehensive assessments. Similar documentation about intimate relationships involving serious but nonlethal incidents should be reviewed to facilitate the identification of risk factors that differentiate lethal from nonlethal IPV.

Third, some of the most important risk factors linked to IPH (e.g., violent jealousness, intensive monitoring and control, threats to kill, nonfatal strangulation, etc.) are not often reported in official documents. All such data are relevant for domestic violence death review teams that seek to inform policy and practice to prevent IPH (Websdale, Ferraro, and Barger 2019). Such risk factors are more often identified via interviews of perpetrators and survivors of IPV. Because official documents are focused on more formal, bureaucratic descriptors of incidents, much of the context pertaining to the relationship between perpetrator and victim goes undocumented. For example, official reports often miss perpetrator behavioral patterns, threats not formally reported, and family and friends' qualitative assessment of whether the perpetrator is/was capable of killing the victim. We strongly recommend interviewing these people. However, collection of interview data for these purposes is often problematic. For example, the California Penal Code Section 11163.5 is not clear on whether members of a death review team are authorized to conduct such interviews; this seems problematic for teams throughout the country (National Domestic Violence Fatality Review Initiative, n.d.). Even if they were authorized, logistics and cost of conducting these interviews might be prohibitive, undermining the sustainability of the effort.

A potentially more promising approach would be to identify points of contact between criminal justice and social service agencies and those involved in IPV where systematic interview mechanisms can be incorporated. For example, first responders could be trained to administer an abbreviated version of the DVSI-R and/or the DA (such as the Lethality Screen) to perpetrators and others who know the intimate partners, with the systematic information obtained included in official reports about IPV incidents (e.g., Messing et al. 2017). As another example, risk assessments could be part of the criminal or civil proceedings involved with acquiring protective or restraining orders, such as those in Connecticut. Having complete, valid, and reliable information about violent intimate relationships upstream may help prevent casualties further downstream.

Our analysis indicates that there are, indeed, several factors that differentiate lethal and nonlethal IPV—an important finding that sheds nuanced light on the reality of intimate violence. The ultimate goal of this work is to provide helpful information to families, friends of vulnerable people, and practitioners who center their work on preventing IPV from escalating to homicide. With this, the work serves as a tool to help keep people, especially those embedded in intimate partnerships, safe.

REFERENCES

Brady, Patrick Q., and Matt R. Nobles. 2017. "The Dark Figure of Stalking: Examining Law Enforcement Response." *Journal of Interpersonal Violence* 32 (20): 3149–73.

Campbell, Jacquelyn C., Nancy Glass, Phyllis W. Sharps, Kathryn Laughon, and Tina Bloom. 2007. "Intimate Partner Homicide: Review and Implications of Research and Policy." *Trauma, Violence, & Abuse* 8:246–69.

Campbell, Jacquelyn C., Jill Messing, and Kirk Williams. 2017. "Prediction of Homicide of and by Battered Women." In *Assessing Dangerousness: Domestic Violence Offenders and Child Abusers*, edited by Jacquelyn Campbell and Jill Messing, 107–38. New York: Springer.

Campbell, Jacquelyn C., Daniel W. Webster, and Nancy Glass. 2009. "The Danger Assessment: Validation of a Lethality Risk Assessment Instrument for Intimate Partner Femicide." *Journal of Interpersonal Violence* 24:653–74.

Campbell, Jacquelyn C., Daniel W. Webster, Jane Koziol-McLain, Carolyn Block, Doris Campbell, Mary Ann Curry, Faye Gary, et al. 2003. "Risk Factors for Femicide in Abusive Relationships: Results from a Multisite Case Control Study." *American Journal of Public Health* 93:1089–97.

Devries, Karen M., Joelle Y. T. Mak, Claudia Garcia-Moreno, Max Petzold, James C. Child, Gail Falder, Stephen Lim, et al. 2013. "The Global Prevalence of Intimate Partner Violence against Women." *Science* 340 (6140): 1527–28.

Dobash, R. Emerson, Russell P. Dobash, Kate Cavanagh, and Juanjo Medina-Ariza. 2007. "Lethal and Nonlethal Violence against an Intimate Female Partner: Comparing Male Murderers to Nonlethal Abusers." *Violence Against Women* 13 (4): 329–53.

Dutton, Donald G., and Greg Kerry. 1999. "Modus Operandi and Personality Disorder in Incarcerated Spousal Killers." *International Journal of Law and Psychiatry* 22:287–99.

Garcia, Lorena, Catalina Soria, and Eric L. Hurwitz. 2007. "Homicides and Intimate Partner Violence: A Literature Review." *Trauma, Violence, & Abuse* 8:370–83.

Gerstenberger, Caryn, Richard Stansfield, and Kirk R. Williams. 2019. "Intimate Partner Violence in Same-Sex Relationships: An Analysis of Risk and Rearrest." *Criminal Justice and Behavior* 46:1515–27.

Goussinsky, Ruhama, and Dalit Yassour-Borochowitz. 2012. "'I Killed Her, But I Never Laid a Finger on Her': A Phenomenological Difference between Wife-Killing and Wife-Battering." *Aggression and Violent Behavior* 17:553–64.

Heckert, D. Alex, and Edward W. Gondolf. 2004. "Battered Women's Perceptions of Risk versus Risk Factors and Instruments in Predicting Repeat Reassault." *Journal of Interpersonal Violence* 19:778–800.

Hilton, N. Zoe, and Grant T. Harris. 2005. "Predicting Wife Assault: A Critical Review and Implications for Policy and Practice." *Trauma, Violence, & Abuse* 6:3–23.

Hilton, N. Zoe, Grant T. Harris, Marnie E. Rice, Carol Lang, Catherine A. Cormier, and Kathryn J. Lines. 2004. "A Brief Actuarial Assessment for the Prediction of Wife Assault Recidivism: The Ontario Domestic Assault Risk Assessment." *Psychological Assessment* 16:267–75.

Matias, Andreia, Mariana Gonçalves, Cristina Soeiro, and Marlene Matos. 2020. "Intimate Partner Homicide: A Meta-analysis of Risk Factors." *Aggression and Violent Behavior* 50:1–12.

Messing, Jill Theresa, Jacquelyn Campbell, Janet Sullivan Wilson, Sheryll Brown, and Beverly Patchell. 2017. "The Lethality Screen: The Predictive Validity of an Intimate Partner Violence Risk Assessment for Use by First Responders." *Journal of Interpersonal Violence* 32:205–26.

Messing, Jill Theresa, and Jonel Thaller. 2013. "The Average Predictive Validity of Intimate Partner Violence Risk Assessment Instruments." *Journal of Interpersonal Violence* 28:1537–58.

National Domestic Violence Fatality Initiative. n.d. "Frequently Asked Questions." Accessed November 5, 2020. https://ndvfri.org/about/faqs/.

Sheehan, Brynn E., Sharon B. Murphy, Mary M. Moynihan, Erin Dudley-Fennessey, and Jane G. Stapleton. 2015. "Intimate Partner Homicide: New Insights for Understanding Lethality and Risks." *Violence against Women* 21:269–88.

Spencer, Chelsea Marie. 2018. *A Meta-analysis of Risk Factors for Intimate Partner Homicide: Examining Male Perpetration and Female Victimization*. Doctoral diss., Kansas State University.

Stansfield, Richard, and Kirk R. Williams. 2014. "Predicting Family Violence Recidivism Using the DVSI-R: Integrating Survival Analysis and Perpetrator Characteristics." *Criminal Justice and Behavior* 41:163–80.

———. 2018. "Coercive Control between Intimate Partners: An Application to Nonfatal Strangulation." *Journal of Interpersonal Violence* 36 (9–10): NP5105–NP5124.

Stark, Evan. 2009. *Coercive Control: The Entrapment of Women in Personal Life*. Oxford: Oxford University Press.

Stockl, Heidi, Karen Devries, Alexandra Rotstein, Naeemah Abrahams, Jacquelyn Campbell, Charlotte Watts, and Claudia Garcia-Moreno. 2013. "The Global Prevalence of Intimate Partner Homicide: A Systematic Review." *Lancet* 382 (9895): 859–65.

Websdale, Neil, Kathleen Ferraro, and Steven D. Barger. 2019. "The Domestic Violence Fatality Review Clearinghouse: Introduction to a New National Data System with a Focus on Firearms." *Injury Epidemiology* 6:1–8.

Williams, Kirk R. 2012. "Family Violence Risk Assessment: A Predictive Cross-Validation Study of the Domestic Violence Screening Instrument-Revised (DVSI-R)." *Law and Human Behavior* 36:120–29.

Williams, Kirk R., and Stephen R. Grant. 2006. "Empirically Examining the Risk of Intimate Partner Violence: The Revised Domestic Violence Screening Instrument (DVSI-R)." *Public Health Reports* 121 (4): 400–408.

Williams, Kirk R., and Richard Stansfield. 2017. "Disentangling the Risk Assessment and Intimate Partner Violence Relation: Estimating Mediating and Moderating Effects." *Law and Human Behavior* 41:344–53.

Williams, Kirk R., Richard Stansfield, and Jacquelyn Campbell. 2021. "Persistence and Potential Lethality in Intimate Partner Violence: Evaluating the Concurrent and Predictive Validity of a Dual Risk Assessment Protocol." *Violence Against Women* 28: 298–315.

10

Gang Homicide in the United States

JOSE ANTONIO SANCHEZ AND DAVID C. PYROOZ

Introduction

Homicide rates in large cities increased by 30 percent in 2020 compared to 2019 (Council on Criminal Justice 2021). Media outlets across the United States—the *Chicago Tribune*, *Denver Post*, *Los Angeles Times*, *New York Times*, and *Wall Street Journal*—speculated frequently about the role of gangs in this rise (Closson 2021; Schmelzer 2021; Jones 2021; Rector and Santa Cruz 2020; Chapman 2020). Even as stay-at-home orders were placed by local governments in response to COVID-19, gang crime did not appear impacted (Brantingham, Tita, and Mohler 2021). This means that gang crime in Los Angeles remained stable after stay-at-home orders were implemented. Los Angeles experienced a 27 percent increase in homicides from 2019 to 2020, and leaders such as Police Chief Michel Moore claimed that gang conflicts were driving much of the violence (Cain 2021). Research has demonstrated that gangs account for a significant number of homicides across the United States (Howell et al. 2011). Gang homicide, at the extreme end of the violence spectrum, can "raise community concerns, elicit political reaction, and trigger suppressive responses by law enforcement" (Maxson, Curry, and Howell 2002, 11), commanding the interest of criminologists.

In this chapter, we take stock of research on gang homicide. First, we discuss theoretical frameworks used in the study of gang violence. Second, we speak to how gang homicides differ from other types of homicide. Third, we cover how gang homicides are measured by researchers and law enforcement (the primary source for gang homicide data). We then focus on what data is available to study gang homicides and their associated strengths and limitations. Fourth, we provide an overview of the prevalence and trends of gang homicides. We conclude this chapter with a brief discussion of strategies that have been implemented to address gang violence.

Theories of Gang Violence

Gang scholars have most commonly focused on theorizing gang emergence and duration (e.g., Cohen 1955; Cloward and Ohlin 1960; Thrasher 1927; for a review see Decker, Pyrooz, and Densley 2022). Unfortunately, the same cannot be said about gang violence (Decker and Curry 2002). That is not to say the cupboard is bereft of any theoretical work, and thus we draw on Short's (1985; 1998) influential statements on levels and explanations to organize our discussion on theories centered on (1) the community level; (2) group processes; and (3) the individual.

Community-level explanations focus on the composition and contextual features of neighborhoods as leading to higher levels of violence including gang homicide, what Papachristos, Hureau, and Braga (2013) call "the corner." Curry and Spergel (1988) built on a social disorganization framework to explain gang homicides. Their study was one of the first to ground gang homicide in criminological theory. They argued that neighborhoods with higher levels of social disorganization—brought on by shifting population, mobility, or economic change—could be linked to higher levels of gang crime, including homicide. Studies on gang violence have found support for social disorganization theory finding that disadvantaged communities are more likely to experience high levels of gang violence (e.g., Mares 2010; Kubrin and Wadsworth 2003; Rosenfeld, Bray, and Egley 1999). However, levels of violence vary within neighborhoods. Indeed, Papachristos and Kirk (2006) found that not all similar neighborhoods experience similar levels of gang violence. Macrolevel studies of gang violence have found that gang violence is not randomly distributed but rather concentrated in low socioeconomic status (SES) neighborhoods (Valasik et al. 2017) and that low SES and population heterogeneity contributes to more gang members, leading to higher rates of gang homicide (Pyrooz 2012).

Unlike community-level explanations, mesolevel theories posit that gang violence is an outcome of group processes endogenous to the gang. Short and Strodtbeck (1965) wrote the seminal book on group process, *Group Process and Gang Delinquency*, in which they observed that microsocial processes within gangs and dynamics between gangs can explain violent behavior. From this work emerged the idea of violence arising from gang members, especially leaders, feeling like their position is under threat. Decker (1996) found that gang violence reflects the weak leadership often found in gangs and the process of collectively identifying a threat. The threat serves as a unifier for the gang, which mobilizes and engages in a violent event. Klein (1969) offered a variant of the group process explanation centered on group cohesion, postulating that groups with higher levels of cohesion engage in more crime. Group processes have been historically understudied; however, there is evidence that group process is a viable theoretical framework for gang violence (Hughes 2013; Hughes, Schaible, and Kephart 2021; Papachristos, Hureau, and Braga 2013). Hughes (2013) found evidence contradicting Klein's argument of group cohesion, but others have argued that group cohesion remains critical for studying gang violence (Papachristos 2013; Hennigan and Sloane 2013).

Theories at the individual level are perhaps the most lacking in gang violence research. These theories postulate that there is nothing special about the communities or gangs causing violence; rather, people who join gangs already maintain high propensity for violence, and their involvement in gangs is incidental or a result of these individual deficits. Scholars such as Yablonsky (1962) and Gottfredson and Hirschi (1990) argued that gang members are simply adolescents with a propensity for offending, because they are sociopaths or due to low self-control, banding together. The research on individual differences is mixed. Klein (1971) refuted Yablonsky's account of the violent gang, stating that there is no support for such a claim. Pyrooz and colleagues (2021) found evidence contradicting the central arguments of self-control. More generally, researchers have found an enhancement effect of gang membership on violence, where selection has a minor but nontrivial influence while facilitation has a larger influence (Melde and Esbensen 2013; Pyrooz et al. 2016; see Thornberry et al. 2003 for a discussion on selection, facilitation, and enhancement). However, there is some support that individual characteristics such as behavioral disorders contribute (DeLisi, Drury, and Elbert 2019). Lifestyle theory (Hindelang, Gottfredson, and Garofalo 1978) has also been, at least partially, supported as a viable theory of violent offending and victimization (e.g., Taylor et al. 2007; Wu and Pyrooz 2016).

Homicide Incident Characteristics: Are Gang Homicides Actually Different?

In one of the first studies to examine individual *and* incident characteristics, Maxson, Gordon, and Klein (1985) compared gang homicides to nongang homicides in Los Angeles using data from the police and sheriff's departments. The study revealed several key differences between gang homicides and nongang homicides: (1) gang homicides are more likely to involve the use of a firearm; (2) they are more likely to occur in public settings; (3) suspects and victims are generally younger; and (4) suspects and victims tend to be racial/ethnic minorities. Subsequent research has supported the findings of Maxson and colleagues (1985) while simultaneously shedding light on further nuances, such as the spatiotemporal characteristics of gang homicides.

The pervasiveness of firearms in gang violence has been widely documented (e.g., Decker and Pyrooz 2010a; Bjerregaard and Lizotte 1995). The link between gangs and guns is strong. A study using nationally representative longitudinal data highlighted how the association between gang membership and gun carrying is relatively stable across sex and race/ethnicity (Tigri et al. 2016). Miller (1975) argued that increased accessibility to firearms alters the landscape of gang violence by drastically increasing the potential lethality of incidents. Indeed, gun use has become a signature characteristic of gang life. Hutson and colleagues (1995) reported that gang killings included the use of a firearm 71 percent of the time in 1979—by 1994, it was about 95 percent of the time.

Most gang homicides are set in public spaces. In the Maxson, Gordon, and Klein (1985) study, over 70 percent of homicides in both datasets occurred in public. A more recent study of gang homicide by Valasik and colleagues (2017) in East Los Angeles found that almost 68 percent of 844 gang homicides were carried out on the street. A study of distances traveled by homicide victim and suspect revealed that gang members, both victims and suspects, are more likely to travel greater distances than other homicide categories, such as drug-related incidents. Additionally, victims of gang homicides are most often away from home, running errands, or hanging out, and suspects usually travel to engage in a crime (Pizarro, Corsaro, and Yu 2007). This study further supports the public nature of gang homicides. Gang violence not only occurs in public, but it also tends to be concentrated in geographic locations, mainly areas of social disadvantage (Mares 2010; Valasik et al. 2017).

Differences between gang and nongang homicide in the demographics of perpetrators and victims also exist. Gang homicides tend to be perpetrated by Black and Hispanic people (Maxson, Gordon, and Klein 1985; Pizarro and McGloin 2006; Papachristos 2009). Gangs are disproportionately composed of racial/ethnic minorities, which makes this observation unsurprising. Of course, some such observations—when relying on law enforcement data—reflect biases built into policy and practice (Esbensen and Winfree 1998; Esbensen and Carson 2012; Reid and Valasik 2020). Victims and perpetrators of gang homicide tend be younger in age than participants in nongang homicide (Maxson, Gordon, and Klein 1985; Decker and Curry 2002). Still, it is important to note that gang homicides typically involve participants who are older than the average gang member (Maxson 1999; Pyrooz 2014).

Victims and perpetrators of gang homicide have different relationships than those in nongang homicide. There is greater likelihood of the victim having had previous interaction with the perpetrator. In fact, research suggests that intragang killings are not uncommon (e.g., Pizarro and McGloin 2006; Valasik and Reid 2021). Studies have also shown that gang violence tends to be concentrated within networks linking gang members and gangs with one another (e.g., Papachristos, Hureau, and Braga 2013). Chicago and Boston demonstrate similarities in that gangs from both cities form one large network that ties most of the gangs together (Papachristos, Hureau, and Braga 2013). To this end, Papachristos and colleagues state that "in this sense, gang violence is a highly connected and structured phenomenon" (2013, 438).

Measurement of Gang Homicide

In late July 2020, a thirty-four-year-old purported gang member in Denver shot and killed a man near a food truck. The shooter was operating under the impression that the victim was from a rival gang and had been responsible for a previous shooting (Oravetz 2020). In an incident that occurred in February 2021, a twenty-eight-year-old man who had admitted to being a gang member killed someone in a personal dispute over $20 (Nicholson 2021). These two cases illustrate one challenge facing researchers: is one, both, or neither a gang homicide?

Researchers who study gangs draw the distinction between homicides that are gang related and those that are gang motivated. In the first incident, the homicide occurred as a result of retaliation. This incident would fall under gang motivated, as it was meant to enact revenge on behalf of the group. The second incident was a personal matter and thus would be considered gang related, as it was not done to further the interests of the gang.

Maxson and Klein (1996) conducted pioneering research on this distinction. They discussed definitional issues related to police jurisdictions across the country and identified gang-member (i.e., gang-related) and gang-motive (i.e., gang-motivated) incidents. Whereas nearly all gang-motivated incidents are gang related, not all gang-related incidents are gang motivated, making gang motivated the more restrictive criterion. This is because determining motive can prove challenging and can be intertwined with homicide clearance by law enforcement. Maxson and Klein compared whether the definitions reveal a different story of the characteristics of gang homicide. They found that jurisdictions using the motive definition maintain 40 percent fewer gang homicides than jurisdictions using the member definition. Unsurprisingly, of 201 gang-related homicides studied by Maxson and Klein, only 120 contained information about a gang motive. When it came to the characteristics of gang homicide, the definition surprisingly did not matter much.

Incident characteristics, such as relationship with the victim, perpetrator demographics, and use of firearms, were invariant across type. This led Maxson and Klein (1996) to advocate for the more inclusive gang-member definition; it could be more valuable to criminologists, as a wider array of crimes and incidents can be studied.

Rosenfeld, Bray, and Egley (1999) provided evidence that contradicted some of Maxson and Klein's (1996) conclusions. They observed a decline of gang-motivated homicides in St. Louis but a continued rise in gang-related homicides. They argued that "the continued rise in gang-affiliated homicides, we suggest, results from increased involvement of gang members—but not gangs—in the drug trade" (513). Unlike Maxson and Klein, Rosenfeld and colleagues coded the incidents themselves as opposed to relying on police classification. A lack of cross-city research on gang homicide definitions has not allowed for generalization or further support for either Maxson and Klein (1996) or Rosenfeld, Bray, and Egley (1999). The contradictory evidence further demonstrates the challenges of incident definition (for violent and drug crimes, see Carson and Hipple 2020).

Data Sources on Gang Homicide

The following constitute the leading data sources in the United States scholars have used to conduct research on gang homicide: the Supplemental Homicide Report (SHR), National Violent Death Reporting System (NVDRS), National Youth Gang Survey (NYGS), and National Death Index (NDI). Each of these data sources has benefits and drawbacks, which we will discuss further. Figure 10.1 illustrates data collection efforts for national gang homicide data.

The SHR is collected as part of the Federal Bureau of Investigation's (FBI) Uniform Crime Report (UCR). The UCR consists of crimes recorded by law enforcement agencies and provided to the FBI to generate national, state, and local crime statistics. The SHR is a supplement to the UCR that focuses on homicide. Its relevance to gang research comes in the form of two measures of gang homicide, "gangland killings" and "juvenile gang killings," which are collected as a homicide circumstance.[1] The current SHR has been in existence since 1976, when it was updated to include more information—including gang homicide data—and to change the unit of analysis to incidents (Maxfield 1989; Riedel 1999). Law enforcement agencies report SHR data on a monthly basis.

The National Gang Center administered the NYGS to collect survey data from a nationally representative sample of law enforcement agencies from 1996 to 2001, including over three thousand agencies in areas ranging from small rural towns to cities over fifty thousand residents, and 2002 to 2012, including almost twenty-four hundred agencies. There are some differences between the 1996 and 2001 data collection years and the 2002 and 2012 years. For example, the 1996–2001 survey asked agencies to report the number of gang homicides that had occurred over the last year and then asked whether that number included only gang-motivated homicides. The 2002–2012 survey included a description of "member-based" (i.e., gang related) or "motive-based" (i.e., gang motivated). Agencies were asked to provide the number of member-based youth gang homicides in their jurisdictions and then asked how many were also motive based. The biggest limitation of the NYGS data is that collection ceased after 2012, which means that scholars are limited to data over a decade old that neglects to provide evidence from when it is most needed to help diagnose the causes of the 2020 rise of homicide.

Two studies have been conducted to assess the validity of NYGS data on gang homicide. Decker and Pyrooz (2010b) compared the SHR and the NYGS data for the hundred largest cities in the United States. They found that the NYGS exhibited satisfactory reliability even for cities without dedicated gang units. The SHR, in contrast, did not. They also found that the data sources were robust enough to conduct comparative research on gang homicide across the United States. A second study on the validity of the NYGS found that while the data are fairly reliable, caution should be taken when using the NYGS to study gang homicides, mainly for cities with populations under two hundred thousand (Katz et al. 2012).

The NVDRS consists of data from law enforcement, medical examiners and coroners, toxicological information, and death certificates. The NVDRS database has not been used often by criminologists in the study of gang homicide. Egley and colleagues (2012) compared the NVDRS to the NYGS and found that the two datasets tracked onto each other fairly well. The NVDRS has, until recently, been spotty in terms of its coverage of areas that classify gang homicides, but the number of states included in data collection has increased gradually. In 2002, only six states were included in data collection; by 2018, the NVDRS was collecting data, including on gang-related homicides, in all fifty states (CDC, n.d.). This led Frazier and colleagues (2017) to present a classification for "gang-like" homicides. The crux of their argument is that gang homicides are underrepresented even when gang-member (or gang-related) definitions are used. To be considered gang-like, an incident had to meet at least three of the four criteria specified by the authors. As expected, there was a substantial increase in the total of gang homicides once gang-like incidents were included.

Given the contention surrounding defining gangs and labeling people/ groups as gang members (see Meehan 2000), this approach to classifying gang-like homicides is controversial. The most glaring issue is that no test for equivalence was presented. Frazier and colleagues briefly mentioned that only 37 percent of the gang-related homicides met their gang-like criteria. The study operated under the assumption that their new criteria was actually capturing what they said it was without providing empirical support. The measure proposed by Frazier and colleagues runs the risk of not capturing gang-related incidents (e.g., domestic violence homicides) or casting too wide a net for incidents (e.g., nongang drug homicides). Further testing is required before its usefulness can be determined.

The NDI is a component of the National Vital Statistics Systems, an annual compilation of information drawn from state-provided death certificates. Death records have been collected from all fifty states, Puerto Rico, DC, and the U.S. Virgin Islands since 1979. The NDI was recently proposed as a viable data source for the study of gang homicide. Tostlebe and colleagues (2021) highlighted the utility of the NDI in criminological research when linked with other data sources, as it allows researchers to determine whether a person is deceased and the cause of death while maintaining national coverage. In linking the NDI with a St. Louis police gang database, the authors found that 285 of the 3,120 gang members in their sample had died and that the cause of death for just under half was assault. Of the 141 people whose death was the result of an assault, 135 deaths involved a firearm. This translated into an age-standardized homicide rate of 950 per 100,000—three times

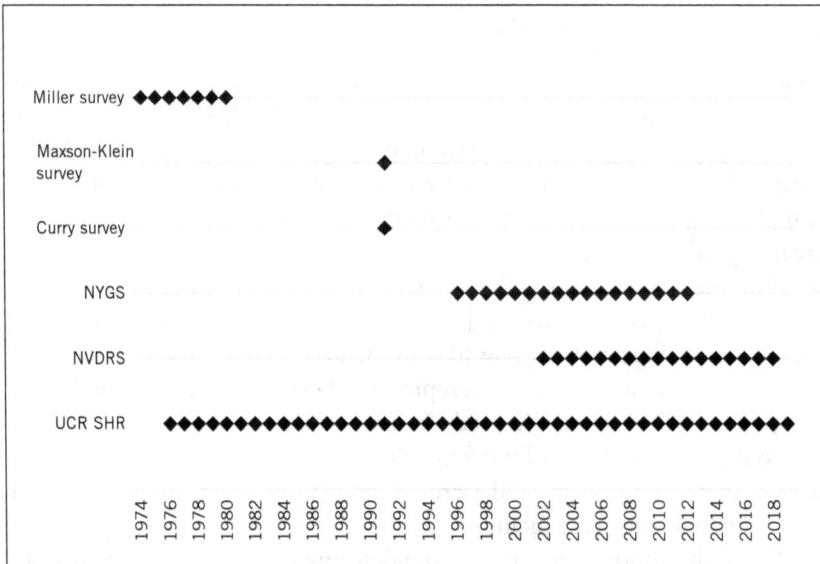

Figure 10.1 Overview of Nationally Representative Data Collected on Gang Homicide (*Sources: Miller [1982]; Klein [1995], Maxson, Woods, and Klein [1996]; nationalgangcenter.gov; cdc.gov/violenceprevention/datasources/nvdrs; fbi.gov/services/ciis/ucr.*)

higher than comparable-age Black males in St. Louis and six times higher than comparable-age Black males in the United States (Pyrooz et al. 2020). Of course, NDI outputs are only as valuable as the inputs. Perhaps the greatest utility is matching large-scale data sources to the NDI, which Chassin and colleagues (2013) did with the data from the Pathways to Desistance study.

The Prevalence and Trends of Gang Homicide

Gang killings make headlines on a daily basis, but how prevalent are they? Several studies have illustrated the prevalence and trends of gang homicide nationally, between multiple cities, and within single cities. Miller (1982) conducted the first national survey to study gang crime that included gang homicide. Miller obtained and illustrated gang homicide data from the United States' nine biggest cities (including Los Angeles, Chicago, and Boston) plus fifty other cities with data available. Miller's study revealed that there was a significant increase in gang homicides from 1967 (181) to 1980 (633). Curry and colleagues (1992) conducted a national study on gang crime in which forty-two jurisdictions across the United States reported a total of 974 gang homicides. Similarly, Maxson (1999) reported findings from the Maxson-Klein survey, which revealed 2,166 gang homicides across 299 American cities. Maxson, Curry, and Howell (2002) looked at national trends using the NYGS and noted some cities had homicide increases from 1996 to 1998 while other cities experienced decreases over the same span. One key finding was that Chicago and Los Angeles dictated national trends. Los Angeles had a major decrease in homicides from 350 in 1991 to 173 in 1998. On the flip side, Chicago had over 100 homicides in 1991 and a spike of 180 in 1998. Despite these differing trends, Chicago and Los Angeles had far and away the most gang homicides, and these dictated their homicide trends.

Egley Jr., Howell, and Harris (2014) published one of the most recent studies examining national trends of gang homicide. There was a 16 percent decrease in gang homicides reported by law enforcement agencies between 2007 (1,975) and 2008 (1,659). However, for 2009 and 2010, homicide numbers spiked to over 2,000. There was a drop to 1,824 in 2011 before another spike to 2,363 in 2012. The report by Egley Jr. and colleagues is limited to aggregated totals and cannot illustrate differences in homicide numbers between different cities. It is thus impossible to tell if the homicides are concentrated within certain geographic locations. The National Gang Center (2013) does break down NYGS data down by city type. Large cities with populations over one hundred thousand reported 61.5 percent of the homicides in 2007 and 67 percent of the homicides in 2012. Howell and colleagues (2011) used NYGS and UCR homicide data to study gang homicides in 247 cities with populations over one hundred thousand. Almost 80 percent of the sample consistently reported gang homicides. Howell and colleagues also found that about 70 percent of the cities in their sample reported that gang homicides made up 20 to 40 percent of their annual homicide totals. Spatial analysis showed that while there were some regional clusters, cities with gang homicides were randomly distributed across the country.

Currently, there are no good ways to map national gang homicide trends. The NYGS was discontinued, and the SHR is too suspect. For example, between 2016 and 2019 (2019 is the most current available SHR data year), Denver reported 244 homicides in the SHR. Of those, only 4 (1.6 percent) were classified as gang related. Meanwhile, the *Denver Post*'s homicide report listed 242 homicides and an average of 15 percent being gang related in that same time span (Schmelzer 2020). It should also be noted that gang homicide increases in the 1990s occurred during a time when homicides in general were dropping (Blumstein and Rosenfeld 1998). Very few studies have compared and contrasted trends in gang homicide to overall homicide or other homicide types, although Valasik et al.'s (2017) research in a Los Angeles policing district is an important exception.

Conclusion

Gang homicide has been an area of interest for academics and policymakers for several decades. Violence is a central part of gang life. Gang members are not only expected to engage in violence but are also more likely to experience victimization. Studies have found that violence is a common reason given by former gang members as to why they left their gang (Decker and Lauritsen 2002; Densley and Pyrooz 2017; Dierkhising, Sanchez, and Gutierrez 2019). What can be done to reduce the high levels of violence observed among gang populations?

Various strategies have been implemented to address gang violence in the form of suppression or intervention. Examples of suppression include gang crackdowns, injunctions, and enhancements (e.g., Yoshino 2008; Ridgeway et al. 2019), which are typically led by police departments through the use of gang units with some empirical support but also criticism (Archbold and Meyer 1999; Ratcliffe and Breen 2011; Valasik, Reid, and Phillips 2016). Focused deterrence approaches to gang homicide—police strategies that target specific offenders and places in hopes of deterring future crime—have shown promise in their effectiveness (for reviews and evaluations see Braga, Weisburd, and Turchan 2018; Sierra-Arevalo, Charette, and Papachristos 2017; Roman 2021).

Examples of intervention types include therapy based (e.g., FFT-G), education or job based (e.g., Conservation Corps), or hospital based (e.g., Caught in the Crossfire) (Becker et al. 2004; Sayegh et al. 2019; Thornberry et al. 2018).

Of course, a combination of suppression and intervention is likely to be the most successful, as posited by the Spergel comprehensive gang model (Spergel 2007). Today, many cities make use of the Spergel model for addressing gangs (Gebo, Bond, and Campos 2015; Pyrooz, Weltman, and Sanchez 2019). Unfortunately, most individual-level gang interventions have not been subjected to rigorous evaluation. This issue has been highlighted for several decades (Miller 1982; Roman, Decker, and Pyrooz 2017; Sanchez, Decker, and Pyrooz 2021). Improvement in this gap is critical because while focused deterrence may show success, it may not provide the long-term solutions communities are seeking (Roman, Decker, and Pyrooz 2017).

NOTE

1. Meena Harris, director of the National Gang Center, has identified funding as the primary reason why the NYGS was cut and for some of the measurement issues with FBI UCR and SHR data (Asher 2017). The National Institute of Justice recently awarded a grant (2020-JX-FX-K007) to launch a new version of the NYGS led by the Rand Corporation.

REFERENCES

Archbold, Carol A., and Michael Meyer. 1999. "Anatomy of a Gang Suppression Unit: The Social Construction of an Organizational Response to Gang Problems." *Police Quarterly* 2 (2): 201–24.

Asher, Jeff. 2017. "Gang Stats Aren't Remotely Reliable, but Voters Keep Hearing about Them Anyway." *FiveThirtyEight*, November 3, 2017. https://fivethirtyeight.com/features /gang-stats-arent-remotely-reliable-but-voters-keep-hearing-about-them-anyway/.

Becker, M., J. Hall, C. Ursic, S. Jain, and D. Calhoun. 2004. "Caught in the Crossfire: The Effects of a Peer-Based Intervention Program for Violently Injured Youth." *Journal of Adolescent Health* 34 (3): 177–83. https://doi.org/10.1016/S1054-139X(03)00278-7.

Bjerregaard, Beth, and Alan J. Lizotte. 1995. "Gun Ownership and Gang Membership." *Journal of Criminal Law and Criminology* 86:37.

Blumstein, Alfred, and Richard Rosenfeld. 1998. "Explaining Recent Trends in US Homicide Rates." *Journal of Criminal Law and Criminology (1973–)* 88 (4): 1175–216.

Braga, Anthony A., David Weisburd, and Brandon Turchan. 2018. "Focused Deterrence Strategies and Crime Control: An Updated Systematic Review and Meta-analysis of the Empirical Evidence." *Criminology & Public Policy* 17 (1): 205–50. https://doi.org /10.1111/1745-9133.12353.

Brantingham, Paul Jeffrey, George E. Tita, and George Mohler. 2021. "Gang-Related Crime in Los Angeles Remained Stable Following COVID-19 Social Distancing Orders." *Criminology & Public Policy* (April): 1745–9133.12541. https://doi.org/10.1111/1745 -9133.12541.

Cain, Josh. 2021. "2020 Was a Deadly One for L.A., with Most Killings in Years." *Daily News*, January 8, 2021. https://www.dailynews.com/2021/01/07/2020-was-a-deadly-one -for-l-a-with-most-killings-in-years.

Carson, Dena, and Natalie Kroovand Hipple. 2020. "Comparing Violent and Non-violent Gang Incidents: An Exploration of Gang-Related Police Incident Reports." *Social Sciences* 9 (11): 199. https://doi.org/10.3390/socsci9110199.

CDC. n.d. "CDC's National Violent Death Reporting System (NVDRS)." Center for Disease Control and Prevention. https://www.cdc.gov/violenceprevention/pdf/NVDRS-factsheet508.pdf.

Chapman, Ben. 2020. "New York City Police to Target Gang Leaders in Campaign against Gun Violence." *Wall Street Journal*, December 13, 2020, sec. US. https://www.wsj.com/articles/new-york-city-police-to-target-gang-leaders-in-campaign-against-gun-violence-11607878818.

Chassin, Laurie, Alex R. Piquero, Sandra H. Losoya, Andre D. Mansion, and Carol A. Schubert. 2013. "Joint Consideration of Distal and Proximal Predictors of Premature Mortality among Serious Juvenile Offenders." *Journal of Adolescent Health* 52 (6): 689–96. https://doi.org/10.1016/j.jadohealth.2012.11.018.

Closson, Troy. 2021. "The Spike in Shootings during the Pandemic May Outlast the Virus." *New York Times*, May 14, 2021, sec. New York. https://www.nytimes.com/2021/05/14/nyregion/shootings-nyc-covid.html.

Cloward, Richard A., and Lloyd E. Ohlin. 1960. *Delinquency and Opportunity: A Study of Delinquent Gangs*. New York: Free Press.

Cohen, Albert Kircidel. 1955. *Delinquent Boys: The Culture of the Gang*. New York: Free Press.

Council on Criminal Justice. 2021. "Impact Report: COVID-19 and Crime." National Commission on COVID-19 and Criminal Justice. January 31, 2021. https://covid19.counciloncj.org/2021/01/31/impact-report-covid-19-and-crime-3/.

Curry, G. D., R. J. Fox, R. A. Ball, and D. Stone. 1992. "National Assessment of Law Enforcement Anti-gang Information Resources." U.S. Department of Justice.

Curry, G. David, and Irving A. Spergel. 1988. "Gang Homicide, Delinquency, and Community." *Criminology* 26 (3): 381–406.

Decker, Scott H. 1996. "Collective and Normative Features of Gang Violence." *Justice Quarterly* 13 (2): 23.

Decker, Scott H., and G. David Curry. 2002. "Gangs, Gang Homicides, and Gang Loyalty: Organized Crimes or Disorganized Criminals." *Journal of Criminal Justice* 30:343–52. https://doi.org/10.1016/s0047-2352(02)00134-4.

Decker, Scott H., and Janet L. Lauritsen. 2002. "Leaving the Gang." In *Gangs in America*, edited by C Ronald Huff, 51–68. Thousand Oaks, CA: SAGE. https://doi.org/10.4135/9781452232201.n4.

Decker, Scott H., and David C. Pyrooz. 2010a. "Gang Violence Worldwide: Context, Culture, and Country." In *Small Arms Survey 2010: Gangs, Groups, and Guns*. 128–55. Cambridge: Cambridge University Press.

———. 2010b. "On the Validity and Reliability of Gang Homicide: A Comparison of Disparate Sources." *Homicide Studies* 14 (4): 359–76. https://doi.org/10.1177/1088767910385400.

Decker, Scott H., David C. Pyrooz, and James A. Densley. 2022. *On Gangs*. 1st ed. Philadelphia: Temple University Press.

DeLisi, Matt, Alan J. Drury, and Michael J. Elbert. 2019. "Do Behavioral Disorders Render Gang Status Spurious? New Insights." *International Journal of Law and Psychiatry* 62 (January): 117–24. https://doi.org/10.1016/j.ijlp.2018.12.007.

Densley, James A., and David C. Pyrooz. 2017. "A Signaling Perspective on Disengagement from Gangs." *Justice Quarterly* August:1–28. https://doi.org/10.1080/07418825.2017.1357743.

Dierkhising, Carly B., Jose A. Sanchez, and Luis Gutierrez. 2019. "'It Changed My Life': Traumatic Loss, Behavioral Health, and Turning Points among Gang-Involved and

Justice-Involved Youth." *Journal of Interpersonal Violence* May:088626051984777. https://doi.org/10.1177/0886260519847779.

Egley, Arlen, Jr., James C. Howell, and Meena Harris. 2014. "Highlights of the 2012 National Youth Gang Survey." Washington DC: Office of Juvenile Justice and Delinquency Prevention. https://ojjdp.ojp.gov/sites/g/files/xyckuh176/files/pubs/248025.pdf.

Egley, Arlen, Jr., John Logan, and D. D. McDaniel. 2012. *Gang Homicides—Five Cities, 2003–2008 (Morbidity and Mortality Weekly Report)*, 46–51. Center for Disease Control and Prevention.

Esbensen, Finn-Aage, and Dena C. Carson. 2012. "Who Are the Gangsters? An Examination of the Age, Race/Ethnicity, Sex, and Immigration Status of Self-Reported Gang Members in a Seven-City Study of American Youth." *Journal of Contemporary Criminal Justice* 28 (4): 465–81.

Esbensen, Finn-Aage, and L. Thomas Winfree. 1998. "Race and Gender Differences between Gang and Nongang Youths: Results from a Multisite Survey." *Justice Quarterly* 15 (3): 505–26. https://doi.org/10.1080/07418829800093861.

Frazier, Leroy, LaVonne Ortega, Nimeshkumar Patel, Jamar Barnes, Alex E. Crosby, and Katherine Hempstead. 2017. "Methods and Findings from the National Violent Death Reporting System for Identifying Gang-Like Homicides, 2005–2008." *Journal of the National Medical Association* 109 (4): 272–78. https://doi.org/10.1016/j.jnma.2017.03.001.

Gebo, Erika, Brenda J. Bond, and Krystal S. Campos. 2015. "The OJJDP Comprehensive Gang Strategy." In *The Handbook of Gangs*, edited by Scott Decker and David Pyrooz, 392–405. Wiley Online Library.

Gottfredson, Michael R., and Travis Hirschi. 1990. *A General Theory of Crime*. Redwood City CA: Stanford University Press.

Hennigan, Karen M., and David Sloane. 2013. "Improving Civil Gang Injunctions: How Implementation Can Affect Gang Dynamics, Crime, and Violence." *Criminology & Public Policy* 12 (1): 7–41. https://doi.org/10.1111/1745-9133.12000.

Hindelang, Michael J., Michael R. Gottfredson, and James Garofalo. 1978. *Victims of Personal Crime: An Empirical Foundation for a Theory of Personal Victimization*. Cambridge, MA: Ballinger.

Howell, James C., Arlen Egley Jr., George E. Tita, and Elizabeth Griffiths. 2011. "US Gang Problem Trends and Seriousness, 1996–2009." Department of Justice, Office of Juvenile Justice and Delinquency Prevention.

Hughes, Lorine A. 2013. "Group Cohesiveness, Gang Member Prestige, and Delinquency and Violence in Chicago, 1959–1962." *Criminology* 51 (4): 795–832. https://doi.org/10.1111/1745-9125.12020.

Hughes, Lorine A., Lonnie M. Schaible, and Timothy Kephart. 2021. "Gang Graffiti, Group Process, and Gang Violence." *Journal of Quantitative Criminology* 38 (3): 365–84. https://doi.org/10.1007/s10940-021-09507-8.

Hutson, H. Range, Deirdre Anglin, Demetrios N. Kyriacou, Joel Hart, and Kelvin Spears. 1995. "The Epidemic of Gang-Related Homicides in Los Angeles County from 1979 through 1994." *Jama* 274 (13): 1031–36.

Jones, Megan. 2021. "Aurora Sees 40% Increase in Shootings in 2020, with Other Crimes up as Well." *Chicago Tribune*, February 7, 2021, sec. Aurora Beacon News, Suburbs. https://www.chicagotribune.com/suburbs/aurora-beacon-news/ct-abn-aurora-crime-rates-2020-st-0207-20210207-rx6zu5evvbfindmt6iqcufg6eq-story.html.

Katz, Charles M., Andrew M. Fox, Chester L. Britt, and Phillip Stevenson. 2012. "Understanding Police Gang Data at the Aggregate Level: An Examination of the Reliability of National Youth Gang Survey Data (Research Note)." *Justice Research and Policy* 14 (2): 103–28. https://doi.org/10.3818/JRP.14.2.2012.103.

Klein, Malcolm W. 1969. "Gang Cohesiveness, Delinquency, and a Street-Work Program." *Journal of Research in Crime and Delinquency* 6 (2): 135–66. https://doi.org/10.1177 /002242786900600204.

———. 1971. *Street Gangs and Street Workers*. Englewood Cliffs, NJ: Prentice-Hall.

Kubrin, Charis E., and Tim Wadsworth. 2003. "Identifying the Structural Correlates of African American Killings: What Can We Learn from Data Disaggregation?" *Homicide Studies* 7 (1): 3–35. https://doi.org/10.1177/1088767902239241.

Mares, Dennis. 2010. "Social Disorganization and Gang Homicides in Chicago: A Neighborhood Level Comparison of Disaggregated Homicides." *Youth Violence and Juvenile Justice* 8 (1): 38–57. https://doi.org/10.1177/1541204009339006.

Maxfield, Michael G. 1989. "Circumstances in Supplementary Homicide Reports: Variety and Validity." *Criminology* 27 (4): 671–96. https://doi.org/10.1111/j.1745-9125.1989 .tb01050.x.

Maxson, Cheryl L. 1999. "Gang Homicide: A Review and Extension of the Literature." In *Homicide: A Sourcebook of Social Research*, edited by M. Dwayne Smith and Margaret A. Zahn, 239–54. Thousand Oaks, CA: SAGE.

Maxson, Cheryl L., G. David Curry, and James C. Howell. 2002. "Youth Gang Homicides." In *Responding to Gangs: Evaluation and Research*, edited by Winfred L. Reed and Scott H. Decker, 107. Washington DC: U.S. Department of Justice, Office of Justice Programs, National Institute of Justice.

Maxson, Cheryl L., Margaret A. Gordon, and Malcolm W. Klein. 1985. "Differences between Gang and Nongang Homicides." *Criminology* 23 (2): 209–22.

Maxson, Cheryl L., and Malcolm W. Klein. 1996. "Defining Gang Homicide: An Updated Look at Member and Motive Approaches." In *Gangs in America*, edited by C. Ronald Huff. Vol. 2. Thousand Oaks, CA: SAGE.

Meehan, Albert J. 2000. "The Organizational Career of Gang Statistics: The Politics of Policing Gangs." *Sociological Quarterly* 41 (3): 337–70.

Melde, Chris, and Finn-Aage Esbensen. 2013. "Gangs and Violence: Disentangling the Impact of Gang Membership on the Level and Nature of Offending." *Journal of Quantitative Criminology* 29 (2): 143–66. https://doi.org/10.1007/s10940-012-9164-z.

Miller, Walter B. 1975. "Violence by Youth Gangs and Youth Groups as a Crime Problem in Major American Cities." U.S. Department of Justice, Law Enforcement Assistance Administration, Office of Juvenile Justice and Delinquency Prevention, National Institute for Juvenile Justice and Delinquency Prevention.

———. 1982. "Crime by Youth Gangs and Groups in the United States." U.S. Department of Justice, Office of Justice Programs, Office of Juvenile Justice and Delinquency Prevention.

National Gang Center. 2013. "Measuring the Extent of Gang Problems." https://www.na tionalgangcenter.gov/survey-analysis/measuring-the-extent-of-gang-problems.

Nicholson, Kieran. 2021. "Man Sentenced to 40 Years in Prison for Aurora Shooting Death over $20 Dispute." *Denver Post* (blog), January 15, 2021. https://www.denverpost.com /2021/01/15/aurora-shooting-death-sentencing/.

Oravetz, Janet. 2020. "Man Charged with Murder after Shooting near Food Truck." *KUSA.com*, July 23, 2020. https://www.9news.com/article/news/crime/man-charged -with-murder-after-shooting-near-food-truck/73-7fa6632d-aacc-4425-a1b1-b458d bea77a3.

Papachristos, Andrew V. 2009. "Murder by Structure: Dominance Relations and the Social Structure of Gang Homicide." *American Journal of Sociology* 115 (1): 74–128. https://doi.org/10.1086/597791.

———. 2013. "The Importance of Cohesion for Gang Research, Policy, and Practice: Civil Gang Injunctions." *Criminology & Public Policy* 12 (1): 49–58. https://doi.org/10.1111/1745-9133.12006.

Papachristos, Andrew V., David M. Hureau, and Anthony A. Braga. 2013. "The Corner and the Crew: The Influence of Geography and Social Networks on Gang Violence." *American Sociological Review* 78 (3): 417–47. https://doi.org/10.1177/0003122413486800.

Papachristos, Andrew V., and David S. Kirk. 2006. "Neighborhood Effects on Street Gang Behavior." *Studying Youth Gangs* 12:63–84.

Pizarro, Jesenia M., Nicholas Corsaro, and Sung-suk Violet Yu. 2007. "Journey to Crime and Victimization: An Application of Routine Activities Theory and Environmental Criminology to Homicide." *Victims & Offenders* 2 (4): 375–94. https://doi.org/10.1080/15564880701568520.

Pizarro, Jesenia M., and Jean Marie McGloin. 2006. "Explaining Gang Homicides in Newark, New Jersey: Collective Behavior or Social Disorganization?" *Journal of Criminal Justice* 34 (2): 195–207. https://doi.org/10.1016/j.jcrimjus.2006.01.002.

Pyrooz, David C. 2012. "Structural Covariates of Gang Homicide in Large U.S. Cities." *Journal of Research in Crime and Delinquency* 49 (4): 489–518. https://doi.org/10.1177/0022427811415535.

———. 2014. "'From Your First Cigarette to Your Last Dyin' Day': The Patterning of Gang Membership in the Life-Course." *Journal of Quantitative Criminology* 30 (2): 349–72. https://doi.org/10.1007/s10940-013-9206-1.

Pyrooz, David C., Ryan K. Masters, Jennifer J. Tostlebe, and Richard G. Rogers. 2020. "Exceptional Mortality Risk among Police-Identified Young Black Male Gang Members." *Preventive Medicine* 141 (December): 106269. https://doi.org/10.1016/j.ypmed.2020.106269.

Pyrooz, David C., Chris Melde, Donna L. Coffman, and Ryan C Meldrum. 2021. "Selection, Stability, and Spuriousness: Testing Gottfredson and Hirschi's Propositions to Reinterpret Street Gangs in Self-Control Perspective." *Criminology* 59 (2): 224–53.

Pyrooz, David C., Jillian J. Turanovic, Scott H. Decker, and Jun Wu. 2016. "Taking Stock of the Relationship between Gang Membership and Offending: A Meta-Analysis." *Criminal Justice and Behavior* 43 (3): 365–97. https://doi.org/10.1177/0093854815605528.

Pyrooz, David C., Elizabeth Weltman, and Jose Sanchez. 2019. "Intervening in the Lives of Gang Members in Denver: A Pilot Evaluation of the Gang Reduction Initiative of Denver." *Justice Evaluation Journal* May:1–25. https://doi.org/10.1080/24751979.2019.1609334.

Ratcliffe, Jerry H., and Clairissa Breen. 2011. "Crime Diffusion and Displacement: Measuring the Side Effects of Police Operations." *Professional Geographer* 63 (2): 230–43. https://doi.org/10.1080/00330124.2010.547154.

Rector, Kevin, and Nicole Santa Cruz. 2020. "L.A.'s Surge in Homicides Fueled by Gang Violence, Killings of Homeless People." *Los Angeles Times*, October 29, 2020, sec. California. https://www.latimes.com/california/story/2020-10-29/gangs-homelessness-cited-in-lapd-report-on-surge-in-killings.

Reid, Shannon E., and Matthew Valasik. 2020. *Alt-Right Gangs: A Hazy Shade of White.* Berkeley: University of California Press.

Ridgeway, Greg, Jeffrey Grogger, Ruth A. Moyer, and John M. MacDonald. 2019. "Effect of Gang Injunctions on Crime: A Study of Los Angeles from 1988–2014." *Journal of Quantitative Criminology* 35 (3): 517–41. https://doi.org/10.1007/s10940-018-9396-7.

Riedel, Marc. 1999. "Sources of Homicide Data: A Review and Comparison." In *Homicide: A Sourcebook of Social Research*, edited by M. Dwayne Smith and Margaret A. Zahn, 75–95. Thousand Oaks, CA: SAGE.

Roman, Caterina G. 2021. "An Evaluator's Reflections and Lessons Learned about Gang Intervention Strategies: An Agenda for Research." *Journal of Aggression, Conflict and Peace Research* 13 (2–3): 146–67

Roman, Caterina G., Scott H. Decker, and David C. Pyrooz. 2017. "Leveraging the Pushes and Pulls of Gang Disengagement to Improve Gang Intervention: Findings from Three Multi-site Studies and a Review of Relevant Gang Programs." *Journal of Crime and Justice* 40 (3): 316–36. https://doi.org/10.1080/0735648X.2017.1345096.

Rosenfeld, Richard, Timothy M. Bray, and Arlen Egley. 1999. "Facilitating Violence: A Comparison of Gang-Motivated, Gang-Affiliated, and Nongang Youth Homicides." *Journal of Quantitative Criminology* 15 (22): 495–516.

Sanchez, Jose Antonio, Scott H. Decker, and David C. Pyrooz. 2021. "Gang Homicide: The Road so Far and a Map for the Future." *Homicide Studies* September:108876792110438. https://doi.org/10.1177/10887679211043804.

Sayegh, Caitlin S., Stanley J. Huey Jr., Janet U. Schneiderman, and Sarah A. Redmond. 2019. "Pilot Evaluation of a Conservation Corps Program for Young Adults." *International Journal of Offender Therapy and Comparative Criminology* 63 (12): 2194–212. https://doi.org/10.1177/0306624X19843424.

Schmelzer, Elise. 2020. "Gang Killings in Denver Spike as Instability and Internal Conflicts Cause Bloodshed." *Denver Post*, September 17, 2020. https://www.denverpost.com/2020/09/17/denver-gang-violence-2020/.

———. 2021. "Denver's 2020 Homicide Numbers Highest in City since 1981 as Police, Communities Navigate 'State of Normlessness.'" *Denver Post*, January 31, 2021. https://www.denverpost.com/2021/01/31/denver-2020-crime-homicides/.

Short, James F. 1985. "The Level of Explanation Problem in Criminology." In *Theoretical Methods in Criminology*, edited by Robert Meier, 51–72. Beverly Hills, CA: SAGE.

———. 1998. "The Level of Explanation Problem Revisited: The American Society of Criminology 1997 Presidential Address." *Criminology* 36 (1): 3–36. https://doi.org/10.1111/j.1745-9125.1998.tb01238.x.

Short, James F., and Fred L. Strodtbeck. 1965. *Group Process and Gang Delinquency*. Chicago: University of Chicago Press.

Sierra-Arevalo, Michael, Yanick Charette, and Andrew V. Papachristos. 2017. "Evaluating the Effect of Project Longevity on Group-Involved Shootings and Homicides in New Haven, Connecticut." *Crime & Delinquency* 63 (4): 446–67. https://doi.org/10.1177/0011128716635197.

Spergel, Irving A. 2007. *Reducing Youth Gang Violence: The Little Village Gang Project in Chicago*. Lanham, MD: Altamira Press.

Taylor, Terrance J., Dana Peterson, Finn-Aage Esbensen, and Adrienne Freng. 2007. "Gang Membership as a Risk Factor for Adolescent Violent Victimization." *Journal of Research in Crime and Delinquency* 44 (4): 351–80. https://doi.org/10.1177/0022427807305845.

Thornberry, Terence P., Brook Kearley, Denise C. Gottfredson, Molly P. Slothower, Deanna N. Devlin, and Jamie J. Fader. 2018. "Reducing Crime among Youth at Risk for Gang

Involvement: A Randomized Trial." *Criminology & Public Policy* 17 (4): 953–89. https://doi.org/10.1111/1745-9133.12395.

Thornberry, Terence P., Marvin D. Krohn, Alan J. Lizotte, Carolyn A. Smith, and Kimberly Tobin. 2003. *Gangs and Delinquency in Developmental Perspective.* Cambridge Studies in Criminology. Cambridge: Cambridge University Press. https://doi.org/10.1017/CBO9780511499517.

Thrasher, Frederic Milton. 1927. *The Gang: A Study of 1,313 Gangs in Chicago.* Chicago: University of Chicago Press.

Tigri, Henry B., Shannon Reid, Michael G. Turner, and Jennifer M. Devinney. 2016. "Investigating the Relationship between Gang Membership and Carrying a Firearm: Results from a National Sample." *American Journal of Criminal Justice* 41 (2): 168–84. https://doi.org/10.1007/s12103-015-9297-3.

Tostlebe, Jennifer J., David C. Pyrooz, Richard G. Rogers, and Ryan K. Masters. 2021. "The National Death Index as a Source of Homicide Data: A Methodological Exposition of Promises and Pitfalls for Criminologists." *Homicide Studies* 25 (1): 5–36. https://doi.org/10.1177/1088767920924450.

Valasik, Matthew, Michael S. Barton, Shannon E. Reid, and George E. Tita. 2017. "Barriocide: Investigating the Temporal and Spatial Influence of Neighborhood Structural Characteristics on Gang and Non-gang Homicides in East Los Angeles." *Homicide Studies* 21 (4): 287–311. https://doi.org/10.1177/1088767917726807.

Valasik, Matthew, and Shannon E. Reid. 2021. "East Side Story: Disaggregating Gang Homicides in East Los Angeles." *Social Sciences* 10 (2): 48. https://doi.org/10.3390/socsci10020048.

Valasik, Matthew, Shannon E. Reid, and Matthew D. Phillips. 2016. "CRASH and Burn: Abatement of a Specialised Gang Unit." Edited by Jane L. Wood. *Journal of Criminological Research, Policy and Practice* 2 (2): 95–106. https://doi.org/10.1108/JCRPP-06-2015-0024.

Wu, Jun, and David C. Pyrooz. 2016. "Uncovering the Pathways between Gang Membership and Violent Victimization." *Journal of Quantitative Criminology* 32 (4): 531–59. https://doi.org/10.1007/s10940-015-9266-5.

Yablonsky, Lewis. 1962. *The Violent Gang.* 1st ed. Baltimore: Penguin Books.

Yoshino, Erin R. 2008. "California's Criminal Gang Enhancements." *Review of Law and Social Justice* 18 (1): 117–52.

11

Drug-Related Homicides

ARNALDO RABOLINI, JOLIEN VAN BREEN, AND MARIEKE LIEM

Introduction

Drugs are generally considered a prominent factor contributing to violent behavior (Caulkins and Kleiman 2011; Collins 1990; EMCDDA and Europol 2016; Ousey and Lee 2007; Varano et al. 2004; Varano and Kuhns 2017). One of the links between drugs and violence is drug circulation, which impacts communities in various regions throughout the world. The crack-cocaine epidemic, for example, is believed to have had a primary role in increased homicide rates in many U.S. cities in the 1980s and 1990s (Blumstein 1995; Blumstein and Rosenfeld 1998; Goldstein, Brownstein, and Ryan 1992). Elsewhere, including in Mexico and Colombia, drug trafficking has been associated with extremely high homicide rates (Durán-Martínez 2015; Alda 2017). Recently, drug-related violence has gained attention from public authorities and researchers in Europe, becoming a security priority for the European Union (European Commission 2020). In short, drug-related violence is a global issue; very few places seem immune to it. In reflecting on developments in drug-related violence and methodological issues in studying this phenomenon, this chapter mostly focuses on the European experience.

The actual nexus between drugs and violence, including homicide—the main focus of this chapter—is more complex and nuanced than it is generally assumed (Reuter 2009). Further, the strength of the link between homicide and drugs varies across space and time and depends on a range of factors, such as specific sociocultural context and type of drug involved. As such, our academic understanding regarding the relationship between drugs and violence, including homicide, is still limited (Varano and Kuhns 2017).

One way to study the link between drugs and homicides is to focus specifically on cases that involve both, such as drug-related homicides (DRH). Studying DRH among all forms of drug-related violence can prove very relevant. Not only is homicide considered the most extreme form of violence—with devastating effects on individuals and communities—but data regarding homicides also are normally more complete and reliable than data about other types of crimes (Smit, de Jong, and Bijleveld 2012). In addition, DRH can provide a better understanding of illegal drug markets and function as an indicator of linked criminal activities (EMCDDA 2020). Most of the crime and violence related to the illegal drug industry remains unreported, and there is little reliable data available at the European level (Groshkova et al. 2021). In this sense, data regarding DRH can inform policy making aimed at countering illegal drug market activity. At the same time, studying DRH presents important methodological challenges, particularly regarding the quality and availability of comparable data. For instance, there is a lack of solid international statistics regarding DRH at the regional level as well as globally.

The aim of this chapter is to outline the most pressing methodological limitations as well as to highlight some next steps and new initiatives to support research on DRH.[1] In what follows, we explain in depth the drugs-violence nexus by looking at trends in the study of this phenomenon, then introduce the main challenges and limitations of researching DRH. Subsequently, we present the European Homicide Monitor (EHM) as a validated instrument for researching DRH. Finally, we give several recommendations on how to move this young research tradition forward.

The Drugs-Violence Nexus: Research Developments

Initially, most work on the drugs-violence nexus focused on individual-level perspectives and the physiological effects of drugs on the propensity of committing violent acts (Asnis, Smith, and Crim 1978; Monteforte and Spitz 1975; Zahn and Bencivengo 1974). It was not until the mid-1980s, with the onset of the crack epidemic, that scholars started considering the systemic effects of drug markets on levels of violence, largely as a result of Goldstein's (1985) seminal work. Goldstein, a sociologist by training, suggested three nonmutually exclusive mechanisms that explain how drugs can be responsible for generating violence: the *psychopharmacological, economic compulsive*, and *systemic* types. The psychopharmacological model points to the direct effects of drugs (and alcohol) on the person as a cause for violence. In some individuals and in certain circumstances, drug consumption can alter perception of reality and induce a state of excitement, irascibility, and irrationality resulting in violent behavior, including homicide (Goldstein 1985). The economic-compulsive explanation comprises acts of violence committed with the purpose of obtaining money to buy drugs, including robberies and stealing. The final type, the systemic, refers to violence resulting from the production, distribution, and consumption of drugs. This includes territorial disputes between dealers, turf wars, robberies of drug dealers and subsequent violent reprisals, punishment for selling phony drugs, punishment of informants, cancellation of debt by punishment, and so on (Goldstein 1985). Goldstein's classification has been widely used in criminological studies globally (Brownstein et al. 1992; Goldstein, Brownstein, and Ryan 1992; Varano et al. 2004; De Bont et al. 2018) and has become a standard-bearer for analyzing the nexus between drugs and violence to the point that it has influenced an entire generation of criminologists (Dickinson 2015; Varano et al. 2004).

Many subsequent studies have relied on Goldstein's tripartite framework, implicitly or explicitly. For instance, each of Goldstein's DRH types has generated its own branch of literature. In terms of psychopharmacological DRH, research has shown that among those who regularly consume substances, the likelihood of homicide incidents occurring is much higher than for the general population (Darke 2010). A study on homicides in Sweden and Finland showed that approximately 20 percent of perpetrators and 10–15 percent of victims are under the influence of drugs when homicide is committed (Granath et al. 2011).

Another noteworthy feature of the literature on psychopharmacological DRH is that it considers not only illegal drugs but also alcohol and prescription drugs (Haggård-Grann et al. 2006; Tihihonen et al. 2015). Many studies concur that alcohol consumption (or the mix of alcohol and other drugs) is associated with higher levels of violent crime and higher homicide rates (Darke 2010; Nash Parker and Auerhahn 1998; Pridemore 2002), though effects of methamphetamines seem less consistent (Kuypers et al. 2020). For instance, van Amsterdam and colleagues (2020) conclude in their empirical review that an important proportion of public violence in Europe is linked to alcohol consumption—more than to drugs use. This development is in line with a more general tendency of countries to veer toward decriminalization of drug consumption and a public health approach in treating drug-related violence. Accordingly, there has been renewed interest in the psychopharmacological dimension of the drug–(lethal) violence nexus, including in legal substances (as discussed previously). This is reflected in important work focusing on the toxicology of homicides (Darke 2010; Kuhns et al. 2014; Kuypers et al. 2020).

In terms of Goldstein's second type, economic-compulsive violence, studies have pointed out that drug users might engage in property crime and violent crime, including homicide, to finance their addiction (see Bennet, Holloway, and Farrington 2008; Chaiken and Chaiken 1990; Inciardi 1990). The overall impact of economic-compulsive violence on homicide levels is not clear, however. Empirical studies have shown that this type of DRH is usually a minority of cases, such as in Finland, the Netherlands, and Sweden (Schönberger et al. 2019). In any case, literature devoted exclusively to this type of DRH is rather limited.

A final development concerns Goldstein's systemic violence, which accounts for an important proportion of drug-related violence, as reflected in the wealth of studies covering this issue (especially since the 1990s). Literature examining the effects of drug markets, in particular for cocaine, on homicide and violence levels has also flourished outside the United States, particularly in Latin America. This region is among the most violent in the world, and a large part of the violence is linked to cocaine trafficking. Many studies have analyzed drug-related violence (and DRH) in Mexico (see Dell 2015; Molzahn, Rios, and Shirk 2012; Reuter 2009), Colombia (Durán-Martínez 2015; Snyder and Durán-Martínez 2009), and Brazil (De Mello 2015; Portella 2019).

In Europe, there has been growing interest in drug-related violence. Recent works have focused on violence linked to cannabis, which plays an important role in drug-related violence and DRH levels (see Moeller and Hesse 2013; Niveau and Dang 2003; Norström and Rossow 2014). A recent study from Sweden shows that between 2016 and 2019, 36 percent of all DRH involved the use of cannabis—a higher percentage than cocaine or other drugs. Most of these cases showed psychopharmacological or systemic components or a combination thereof as most salient (Granath, Galanti, and Magnusson 2022). The recent uptick in research on drug-related violence and DRH in Europe is in part the result of the active role of researchers from the EHM and the prioritization of this phenomenon by the European Monitoring Centre on Drugs and Drug Addiction (EMCDDA).

Challenges and Limitations in Researching DRH

Research on DRH presents numerous challenges. These are partly common to homicide research in general and partly specific to drug-related cases. A first significant limitation when conducting research on DRH comes from lack of uniformity in defining what constitutes a DRH and what specific causal role drugs play in acts of lethal violence. This inconsistency has important consequences: it renders the mere definition and classification of DRH open to interpretation, impacting the way events are registered and thus the available data. There is no clarity regarding what drug-related characteristics police and homicide investigators need to record. Drug elements in homicide cases are often perceived as circumstantial rather than as possible causal mechanisms. Thus, police frequently do not consider such information essential for solving cases. As a consequence, drug-related information is not recorded systematically and is often overlooked entirely (Varano and Kuhns 2017). Already in 1989, Goldstein denounced the inadequacies of registration methods when reporting the drug factor due to "the lack of consensus and standardization in concepts, operational definitions, and empirical indicators" (Goldstein et al. 1989, 654). Even if there have been concrete improvements (some of which are presented in the following paragraph), classification and registration issues still hamper DRH research (De Bont et al. 2018).

One way psychopharmacological DRH has been operationalized is by checking whether the perpetrator, victim, or both were under the influence of any substances at the moment the homicide was committed. Although toxicology tests are—depending on regional and local resources—routinely carried out for homicide victims, in western Europe, for instance, they are seldom done for offenders. This can be attributed to various obstacles: not only does the offender need to be identified, but also tests need to be carried out before the traces of substances are eliminated from the body (Darke 2010). Aside from this basic logistical challenge, there a lack of homogeneity in toxicology tests in terms of drugs tested, as thresholds and protocols have changed over time (Varano and Kuhns 2017). This factor limits the ability to make comparisons. Moreover, there is no consensus in terms of thresholds of substance quantity that can result in violent behavior (Kuypers et al. 2020).

Another important factor hindering research on DRH is the propensity of DRH cases to remain unsolved (Braga, Turchan, and Barao 2018; Liem et al. 2019; Wellford and Cronin 1999). This characteristic exacerbates the already discussed lack of data issue. For instance, Wellford and Cronin (1999) analyzed clearance data relative to homicide cases committed in the twenty largest cities in the United States and concluded that a case is significantly less likely to be solved if it is drug related. Instances of systemic DRH, which often constitute the majority of cases, generally present characteristics that are among the main predictors for lack of clearance in homicide cases: they tend to occur in the criminal milieu, in public spaces, with firearms, and where victims and perpetrators are unknown to each other (Braga, Turchan, and Barao 2018). In a study of homicide clearance in four European countries, Liem et al. (2019) concluded that differences in prevalence of the previously mentioned factors explain variations in homicide clearance between countries. The result is a noticeable amount of missing data regarding the drug component of cases as well as general characteristics of offenders.

Furthermore, the lack of publicly available information regarding the drug dimension in homicide cases inhibits international comparisons (De Bont et al. 2018). For many countries, public health statistics do not contain specific information regarding DRH. In a study conducted by De Bont and colleagues among thirty European countries, only a third provide DRH information (De Bont et al. 2018). Moreover, where this information is included, the categories used for drug relatedness differ in ways that make valid comparisons impossible. As an example, Scotland provides information on the total number of offenders who perpetrated a homicidal act under the influence of drugs, while Germany releases data about number of homicide perpetrators who were known to be habitual drug users or addicts regardless of whether they were under the influence when the homicide was committed (De Bont et al. 2018, 141). The main international sources of homicides statistics, including WHO, UNODC, and Eurostat (at a European level), do not contain statistics regarding DRH (Smit, de Jong, and Bijleveld 2012). Thus, comparability of data regarding the drug relatedness of homicides is an important challenge for researchers.

Overcoming Limitations

Research on DRH has put forward various ways to overcome these limitations. For instance, when it comes to missing data, researchers have either omitted missing data or used computation techniques. As missing data is not randomly distributed, excluding these cases results in considerable bias (Schönberger et al. 2019). It understates and distorts rates of offenders by specific subgroups, as the probability of having missing data is linked to specific offender characteristics (Fox 2004), as well as being an important loss of data in an already relatively limited N size. There is no ideal imputation technique, and "the only really good solution to the missing data problem is not to have any" (Allison 2002, 2). There is no consensus on the best technique to use (Riedel and Regoeczi 2004).

In terms of registration techniques, important advancements have been made at different levels. In the United States, the National Violent Death Reporting System (NVDRS)—a surveillance system for monitoring the occurrence of violent death (recently extended to all fifty states)—includes toxicology tests for decedents who were tested (Ertl et al. 2019). This represents a concrete step forward in improving research on the drug-violence nexus. At the international level, there have been some advances, such as the inclusion of drug-related violence information in the International Classification of Crimes by the UNODC. At the European level, there has been renewed interest in drug-related violence, and numerous concrete steps have been taken to overcome data availability and registration limitations. Some countries, including the UK, Italy, Germany, and Czech Republic, now provide drug-related information in their homicide reporting systems (De Bont et al. 2018).

In response to some of the limitations outlined, a new initiative at the European level has been developed, namely adapting the existing EHM (Granath et al. 2011) in such a way that can capture specific drug-related factors (for an overview and details, see www.europeanhomicide.com). The EHM is a database that systematically collects information about every single homicide case for participating countries; at this moment, it includes Finland, Sweden, the Netherlands, and Switzerland, with EHM compatible monitoring systems in Iceland, Scotland, Estonia, Paris, and the Dutch Caribbean. The data is gathered from existing national homicide monitors of participating countries. Each national dataset gathers data from different sources, which vary according to country: for instance, data from Finland and Sweden come mostly from the police, while the Dutch monitor relies on sources including media sources, public prosecution data, and court documents (Schönberger et al. 2019). The EHM provides a data framework with standardized variables that allows direct comparisons across countries. It contains eighty-five variables, making analysis at the case or individual characteristic level possible, such as relationship between victim and perpetrators, motive, and context of the homicide, as well as trends and patterns (Liem 2021).

Given these features, the EHM is particularly well suited to researching DRH. A pilot study commissioned by the EMCDDA and carried out by a Leiden University team of researchers in 2019 concluded that the current structure of the EHM allows integration of new drug-related variables (Schönberger et al. 2019). Today, the EHM includes information not only on whether the homicide was drug related but also on the extent to which the drug factor was involved in the case. Relying on Goldstein's tripartite framework to define and classify DRH allows for direct comparisons and helps overcome the definitional problem. Furthermore, the EHM incorporates variables and coding that allow capturing of the drug dimension in homicide cases at incident, victim, and perpetrator level.

For each type, the EHM contains specific variables/coding that can easily be scored by practitioners. For psychopharmacological DRH, variables include whether the individual took drugs at the time of the crime, what type of drug, and the quantity. For economic-compulsive types, variables include what the perpetrator was trying to steal (in the case of a robbery killing) and what was obtained. For systemic types, in homicides occurring in the criminal milieu, the coding enables definition of whether the killing occurred in drug-related contexts, such as turf wars, rip deals, or retaliation/revenge (Schönberger et al. 2019).

This set of standardized variables can easily serve as guidelines for those responsible for registration (police detectives, for instance). Moreover, the EHM is an open system that can be updated to include new cases or add information to cases already registered (for instance, when an unsolved case is finally cleared). Cases can be updated based on the many sources from which national homicide monitors draw their data. This can contribute to minimizing the problem of missing data, which in the case of DRH is particularly relevant. Finally, the EHM architecture has the advantage of allowing new countries to join the existing framework (De Bont et al. 2018), and its structure and variables can guide national police agencies in categorizing drug-related information from homicide cases. In this vein, and in accordance with the EHM, the EMCDDA actively promotes uniformity among EU member states in collecting and recording DRH data.

DRH in Finland, the Netherlands, Sweden, and Switzerland

To showcase the potential of using the EHM, we present some of our recent findings comparing DRH in four European countries: Finland, the Netherlands, Sweden, and Switzerland (Schönberger et al. 2019; Markwalder and Walser, email to authors). Although the four countries present similar general characteristics (highly developed, wealthy, stable European democracies with a strong social welfare system), there are clear differences in types of DRH and their prevalent characteristics (see table 11.1).

Data shows that all cases of DRH that occurred in Finland were classified as psychopharmacological. This stands in stark contrast to the Netherlands, where the majority of cases were systemic DRH; only one out of four cases was considered psychopharmacological. In Sweden, although the overwhelming majority of DRH cases could be classified as psychopharmacologi-

TABLE 11.1 NUMBER OF HOMICIDES EXAMINED AND SCOPE OF DRUG-RELATED CASES IN PARTICIPATING COUNTRIES

	Finland (2014–2015)		The Netherlands (2012–2016)		Sweden (2013–2014)		Switzerland (2010–2014)		Combined	
	N	%	N	%	N	%	N	%	N	%
Total cases examined	170	100	644	100	168	100	186	100	982	100
Drug-related homicide*	83	49	186	51	74	49	23	15.9	343	50
Psychopharmacological	83	100	44	24	66	89	21	91.3	*193*	*56*
Economic-compulsive	2	2	13	7	10	14	2	8.7	*25*	*7*
Systemic	11	13	116	63	22	30	4	17.4	*149*	*43*
Non-drug-related homicide	87	51	181	49	78	51	122	84.1	346	50
Total known	170	100	367	57	152	90	145	78	689	70
Unknown	0	0	277	43	16	10	41	22	293	30

Source: Schönberger, Liem, Kivivuori, Lehti, Granath, and Suonpää 2018; Markwalder, email to authors, December 2021.
*Because of the nonmutually exclusive nature of DRH categories, the percentages in italics do not add up to 100 percent.

cal, almost a third were also systemic (the types are not mutually exclusive). Similarly, in Switzerland, the overwhelming majority of DRH cases were psychopharmacological, while a handful were classified as systemic and only one case as economic compulsive. These variations can partly be explained by the countries' different positions in the drug market chain. For instance, the Netherlands is one of Europe's main producers of synthetic drugs and one of the most important transit points in the cocaine and heroin supply chain (EMCDDA and Europol 2016). Taking this into consideration, it is unsurprising that most of its DRH are systemic (Schönberger et al. 2019).

Looking at the characteristics of DRH at the case level, DRH in the Netherlands tended to occur in public spaces and were committed mostly with firearms. In the Nordic countries, most DRH occurred indoors, between intimate partners, friends, or acquaintances, and carried out with a knife (or sharp object). Similarly, in Switzerland, the large majority of DRH were committed using a knife, taking place in a private location. These differences reflect variations in type of DRH. Psychopharmacological cases (the majority in Finland, Sweden, and Switzerland), which involve individuals under the influence of drugs or alcohol, tended to occur indoors between intimate partners or people well known to each other. Systemic homicides, on the other hand, were usually linked to disputes within the drug markets and likely to involve organized crime. As such, data show that tend to occur outdoors, between young males, and with firearms (see table 11.2).

Use of the EHM is, however, not without limitations. First, the EHM relies on data collected from various sources, including police, media, court files, and other sources not intended for research purposes (Liem 2021). Thus, there is a risk of losing important information or interpreting information differently when translating sources into the EHM format. Partly as a result of this, the EHM tends toward a lowest common denominator (Liem 2021). A clear example is the category "other" as type of homicide—an important percentage of type of homicides appears as "other" in the EHM.

Finally, one of the strongest features of the EHM—the granularity of data and diverse range of sources it relies on—entails an important challenge: it is a lengthy and time-consuming effort. Recording information at the individual level requires going through different types of official documents, sometimes retroactively. This has been the case for many drug-related variables added more recently, such as relative to type of drug. For example, in Sweden, police usually carry out toxicology tests on homicide victims and on perpetrators when they are arrested in near time (Sven Granath, email to authors, November 2021). However, police do not register this information in a way that can be digitally merged into the EHM. Thus, in order to include such data into the EHM, researchers need to go through the court or investigation documents. This information, which may be available for psychopharmaco-

TABLE 11.2 DRUG-RELATED HOMICIDE INCIDENT, PERPETRATOR, AND VICTIM CHARACTERISTICS IN PARTICIPATING COUNTRIES

	Finland (2014–2015)		The Netherlands (2012–2016)		Sweden (2013–2014)		Switzerland (2010–2014)	
	Number (total=83)	%	*Number (total=186)*	%	*Number (total=74)*	%	*Number (total=23)*	%
Crime scene								
Private home	46	55	66	36	39	53	14	60.9
Public (or outdoor) area	20	24	104	56	33	44	6	26.1
Other	17	21	16	8	2	3	2	8.7
Unknown	0	—	0	—	0	—	1	4.3
Modus operandi								
Firearm	16	19	101	54	29	39	6	26.1
Knife or sharp weapon	32	39	47	25	31	42	14	60.9
Blunt object	8	10	7	4	4	5	1	4.3
Strangulation or suffocation	8	10	15	8	3	4	1	4.3
Hitting without weapon	13	15	9	5	6	9	0	0
Other	6	7	7	4	1	1	0	0
Unknown	0	—	0	—	0	—	1	4.3
Evidence of drug ingestion								
Victim only	14	17	—	—	21	28	0	0
Perpetrator only	25	29	—	—	11	15	9	39.1
Both	22	27	—	—	24	33	7	30.4
None	22	27	—	—	18	24	2	8.7
Unknown	0	—	—	—	0	—	5	21.7
Age of perpetrator (years)								
< 18	1	1	5	3	2	4	0	0
18–24	16	20	21	11	17	30	10	43.5
25–34	27	33	55	30	26	46	6	26.1
35–44	22	27	41	22	7	12	2	8.7
> 45	16	19	64	34	5	8	4	17.4
Unknown	1	—	0	—	17	—	1	4.3
Relationship between perpetrator and victim								
Family member	4	4	29	19	4	8	4	17.2

(continued)

TABLE 11.2 (continued)								
	Finland		The Netherlands		Sweden		Switzerland	
	(2014–2015)		(2012–2016)		(2013–2014)		(2010–2014)	
	Number (total=83)	%	Number (total=186)	%	Number (total=74)	%	Number (total=23)	%
(ex) intimate partner	12	15	36	24	5	10	4	17.4
Friend or acquaintance	36	44	44	29	32	64	7	30.4
Drug customer	0	0	3	2	0	0	1	4.3
Drug dealer	0	0	3	2	0	0	1	4.3
Other previously known	17	21	20	14	0	0	0	0
Stranger	13	16	14	10	9	18	4	17.4
Unknown	1	—	37	—	24	—	2	8.7
Victim's gender								
Female	13	16	35	19	9	12	5	21.7
Male	70	84	151	81	65	88	18	78.3
Age of victim (years)								
< 18	3	4	7	4	2	3	1	4.3
18–24	4	5	22	12	11	15	5	21.7
25–34	22	27	56	30	29	39	11	47.8
35–44	23	28	39	21	6	7	3	13
> 45	31	38	62	33	26	36	3	13
Unknown	0	—	0	—	0	—	0	—

logical DRH (as it implies the presence of a substance), is quite difficult to retrieve in the case of economic-compulsive or systemic DRH (for instance, in the robbery of a drug dealer). This difficulty is even more pronounced for multidimensional DRH (cases that can be classified as more than just one type) and in establishing and recording polydrug use.

Conclusion

The relationship between drugs and violence is supported by a wealth of existing scientific research. DRH constitutes a complex phenomenon, and its study presents many methodological challenges, mostly regarding the quality and availability of data. This makes analysis at the case, victim, and perpetrator level all but impossible and undermines the research enterprise.

Moving forward, certain challenges need to be addressed in order to improve our understanding of this phenomenon. First, it is important that information regarding the drug dimension of homicide cases is thoroughly and correctly registered by police and forensic authorities. This information should be registered following a series of simple, straightforward variables apt to capture the role of drugs in the homicide case. This process may require initial training and instructing effort that can be time consuming (and costly) but can greatly improve data gathering. Moreover, data should be made available for research purposes and presented and organized in a standardized way that allows for comparisons. Finally, data should be disaggregated so that analysis at the individual and case level can be carried out. In this sense, the EHM represents a solid model to guide registration and coding of DRH. Toxicology tests should be standardized and made publicly available. Moreover, they should include dosage and purity data, as well as measure the temporal proximity to the violent act to control for intoxication decay (Kuhns and Clodfelter 2009).

What should we, as a field, move toward? And what is necessary to advance our understanding of this multifaceted and complex phenomenon? The answer, we believe, is prioritizing the issue on multiple levels, strengthening the cooperation between researchers, practitioners, and policy makers. Efforts such as those by the NVDRS or the EHM show that there are concrete steps possible and feasible to improve the availability of data. More resources should be devoted to training those responsible for registering information of homicide cases, as well as to researchers dedicated to the analysis of this data; strengthened international coordination would allow for comparisons between countries and regions. These concrete actions would provide new possibilities for furthering research on DRH.

NOTE

1. With contributions from the European Homicide Monitor Network: Janne Kivivuori, Martti Lehti, Karoliina Suonpää, Nora Markwalder, and Sven Granath.

REFERENCES

Alda, Erik. 2017. "Drivers of Homicide in Latin America and the Caribbean: Does Relative Political Capacity Matter?" In *The Handbook of Homicide*, edited by Fiona Brookman, Edward R. Maguire, and Mike Maguire, 432–50. Hoboken, NJ: John Wiley & Sons.

Allison, Paul D. 2002. *Missing Data*. Thousand Oaks, CA: Sage.

Asnis, Stephen F., Roger C. Smith, and D. Crim. 1978. "Amphetamine Abuse and Violence." *Journal of Psychedelic Drugs* 10 (4): 371–77.

Bennet, Trevor, Katy Holloway, and David Farrington. 2008. "The Statistical Association between Drug Misuse and Crime: A Meta-Analysis." *Aggression and Violent Behavior* 13:107–18.

Blumstein, Alfred. 1995. "Youth Violence, Guns, and the Illicit-Drug Industry." *Journal of Criminal Law and Criminology* 86 (1): 10–36.

Blumstein, Alfred, and Richard Rosenfeld. 1998. "Explaining Recent Trends in US Homicide Rates." *Journal of Criminal Law and Criminology* 88 (4): 1175–216.

Braga, Anthony A., Brandon Turchan, and Lisa Barao. 2018. "The Influence of Investigative Resources on Homicide Clearances." *Journal of Quantitative Criminology* 35:337–64.

Brownstein, Henry H., Hari R. Shiledar Baxi, Paul J. Goldstein, and Patrick J. Ryan. 1992. "The Relationship of Drugs, Drug Trafficking, and Drug Traffickers to Homicide." *Journal of Crime and Justice* 15 (1): 25–44.

Caulkins, Jonathan P., and Mark A. R. Kleiman. 2011. "Drugs and Crime." In *The Oxford Handbook of Crime and Criminal Justice*, edited by Michael Tonry, 275–320. Oxford: Oxford University Press.

Chaiken, Jan M., and Marcia R. Chaiken. 1990. "Drugs and Predatory Crime." *Crime and Justice* 13:203–39.

Collins, James J. 1990. "Summary Thoughts about Drugs and Violence." In *Drugs and Violence: Causes, Correlates, and Consequences*, by M. De La Rosa, E. Lambert, and B. Gropper, 265–75. Rockville: U.S. Department of Health and Human Services.

Darke, Shane. 2010. "The Toxicology of Homicide Offenders and Victims: A Review." *Drug and Alcohol Review* 29:202–15.

De Bont, Roel, Teodora Groshkova, Andrew Cunningham, and Marieke Liem. 2018. "Drug-Related Homicide in Europe—First Review of Data and Sources." *International Journal of Drug Policy* 56:137–43.

Dell, Melissa. 2015. "Trafficking Networks and the Mexican Drug War." *American Economic Review* 105 (6): 1738–79.

De Mello, João. M. 2015. "Does Drug Illegality Beget Violence? Evidence from the Crack-Cocaine Wave in São Paulo." *Economía*, 157–85.

Dickinson, Timothy. 2015. "Exploring the Drugs/Violence Nexus among Active Offenders: Contributions from the St. Louis School." *Criminal Justice Review* 40 (1): 67–88.

Durán-Martínez, Angélica. 2015. "Drugs around the Corner: Domestic Drug Markets and Violence in Colombia and Mexico." *Latin American Politics and Society* 57 (3): 122–46.

———. 2017. *The Politics of Drug Violence: Criminals, Cops and Politicians in Colombia and Mexico*. Oxford: University Press.

EMCDDA. 2020. *Drug-Related Homicide in Europe: Data Protocol*. Technical Report. Luxembourg: Publications Office of the European Union.

EMCDDA and Europol. 2016. *EU Drug Markets Report: In-depth Analysis*. Accessed October 2021. http://www.emcdda.europa.eu/system/files/publications/2373/TD021607 2ENN.PDF.

Ertl, Allison, Kameron Sheats, Emiko Petrosky, Carter Betz, Keming Yuan, and Katherine Fowler. 2019. "Surveillance for Violent Deaths—National Violent Death Reporting System, 32 States, 2016." *MMWR Surveillance Summaries* 68 (9): 1–36.

European Commission. 2020. "Communication from the Commission to the European Parliament, the Council, the European Economic and Social Committee and the Committee of the Regions. EU Agenda and Action Plan on Drugs 2021–2025." July 24. Accessed 2021.

Fox, James Alan. 2004. "Missing Data Problems in the SHR." *Homicide Studies* 8 (3): 214–54.

Friman, Richard. 2009. "Drug Markets and the Selective Use of Violence." *Crime, Law and Social Change* 52:285–95.

Goldstein, Paul J. 1985. "The Drugs/Violence Nexus: A Tripartite Conceptual Framework." *Journal of Drug Issues* 15 (4): 493–506.

Goldstein, Paul J., Hery H. Brownstein, and Patrick J. Ryan. 1992. "Drug-Related Homicide in New York: 1984 and 1988." *Crime and Delinquency* 38 (4): 459–576.

Goldstein, Paul J., Henry H. Brownstein, Patrick J. Ryan, and Patricia A. Bellucci. 1989. "Crack and Homicide in New York City, 1988: A Conceptually Based Event Analysis." *Contemporary Drug Problems* 16 (4): 651–88.

Granath, S., M. R. Galanti, and C. Magnusson. 2022. *Inslag av cannabisbruk och cannabishantering vid dödligt våld i Stockholm och i Sverige [Cannabis-Related Homicide in Stockholm and Other Parts of Sweden 2008–2019]*. Stockholm: Centrum för epidemiologi och samhällsmedicin, Region Stockholm.

Granath, S., S. Ganpat, J. Hagstedt, J. Kivivuori, M. Lehti, M. Liem, et al. 2011. *Homicide in Finland, the Netherlands and Sweden: A First Study on the European Homicide Monitor Data*. Stockholm: Brå, Swedish National Council for Crime Prevention.

Groshkova, Teodora, Marieke Liem, Andrew Cunningham, Roumen Sedefov, and Paul Griffiths. 2021. "Drug-Related Violence: Will COVID-19 Drive Better Data for Safer and More Secure EU?" *International Journal of Drug Policy* 93 (July): 103143.

Haggård-Grann, Ulrika, Johan Hallqvist, Niklas Langstrom, and Jette Moller. 2006. "The Role of Alcohol and Drugs in Triggering Criminal Violence: A Case Cross-Over Study." *Addict* 101:100–108.

Inciardi, James A. 1990. "The Crack-Violence Connection within a Population of Hard-Core Adolescent Offenders." In *Drugs and Violence: Causes, Correlates, and Consequences*, edited by Mario De La Rosa, Elizabeth Lambert, and Bernard Gropper. Rockville: U.S. Department of Health and Human Services.

Johson, Bruce D., Andrew Golub, and Jeffrey Fagan. 1995. "Careers in Crack, Drug Use, Drug Distribution and Nondrug Criminality." *Crime and Delinquency* 41 (3): 275–95.

Kuhns, Joseph, and Tammatha Clodfelter. 2009. "Illicit Drug Related Psychopharmacological Violence: The Current Understanding within a Causal Context." *Aggression and Violent Behavior* 14 (1): 69–78.

Kuhns, Joseph, M. Lyn Exum, Tammatha Clodfelter, and Martha Bottia. 2014. "The Prevalence of Alcohol Involved Homicide Offending: A Meta-analytic Review." *Homicide Studies* 18 (3): 251–70.

Kuypers, K., R. Verkes, W. van den Brink, J. Arnsterdam, and J. Ramaekers. 2020. "Intoxicated Aggression: Do Alcohol and Stimulants Cause Dose-Related Aggression? A Review." *European Neuropsychopharmacology* 30:114–47.

Lappi-Seppälä, Tapio, and Martti Lehti. 2014. "Cross-Comparative Perspectives on Global Homicide Trends." *Crime and Justice* 43 (1): 135–230.

Liem, Marieke. 2017. "Homicide in Europe." In *Handbook on Homicide*, edited by Fiona Brookman, Edward Maguire, and Mike Maguire, 289–307. Chichester: Wiley.

———. 2021. "Balkanisation in European Homicide Research." In *Violence in the Balkans*, edited by Anna-Maria Getoš Kalac, 11–22. Cham, Switzerland: Springer.

Liem, Marieke C., Karoliina Suonpää, Martti Lehti, Janne Kivivuori, Sven Granath, Simone Walser, and Martin Killias. 2019. "Homicide Clearance in Western Europe." *European Journal of Criminology* 16 (1): 81–101.

Lindqvist, Per. 1991. "Homicides Committed by Abusers of Alcohol and Illicit Drugs." *British Journal of Addiction* 86:321–26.

Moeller, Kim, and Morten Hesse. 2013. "Drug Market Disruption and Systemic Violence: Cannabis Markets in Copenhagen." *European Journal of Criminology* 10 (2): 206–21.

Molzahn, Cory, Viridiana Rios, and David A. Shirk. 2012. *Drug Violence in Mexico: Data and Analysis Through 2011*. Special Report. San Diego: Trans-Border Institute, Joan B. Kroc School of Peace Studies.

Monteforte, J. R., and W. U. Spitz. 1975. "Narcotic Abuse among Homicides in Detroit." *Journal of Forensic Sciences* 20:186–90.

Nash Parker, Robert, and Kathleen Auerhahn. 1998. "Alcohol, Drugs, and Violence." *Annual Review of Sociology* 24:291–311.

Niveau, Gérard, and Cécile Dang. 2003. "Cannabis and Violent Crime." *Medicine, Science and the Law* 4 (2): 115–21.

Norström, Thor, and Ingeborg Rossow. 2014. "Cannabis Use and Violence: Is There a Link?" *Scandinavian Journal of Public Health* 42 (4): 358–63.

Ousey, Graham, and Matthew Lee. 2002. "Examining the Conditional Nature of the Illicit Drug Market-Homicide Relationship: A Partial Test of the Theory of Contingent Causation." *Criminology* 40 (1): 73–102.

——. 2007. "Homicide Trends and Illicit Drug Markets: Exploring Differences across Time." *Justice Quarterly* 24 (1): 48–79.

Portella, Daniel D. A., Edna M. D. de Araújo, Nelson F. de Oliveira, Joselisa M. Chaves, Washington J. S. da Franca Rocha, and Dayse D. Oliveira. 2019. "Intentional Homicide, Drug Trafficking and Social Indicators in Salvador, Bahia, Brazil." *Ciencia and Saude Coletiva* 24:631–39.

Pridemore, William. 2002. "Vodka and Violence: Alcohol Consumption and Homicide Rates in Russia." *American Journal of Public Health* 92 (12): 1921–30.

Reuter, Peter. 2009. "Systemic Violence in Drug Markets." *Crime Law Soc Change* 52:275–84.

Riedel, Marc, and Wendy Regoeczi. 2004. "Missing Data in Homicide Research." *Homicide Studies* 8 (3): 163–92.

Schönberger, H., M. Liem, J. Kivivuori, M. Lehti, S. Granath, and K. Suonpää. 2019. *Drug-Related Homicide in Europe: A Pilot Study*. Lisbon: EMCDDA Papers.

Shaw, Jenny, Isabelle Hunt, Sandra Flynn, et al. 2006. "The Role of Alcohol and Drugs in Homicides in England and Wales." *Addiction* 101 (8): 1117–24.

Smit, Paul, Rinke de Jong, and Catrien C. J. Bijleveld. 2012. "Homicide Data in Europe: Definitions, Sources, and Statistics." In *Handbook of European Homicide Research*, edited by Marieke Liem and William Pridemore, 5–23. New York: Springer.

Snyder, Richard, and Angélica Durán-Martínez. 2009. "Drugs, Violence, and State-Sponsored Protection Rackets in Mexico and Colombia." *Colombia Internacional* 70:61–91.

Tiihonen, J., M-R. Rautiainen, H. M. Ollila, E. Repo-Tiihonen, M. Virkkunen, A. Palotie, O. Pietiläinen et al. "Genetic Background of Extreme Violent Behavior." *Molecular Psychiatry* 20:786–92.

Van Amsterdam, Jan G. C., Johannes G. Ramaekers, Robbert-Jan Verkes, Kim P. C. Kuypers, Anne Goudriaan, and Wim van den Brink. 2020. "Alcohol- and Drug-Related Public Violence in Europe." *European Journal of Criminology* 17 (6): 806–25.

Varano, Sean P., and Joseph B. Kuhns. 2017. "Drug-Related Homicide." In *The Handbook of Homicide*, by Fiona Brookman, Edward Maguire, and Mike Maguire, 89–104. John Wiley & Sons.

Varano, Sean P., John McCluskey, Justin W. Patchin, and Timothy S. Bynum. 2004. "Exploring the Drug-Homicide Connection." *Journal of Contemporary Criminal Justice* 20 (4): 369–92.

Wellford., C., and J. Cronin. 1999. *An Analysis of Variables Affecting the Clearance of Homicides: A Multistate Study*. Washington, DC: Justice Research and Statistics Association.

Zahn, Margaret, and M. Bencivengo. 1974. "Violent Death: A Comparison between Drug Users and Nondrug Users." *Addictive Diseases* 1:283–96.

12

Firearms and Homicide

ELIZABETH GRIFFITHS AND DANIEL SEMENZA

Introduction

In 2019, three-quarters of all homicides in the United States were carried out with a firearm (see fig. 12.1). As such, homicide research is effectively gun research. Yet despite all we know about victims, offenders, circumstances, community conditions, motivations, types, and locations of homicides in America, perhaps the most common factor among lethal violence incidents—the use of a gun—is the most methodologically and ideologically fraught for researchers. This reality is, in part, because firearm ownership is specifically protected under the Bill of Rights, and thus regulation and oversight of gun purchase, ownership, and transfer in the form of robust gun control is a political quagmire. The methodological problems that researchers face in studying gun violence are therefore inexorably bound to the cultural and legal context of the United States.

This chapter explores the methodological challenges of researching gun violence in the United States, fatal shootings specifically, across three domains: (1) mesolevel or community-based research on gun availability and associated rates of gun violence; (2) the instrumentality or lethality of guns in violent situations vis-à-vis the intentions of offenders; and (3) the role of forensic science in solving cases and linking guns to specific shooters. We evaluate each of these domains in turn, with an eye toward existing methodological dilemmas and potential solutions for scholars studying gun homicide. As suggested by President Biden in April of 2021 as he unveiled his executive

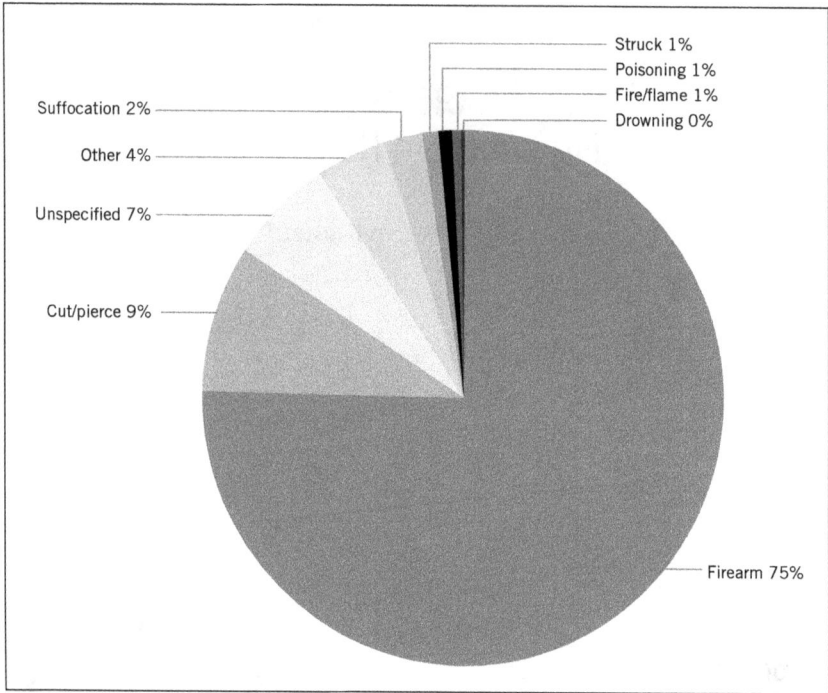

Figure 12.1 Proportion of U.S. Homicides by Weapon Type, 2019 (*Source: NCHS Vital Statistics System for numbers of deaths. Bureau of Census for population estimates. https://wisqars-viz.cdc.gov:8006/explore-data/home. Accessed April 7, 2021.*)

actions on firearms, gun violence is an American epidemic and an "international embarrassment" that must be stemmed by good policy. Strong policies are evidence based, yet gun violence researchers are handcuffed by a variety of impediments, primarily to data collection, that hinder comprehensive study. We outline a number of challenges and suggestions for change to advance research on firearm homicide in America.

Does the Availability of Firearms Elevate Homicide?

One long-standing challenge in studying firearm homicide is determining whether and how access to firearms influences rates of fatal violence across time and place. This issue has been the focus of substantial criminological research since the late 1970s (Cook 1979) and has garnered close attention among public health and injury epidemiologists since the early 1990s (Azrael et al. 2004; Hepburn and Hemenway 2004; Kellerman et al. 1993). Three key methodological concerns are paramount: (1) data availability; (2) prevalence measurement; and (3) available scale of analysis across social ecology and over time.

Data on Gun Ownership and Firearm Availability

The United States has uniquely high rates of both firearm ownership and homicide compared to peer industrialized nations. Recent estimates suggest there are almost four hundred million guns in circulation in the United States, comprising roughly half of the world's gun stock despite the United States only making up about 4 percent of the global population (Karp 2018). The United States also has high rates of homicide compared to similarly developed nations (UNODC 2019). Given these two notable distinctions, researchers have logically surmised that firearm prevalence and homicide are related. Greater firearm ownership in the general population should make it easier for potential criminals to acquire firearms, and the use of firearms in violent situations leads to a greater number of fatalities (Cook 1979; McDowall 1991). Others scholars, however, have claimed that firearm prevalence may actually reduce homicide incidents by encouraging defensive uses to stop fatal attacks (Cook, Ludwig, and Hemenway 1997; Kleck 2021). Tests of these competing assertions generally find that firearm availability increases homicide risk (Hemenway and Miller 2000; Hepburn and Hemenway 2004), although some find no statistically significant relationship (Kates and Polsby 2000) or a negative relationship (Lott 2013). The most scientifically rigorous research, however, shows that firearm prevalence is associated with an increase in homicides (Cook, Ludwig, and Hemenway 1997; Hemenway and Azrael 2000). A key reason for the discrepancy among these findings is lack of appropriate data.

In the United States, there has never been a systematic form of record-keeping to track firearm registration or ownership. Most states do not systematically document who purchases a firearm and how the firearm is transacted. Without systematic tracking, it is difficult to quantify and trace firearms in the United States, and even broad national estimates come with a high degree of uncertainty (Karp 2018). Thus, the basic questions of how many guns exist in the United States and who owns them cannot be answered through administrative registration data. In the absence of a national registration system, researchers have attempted to leverage survey data to establish rough estimates of the general firearm stock in the country. With a few exceptions, such as the General Social Survey (Smith and Son 2019) and the National Firearm Survey (Azrael et al. 2017), most assessments are not nationally representative or do not provide adequate information to estimate ownership in smaller areas such as counties, cities, or census tracts. Even the results of nationally representative surveys must be considered with significant caveats given the likelihood of under- or overreporting among respondents (Azrael et al. 2017).

In lieu of a national registry or consistent, nationally representative survey, firearm tracking and tracing has fallen under the purview of the Bureau of Alcohol, Tobacco, Firearms, and Explosives (ATF). However, guns are not required to be registered with the ATF unless they are subject to the National Firearms Act (weapons and accessories subject to this legislation include machine guns, short-barreled rifles, and silencers). And firearms are only traced by the ATF at the request of law enforcement agencies (Cook and Braga 2001). Proper tracing is complicated by the fact that although firearms start out as legally manufactured or imported and are introduced into the primary market by federally licensed dealers (Azrael et al. 2017), they are often exchanged through informal private sales, theft, borrowing, gifts, or inheritance. Thus, a clear understanding of not only how many firearms are in the country but exactly who has them in their possession at any given time remains elusive for researchers and law enforcement practitioners.

Measurement Challenges

As a result of data deficiencies, researchers are forced to construct proxy measurements for the prevalence of firearm ownership and availability. Studies have proposed an array of measures to approximate firearm availability both within the United States and around the world (Kleck 2004; Azrael, Cook, and Miller 2004), including the proportion of suicides carried out with a firearm (FS/S) (Cook 1979; McDowall 1991), survey estimates (Miller, Azrael, and Hemenway 2002), concentration of federally licensed firearm dealers (FFLs) (Haviland et al. 2021; Semenza, Stansfield, and Link 2020; Stansfield, Semenza, and Steidley 2021; Steidley, Ramey, and Shrider 2017), and subscription rates to the magazine *Guns & Ammo* (Duggan 2001). The proportion of suicides committed with a firearm (FS/S) is generally recognized as the best proxy for measuring firearm availability in the absence of direct or survey-based measures, though it depends on the level of analysis in question (Azrael, Cook, and Miller 2004; Haviland et al. 2021; Kleck 2004).

More recently, researchers have attempted to account for both legal and illegal firearm availability to examine variation in homicide rates, since most states do not require permits to purchase or own firearms (Stansfield, Semenza, and Steidley 2021). As such, solely focusing on registered firearms acquired legally is a poor means of estimating total availability (Yu, Lee, and Pizarro 2020). In attempting to disaggregate the availability of legal and illegal firearms, researchers have used illegal proxies such as the number of guns reported stolen by the police (Dierenfeldt, Brown, and Roles 2017; Stolzenberg and D'Alessio 2000) or the total number of firearms recovered by the police

(Yu, Lee, and Pizarro 2020). Proxies like the proportion of suicides with a firearm cannot distinguish the legality of firearms, yet this distinction is critical, as legal and illicit gun markets operate differently and violent offenders typically obtain guns through illegal private transactions (Cook 2018; Cook et al. 2007). Clearly, measuring firearm prevalence to analyze the influence of gun availability on homicide remains an imperfect science.

Scale of Analysis and Lack of Longitudinal Data

A final methodological concern related to gun prevalence and homicide pertains to the scale and temporal nature of analysis. In public health scholarship, researchers have established a robust relationship between firearm ownership in the home and risk of homicide (Anglemeyer, Horvath, and Rutherford 2014; Kellerman et al. 1993). Others have identified a relationship between firearm availability and homicide at broader levels of the social ecology, such as nations, states, cities, and counties (Hemenway and Miller 2000; Hepburn and Hemenway 2004; Zimmerman and Fridel 2020). It can be reasonably concluded that firearm prevalence at both the micro- and macrolevel increases the risk of homicide. However, nationally representative estimates of firearm prevalence do not typically provide detail on firearm ownership at key mesolevels of the social ecology, such as neighborhoods or city blocks. Data and research on firearm availability consequently focus on micro- (e.g., household) and macrolevel (e.g., city or higher) estimates of prevalence without sufficient attention to midrange tiers of ecological analysis.

The issue of mesolevel analysis extends beyond firearm availability and affects the study of homicide more broadly in the United States. Presently, the definitive source of homicide data is the FBI's Uniform Crime Report (UCR), which tracks crime data from individual police agencies across the country. However, these data are aggregated up to the level of jurisdiction for policing agencies without geographical coding within the city, making it impossible to establish small-area estimates for homicide rates in neighborhoods (Fay and Diallo 2012). Although national, state, and city-level estimates of firearm prevalence and homicide rates contribute to a better collective understanding of the availability-homicide link, homicide varies considerably across neighborhoods, and crime reduction programs are most effectively carried out within local jurisdictions. Homicides cluster in particular communities and hot spots (Braga et al. 2019; Griffiths and Chavez 2004), diffuse throughout local neighborhood networks (Papachristos, Braga, and Hureau 2012), and disproportionately affect disadvantaged communities of color (Papachristos and Wildeman 2014). Given this reality, estimating firearm availability in conjunction with homicide rates at state, county, or city levels obscures important neighborhood variation that drives vastly disparate community experiences of fatal violence.

A handful of studies have attempted to account for this gap in understanding by establishing neighborhood-level proxies for firearm prevalence and homicide. Studies in cities like Newark and Detroit have examined how firearm availability in a given locale corresponds to homicide rates in that area (McDowall 1991). Yu and colleagues (2020), for example, have found that local-level estimates of illegal firearm availability correspond to higher rates of homicide in Newark neighborhoods. Nevertheless, there remains no systematic way to track firearm availability (legal or illicit) in neighborhoods in a nationally representative manner. Even the most validated proxy of firearm prevalence, FS/S, is not available at the neighborhood-level because data on suicide in the United States are aggregated by county (National Center for Health Statistics 2011). Despite critical efforts of past researchers to generate small-area homicide estimates at a given point in time for a representative sample of U.S. cities (Peterson and Krivo 2010), neighborhood-level homicide rates are not collected for the entire country at regular intervals and must therefore be obtained on an ad hoc basis for specific jurisdictions with the beneficence of local police departments.

Finally, much of the research on the relationship between firearm availability and homicide has relied on cross-sectional data (Hepburn and Hemenway 2004). Lack of data uniformity and availability over time compounds difficulties in establishing a longitudinal relationship between firearm prevalence and homicide at any level of the social ecology, rendering it difficult to specify causal mechanisms—even though the main association appears robust across studies (Cook 2018). This difficulty may be particularly important because, as Kleck (2021) notes, cross-sectional studies cannot distinguish the effect of gun availability on violence from the effect of violence on gun acquisition. As such, there remains little consensus on how firearm prevalence affects rates of homicide over time at most ecological levels of analysis, with the greatest dearth of understanding at the meso- or neighborhood level.

Do Offenders Who Attack with Guns Intend for the Victim to Die?

One central philosophical dilemma that animates the gun availability–homicide debate is the question of instrumentality (Braga and Cook 2018; Braga et al. 2021; Zimring 1968; 1972). Lethal violence may be higher in the United States because homicide offenders have greater access to guns, making killing easier, or because there is some cultural difference that encourages lethal violence here and not elsewhere. In the latter case, homicides committed by guns would be homicides committed by other means in the absence of widespread firearm availability. The instrumentality question centers, then, on the extent to which homicide might be significantly reduced if the most lethal of weapons—guns—were less available. This debate is of central importance to researchers who study the link between guns and homicide primarily because it speaks to intent to kill. In this section, we briefly outline the instrumentality argument before considering whether and how researchers might directly measure offender intentions.

Instrumentality: The Lethality of Firearms

Research on the instrumentality of firearms grows from Zimring's (1968; 1972) seminal work, in which he argues that guns independently contribute to fatalities by virtue of their lethality. Said differently, the dangerousness of the weapon makes what would be nonfatal violent encounters fatal. The motivation for lethal violence in at least some homicides, he argues, is ambiguous rather than "deliberate and determined," and "if the probable substitute for firearms in these situations is less likely to lead to death, then the elimination of guns would reduce the number of homicides" (Zimring 1968, 722). Homicide incidents that would otherwise be assaults result in death due to the ease and distance by which shooters can cause fatal injury. To reach these conclusions, Zimring (1968; 1972) shows that homicides are overwhelmingly (70 percent) a consequence of a single gunshot wound rather than many and that more than half (54 percent) involve drinking by the victim, the offender, or both in advance of the attack. Taken together, this suggests an impulsivity in the act and a lack of intention to ensure that the victim dies. There is little to suggest that gun homicides markedly differ from either gun assaults or homicides carried out with other weapons.

One might assume that death is intended in interpersonal attacks carried out with a gun rather than a less-lethal weapon, but empirical evidence suggests that wounds in shootings are actually more likely to be located on nonvital areas of the body, such as the extremities, compared to attacks with knives or other weapons (Zimring 1968). Likewise, Braga and Cook (2018) find that features of shootings involving medium and large-caliber guns are virtually indistinguishable from features of shootings involving small-caliber guns—save for the number of fatalities. This lends support for the notion that it is not offenders determined to kill who select more lethal firearms; instead, offenders who shoot victims with larger caliber guns are more likely to fatally injure their opponents than shooters who attack with smaller caliber guns. While scholars might have reached convincing conclusions that the lethality of the weapon, or its instrumentality, is a major factor contributing to elevated rates of homicide (Braga et al. 2021), these conclusions are not based on direct evidence about motivation to kill as articulated by offenders themselves.

Measuring Fatal Intentions

Psychological, symbolic interactionist, and phenomenological traditions might be especially valuable for estimating offender intentionality in fatal and non-fatal attacks with a gun (Collins 2008; Katz 1988). Purposefully measuring intent can help answer various questions: Can the attacker's aim or motivation at the time of the offense be discerned? How driven is the attacker to injure or kill? Recent evidence suggests that roughly two-thirds of victims of intimate partner violence experience routine displays of firearms and threats of their use during incidents of domestic violence (Adhia et al. 2021), contributing to the notion that guns may be employed for a variety of outcomes, only some of which are fatal. Likewise, robberies are both less likely to lead to any injury and more likely to lead to death when committed with a gun than any other weapon (Cook 1987). Brandishing guns can have the effect of reducing resistance and thus injury during robberies through the elevated threat of death alone. Therefore, intent to kill (or injure) cannot be discerned primarily as a function of weapon choice.

There are no existing data repositories from which researchers can directly identify and catalog intent to kill during violent interactions, either in small research settings or in any nationally representative way (but see Collins 2008; Luckenbill 1977). As a result, scholars have had to be creative in comparing events that end in homicide from violent events that do not to estimate intent. Naturalistic observation would be ideal, but this data collection task is nearly impossible for homicide researchers given homicides rarity and the extent to which fatal violence happens in private settings (Graham et al. 2006). It has recently been made slightly easier by the greater number of violent incidents being caught on camera, either through CCTV on the street or with the private cell phones of people on the scene when violence erupts (Collins 2008).

In a careful review of the literature, we identified only one study in which the authors used systematic social observation to measure variability in intent to injure and severity of harm in aggressive acts, in this case carried out by patrons in barroom settings (Graham et al. 2006). In the study, Graham and colleagues (2006) observed 1,052 incidents in which 1,754 patrons engaged in some form of aggression toward others across 118 bars and clubs in Toronto, Ontario. Acts of aggression ranged from very minor expressions of anger or disapproval to more serious physical aggression, like punching or kicking. Despite their efforts to ascertain intent to injure in these interactions, the authors note that more work is needed as "it is the context, intent, and level of force that give the act meaning" (Graham et al. 2006, 292).

Retrospective interviews and, to a lesser extent, surveys or criminal case files may provide another source of data on actors' intentions to injure when they commit violence (Felson, Ribner, and Siegel 1984; Graham et al. 2006).

Aside from the retrospective and social desirability response biases (Poltavski et al. 2018) that may color respondents' perceptions of their intentions at an earlier time, Chapman (2001) showcases the problem of measurement effects in assessing intent, including measurement reactivity and self-generated validity (Feldman and Lynch 1988). Even if researchers could trust that social desirability and response biases (particularly for those in prison) are not corrupting the data, asking people to retrospectively distinguish intentions from goals and realized outcomes may lead to a reinterpretation of the meaning of their actions at the time of the offense (Chapman 2001). Directly measuring intent to kill should be a focus of future research on gun violence, even if it involves difficult or novel data collection efforts.

Why Should Firearms-Related Forensics be a Focus of Homicide Researchers?

As media attention to the global COVID-19 pandemic began to wane, reports of public mass shootings reemerged in the United States. These incidents of violence provide fodder for gun control advocates in public policy debates, often focusing on a wide range of issues including reducing access to firearms, requiring stronger background checks, enlarging the list of exclusionary criteria for gun ownership, emphasizing firearm accessories such as bump stocks or silencers, and raising awareness of technological innovations and modifications that make it harder to trace firearms (e.g., ghost guns or 3D-printed firearms). Scholarship on gun homicide has historically focused on issues of access, prevalence, and lethal intent to the exclusion of critically evaluating the role of firearms-related forensic evidence in solving cases and its reliability in identifying perpetrators. Homicide researchers have tended to treat forensic science as the purview of natural scientists or law enforcement. Yet the oversized role of forensics in indicating guilt in criminal trials suggests that gun violence researchers might contribute to debates about the value and drawbacks of various types of forensics for criminal case processing.

Evaluating the Production of Evidence

According to popular logic, prosecutors prefer and juries increasingly demand forensic evidence in criminal cases to secure convictions. Despite the fact that witness testimony constitutes the bulk of direct evidence in criminal trials, it is science—or evidence that has the aura of science—in which factfinders feel the most confident (Ling, Kaplan, and Berryessa 2021; Nir and Griffiths 2018). Scientific evidence is viewed as much more credible and less fallible than other types of evidence in trials, yet this credibility may be oversold (Cole 2010). One standard phrase used by forensic experts in court, for example, is that their findings are accurate to "a reasonable degree of scientific certainty" (Epstein 2018). Such terminology has been soundly criticized by the National Commission on Forensic Science (2016), which holds that

> Such statements have no scientific meaning and may mislead factfinders when deciding whether guilt has been proved beyond a reasonable doubt. Outside of the courts, this phrasing is not routinely used in scientific disciplines. In the courtroom setting, the phrase's reference to "certainty" risks misleading or confusing the factfinder.

Another concern is the size and scope of the evidentiary packet, which is central to criminal trials. Cooney (1994) has argued that—contrary to the notion that there is a quantifiable amount of existing evidence in criminal cases that law enforcement merely identifies, collects, and documents—the amount and types of evidence marshaled in certain kinds of criminal cases varies by the social status characteristics of victims and offenders. More serious offenses result in pressure on law enforcement to investigate, locate, and produce incriminating evidence. Homicide investigations thus receive greater attention in terms of time, effort, and resources by police than other types of offenses, including nonfatal gun assaults (Cook et al. 2019). Cook and colleagues (2019) show that clearance rates for gun homicides (43 percent) are more than twice as high as for nonlethal gun assaults (19 percent)—a discrepancy that emerges more than two days into the investigation. They note that the extra time and resources that detectives direct at gun homicides versus nonfatal shootings result in a greater quantity of evidence collected at the crime scene and beyond, including call records, latent prints, and ballistics reports, in the days or weeks that follow the event (Cook et al. 2019). Police effort and forensic advances are thus important avenues for clearing homicides; as such, the reliability of firearms forensics is germane not only for forensic experts but also for social scientists who study gun homicide.

Evaluating the Effectiveness of Firearm Forensic Sciences

The National Academy of Sciences (National Research Council 2009, 4) produced a comprehensive report on forensic science in the United States and called attention to the fact that

> Many crimes that may have gone unsolved are now being solved because forensic science is helping to identify the perpetrators. Those advances, however, also have revealed that, in some cases, substan-

tive information and testimony based on faulty forensic science analyses may have contributed to wrongful convictions of innocent people. This fact has demonstrated the potential danger of giving undue weight to evidence and testimony derived from imperfect testing and analysis. Moreover, imprecise or exaggerated expert testimony has sometimes contributed to the admission of erroneous or misleading evidence.

This assertion is particularly fitting for some of the various types of forensic examination of firearms, including compositional analysis of bullet lead, toolmark and pattern matching, distance estimates, weapon operability, and gunshot residue tests.

Firearm examination is among the most common services of crime laboratories (National Research Council 2009), and while some methods stand on highly questionable scientific foundations, each has contributed to numerous convictions. For example, in cases where a bullet was found at a scene but was too mangled or fragmented to conduct striation matching, the FBI, for more than three decades, conducted compositional analyses of bullet lead. In essence, if the chemical compounds identified in the crime-scene bullet "sufficiently" matched the chemical composition of ammunition found in the possession of the accused, forensic scientists would testify in court that the bullet at the scene likely came from the same source (National Research Council 2004). To jurors, this was damning evidence. Unfortunately, there is little empirical basis to substantiate this methodology in the scientific literature, a great deal of subjectivity in examiners' conclusions, and too incomplete a database on the elemental compositions of ammunition to ascertain how probative an apparent match actually is in linking a suspect to a crime scene.

One of the most problematic aspects of many forensic sciences is that they grew not from scientific enterprises outside of law enforcement but from heuristic hunches about how to match individuals to objects found at crime scenes—what Saks and Koehler (2005) call the "individualization sciences." Ballistics testimony generally relies on toolmark identification, whether striations on bullets from a gun barrel or markings on cartridge cases left by firing pins (National Research Council 2009). Advocates claim that when there is no discernible difference in patterns, the gun in question must have been the weapon used in the offense. But these and other individuation sciences rely on an "assumption of discernible uniqueness," stipulating that "two indistinguishable marks must have been produced by a single object . . . to the exclusion of all others in the world" (Saks and Koehler 2005, 892). There is no estimation of error rates, attention to protocols for proficiency testing of technicians, or recognition about the probabilistic nature or subjectivity of a match (National Research Council 2008). Instead, jurors are led to believe that the evidence definitively links the defendant to the crime; it is treated as persuasive evidence of guilt.

We underscore the pitfalls of and overreliance on firearm forensic science in homicide cases to illustrate a significant blind spot in social scientific research on gun violence. Legal scholars, medical examiners, and forensic technicians all have seats at the table for discussions about reliability, best practices, and scientific standards of firearm forensics. Given the proportion of homicides involving guns, it is time for social scientists and gun violence scholars in particular to wade into the debate about the oversized confidence in and reliance on certain types of firearm forensics in criminal case processing (for an exception, see National Research Council 2008). In many ways, high-quality social science is a key mechanism of accountability for the function (and dysfunction) of the criminal justice system. This effort is equally important for the use of forensic evidence in firearm homicide cases.

Recommendations for Improving Research on Firearm Homicide

In this chapter, we examined a series of big-picture questions about the state of research on firearms and gun homicide. Methodological issues such as measuring the prevalence of firearms at various ecological scales and over time as well as estimating instrumentality separately from intent to injure are long-standing concerns of homicide researchers (Cook 1979; Cook, Ludwig, and Hemenway 1997; McDowall 1991; Zimring 1968; 1972). The data availability and measurement issues noted point to a clear need for a comprehensive registration system for firearms in the United States. However, political interests, lobbying from firearms groups such as the National Rifle Association (NRA), and financial barriers have precluded the establishment of this kind of database despite the fact that a national registry would offer a key source of data for researchers and could reduce gun-related deaths (Chapman and Alpers 2013). In 2020, National Opinion Research Center (NORC) at the University of Chicago provided guidelines for establishing an improved firearms data infrastructure (Roman 2020). One key recommendation was the development of a semiannual random household survey of American firearm ownership to measure firearm ownership, carriage, risk perception, and access to firearms. Investment in a regular, nationally representative survey would vastly improve issues of data availability and measurement for firearm prevalence, even if a national registration system is not financially or politically feasible.

Homicide researchers have made impressive strides in investigating the types, locations, and circumstances of violent incidents, but one central question that remains under debate is whether the United States has dramatically higher rates of fatal violence compared to peer industrialized nations because America has more guns (Braga et al. 2021). Future data collection efforts should center on establishing intent to harm more directly via retrospective interviews, systematic social observations, or video recordings of lethal violence. Intention is, after all, the other half of the instrumentality debate.

Finally, social scientists have paid little attention to an equally important aspect of homicide investigations: forensic evidence. In general, homicide scholars need to take a critical look at how forensic scientists link people to specific guns and the degree to which they can do so accurately (Saks and Koehler 2005). A small but growing body of research highlights the necessity of exploring biases in forensic testing (Dror and Charlton 2006), differentials in the selection of forensic evidence for testing by law enforcement (Cowan and Koppl 2010), comparison database size and comprehensiveness (De Ceuster and Dujardin 2015), and related statistical and ethical issues (Cole 2010). Not surprisingly, in a recent report by former President Obama's Council of Advisors on Science and Technology, the assembled expert committee determined that "insufficient studies exist with the required quality and quantity to provide sufficient foundational validity or to estimate the reliability of [firearm examination] method[s] as applied" (Mattijssen 2020, 389).

A perhaps unsatisfactory but nonetheless unifying theme of this chapter, then, is a call for new and better data collection efforts to answer some of the most pressing questions of scholars who study homicides involving guns. Fortunately, the current political climate and President Biden's recent announcement of major funding directed at community gun violence intervention and reduction strategies may encourage homicide scholars to embark on efforts to collect reliable national estimates of gun availability, design studies that more directly operationalize intent to kill, and delve into areas of research related to homicide investigation and prosecution, including the forensic sciences. Heretofore, such research has largely been left to fields outside of the social sciences, such as law enforcement, legal scholars, and forensic scientists themselves. Allowing the discussion to be framed by those most directly involved in the criminal justice system can curb critical examination. Greater attention to the issues raised in this chapter may lead to the development of empirically based social policies that can be leveraged to stem America's gun violence epidemic.

REFERENCES

Adhia, Avanti, Vivian H. Lyons, Caitlin A. Moe, Ali Rowhani-Rahbar, and Frederick P. Rivara. 2021. "Nonfatal Use of Firearms in Intimate Partner Violence: Results of a National Survey." *Preventive Medicine* 147 (June): 1–7.

Anglemyer, Andrew, Tara Horvath, and George Rutherford. 2014. "The Accessibility of Firearms and Risk for Suicide and Homicide Victimization among Household Members: A Systematic Review and Meta-Analysis." *Annals of Internal Medicine* 160 (2): 101–10.

Azrael, Deborah, Philip J. Cook, and Matthew Miller. 2004. "State and Local Prevalence of Firearms Ownership Measurement, Structure, and Trends." *Journal of Quantitative Criminology* 20 (1): 43–62.

Azrael, Deborah, Lisa Hepburn, David Hemenway, and Matthew Miller. 2017. "The Stock and Flow of U.S. Firearms: Results from the 2015 National Firearms Survey." *RSF: The Russell Sage Foundation Journal of the Social Sciences* 3 (5): 38–57.

Braga, Anthony A., and Philip J. Cook. 2018. "The Association of Firearm Caliber with Likelihood of Death from Gunshot Injury in Criminal Assaults." *JAMA Network Open* 1 (3): e180833.

Braga, Anthony A., Elizabeth Griffiths, Keller Sheppard, and Stephen Douglas. 2021. "Firearm Instrumentality: Do Guns Make Violent Situations More Lethal?" *Annual Review of Criminology* 4:147–64.

Braga, Anthony A., Brandon Turchan, Andrew V. Papachristos, and David M. Hureau. 2019. "Hot Spots Policing of Small Geographic Areas Effects on Crime." *Campbell Systematic Reviews* 15 (3): e1046.

Chapman, Kenneth J. 2001. "Measuring Intent: There's Nothing 'Mere' about Mere Measurement Effects." *Psychology & Marketing* 18 (8): 811–41.

Chapman, Simon, and Philip Alpers. 2013. "Gun-Related Deaths: How Australia Stepped off 'The American Path.'" *Annals of Internal Medicine* 158 (10): 770–71.

Cole, Simon A. 2010. "Forensic Identification Evidence: Utility without Infallibility." *Criminology & Public Policy* 9 (2): 375–79.

Collins, Randall. 2008. *Violence: A Micro-sociological Theory*. Princeton, NJ: Princeton University Press.

Cook, Philip J. 1979. "The Effect of Gun Availability on Robbery and Robbery Murder." *Policy Studies Review Annual* 3:743–81.

———. 1987. "Robbery Violence." *Journal of Criminal Law and Criminology* 78 (2): 357–76.

———. 2018. "Gun Markets." *Annual Review of Criminology* 1:359–77.

Cook, Philip J., and Anthony A. Braga. 2001. "Comprehensive Firearms Tracing: Strategic and Investigative Uses of New Data on Firearms Markets." *Arizona Law Review* 43:277–309.

Cook, Philip J., Anthony A. Braga, Brandon S. Turchan, and Lisa M. Barao. 2019. "Why Do Gun Murders Have a Higher Clearance Rate Than Gunshot Assaults?" *Criminology & Public Policy* 18 (3): 525–51.

Cook, Philip J., Jens Ludwig, and David Hemenway. 1997. "The Gun Debate's New Mythical Number: How Many Defensive Uses per Year?" *Journal of Policy Analysis and Management* 16 (3): 463–69.

Cook, Philip J., Jens Ludwig, Sudhir Venkatesh, and Anthony A. Braga. 2007. "Underground Gun Markets." *Economic Journal* 117 (524): F588–F618.

Cooney, Mark. 1994. "Evidence as Partisanship." *Law & Society Review* 28 (4): 833–58.

Cowan, E. James, and Roger Koppl. 2010. "An Economic Perspective on 'Unanalyzed Evidence in Law Enforcement Agencies.'" *Criminology & Public Policy* 9 (2): 411–19.

De Ceuster, Jan, and Sylvain Dujardin. 2015. "The Reference Ballistic Imaging Database Revisited." *Forensic Science International* 248:82–87.

Dierenfeldt, Rick, Timothy C. Brown, and Rocio A. Roles. 2017. "Re-considering the Structural Covariates of Gun Crime: An Examination of Direct and Moderated Effects." *Deviant Behavior* 38 (2): 208–25.

Dror, Itiel E., and David Charlton. 2006. "Why Experts Make Errors." *Journal of Forensic Identification* 56 (4): 600–616.

Duggan, Mark. 2001. "More Guns, More Crime." *Journal of Political Economy* 109 (5): 1086–114.

Epstein, Jules M. 2018. "Reasonable Certainty: A Term It Is Certainly Reasonable to Repudiate." *Criminal Justice* 33 (3): 39–40.

Fay, Robert E., and Mamdou S. Diallo. 2012. "Small Area Estimation Alternatives for the National Crime Victimization Survey." In *Proceedings of the Section on Survey Research Methods*. American Statistical Association, 3742–56. http://www.asasrms.org/Proceedings/y2012/Files/304438_73111.pdf.

Feldman, Jack M., and John G. Lynch. 1988. "Self-Generated Validity and Other Effects of Measurement on Belief, Attitude, Intention, and Behavior." *Journal of Applied Psychology* 73 (3): 421–35.

Felson, Richard B., Stephen A. Ribner, and Merryl S. Siegel. 1984. "Age and the Effect of Third Parties during Criminal Violence." *Sociology and Social Research* 68 (4): 452–62.

Graham, Kathryn, Paul F. Tremblay, Samantha Wells, Kai Pernanen, John Purcell, and Jennifer Jelley. 2006. "Harm, Intent, and the Nature of Aggressive Behavior: Measuring Naturally Occurring Aggression in Barroom Settings." *Assessment* 13 (3): 280–96.

Griffiths, Elizabeth, and Jorge M. Chavez. 2004. "Communities, Street Guns, and Homicide Trajectories in Chicago, 1980–1995: Merging Methods for Examining Homicide Trends across Space and Time." *Criminology* 42 (4): 941–78.

Haviland, Miriam J., Emma Gause, Frederick P. Rivara, Andrew G. Bowen, Amelia Hanron, and Ali Rowhani-Rahbar. 2021. "Assessment of County-Level Proxy Variables for Household Firearm Ownership." *Preventive Medicine* 148:106571.

Hemenway, David, and Deborah Azrael. 2000. "The Relative Frequency of Offensive and Defensive Gun Uses: Results from a National Survey." *Violence and Victims* 15 (3): 257–72.

Hemenway, David, and Matthew Miller. 2000. "Firearm Availability and Homicide Rates across 26 High-Income Countries." *Journal of Trauma and Acute Care Surgery* 49 (6): 985–88.

Hepburn, Lisa M., and David Hemenway. 2004. "Firearm Availability and Homicide: A Review of the Literature." *Aggression and Violent Behavior* 9 (4): 417–40.

Karp, Aaron. 2018. *Estimating Global Civilian-Held Firearms Numbers*. Briefing Paper. Small Arms Survey. Geneva, Switzerland. https://www.club-caza.com/enprofundidad/archivos/SAS-BP-Civilian-Firearms-Numbers.pdf.

Kates, Don B., and Daniel D. Polsby. 2000. "Long-Term Nonrelationship of Widespread and Increasing Firearm Availability to Homicide in the United States." *Homicide Studies* 4 (2): 185–201.

Katz, Jack. 1988. *Seductions of Crime: A Chilling Exploration of the Criminal Mind—From Juvenile Delinquency to Cold Blooded Murder*. New York: Basic Books.

Kellermann, Arthur L., Frederick P. Rivara, Norman B. Rushforth, Joyce G. Banton, Donald T. Reay, Jerry T. Francisco, Ana B. Locci, Janice Prodzinski, Bela B. Hackman, and Grant Somes. 1993. "Gun Ownership as a Risk Factor for Homicide in the Home." *New England Journal of Medicine* 329 (15): 1084–91.

Kleck, Gary. 2004. "Measures of Gun Ownership Levels for Macro-level Crime and Violence Research." *Journal of Research in Crime and Delinquency* (41) 1: 3–36.

———. 2021. "The Continuing Vitality of Flawed Research on Guns and Violence: A Comment on Fridel (2020)." *Justice Quarterly* 38 (5): 916–24. https://doi.org/10.1080/0741 8825.2020.1823455.

Ling, Shichun, Jacob Kaplan, and Colleen M. Berryessa. 2021. "The Importance of Forensic Evidence for Decisions on Criminal Guilt." *Science & Justice* 61 (2): 142–49.

Lott, John R. 2013. *More Guns, Less Crime: Understanding Crime and Gun Control Laws*. Chicago: University of Chicago Press.

Luckenbill, David F. 1977. "Criminal Homicide as a Situated Transaction." *Social Problems* 25 (2): 176–86.

Mattijjssen, Erwin J. A. T. 2020. "Interpol Review of Forensic Firearm Examination 2016–2019." *Forensic Science International: Synergy* 2:389–403.

McDowall, David. 1991. "Firearm Availability and Homicide Rates in Detroit, 1951–1986." *Social Forces* 69 (4): 1085–101.

Miller, Matthew, Deborah Azrael, and David Hemenway. 2002. "Rates of Household Firearm Ownership and Homicide across U.S. Regions and States, 1988–1997." *American Journal of Public Health* 92 (12): 1988–93.

National Center for Health Statistics. 2011. *WISQARS Injury Mortality Reports, 1999–2007*. National Center for Inquiry Prevention and Control. http://webappa.cdc.gov /sasweb/ncipc/mortrate10_sy.html.

National Commission on Forensic Science. 2016. *Testimony Using the Term "Reasonable Scientific Certainty."* National Institute of Standards and Technology. https://www .justice.gov/archives/ncfs/page/file/641331/download.

National Research Council. 2004. *Forensic Analysis: Weighing Bullet Lead Evidence*. National Academies Press. https://www.nap.edu/catalog/10924/forensic-analysis-weigh ing-bullet-lead-evidence.

———. 2008. *Ballistic Imaging*. National Academies Press. https://www.nap.edu/catalog /12162/ballistic-imaging.

———. 2009. *Strengthening Forensic Science in the United States: A Path Forward*. National Academies Press. https://www.ojp.gov/pdffiles1/nij/grants/228091.pdf.

Nir, Esther, and Elizabeth Griffiths. 2018. "Sentencing on the Evidence." *Criminal Justice Policy Review* (29) 4: 365–90.

Papachristos, Andrew V., Anthony A. Braga, and David M. Hureau. 2012. "Social Networks and the Risk of Gunshot Injury." *Journal of Urban Health* 89 (6): 992–1003.

Papachristos, Andrew V., and Christopher Wildeman. 2014. "Network Exposure and Homicide Victimization in an African American Community." *American Journal of Public Health* 104 (1): 143–50.

Peterson, Ruth D., and Lauren J. Krivo. 2010. *Divergent Social Worlds: Neighborhood Crime and the Racial-Spatial Divide*. New York: Russell Sage Foundation.

Poltavski, Dmitri, Richard Van Eck, Austin T. Winger, and Charles Honts. 2018. "Using a Polygraph System for Evaluation of the Social Desirability Response Bias in Self-Report Measures of Aggression." *Applied Psychophysiological Biofeedback* 43 (4): 309–18.

Roman, J. K. 2020. *A Blueprint for a U.S. Firearms Data Infrastructure*. Bethesda: NORC at the University of Chicago. https://www.norc.org/PDFs/Firearm%20Data%20Infra structure%20Expert%20Panel/A%20Blueprint%20for%20a%20U.S.%20Firearms%20 Data%20Infrastructure_NORC%20Expert%20Panel%20Final%20Report_October %202020.pdf.

Saks, Michael J., and Jonathan J. Koehler. 2005. "The Coming Paradigm Shift in Forensic Identification Science." *Science* 309 (5736): 892–95.

Semenza, Daniel C., Richard Stansfield, and Nathan W. Link. 2020. "The Dynamics of Race, Place, and Homicide Context in the Relationship between Firearm Dealers and Gun Violence." *Justice Quarterly* 39 (1): 134–51. https://doi.org/10.1080/07418825.2019 .1707858.

Smith, Tom W., and Jaesok Son. 2019. *Trends in Gun Ownership in the United States, 1972–2018.* Chicago: NORAC at the University of Chicago. https://gssdataexplorer .norc.org/documents/905/download.

Stansfield, Richard, Daniel C. Semenza, and Trent Steidley. 2021. "Public Guns, Private Violence: The Association of City-Level Firearm Availability and Intimate Partner Homicide in the United States." *Preventive Medicine* 148 (July): 106599. https://doi.org /10.1016/j.ypmed.2021.106599.

Steidley, Trent, David M. Ramey, and Emily A. Shrider. 2017. "Gun Shops as Local Institutions: Federal Firearms Licensees, Social Disorganization, and Neighborhood Violent Crime." *Social Forces* 96 (1): 265–98.

Stolzenberg, Lisa, and Stewart J. D'Alessio. 2000. "Gun Availability and Violent Crime: New Evidence from the National Incident-Based Reporting System." *Social Forces* 78 (4): 1461–82.

UNODC. 2019. *Global Study on Homicide 2019.* Vienna: United Nations Office on Drugs and Crime. https://www.unodc.org/documents/data-and-analysis/gsh/Booklet1.pdf.

Yu, Sung-suk Violet, Daiwon Lee, and Jesenia M. Pizarro. 2020. "Illegal Firearm Availability and Violence: Neighborhood-Level Analysis." *Journal of Interpersonal Violence* 35 (19–20): 3896–4012.

Zimmerman, Gregory M., and Emma E. Fridel. 2020. "Contextualizing Homicide-Suicide: Examining how Ecological Gun Availability Affects Homicide-Suicide at Multiple Levels of Analysis." *Homicide Studies* 24 (2): 151–77.

Zimring, Frank E. 1968. "Is Gun Control Likely to Reduce Violent Killings?" *University of Chicago Law Review* 35 (4): 721–37.

———. 1972. "The Medium Is the Message: Firearm Caliber as a Determinant of Death from Assault." *Journal of Legal Studies* 1 (1): 97–123.

Zimring, Franklin E., and Gordon Hawkins. 1999. *Crime Is Not the Problem: Lethal Violence in America.* Oxford: Oxford University Press.

13

U.S. Homicide Inequalities across Race, Ethnicity, and Gender

Shytierra Gaston

Introduction

Within the contexts of mortality and crime, homicides are relatively rare. In 2019, for example, the Centers for Disease Control and Prevention (CDC) reported 2,854,838 deaths nationally. Of them, 19,141—0.67 percent—resulted from homicide (CDC 2021; Kochanek, Xu, and Arias 2020). During that same year, the Federal Bureau of Investigation (FBI) reported 1,203,808 violent index crimes, 16,425—1 percent—of which were homicides (FBI UCR 2019, table 1). These figures do not account for the multimillion crimes of other types committed annually or the fact that crimes known to police constitute a small, nonrandom, nonrepresentative subset of all U.S. crimes. Because homicide is the most reliably, consistently measured offense, one can reasonably deduce that homicide comprises far less than 1 percent of all the nation's crimes.

Though a relatively rare crime and mortality type, homicide constitutes a serious public safety and public health problem; it is a feature that sets the United States apart from comparable industrialized nations due to its high prevalence (Messner and Rosenfeld 2013). Homicide is profoundly consequential, wreaking devastating havoc on families, communities, and broader society. Children and families of homicide victims are left to confront the trauma, grief, and economic consequences of tragically losing a loved one. Homicide undermines the safety and well-being of communities and societies, contributing to economic divestment and social disruption that perpetuate disadvantage and marginalization (Abt 2019). In addition, homicide is costly to taxpayers. A study estimating the financial cost of crime among a sample of convicted and incarcerated perpetrators found that every murder offense produced an average estimated cost of $17.3 million, more than 50 times the cost of armed robbery and 119 times that of aggravated assault (DeLisi et al. 2010, 506).

Although infrequent in the aggregate, homicide—and its accompanying harms—imposes a heavy toll on certain segments of the population due to its unequal distribution and tendency to concentrate among people and places of color. At the macrolevel, homicide occurs disproportionately in the South, urban areas, and structurally disadvantaged neighborhoods—where people of color are more likely to live (CDC 2021; Krivo and Peterson 2000). Because of these racialized geographic patterns, at the microlevel, people of color—specifically Black, Native, and Hispanic Americans—face the greatest risk of homicide involvement as victims and, according to results from limited data, as perpetrators (Fox and Zawitz 2004). For youth aged fifteen to twenty-four years old, homicide is the leading cause of death among Black males and the second leading cause of death among Black females and Hispanic males (CDC 2018, 47, 113, 124). Black men are killed at a higher rate than any other race/ethnic-gender subgroup (Gaston and Sewell 2020). Black women face the highest homicide risk among women, and their rates exceed those of White men (Gaston and Sewell 2020). Scholars have observed high homicide rates among Native Americans (Herne, Maschino, and Graham-Phillips 2016), but their homicide risks are significantly understudied, especially in recent decades, by gender and relative to other racial/ethnic groups.

Despite considerable public and scholarly attention to homicide, the literature contains significant knowledge gaps regarding homicide inequalities by race, ethnicity, and gender. Most race scholarship focuses solely on Black and White Americans, obscuring homicide patterns across a full spectrum of racial and ethnic identities. Moreover, theories and analyses on race/ethnicity and homicide are largely disjointed from those on gender and homicide, masking important risks and stalling understanding of homicide at the intersection of race, ethnicity, and gender. These knowledge gaps are largely attributable to persistent data limitations that preclude nuanced studies of race, ethnicity, and gender in homicide research.

The goal of this chapter is to describe the nature and extent of homicide victimization trends by race, ethnicity, and gender. This fundamental task serves as a foundation to explanatory studies, theory building, and policy prescriptions while identifying knowledge gaps that would advance the homicide literature. To accomplish this goal, I compile national mortality data and describe thirty-year homicide victimization trends from 1990 to 2019 by race, ethnicity, and gender among ten subgroups comprising five races/

ethnicities and two genders. Specifically, I describe homicide rates by race/ethnicity and race/ethnicity-gender as well as comparing disparities between subgroups. I start by situating these race/ethnic and gender-specific trends within theoretical explanations and describe the research methodology.

Explaining Homicide Inequalities across Race, Ethnicity, and Gender

Historical Foundations

The United States was founded on and is sustained by violence and racial oppression targeted at groups of color. As part of colonization of the lands now known as the United States of America, European colonizers committed heinous acts of violence and genocide against Native peoples, robbed them of lands and resources, and forcibly removed them from their territories (Perry 2008). The colonizers' goal of establishing a new society by invading preexisting ones was furthered by the transatlantic slave trade, in which the White ruling class—including the so-called founding fathers—kidnapped African people from their continent and exploited them for free labor (Alexander 2010). This system was sustained by a variety of social control tactics including violence in the form of battery, rape, and murder. After emancipation, anti-Black violence and racial control continued for decades through state-sanctioned systems and practices such as racial lynchings, Black codes, convict leasing, Jim Crow, northern and southern segregation, and ghettoization (Alexander 2010; Ivanov 1985). In addition to targeted violence and oppression against Native and Black Americans, the U.S. government at various levels has sponsored racial discrimination, lynchings, and segregation known as "Juan Crow" against Hispanic/Latinx groups, such as Mexicans and Puerto Ricans (Martinez 2018; Martinez 2019). Thus, the disproportionate homicides that Black, Native, and Hispanic Americans experience today are part of America's enduring legacy of violently victimizing and oppressing them and correspond to their position in the racial-social order.

Structural Disadvantage

From these historical systems of violence and racist oppression stem conditions known today to cause violence. Specifically, economic exploitation, segregation in deprived neighborhoods, and relegation to the bottom of the racial-social hierarchy have made Black, Native, and Hispanic Americans vulnerable to violence as perpetrators, victims, and as an adaptive response to socioeconomic deprivation. Scholars identify concentrated structural disadvantage as the most robust correlate of homicide in the aggregate and by race/ethnicity. According to social disorganization theory, geographic concentrations of poverty, unemployment, residential turnover, racial segregation, and family disruption correspond with homicide rates (Kaufman 2005; Krivo and Peterson 2000; McNulty and Bellair 2006; Morenoff, Sampson, and Raudenbush 2005; Sampson and Wilson 1995; Unnever and Gabbidon 2011). These structural disadvantages have also been linked to race/ethnic-specific homicide among Black, White, Hispanic, Native, and Asian Americans, although to varying degrees (Bachman 1991; Chauhan et al. 2011; Kaufman 2005; Krivo and Peterson 2000; Lanier 2010; Martínez 2014; Phillips 2002; Velez, Krivo, and Peterson 2003; Wu 2009). The mechanisms linking structural disadvantage to homicide include the formation of violent subcultures and the weakening of informal social control. Violence becomes a means through which residents adapt to and survive socioeconomic deprivation and its accompanying strains, fostering a subculture in which interpersonal violence is acceptable and expected (Anderson 1999). The concentration of structural disadvantages disrupts informal social control and the ability for neighborhoods to regulate themselves against violence (Morenoff, Sampson, and Raudenbush 2001). This concentrated disadvantage, coupled with disproportionate police oppression, increases the chances of residents taking matters into their own hands and enacting violence when problems or disputes arise instead of relying on formal social control mechanisms such as law enforcement (Anderson 1999).

Intersectional Disadvantage

Structural theories generally aim to explain violence in the aggregate or by race/ethnicity while overlooking gendered systems of oppression, such as patriarchy, which are critical to understanding violence (Pease 2019). Although studies have empirically linked structural disadvantage to homicide by race, ethnicity, and gender separately, conceptual and empirical advancements at the intersection of these identities are scant. This deficiency obscures subgroup-specific homicide risks and patterns and stalls preventative and interventive endeavors to reduce homicide, underscoring the need to integrate structural and intersectional perspectives. Intersectional research acknowledges the fact that individuals occupy multiple, rather than single, social identities that confer disadvantages and privileges (Crenshaw 1989). Intersectionality illuminates the ways in which oppression is experienced distinctly among individuals occupying multiple marginalized social locations, such as Black American women and Native American women, who experience racism-sexism distinct from the racism experienced by their male counterparts and the sexism White women face. The multiplicity of systems of power related to race, ethnicity, and gender create different structural arrangements relevant throughout social life (Potter 2013), including in homicide risk (Burgess-Proctor 2006; Parker 2008; Parker and Hefner 2015; Potter 2006; 2015; Haynie and Armstrong 2006). While prior studies have found a relationship between structural disadvantage and homicide among women, including by race (Parker and Hefner 2015; Steffensmeier and Haynie 2000), results vary in strength and significance of structural variables and by women subgroup, suggesting the need to further investigate intersectionally specific homicide covariates.

Data and Method

To accomplish the analytic goal of describing homicide trends by race, ethnicity, and gender, I compiled homicide data from the CDC's Fatal Injury Reports housed in the Web-Based Injury Statistics Query and Reporting System (WISQARS). This public health data source offers reliable race/ethnic/gender-specific intersectional data on the nation's homicides. It overcomes significant limitations of FBI homicide data conventionally used in the literature (Loftin, McDowall, and Fetzer 2008). For example, although race data are available for arrests—indicators of police behavior, not crimes—the FBI UCR does not report the race of victims or perpetrators of known crimes. Such information is available through the FBI SHR, but the race and ethnicity of crime victims and perpetrators are inconsistently recorded, and Hispanic Americans are designated as White. Known as the "Hispanic Effect," this consequential measurement limitation plagues race-homicide research and has been shown to inflate non-Hispanic White homicide rates, underestimate disparities between non-Hispanic Whites and other racial/ethnic groups, and preventing Hispanic-specific analyses (Gaston and Sewell 2020; Steffensmeier et al. 2011). While WISQARS overcomes this significant, longstanding limitation that has stalled homicide research (Gaston and Sewell 2020), it too has caveats that must be considered when interpreting results. For example, WISQARS data are collected and reported by local health departments. Therefore, it is possible that classification and data collection processes vary across jurisdictions and over time, although the legal definition of homicide has not changed considerably since 1950. Moreover, WISQARS provides data on homicide *victimization* and is unable to offer information about homicide perpetrators or circumstances. Because homicide events tend to be intraracial (Fox and Zawitz 2004), criminologists commonly infer that results about race and homicide victimization can be generalized to understand race and homicide perpetration. Nevertheless, improved data collections are needed to resolve this limitation in the event that this conventional wisdom does not fully hold and important race/ethnic/gender-specific patterns are being masked.

From WISQARS, I gathered national-level race/ethnic and gender-specific homicide counts, population size, and rates from 1990 to 2019. WISQARS began including Hispanic origin in 1990. Because homicide data prior to 1990 are confounded by the Hispanic Effect, the current analysis starts in 1990. The analysis describes longitudinal homicide rates among ten racial/ethnic/gender subgroups, including women and men of the following five races/ethnicities: Black American, Native American, Hispanic American, White American, and Asian American.[1] Victims of Hispanic origin are excluded from the racial groups and comprise their own mutually exclusive category.

In the following discussion of the results, I describe homicide victimization trends during the thirty-year period for the subgroups by race/ethnicity and by race/ethnicity/gender. Age-adjusted rates from WISQARS are presented instead of crude rates because, as Selvin, Sacks, and Merrill (1980) note, homicide is unequally distributed across age. Using age-adjusted rates overcomes the limitation of producing misleading results influenced by age distribution and standardizes the homicide rate, allowing for more meaningful comparisons across subgroups.

Results

Homicide by Race and Ethnicity

Homicide research is generally conducted in the aggregate and, to a lesser degree, by race or gender. The race literature centers a Black-White dichotomy that highlights Black Americans' disproportionate involvement in homicide offending and victimization (Fox and Zawitz 2004; LaFree 1995; LaFree, Baumer, and O'Brien 2010; Parker 2008; Velez, Krivo, and Peterson 2003). A smaller number of studies examines ethnicity, revealing that Hispanic Americans' homicide involvement is intermediate to that of Black and White Americans (Langley and Sugarmann 2018). Analyses of Native and Asian American homicide are even sparser, making it difficult to ascertain their risks relative to the other three subgroups.

Figure 13.1 depicts age-adjusted homicide victimization rates from 1990 to 2019 for Black, Hispanic, Native, White, and Asian Americans juxtaposed to those for the total U.S. population. During the thirty-year period, the average annual total homicide rate—annual rates averaged over thirty years—was 6.64 per 100,000 residents. The total homicide rate fluctuated between a low of 5.06 in 2014 and a peak of 9.89 in 1991. The early 1990s was a period

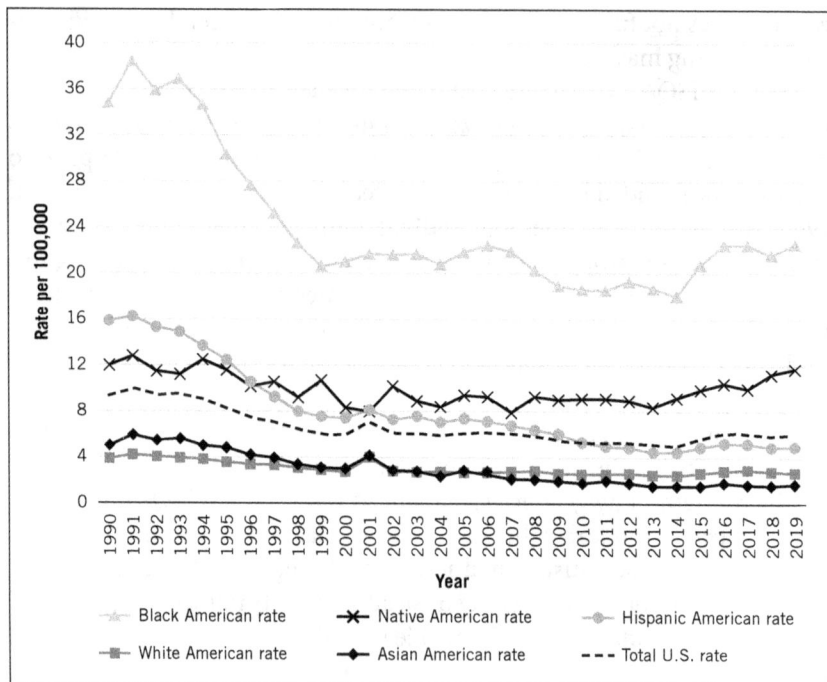

Figure 13.1 Race/Ethnic-Specific Age-Adjusted Homicide Victimization Rates, 1990–2019

of homicide highs followed by precipitous homicide declines to levels not seen since the 1960s, a phenomenon coined the "Great Crime Decline" (Zimring 2007). Homicide rates stabilized in the early 2000s, except for an uptick in 2001 due to the September 11 terrorist attacks. Homicide declined again from 2007 to 2014 before an abrupt uptick in 2015. Between 2014 and 2015, homicide rates spiked from 5.06 to 5.64 per 100,000 residents—an 11.57 percent increase—and grew to 6.01 by 2019. Although homicide *rates* remain among historic lows, the one-year increase from 2014 to 2015 was nearly unprecedented and the largest seen since 1968 with the exception of 2001 (Rosenfeld 2016; Rosenfeld et al. 2017).

These total homicide rates and trends for the aggregate population are commonly the focus in the literature and public discourse. As shown in figure 13.1, when disaggregated by race and ethnicity, important race/ethnic-specific patterns are revealed. During the series, Black Americans consistently had the highest homicide rates, while White and Asian Americans rivaled at lowest risk. Black age-adjusted homicide rates ranged from 18.03 to 38.43 per 100,000 Black Americans, with an average annual rate of 24.09 (nearly quadruple that for the total population). These high risks starkly contrast low homicide rates for White Americans, which ranged between 2.46 and 4.22, and for Asian Americans, which ranged from 1.55 to 5.90. Both of these trend lines fell well below the trend for the total population. On the other hand, Native and Hispanic American homicide risks were intermediate to Black homicide and White and Asian homicide, alternating between second and third greatest risk during the 1990s, with Native Americans consistently having the second highest homicide rates thereafter. Native American homicide rates ranged from 7.92 to 12.76 with an annual average of 9.96. Hispanic American homicide rates fluctuated between 4.48 and 16.20 with an annual average of 8.14. During the time series, Native American homicide was consistently above the total trend line; Hispanic American homicide converged with the total homicide rate throughout the 1990s and 2000s, falling below the total rate in 2011.

In addition to race/ethnic differences in homicide *levels*, figure 13.1 reveals important racial/ethnic differences in homicide *fluctuation*. As one example, the extent of the Great Crime Decline varied across groups. Between 1993 and 2000, Hispanic, Asian, and Black Americans experienced the largest declines, by 50 percent, 47 percent, and 43 percent respectively, in comparison to 30 percent and 26 percent decreases in White and Native homicide, respectively. Whereas homicide among most groups dropped constantly during this period, the decline in Native American homicide was a function of several sharp increases and decreases. Moreover, the recent homicide rise was experienced unequally across race/ethnicity. From 2014 to 2019—during the American policing crisis (Gaston, Cunningham, and Gillezeau 2019; Rosenfeld et al. 2017)—homicide rates increased most dramatically among Native and Black Americans, by 27 percent and 25 percent respectively, compared to 10 percent each among Hispanic, White, and Asian Americans. Given that Black and Native Americans are disproportionately subjected to racialized policing, these patterns raise questions about whether the policing crisis exacerbated their homicide risks. Together, the trend lines in figure 13.1 show that total homicide in the aggregate masks important race/ethnic-specific homicide risks and fluctuations, pointing to the need for more nuanced research by race/ethnicity. Notably, Black homicide is exceptionally and consistently high, appearing to drive the largest share of total homicide in the aggregate.

A handful of longitudinal race/ethnic-specific homicide studies suggest that race and ethnic disparities in homicide have markedly declined in recent decades (Cook and Laub 2002; Fox and Zawitz 2004; LaFree 1995; LaFree, Baumer, and O'Brien 2010; LaFree, O'Brien, and Baumer 2006; Parker 2008; Rosenfeld and Fox 2019; Tonry and Melewski 2008). However, this literature is generally confounded by the Hispanic Effect and focuses nearly exclusively on Black and White Americans. Studies by Steffensmeier et al. (2011),

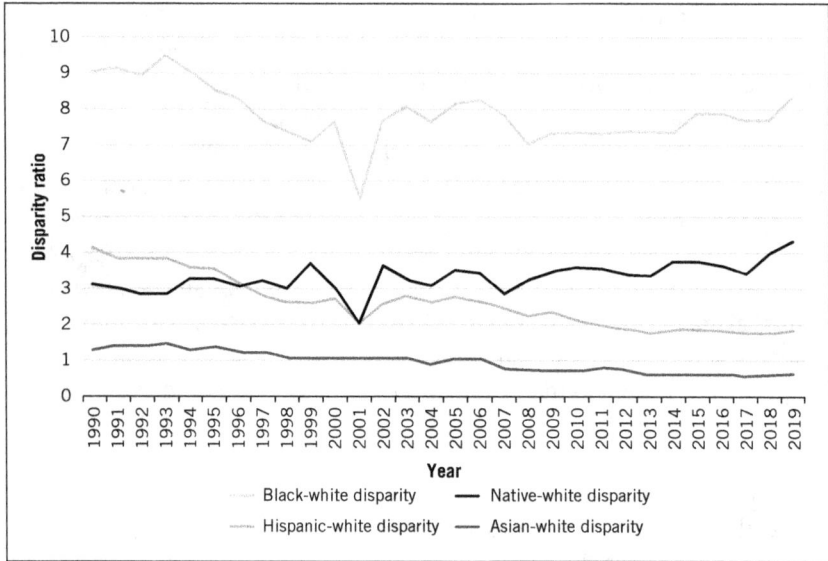

Figure 13.2 Racial/Ethnic Homicide Victimization Disparity Ratios, 1990–2019

Light and Ulmer (2016), and Gaston and Sewell (2020) demonstrate that claims of Black-White convergence are overstated. Further, this literature leaves more to be learned about levels and changes in race/ethnic disparities among a broader spectrum of races/ethnicities.

Figure 13.2 displays homicide disparity ratios by race/ethnicity between 1990 and 2019 for the five racial/ethnic groups. Age-adjusted rates for each race/ethnicity were divided by those of White Americans, the reference group. The trends reveal stark racial/ethnic disparities, the largest being between Black and White Americans. During the thirty-year period, an annual average of 7.85 Black Americans were killed for every White American, a disparity ratio fluctuating between a low of 5.42 in 2001 and a high of 9.47 in 1993. Homicide inequalities for Hispanic and Native Americans were less stark than Black Americans', although both groups' homicide rates multiplied those of White Americans. The Native-White disparity was second highest during most of the series, with an annual average of 3.31 Native homicides per White homicide; disparity ratios ranged between 1.99 in 2001 and 4.32 in 2019. An annual average of 2.58 Hispanics were killed for every White killing, a disparity that fluctuated between 1.74 in 2018 and 4.11 in 1990. The lowest disparity was among Asian Americans, the only group whose homicide risk has ever been lower than White Americans'. The annual average Asian-White disparity was 0.95, ranging between 0.57 in 2017 and 1.44 in 1993. While prior studies assert substantial decreased racial/ethnic disparities in homicide, figure 13.2 disputes this claim with the exception of slight convergence in Hispanic-White and Asian-White homicide in the past decade. For the two racial/ethnic groups at greatest risk of homicide—Black and Native Americans—disparities in homicide between White Americans have not decreased to the degree described in many prior studies. In fact, in most years between 2014 and 2019—during the policing crisis—homicide inequalities grew sharply: 15 percent between Native and White Americans and 14 percent between Black and White Americans, in comparison to virtually no change in Hispanic-White (+0.31 percent) and Asian-White disparities (+0.10 percent).

Homicide at the Intersection of Race, Ethnicity, and Gender

While some studies have examined the influence of race/ethnicity and gender on homicide separately, intersectional approaches to theorizing and analyzing race/ethnicity and gender jointly have lagged. Exceptions include the emphasis often placed on homicide of young Black males. Empirical and public attention to homicide among young Black men has far outpaced attention for other racial/ethnic/gender subgroups, such as for women who are Black, Native, Hispanic, White, or Asian and men who are Native, Hispanic, White, or Asian.

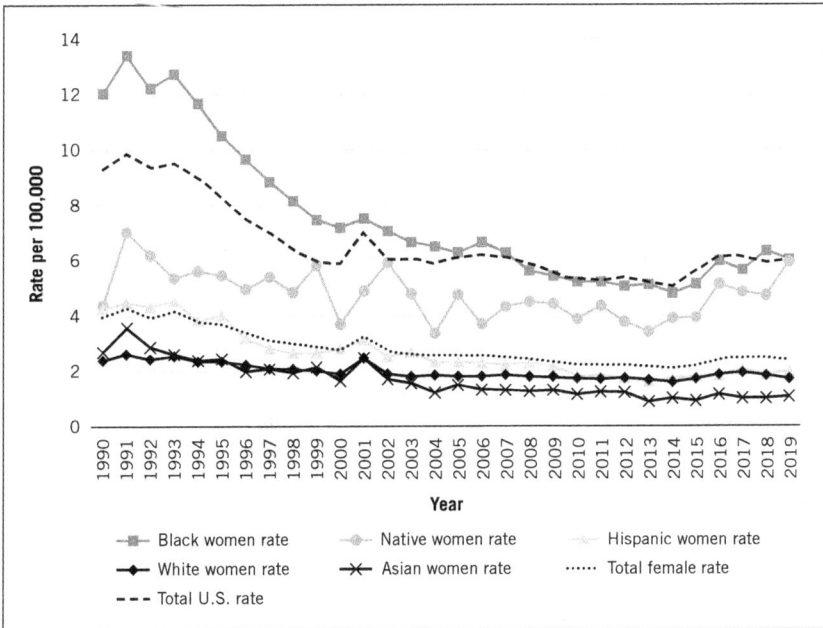

Figure 13.3 Race/Ethnic and Women-Specific Age-Adjusted Homicide Victimization Rates, 1990–2019

Figure 13.3 depicts age-adjusted homicide rates for women by race and ethnicity between 1990 and 2019. These are presented alongside total homicide and total female homicide trends. Throughout the thirty-year period, Black women consistently had the highest homicide risk among women, ranging from a low of 4.84 in 2014 to a high of 13.42 in 1991 per 100,000 Black American women. Their annual average rate of 7.55, 1.14 times that for the total population and 3.15 times that for the total female population, was the only one to exceed rates for the total aggregate population, at least until the last decade, when both trend lines converged. Native American women homicide ranked second highest among female homicide, ranging from a low of 3.37 in 2004 to a high of 7.02 in 1991. Native women homicide rates were noticeably lower than those for Black women for most years until both trends began converging around 2007, becoming nearly identical in 2019 at a rate of 5.97 and 6.04, respectively. On the other hand, Asian women had the lowest homicide risk among women for most of the series, ranging from 0.89 in 2013 to 3.58 in 1991. Asian women's trends were relatively similar to White women's during the 1990s before decreasing and diverging starting in 2002, becoming the lowest for the remainder of the series. Hispanic women homicide was third highest during most years, ranging from 1.58 in 2013 to 4.55 in 1993 in comparison to a range of 1.61 in 2014 and 2.60 in 1991 for White women. However, trends for Hispanic women and White women converged and became nearly identical in the last decade. Between 2010 and 2019, for example, the annual average homicide rates were 1.81 and 1.76 for Hispanic and White women respectively.

Homicide fluctuated notably among women subgroups. During the Great Crime Decline (between 1993 and 2000), Black women's homicide rate changed more substantially, dropping from 12.74 to 7.20, a rate change of 43 percent in comparison to 38 percent for Hispanic women, 37 percent for Asian women, 31 percent for Native women, and 25 percent for White women. Recent upticks in homicide were also unequal among women. During the policing crisis from 2014 to 2019, homicide increased among all women—but by a dramatic 53 percent increase among Native women and 25 percent increase among Black women compared to 15 percent among Hispanic women, 7 percent among White women, and 6 percent among Asian women. In 2019, when homicide rates changed by a single-digit percentage over the previous year among most women (between -6 percent and +7 percent), the Native women homicide rate was exceptional in its an astonishing one-year increase of 26 percent. These findings underscore the need to focus on homicide among Native and Black women.

Figure 13.4 depicts age-adjusted homicide trends for men by race and ethnicity between 1990 and 2019 relative to total homicide and total male homicide trends. Because Black men's homicide rates were substantially higher

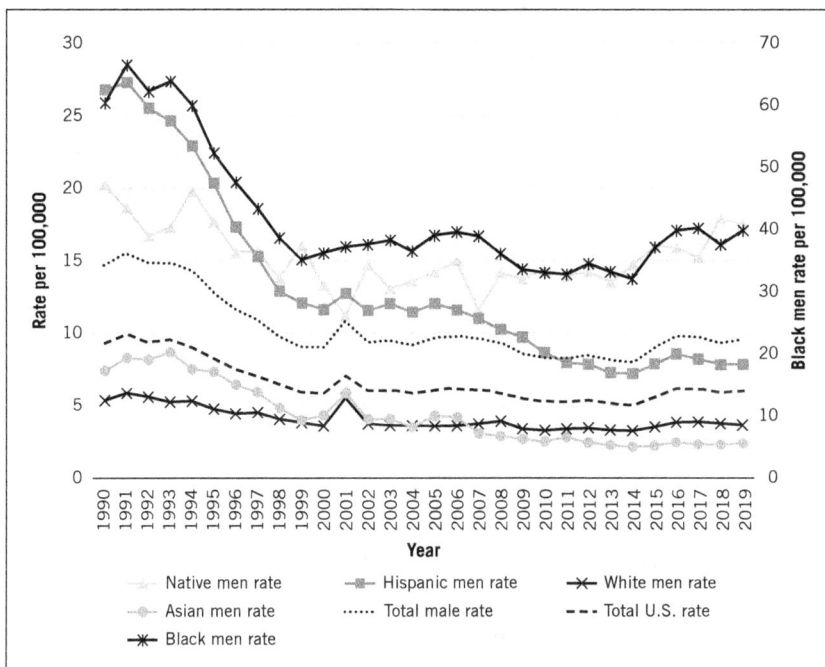

Figure 13.4 Race/Ethnic and Men-Specific Age-Adjusted Homicide Victimization Rates, 1990–2019

than other groups', their trend line is plotted on the secondary vertical axis. Like Black women, Black men consistently had the highest homicide risk among their gender. Black male homicide rates ranged from a low of 32.07 in 2014 to a high of 66.56 in 1991 per 100,000 Black American men. They had an annual average rate of 42.16, multiplying the total population rate by 6.35 and the total male population rate by 4.05. Although Native women had the second highest and Hispanic women the third highest homicide risks among their gender, trends for Native men and Hispanic men alternated between second and third highest during the series. Homicide rates among Native men ranged from a low of 11.19 in 2001 and a high of 20.21 in 1990 compared to a low of 7.21 in 2014 and a high of 27.28 in 1991 among Hispanic men. The annual average Native male homicide rate of 15.30 was more than double that for the total population, and the annual average rate of 13.28 for Hispanic men was twice that for the total population. Hispanic male homicide dropped sharply in the 1990s, stabilized during the early 2000s, and declined again during the remaining series, converging with the total homicide trend line. Notably, as homicide declined among most subgroups, Native American men homicide followed a different trend, exhibiting a series of sharp, short-term upticks and downturns before stabilizing between 2008 and 2013 and increasing thereafter. From 2013 to 2019, Native men homicide rates increased by 29 percent, from 13.51 to 17.50.

Like trends for Asian and White women, Asian and White men homicide rates were largely comparable during the series. Asian men homicide rates ranged from a low of 2.16 in 2014 to a high of 8.68 in 1993, with an annual average rate of 4.39, whereas White men homicide ranged from a low of 3.30 in 2014 to a high of 5.87 in 1991, with an annual average of 4.11. The homicide rate of Asian men exceeded White men's during most of the 1990s and then converged between 1998 and 2006 before becoming the lowest during the remainder of the series. While homicide rates among Black, Native, and Hispanic men exceeded the total homicide trend, homicide rates among Asian and White men were beneath it.

At least three patterns are noteworthy. First, homicide risks are the highest among Black men, Native men, and Hispanic men. However, Black men's homicide is substantially higher and disparate relative to any male group. Second, Black women have the fourth highest homicide risk among the ten racial/ethnic/gender subgroups. In addition to having the greatest homicide risk among women, Black women are at greater risk of being killed than men who are White or Asian. Third, Native women homicide not only exceeds that of Hispanic, Asian, and White women but has also exceeded White and Asian male homicide in recent years. These patterns among Black and Native women refute common claims that women are at lower risk of homicide than men (Fox and Fridel 2017).

Future Directions for Research

In this chapter, I summarized salient theoretical explanations of homicide risks across racial/ethnic and gender lines and presented findings from an analysis of national homicide inequalities from 1990 to 2019 among ten racial/ethnic/gender subgroups: Black women and men, Native women and men, Hispanic women and men, White women and men, and Asian women and men. Overall, the results reveal important patterns by race, ethnicity, and gender that have been masked in analyses of aggregate homicide trends and by long-standing data limitations that preclude a complete understanding of homicide inequalities. A major takeaway is that homicide risks and trends vary substantially by race, ethnicity, and gender, pointing to a greater need for intersectional homicide research beyond the aggregate population. Accomplishing this goal, however, is contingent on the availability of reliable data. Government agencies at all levels must improve the quality of homicide data in a way that facilitates nuanced, sophisticated homicide analyses by race, ethnicity, and gender at various units and levels of analysis, over various time periods, and by homicide type and circumstance.

Moving beyond the Black male–White male dichotomy in homicide research is necessary. Contrary to findings in prior studies, racial/ethnic disparities have not narrowed substantially in the past three decades and have even increased in recent years between Black and White Americans and Native and White Americans. Moreover, while Black men's exorbitantly high homicide risk is well documented, this study reveals the need for experts to center Black women, who are at greatest risk of being killed among women, as well as Native women and men, whose homicide rates are generally second highest and have increased substantially in recent years when other groups' have decreased or stabilized. Notably, Black women and Native women are at greater risk of being murdered than women of other races *and* men who are White or Asian, especially in recent years. Considering the large homicide rises among Black and Native women and men during the recent policing crisis (2014–2019), investigating the impact of police violence and illegitimacy on homicide among these subgroups is a fruitful avenue for future research. Finally, while it is commonly understood that Hispanic homicide is intermediate to Black and White homicide as the second highest rate, a broader examination of race and gender complicates this conventional wisdom. Hispanic male homicide has been the *third* highest among the ten subgroups for nearly two decades, and Hispanic women's homicide risk has become identical to White women's over time.

Together, these findings expand and challenge extant knowledge about homicide by race, ethnicity, gender. In addition to expanding homicide research empirically, the current study highlights the need to revisit homicide theories and their efficacy in light of homicide inequalities among racial/ethnic/gender subgroups that have been historically underrepresented in homicide research. Such theoretical redevelopment might require expanding, refining, or merging preexisting theories or developing new ones. Whatever the case, viable theories should account for systems of racialized-gendered oppressions and privileges. Empirical and theoretical efforts that account for the race/ethnic-gender intersectionality of homicide might be better suited to informing policy prescriptions that effectively, safely, and fairly reduce homicide and make communities safer for all.

NOTE

1. "Native American" includes victims classified as American Indian or Alaskan Native. "Asian" includes victims classified as Asian or Pacific Islander. Although I use gender terms such as "women" and "men," homicide victims are identified by sex—female or male. I use gender and sex designations interchangeably.

REFERENCES

Abt, Thomas. 2019. *Bleeding Out: The Devastating Consequences of Urban Violence—and a Bold New Plan for Peace in the Streets.* New York: Basic Books.

Alexander, Michelle. 2010. *The New Jim Crow: Mass Incarceration in the Age of Colorblindness.* New York: The New Press.

Anderson, Elijah. 1999. *Code of the Street: Decency, Violence, and the Moral Life of the Inner City.* New York: W. W. Norton.

Bachman, Ronet. 1991. "An Analysis of American Indian Homicide: A Test of Social Disorganization and Economic Deprivation at the Reservation County Level." *Journal of Research in Crime and Delinquency* 28 (4): 456–71. https://doi.org/10.1177/00224278910 28004006.

Burgess-Proctor, Amanda. 2006. "Intersections of Race, Class, Gender, and Crime: Future Directions for Feminist Criminology." *Feminist Criminology* 1 (1): 27–47. https:// doi.org/10.1177/1557085105282899.

CDC. 2018. "NVSS—Mortality Tables—Leading Causes of Death—LCWK1_HR." Deaths, Percent of Total Deaths, and Death Rates for the 15 Leading Causes of Death in 5-year Age Groups, by Race and Hispanic Origin, and Sex: United States, 2015–2017. LCWK1 _HR_2017. Centers for Disease Control and Prevention. National Center for Health Statistics. https://www.cdc.gov/nchs/data/dvs/lcwk/lcwk1_hr_2017-a.pdf.

———. 2021. "Underlying Cause of Death, 1999–2019, D99F056." Centers for Disease Control and Prevention. National Vital Statistics System—Mortality Data (2019) via CDC WONDER. https://wonder.cdc.gov/controller/saved/D76/D99F056.

Chauhan, Preeti, Magdalena Cerdá, Steven F. Messner, Melissa Tracy, Kenneth Tardiff, and Sandro Galea. 2011. "Race/Ethnic-Specific Homicide Rates in New York City: Evaluating the Impact of Broken Windows Policing and Crack Cocaine Markets." *Homicide Studies* 15 (3): 268–90. https://doi.org/10.1177/1088767911416917.

Cook, Philip J., and John H. Laub. 2002. "After the Epidemic: Recent Trends in Youth Violence in the United States." *Crime and Justice* 29 (January): 1–37. https://doi.org /10.1086/652218.

Crenshaw, Kimberle. 1989. "Demarginalizing the Intersection of Race and Sex: A Black Feminist Critique of Antidiscrimination Doctrine, Feminist Theory and Antiracist Politics." *University of Chicago Legal Forum* 1989:139.

DeLisi, Matt, Anna Kosloski, Molly Sween, Emily Hachmeister, Matt Moore, and Alan Drury. 2010. "Murder by Numbers: Monetary Costs Imposed by a Sample of Homicide Offenders." *Journal of Forensic Psychiatry & Psychology* 21 (4): 501–13. https://doi .org/10.1080/14789940903564388.

FBI UCR. 2019. "Offenses Known to Law Enforcement." Federal Bureau of Investigation. Uniform Crime Reports. https://ucr.fbi.gov/crime-in-the-u.s/2019/crime-in-the-u.s .-2019/topic-pages/offenses-known-to-law-enforcement.

Fox, James Alan, and Emma E. Fridel. 2017. "Gender Differences in Patterns and Trends in U.S. Homicide, 1976–2015." *Violence and Gender* 4 (2): 37–43. https://doi.org/10 .1089/vio.2017.0016.

Fox, James Alan, and Marianne W. Zawitz. 2004. *Homicide Trends in the United States: 2000 Update.* NCJ 204885. Washington, DC: Bureau of Justice Statistics. https://www .bjs.gov/content/pub/pdf/htus00.pdf.

Gaston, Shytierra, Jamein P. Cunningham, and Rob Gillezeau. 2019. "A Ferguson Effect, the Drug Epidemic, Both, or Neither? Explaining the 2015 and 2016 U.S. Homicide

Rises by Race and Ethnicity." *Homicide Studies* 23 (3): 285–313. https://doi.org/10.1177/1088767919849642.

Gaston, Shytierra, and CheyOnna Sewell. 2020. "Parsing out the 'Hispanic Effect' in Disaggregated Homicide Trends at the Intersection of Race, Ethnicity, and Gender from 1990 to 2016." *Homicide Studies* July:1088767920939312. https://doi.org/10.1177/1088767920939312.

Haynie, Dana L., and David P. Armstrong. 2006. "Race and Gender-Disaggregated Homicide Offending Rates Differences and Similarities by Victim-Offender Relations across Cities." *Homicide Studies* 10 (1): 3–32. https://doi.org/10.1177/1088767905281518.

Herne, Mose A., Alexandra C. Maschino, and Anita L. Graham-Phillips. 2016. "Homicide among American Indians/Alaska Natives, 1999–2009: Implications for Public Health Interventions." *Public Health Reports* 131 (4): 597–604. https://doi.org/10.1177/0033354916662219.

Ivanov, Robert Fedorovich. 1985. *Blacks in United States History*. Moscow: Progress.

Kaufman, Joanne M. 2005. "Explaining the Race/Ethnicity–Violence Relationship: Neighborhood Context and Social Psychological Processes." *Justice Quarterly* 22 (2): 224–51. https://doi.org/10.1080/07418820500088986.

Kochanek, Kenneth D., Jiaquan Xu, and Elizabeth Arias. 2020. "Mortality in the United States, 2019." NCHS Data Brief 395. U.S. Department of Health and Human Services. Centers for Disease Control and Prevention. National Center for Health Statistics. https://www.cdc.gov/nchs/data/databriefs/db395-H.pdf.

Krivo, Lauren J., and Ruth D. Peterson. 2000. "The Structural Context of Homicide: Accounting for Racial Differences in Process." *American Sociological Review* 65 (4): 547–59. https://doi.org/10.2307/2657382.

LaFree, Gary. 1995. "Race and Crime Trends in the United States, 1946–1990." In *Ethnicity, Race, and Crime*, edited by Darnell F. Hawkins, 169–93. Albany: State University of New York Press.

LaFree, Gary, Eric P. Baumer, and Robert O'Brien. 2010. "Still Separate and Unequal? A City-Level Analysis of the Black-White Gap in Homicide Arrests since 1960." *American Sociological Review* 75 (1): 75–100.

LaFree, Gary, Robert M. O'Brien, and Eric Baumer. 2006. "Is the Gap Between Black and White Arrest Rates Narrowing? National Trends for Personal Contact Crimes, 1960–2003." In *The Many Colors of Crime: Inequalities of Race, Ethnicity, and Crime in America*, edited by Ruth D. Peterson, Lauren J. Krivo, and John Hagan, 179–98. New York: NYU Press.

Langley, Marty, and Josh Sugarmann. 2018. *Hispanic Victims of Lethal Firearms Violence in the United States*. Washington, DC: Violence Policy Center. http://www.vpc.org/studies/hispanic18.pdf.

Lanier, Christina. 2010. "Structure, Culture, and Lethality: An Integrated Model Approach to American Indian Suicide and Homicide." *Homicide Studies* 14 (1): 72–89. https://doi.org/10.1177/1088767909352829.

Light, M. T., and J. T. Ulmer. 2016. "Explaining the Gaps in White, Black, and Hispanic Violence since 1990: Accounting for Immigration, Incarceration, and Inequality." *American Sociological Review* 81 (2): 290–315. https://doi.org/10.1177/0003122416635667.

Loftin, Colin, David McDowall, and Matthew D. Fetzer. 2008. "A Comparison of SHR and Vital Statistics Homicide Estimates for U.S. Cities." *Journal of Contemporary Criminal Justice* 24 (1): 4–17. https://doi.org/10.1177/1043986207312585.

Martinez, Marlene. 2019. "Juan Crow." *Measure: An Undergraduate Research Journal* 3 (October): 10–24. https://measure-ojs-shsu.tdl.org/measure/index.php/measure/article /view/41.

Martinez, Monica Muñoz. 2018. *The Injustice Never Leaves You: Anti-Mexican Violence in Texas.* Cambridge: Harvard University Press.

Martínez, Ramiro. 2014. *Latino Homicide: Immigration, Violence, and Community.* New York: Routledge. https://doi.org/10.4324/9781315776064.

McNulty, Thomas, and Paul Bellair. 2006. "Explaining Racial and Ethnic Differences in Serious Adolescent Violent Behavior." *Criminology* 41 (3): 709–47.

Messner, Steven F., and Richard Rosenfeld. 2013. *Crime and the American Dream.* 5th ed. Belmont, CA: Wadsworth.

Morenoff, Jeffrey D., Robert J. Sampson, and Stephen W. Raudenbush. 2001. "Neighborhood Inequality, Collective Efficacy, and the Spatial Dynamics of Urban Violence." *Criminology* 39 (3): 517–58. https://doi.org/10.1111/j.1745-9125.2001.tb00932.x.

Parker, Karen F. 2008. *Unequal Crime Decline.* New York: New York University Press.

Parker, Karen F., and M. Kristen Hefner. 2015. "Intersections of Race, Gender, Disadvantage, and Violence: Applying Intersectionality to the Macro-level Study of Female Homicide." *Justice Quarterly* 32 (2): 1–32. https://doi.org/10.1080/07418825.2012.761719.

Pease, Bob. 2019. *Facing Patriarchy: From a Violent Gender Order to a Culture of Peace.* 1st ed. N.p.: Zed Books.

Perry, Barbara. 2008. *Silent Victims: Hate Crimes against Native Americans.* Tucson: University of Arizona Press.

Phillips, Julie A. 2002. "White, Black, and Latino Homicide Rates: Why the Difference?" *Social Problems* 49 (3): 349–73. https://doi.org/10.1525/sp.2002.49.3.349.

Potter, Hillary. 2006. "An Argument for Black Feminist Criminology Understanding African American Women's Experiences with Intimate Partner Abuse Using an Integrated Approach." *Feminist Criminology* 1 (2): 106–24. https://doi.org/10.1177/15570 85106286547.

———. 2013. "Intersectional Criminology: Interrogating Identity and Power in Criminological Research and Theory." *Critical Criminology* 21 (3): 305–18. https://doi.org /10.1007/s10612-013-9203-6.

———. 2015. *Intersectionality and Criminology: Disrupting and Revolutionizing Studies of Crime.* 1st ed. New York: Routledge.

Rosenfeld, Richard. 2016. *Documenting and Explaining the 2015 Homicide Rise: Research Directions.* NCJ 249895. Washington, DC: National Institute of Justice.

Rosenfeld, Richard, and James Alan Fox. 2019. "Anatomy of the Homicide Rise." *Homicide Studies* 23 (3): 202–24. https://doi.org/10.1177/1088767919848821.

Rosenfeld, Richard, Shytierra Gaston, Howard Spivak, and Seri Irazola. 2017. *Assessing and Responding to the Recent Homicide Rise in the United States.* NCJ 251067. Washington, DC: National Institute of Justice. https://www.ncjrs.gov/pdffiles1/nij/251067 .pdf.

Sampson, Robert J., and William Julius Wilson. 1995. "Toward a Theory of Race, Crime, and Urban Inequality." *Crime and Inequality,* edited by John Hagan and Ruth D Peterson, 37–56. Stanford, CA: Stanford University Press.

Selvin, S., S. T. Sacks, and D. W. Merrill. 1980. *Standardization of Age-Adjusted Mortality Rates.* LBL-10323. Berkeley: California University, Lawrence Berkeley Lab. https:// doi.org/10.2172/5277554.

Steffensmeier, Darrell, Ben Feldmeyer, Casey T. Harris, and Jeffery T. Ulmer. 2011. "Reassessing Trends in Black Violent Crime, 1980–2008: Sorting Out the 'Hispanic Effect' in Uniform Crime Reports Arrests, National Crime Victimization Survey Offender Estimates, and U.S. Prisoner Counts." *Criminology* 49 (1): 197–251. https://doi .org/10.1111/j.1745-9125.2010.00222.x.

Steffensmeier, Darrell, and Dana Haynie. 2000. "Gender, Structural Disadvantage, and Urban Crime: Do Macrosocial Variables Also Explain Female Offending Rates?" *Criminology* 38 (2): 403–38. https://doi.org/10.1111/j.1745-9125.2000.tb00895.x.

Tonry, Michael, and Matthew Melewski. 2008. "The Malign Effects of Drug and Crime Control Policies on Black Americans." *Crime and Justice* 37 (1): 1–44. https://doi.org /10.1086/588492.

Unnever, J. D., and S. L. Gabbidon. 2011. *A Theory of African American Offending: Race, Racism, and Crime.* 1st ed. New York: Routledge.

Velez, Maria B., Lauren J. Krivo, and Ruth D. Peterson. 2003. "Structural Inequality and Homicide: An Assessment of the Black-White Gap in Killings." *Criminology* 41 (3): 645–72. https://doi.org/10.1111/j.1745-9125.2003.tb01000.x.

Wu, Bohsiu. 2009. "Intimate Homicide between Asians and Non-Asians: The Impact of Community Context." *Journal of Interpersonal Violence* 24 (7): 1148–64. https://doi .org/10.1177/0886260508322191.

Zimring, Franklin E. 2007. *The Great American Crime Decline.* 1st ed. Oxford: Oxford University Press.

14

The Empirics of Immigration and Homicide

Evidence from California and Texas

MICHAEL T. LIGHT, LAURA BOISTEN, AND JUNGMYUNG KIM

Introduction

Immigrant criminality, especially serious criminality (e.g., homicide), is one of the most controversial issues in U.S. society. Concerns over crime and public safety have not only motivated some of the most divisive immigration policies in recent decades[1] but are also at the fore of political and legal debates. In his 2019 State of the Union address, for example, former president Trump stated that "year after year, countless Americans are murdered by criminal illegal aliens." And as recently as January 2021, the Texas attorney general sued the federal government for proposing a hundred-day moratorium on most deportations, arguing that "a near-complete suspension of deportations would only serve to endanger Texans and undermine federal law" (Ken Paxton 2021).[2]

Against this backdrop, it is unsurprising that the study of immigration and crime has been a key focus of criminological inquiry. Research in this area tends to fall within two broad categories. The first examines the macrolevel relationship between immigration and crime at multiple units of aggregation (e.g., counties, cities, neighborhoods). A recent meta-analysis of this body of work by Ousey and Kubrin (2018) found that the overall relationship between immigration and crime is negative and weak, but this association varies considerably depending on the type of crime, unit of analysis, and temporal design of the study. While this research evidences both theoretical depth and methodological sophistication, it can only indirectly speak to the central question motivating much of the ongoing controversy regarding immigrant criminality: do immigrants commit a disproportionate share of serious crime relative to native-born Americans?

The second body of research partially answers this question by using microlevel data to compare the criminality of immigrants and native-born U.S. citizens, often through a variety of youth surveys. This research generally finds lower criminal involvement among immigrants relative to their native-born peers (Stowell and Dipietro 2014), a result replicated in well-known surveys such as the Project on Human Development in Chicago Neighborhoods (PHDCN) (Sampson, Morenoff, and Raudenbush 2005), the Children of Immigrants Longitudinal Study (CILS) (Rumbaut, Massey, and Bean 2006), the National Longitudinal Survey of Youth (NLSY) (Bersani 2014), and the National Longitudinal Study of Adolescent to Adult Health (Add Health) (Rima et al. 2019). Despite the valuable contributions of this scholarly corpus, important gaps remain in our understanding of immigrant criminality. Most notably, few surveys allow for a detailed examination of the most serious forms of violence, such as homicide, because these are rare relative to other forms of crime and surveys of self-reported delinquency often exclude the most serious offenses (Hindelang, Hirschi, and Weis 1979).

It is likely for these reasons that much of the research on homicide draws from official crime statistics, such as the FBI's Supplementary Homicide Reports (Tostlebe et al. 2021).[3] When it comes to immigration research, however, most official crime sources are inadequate due to lack of information on immigration status. Of the most widely utilized crime data sources, neither the Uniform Crime Reports, National Crime Victimization Survey, or National Incident-Based Reporting System record information about nativity or immigration status. Immigration status is also inconsistently recorded in prison populations. For example, in 2016, California, Nevada, New Hampshire, North Dakota, and Oregon did not report information on the number of immigrants in their prison populations to the Bureau of Justice Statistics (BJS), while other states "likely provided undercounts" (Carson 2018, 13). The few studies that have leveraged official crime statistics to examine homicide offending by immigration status are often drawn from a single, highly select jurisdiction, such as Miami (Martinez and Lee 2000; Nielson et al. 2005; but see Light, He, and Robey 2020 for an exception).

Thus, dual data constraints obscure the picture of immigration and homicide: surveys that include immigrant criminality rarely inform our understanding of serious violence, while official crime statistics often omit information on immigration status. The result is a lack of information to address basic questions regarding comparative rates of lethal violence between immigrants and U.S.-born citizens. Our goal in this chapter is to fill this gap. Using uniquely detailed criminal history information for all arrests in California and Texas between 2006 and 2018, we aim to provide an empirical foundation for general criminological literature on the immigration-homicide nexus by establishing facts about its key dimensions: Do immigrants have more violent criminal pasts than native-born citizens? How does the immigrant homicide rate compare to the native-born rate? Do these relationships differ by race, ethnicity, or national origin? How have immigrant homicide rates changed in recent years? Is the homicide rate different for undocumented immigrants? Given the amount of public and political acrimony surrounding immigrant criminality, systematic answers to each of these questions are long overdue.

Data Sources

California and Texas are advantageous research settings for understanding crime and immigration. They are home to roughly 20 percent of the total U.S. population and 35 percent of the immigrant population.[4] Both states are sites of intense federal immigration enforcement initiatives. Indeed, the federal government paid California more than any other state to hold criminal aliens in 2017—and Texas the third most.[5] Interestingly, California and Texas have taken markedly different approaches to collaborating with federal immigration authorities in recent years. Perhaps nowhere is this juxtaposition better illustrated than in the immigration-related bills both states passed in 2017. That year, Texas legislators signed SB 4 into law, attempting to abolish sanctuary policies by holding local officials criminally liable for refusing to accommodate the federal government's requests to help enforce immigration law (Hing 2017). California, on the other hand, enacted SB 54, declaring the state a sanctuary by limiting cooperation with immigration authorities and preventing state and local police from holding people for immigration violations alone (Ulloa 2017). These differences provide an interesting contrast to inform how state-level contexts condition the immigration-homicide relationship.

Our Texas data come from the Computerized Criminal History (CCH) database provided by the Texas Department of Public Safety (DPS), which by law requires local jurisdictions to provide case processing information for all felony, class A, and class B misdemeanor arrests throughout the state. The CCH includes rich information on defendant, date of arrest, arresting agency, level of offense, criminal statute, and complete criminal history over a person's lifetime. Critical for this study, inquiries into citizenship and place of birth are mandatory parts of the jail booking process in Texas and are thus included in the CCH database. In addition, starting in June 2011, the DPS started collecting immigration status information from the Department of Homeland Security (DHS). The DHS runs the biometric information on arrestees through its IDENT database so that Immigration and Customs Enforcement (ICE) can determine the person's immigration status and whether the individual is a priority for removal. In our analysis, we define native-born citizens as people who were born in the United States, are U.S. citizens, and are not recorded in the CCH database as "legal" or "illegal" immigrants. All other individuals are classified as immigrants. We also conduct subanalyses to examine heterogeneity among immigrants according to CCH classifications of undocumented and lawful immigrants. For technical details on the CCH data, see Light, He, and Robey (2020).

The primary data source for California is the Criminal Offender Record Information (CORI) provided by the California Department of Justice. Like the CCH, the CORI database contains information on citizenship and nativity and is legally required to include complete criminal records for those with criminal justice contact throughout California. Unlike the Texas database, CORI does not include information on legal status, and thus our inquiry into differences by documentation status centers on Texas.

In both the CCH and CORI datasets, we focus on violent and homicide arrest charges.[6] To harmonize crime definitions across the states, we use the National Crime Information Center (NCIC) offense classifications.[7] The sole difference between our approach and the NCIC codes is that we exclude misdemeanor offenses in our definition of homicide and violent crime. We classify felony arrests with offense codes listed as "violent crime" as our measure of violence (this includes homicide, kidnapping, sexual assault, robbery, simple and aggravated assault, terroristic threat, and extortion with human injury). Felony arrests for murder and negligent manslaughter are classified as homicides. These measures serve as the numerators for our crime rate calculations.[8] Population figures come from the U.S. Census' American Community Survey (ACS) one-year estimates.[9] Consistent with common usage, we classify individuals as nonimmigrants if they were born in the United States or were born abroad to American parents. Naturalized and non-U.S. citizens are both classified as immigrants in our study. We use the same classifications for both Texas and California to get respective total immigrant population counts as well as the native-born citizen count. Regarding undocumented immigrants, the ACS does not provide estimates of documented and undocumented immigrants. We thus use data from the Center for Migration Studies (CMS), which provides annual estimates of the undocumented population by state and is one of the primary data sources in previous research on undocumented immigration and crime (Light and Miller 2018; Light, He, and Robey 2020).

Data Findings

Violent Crime and Homicide Rates

Figure 14.1 displays violent felony crime and homicide rates between 2006 and 2018 in Texas by immigration status. Beginning with violent crimes in the top panel, U.S.-born citizens are moderately more likely to be arrested for a violent felony (per 100,000) across the entire study period. Over time, this gap widens. In 2006, the violent crime rate among immigrants is roughly 15 percent less than the violent crime rate among nonimmigrants. By 2018, the immigrant rate of violence is 33 percent less, largely due to an increase in violent arrests among U.S.-born citizens (from 190.3 per 100,000 in 2006 to 230.7 in 2018) and a steady rate of violence among immigrants (from 162.5 per 100,000 in 2006 to 155.1 in 2018). As indicated in the bottom panel, the homicide rate among immigrants and nonimmigrants in Texas slowly decreases over the period. As in the overall rates of violence, immigrants consistently exhibit lower rates of homicide offending than U.S.-born citizens (though the gaps are relatively modest most years).

Turning to figure 14.2, the relative offending gap between immigrants and nonimmigrants in California is more noticeable. Between 2006 and 2018, violent crime rates per 100,000 individuals are 205.9 for the U.S.-born

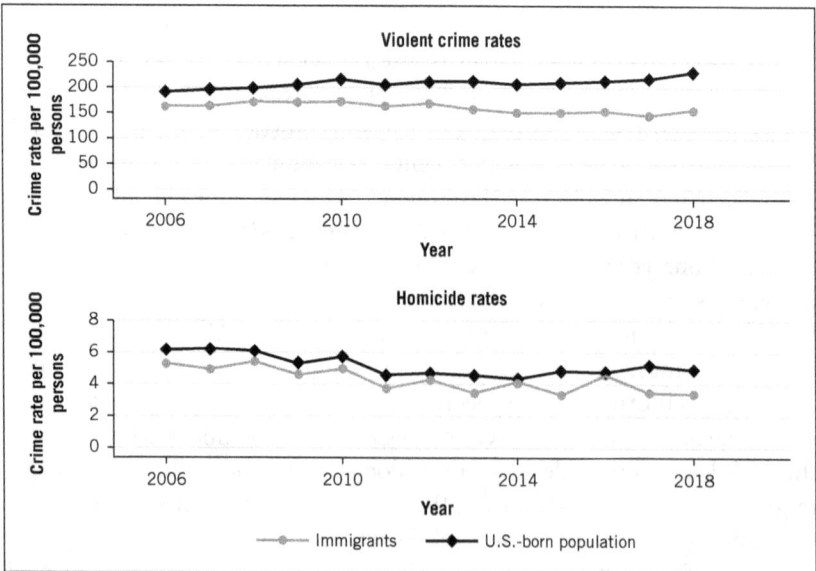

Figure 14.1 Violent Crime Rates in Texas by Immigration Status

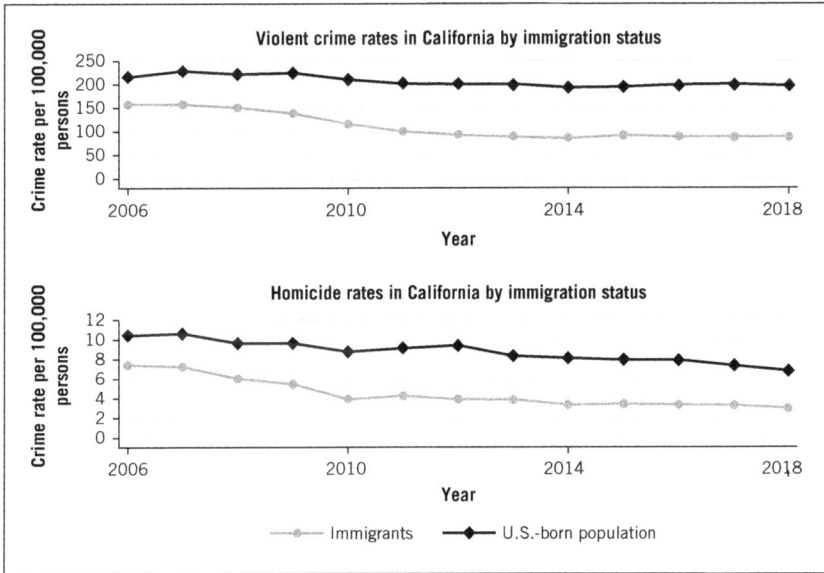

Figure 14.2 Violent Crime Rates in California by Immigration Status

population and 110.5 for immigrants. Stated differently, the U.S.-born population is about 1.9 times more likely to be arrested for violent crimes than immigrants. For homicides (bottom panel), the rates for U.S.-born citizens and immigrants over the period were 8.7 and 4.5 (per 100,000), respectively. Correspondingly, the U.S.-born population is 1.9 times more likely to be arrested for homicide compared to immigrants in California. Over time, we observe a general crime decline; this trend is stronger among immigrants. The decrease in violent crime is around 10 percent for the U.S.-born population (216.3 in 2006 and 196.7 in 2018) but about 45 percent for immigrants (157.6 in 2006 and 87.4 in 2018). The homicide rate shows a similar pattern. Homicide rates decrease by about 35 percent for the U.S.-born population (10.4 to 6.8), while the decline among immigrants is considerably more marked (60 percent, from 7.4 to 3.0).

Comparing figures 14.1 and 14.2, we see that since 2010, immigrant homicide rates in Texas and California have been comparable. This is not the case for violent crime, however, where immigrants generally exhibit lower arrest rates in California relative to Texas. The magnitude of this difference is sizable. Between 2006 and 2018, the immigrant violent arrest rate in California is 31 percent lower than in Texas (110.5 per 100,000 in California versus 160.7 per 100,000 in Texas).

Race, Ethnicity, and National Origin

Table 14.1 shows homicide rates by race and ethnicity for immigrants in Texas. For this fine-grain analysis, we use the average number of homicides between 2014 and 2018 to ensure enough cases (we use the average population of each racial/ethnic group in Texas over this same period). We observe significant differences not only across racial groups but also by immigration status among those in the same racial category. For white people, the homicide rate among immigrants is considerably higher (the gap is -4.10 per 100,000). For Hispanic and Asian people, homicide rates for immigrants and U.S.-born citizens are comparable. Among Black individuals, however, homicide rates are substantially higher for U.S.-born individuals—over three times higher than for Black immigrants. This same pattern is true among individuals in the category "other races," but to a lesser extent (the U.S.-born homicide rate among other races is only about two times greater than other race immigrants in Texas).

Table 14.1 also shows homicide rates by national origin in Texas. For this analysis, we examine the ten largest immigrant groups by population between 2014 and 2018. Immigrants from all ten countries listed have lower homicide rates than native-born U.S. citizens. Among these groups, however, there is considerable variation, ranging from 3.9 (per 100,000) among Guatemalan immigrants to 0 among Chinese immigrants. This latter finding is noteworthy. Over a five-year period, there is not a single recorded homicide arrest of a Chinese immigrant in Texas despite a yearly average population of 103,190. Mexico is by far the largest immigrant group living in Texas with a yearly average of roughly 2.5 million between 2014 and 2018. However, three countries of origin have a higher homicide rate than Mexico (2.2): Honduras (2.7), El Salvador (3.6), and Guatemala (3.9).

TABLE 14.1 HOMICIDE RATES BY SOCIODEMOGRAPHIC GROUP: TEXAS, 2014–2018							
Immigrant Status and Race/Ethnicity				National Origin			
	U.S.-Born	Immigrant	Difference	Country	Homicide	Country	Homicide
White	2.69	6.79	−4.10	Guatemala	3.85	India	0.64
Black	10.95	3.56	7.39	El Salvador	3.63	Pakistan	0.70
Hispanic	3.32	3.43	−0.11	Honduras	2.71	Vietnam	0.23
Asian	0.54	0.62	−0.08	Mexico	2.19	Philippines	0.19
Other Race	1.32	0.67	0.65	Nigeria	0.80	China	0.00
Overall	4.82	3.81	1.01	United States	4.82		

Note: The unit of analysis is a charge at arrest, not an individual. Immigrants include naturalized U.S. citizens.

TABLE 14.2 HOMICIDE RATES BY SOCIODEMOGRAPHIC GROUP: CALIFORNIA, 2014–2018

Immigrant Status and Race/Ethnicity				National Origin			
	U.S.-Born	Immigrant	Difference	Country	Homicide	Country	Homicide
White	2.75	0.65	2.10	El Salvador	4.55	Philippines	0.89
Black	29.05	13.98	15.07	Mexico	4.43	China	0.85
Hispanic	24.65	10.85	13.79	Guatemala	2.93	Iran	0.74
Asian	2.05	0.71	1.34	Korea	1.78	India	0.49
Other Race	3.51	12.36	−8.85	Vietnam	1.48	Taiwan	0.32
Overall	7.58	3.28	4.30	United States	7.58		

Note: The unit of analysis is a charge at arrest, not an individual.

Table 14.2 shows how the immigration gap in homicide rates differs by race and ethnicity in California from 2014 to 2018. Immigrants show lower homicide rates across all racial groups except for "other races," partly due to that group's small size and thus higher outlier influence (the immigrant gap among white population: 2.1, Black population: 15.1, Hispanic: 13.8, Asian: 1.3, other race: -8.9). Furthermore, we examine homicide differences by national origin among immigrants. As with Texas, we focus on the top ten countries of origin by population size in California. Unsurprisingly, the focal countries are Latin American and Asian. The results suggest that immigrants from Latin American countries (El Salvador: 4.6, Mexico: 4.4, Guatemala: 2.9) tend to have higher homicide rates than immigrants from Asian countries (Korea: 1.8, Vietnam: 1.5, Philippines: 0.9, China: 0.9, Iran: 0.7, India: 0.5, Taiwan: 0.3). Immigrants from all these countries show lower homicide rates than the U.S.-born population (7.6 from 2014 to 2018).

Criminal History Profile

Tables 14.3 and 14.4 answer questions about the extensiveness of immigrants' criminal records relative to native citizens' records. Specifically, these tables report the number of prior felony and misdemeanor arrests, arrests for violence, felony and misdemeanor convictions, and prison sentences by immigrant status. The tables include the criminal history profiles for individuals arrested between 2006 and 2018, though it is important to note that arrests, convictions, and incarcerations that occurred before 2006 are included in these records.[10]

Table 14.3 shows criminal histories in Texas. Prior to the current offense, immigrants arrested for a violent crime had fewer arrests and convictions than U.S.-born citizens (shown on the left side of table 14.3). Specifically, the

TABLE 14.3 ARREST/CONVICTION HISTORIES OF VIOLENT CRIME AND HOMICIDE CASES BY IMMIGRATION STATUS: TEXAS

	Violent Crime				Homicide			
	U.S.-Born Population		Immigrants		U.S.-Born Population		Immigrants	
	Mean	SD	Mean	SD	Mean	SD	Mean	SD
Number of prior arrests	3.89	3.56	2.09	2.81	3.44	3.37	1.94	2.70
Number of prior violent felony arrests	0.72	1.56	0.39	1.21	0.66	1.48	0.36	1.07
Number of prior misd. arrests	2.41	2.73	1.37	2.09	1.86	2.36	1.06	1.72
Number of prior felony arrests	1.46	2.03	0.69	1.41	1.43	1.96	0.77	1.51
Number of prior misd. convictions	1.68	2.39	0.86	1.66	1.24	2.01	0.65	1.36
Number of prior felony convictions	0.63	1.36	0.26	0.81	0.61	1.28	0.28	0.85
Number of prior sentences	0.49	1.03	0.17	0.58	0.49	1.01	0.19	0.60
Observations	594,159		89,584		14,637		2,374	

Note: The unit of analysis is a charge at arrest, not an individual. Immigrants include naturalized U.S. citizens.

results show that on average, native-born citizens have almost twice as many prior arrests than immigrants (3.9 for U.S. citizens and 2.1 for immigrants) and over twice as many past felony convictions (0.6 for U.S. citizens and 0.3 for immigrants). Perhaps more important for our inquiry, U.S.-born citizens are nearly two times more likely to have been arrested for a prior violent felony than immigrants (0.7 for U.S.-born citizens and 0.4 for immigrants).

The results among homicide offenders on the right panel of table 14.3 tell a similar story. On average, immigrants tend to have fewer arrests, convictions, and prison sentences prior to arrest for a homicide. Interestingly, the number of prior violent arrests is quite small for both groups (0.7 for citizens and 0.4 for immigrants), but there is substantial overlap in the distribution as indicated by the relatively large standard deviations (1.5 for citizens and 1.1 for immigrants).

Table 14.4 displays criminal histories for arrestees by immigration status in California. Consistent with the findings in Texas, among those arrested for a violent crime, immigrants have considerably fewer prior criminal cases. Throughout various measures of criminal history, including prior violent arrests, the U.S-born population tends to have between 1.5 and 2.5 times as many prior cases as immigrants. We observe essentially the same pattern among homicide cases, where criminal histories among immigrants tend to be considerably less extensive.

Undocumented Immigrants

Going beyond immigration status, table 14.5 shows criminal history profiles for violent felony arrests and homicide arrests by legal status. It is important

TABLE 14.4 ARREST/CONVICTION HISTORIES OF VIOLENT CRIME AND HOMICIDE CASES BY IMMIGRATION STATUS: CALIFORNIA

	Violent Crime				Homicide			
	U.S.-Born Population		Immigrants		U.S.-Born Population		Immigrants	
	Mean	SD	Mean	SD	Mean	SD	Mean	SD
Number of prior arrests	3.87	4.08	2.48	3.02	2.99	3.23	1.90	2.19
Number of prior violent felony arrests	0.74	1.33	0.40	0.93	0.57	0.99	0.33	0.70
Number of prior misd. arrests	1.37	2.26	0.86	1.75	0.88	1.67	0.54	1.20
Number of prior felony arrests	2.51	2.45	1.62	1.76	2.11	2.15	1.37	1.45
Number of prior misd. convictions	2.19	2.94	1.61	2.49	1.57	2.44	1.21	2.05
Number of prior felony convictions	2.15	3.16	1.05	2.22	2.05	3.01	1.06	2.11
Number of prior sentences	1.07	2.12	0.44	1.33	1.05	1.97	0.47	1.22
Observations	1,438,067		314,419		33,053		6,539	

Note: The unit of analysis is a charge at arrest, not an individual.

to note that this table only includes those arrested between 2012 and 2018 due to lack of legal status information prior to this time. The results in table 14.5 display a clear trend: native-born citizens are arrested and convicted of more crimes prior to either a homicide or violent arrest than documented or undocumented immigrants. Prior to a homicide or violent felony arrest, native-born citizens have over 1.5 times as many previous arrests as documented immigrants. Relative to undocumented immigrants, U.S.-born citizens have about three times as many prior arrests. This difference is more glaring when looking at prior violent felony arrests. Prior to an arrest for a violent crime, U.S.-born citizens are roughly four times more likely to have been previously arrested for a violent felony than undocumented immigrants. Among those arrested for homicide, U.S.-born citizens are twice as likely to have a violent felony arrest in their criminal history than undocumented immigrants. Focusing on the two immigrant groups, undocumented immigrants have less extensive criminal histories than documented immigrants without exception.

Moving beyond prior criminality, how do crime rates compare for those with different legal statuses? The top and bottom panels of figure 14.3 answer this question by showing violent felony and homicide arrests by legal status in Texas.[11] The obvious pattern is that violent crime rates for undocumented and documented immigrants have been lower than those for native-born citizens in recent years. Undocumented immigrants have substantially lower violent crime rates than both documented immigrants and U.S.-citizens. Rates of violence for each group are fairly steady over the period. Homicide rates tell a different story. Undocumented immigrants again have lower rates than both lawful immigrants and native-born citizens. However, the homicide rate

TABLE 14.5 ARREST/CONVICTION HISTORIES OF VIOLENT CRIME AND HOMICIDE CASES BY DOCUMENTATION STATUS: TEXAS

| | Violent Crime | | | | | | Homicide | | | | | |
| | U.S.-Born Population | | Documented Immigrants | | Undocumented Immigrants | | U.S.-Born Population | | Documented Immigrants | | Undocumented Immigrants | |
	Mean	SD	Mean	SD	Mean	SD	Mean	SD	Mean	SD	Mean	SD
Number of prior arrests	4.05	3.61	2.53	3.11	1.31	2.00	3.60	3.46	2.27	3.04	1.36	1.81
Number of prior violent felony arrests	0.82	1.68	0.53	1.44	0.19	0.77	0.73	1.55	0.43	1.18	0.35	0.98
Number of prior misd. arrests	2.61	2.85	1.68	2.39	0.93	1.55	2.05	2.52	1.26	1.92	0.87	1.43
Number of prior felony arrests	1.60	2.17	0.92	1.68	0.37	0.96	1.59	2.12	0.96	1.86	0.45	0.77
Number of prior misd. convictions	1.81	2.51	1.02	1.88	0.61	1.28	1.37	2.18	0.76	1.55	0.50	1.04
Number of prior felony convictions	0.71	1.48	0.35	1.00	0.12	0.53	0.68	1.40	0.37	0.97	0.10	0.39
Number of prior sentences	0.51	1.08	0.23	0.69	0.07	0.33	0.52	1.07	0.24	0.71	0.06	0.29
Observations	343,557		37,863		11,940		7,624		1,002		230	

Note: The unit of analysis is a charge at arrest, not an individual. Years 2012–2018. Documented immigrants include naturalized U.S. citizens.

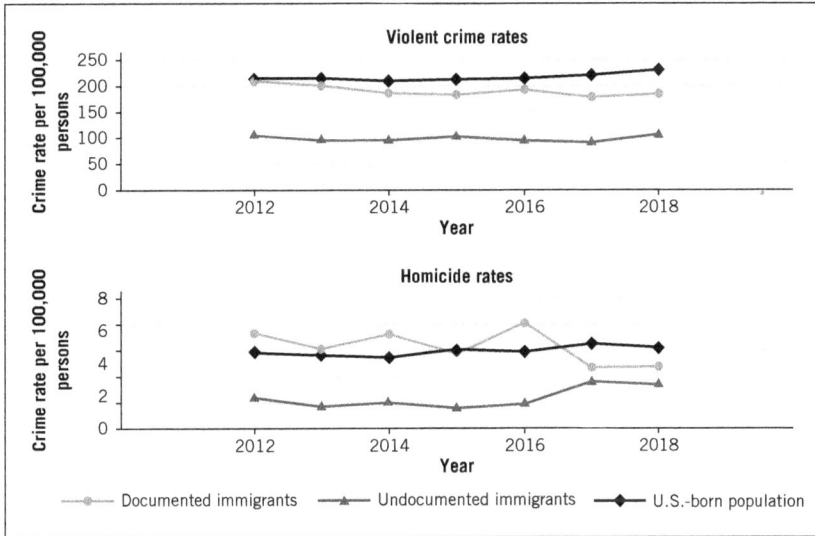

Figure 14.3 Violent Crime Rates in Texas by Legal Status

for documented immigrants fluctuates much more and is at times higher than the rate of U.S-citizens (2012–2014 and 2016). The rate for the U.S.-born population is relatively stable over the period, while the homicide rate for undocumented immigrants hovers around two (per 100,000) until 2016 and then increases to roughly three in 2017 and 2018.

Discussion

This chapter leverages rich criminal justice data from the two largest immigrant destinations in the United States to establish basic facts about immigrants and serious violent crime. This effort to get the facts right yields several important findings, summarized as follows:

- Immigrants generally exhibit lower rates of serious violent crime in California and Texas. This is true for overall rates of violence and homicide.
- Violent crime rates among immigrants in California are lower than among immigrants in Texas, and the relative gap between rates for native and foreign-born individuals is considerably larger in California. Immigrant homicide rates are more comparable in Texas and California, particularly since 2010.
- In both states, there is substantial heterogeneity in the immigration-homicide relationship by race/ethnicity and national origin.

Generally speaking, immigrants from Asian countries have especially low rates of homicide offending.

- In Texas, undocumented immigrants have lower rates of violence and homicide offending than lawful immigrants and native-born citizens especially. This is true for every year we have data.
- Relative to the U.S.-born population, the criminal histories of immigrants arrested for violent crimes are both less extensive and less severe. Among the foreign born, undocumented immigrants have the least serious criminal records.

Each of these points is necessarily descriptive, but as criminologist Robert Sampson (2008, 30) notes, "descriptive facts are at the heart of sound social science, a first step in any causal inquiry." Having laid out some fundamental contours of the immigration-violence nexus in the contemporary United States, the critical next step is for researchers to build off this foundation and examine why we observe these patterns. In this vein, our results point to several fruitful areas for subsequent research.

The first area is deportation. Federal immigration enforcement is increasingly dependent on state and local criminal justice authorities to funnel criminal aliens into removal proceedings (Eagly 2013), making local police the gatekeepers of both the criminal justice system and immigration courts (Motomura 2011). As Supreme Court Justice John Paul Stevens wrote in *Padilla v Kentucky* (559 U.S. 356 2010), "the 'drastic measure' of deportation or removal, is now virtually inevitable for a vast number of noncitizens convicted of crimes." This is especially true for immigrants convicted of serious violent crimes—even in California, which does not shield violent offenders from federal immigration authorities.[12] Thus, on top of criminal punishment, fear of deportation may deter criminal wrongdoing. Deportation likely informs our criminal history findings as well; it is plausible that immigrants with the most severe criminal histories were deported and thus excluded from our data. As the immigration and criminal justice systems become increasingly intertwined, we think a concerted focus on deportation in immigration-violence research is imperative.

Given the observed differences between California and Texas, we think emphasis on the context of reception is also warranted. For example, Lyons, Vélez, and Santoro (2013) suggest that immigrants generally commit fewer crimes in areas that provide greater immigrant political opportunities, such as those that provide sanctuary to immigrants. This view generally aligns with Stowell and Dipietro's (2014, 524) argument that "social contexts inhospitable or unwelcoming of immigrants may potentially carry the unanticipated consequences of increased levels of violent deviance." Do the markedly different policy stances toward immigrants in California and Texas help explain the observed differences in immigrant violent crime in these states? Our findings cannot answer this question, but they do provide suggestive evidence in favor of this view. More broadly, we think the differential embrace of heightened immigration enforcement between California and Texas in recent years provides a useful research setting to understand how the context of reception shapes immigrant crime patterns. This contrast can shed light on the efficacy of immigration enforcement policies to reduce immigrant criminality.

Lastly, despite growing calls for researchers to consider the tremendous heterogeneity within immigrant populations and theoretical reasons to expect significant variation in immigrant criminality based on factors such as race/ethnicity, national origin, and documentation status, the foreign-native dichotomy still predominates in immigration-crime research. The results presented here add empirical validity for theoretical motivations to move beyond this approach. In our assessment, differences by national origin present remarkably interesting criminological questions. Take our results regarding several Asian immigrant groups, for example. From 2014 to 2018, there were a total of 11,517,131 immigrants from China, Philippines, and Vietnam living in Texas and California (1,915,081 in Texas and 9,602,050 in California, based on the aggregate total population of these groups from 2014 to 2018), yet we observe only 103 homicide charges among these groups (3 in Texas and 100 in California). This amounts to a combined homicide rate of 0.9 per 100,000, roughly 80 percent below the national average.[13] Understanding what constellation of factors accounts for these notably low rates, such as differences in human capital, neighborhood resources, family structures, and cultural values, is a paramount criminological question. While each of these aforementioned areas presents great theoretical and methodological challenges, they also represent promising research frontiers.

NOTES

1. In defending the passage of Arizona's controversial SB 1070 law, which requires that state law enforcement officers attempt to determine individuals' immigration status during lawful stops, then governor Jan Brewer stated, "We cannot afford all this illegal immigration and everything that comes with it, everything from the crime and to the drugs and the kidnappings and the extortion and the beheadings and the fact that people can't feel safe in their community. It's wrong!" (Farley 2010). The Department of Homeland Security's Secure Communities Program (S-Comm) is another prominent example of a policy motivated by concerns about crime. This program was designed as a crime fighting initiative to enhance the ability of Immigration and Customs Enforcement (ICE) to identify and deport criminal aliens by checking biometric information from arrested suspects in state and local jurisdictions for immigration violations (Miles and Cox 2014).

2. An amicus brief filed in this case on behalf of Advocates for Victims of Illegal Alien Crime further argued that "DHS's abdication of its duties will surely make these crime statistics increase and Texas will be left picking up the pieces. The State of Texas and her

citizens pay the price for these crimes in the form of the victim's emotional toll and the tax dollars spent processing the accused through the justice system and ultimately incarcerating them in Texas' prisons. These are crimes that would not have occurred if these individuals were not in the country" (Civil Action No. 6:21-cv-0003, Document 77).

3. A related body of research examines homicide victimization rates using death certificates (Light and Ulmer 2016; also see Tostlebe et al. 2021 for a useful discussion of using death certificates in homicide research).

4. United States Census Bureau. "April 2010 Census Table 1. Annual Estimates of the Resident Population for the United States, Regions, States, and Puerto Rico: April 1, 2010 to July 1, 2019." Accessed February 23, 2021. https://www.census.gov/data/tables/time-series/demo/popest/2010s-state-total.html.

5. Accessed here: https://bja.ojp.gov/program/state-criminal-alien-assistance-program-scaap/archives.

6. We restrict the sample by omitting juvenile offenders. In Texas, the age at which an offender can be tried as an adult is seventeen; in California, the age is sixteen (Interstate Commission for Juveniles).

7. We use the following NCIC definitions: https://secure.ssa.gov/poms.nsf/lnx/0202613900.

8. We externally validated the crime statistics reported here with official published reports in each state. We compared our Texas arrests with the total number of arrests published by the DPS. From 2006 to 2018, there is a correlation of 0.97. We also compared the homicide rates to the official DPS reports (Texas Crime Analysis 2 for years 2010–2018 and the Annual Report of UCR for years 2006–2009). However, it should be noted that these do not use the same definition we do, as they report a murder rate rather than a homicide rate. The most important difference is that we include any individual who was arrested regardless of whether the arrest led to a conviction or whether the classification changed later on in the prosecution process, while these reports report a crime rate rather than an arrest rate. Cleared cases and multiple offenders are not reflected in the Texas DPS statistics. Furthermore, yearly murder rates reported by DPS are slightly different, as "attempted murder and assaults with the intent to kill are not counted as murder, but are included in UCR as aggravated assaults. Suicides, accidental deaths, and justifiable homicides are also excluded from the murder classification." Over our study period, our homicide rate and the DPS murder rate show a correlation of 0.75.

For California data, we compared our figures with those in the *Crime in California 2018* report published by the California Department of Justice (California Department of Justice 2019). The crime statistics in our data show some differences with the California Department of Justice. The overall violent crime rate between 2006 and 2018 is 180.1, and the homicide rate is 7.6, which is different from the statistics in *Crime in California 2018* (444.1 for violent crime rates and 5.1 for homicide rates during the same period). This difference can be attributed to four main factors. First and foremost, the reports define homicide and violent crime using UCR classifications rather than NCIC crime codes. When we apply the UCR definitions of homicide and violent crime to the CORI data, our results are satisfyingly close to those reported in the *Crime in California 2018* report. Second, the crime rates collected from our data are not based on reporting of crimes but on actual arrests made for crimes, and there could be multiple offenders for the same reported crime. In California, 15 percent of homicide cases had the same arrest agency and the arrest date. Considering multiple offenders could be arrested on different dates, the possibility of multiple offenders in one crime could be even larger. Unfortunately, we do not have information on how multiple offenders are involved in one crime to examine the impact of this possibility. Third, using a charge rather than an arrest as the unit of analysis also helps explain the difference between our analysis and that of the California Department of Justice. Last, we focus on felony offenses to define violent crimes, which is different from *Crime in California 2018*. Combined, these factors help explain the aforementioned differences. Our trends over time are similar to the official reports, showing steady decrease of violent crime and homicide rates since 2006 (correlation 0.86 for violent crime and 0.9 for homicide). This gives evidence that the pattern examined here shows consistency with external sources.

9. Accessed via IPUMS: https://usa.ipums.org/usa/.

10. All criminal history measures are capped at ten to reduce the influence of outliers.

11. Homicide trends for each group and overall pattern are consistent with Light, He, and Robey (2020). See Light, He, and Robey (2020) appendix section 2 figure S1 for a similar graph using a slightly different definition of homicide.

12. California's SB 54 gives law enforcement officials the discretion to cooperate with immigration authorities if the individual has been convicted of a "serious or violent felony."

13. The national homicide rate during the same period is 5.0 on average, according to the FBI.

REFERENCES

Bersani, Bianca. 2014. "An Examination of First and Second Generation Immigrant Offending Trajectories." *Justice Quarterly* 31 (2): 315–43.

Carson, A. E. 2018. "Prisoners in 2016." News Release, NCJ251149. https://bjs.ojp.gov/library/publications/prisoners-2016.

Eagly, Ingrid V. 2013. "Criminal Justice for Noncitizens: An Analysis of Variation in Local Enforcement." *NYU Law Review* 88:1126.

Hindelang, Michael J., Travis Hirschi, and Joseph G. Weis. 1979. "Correlates of Delinquency: The Illusion of Discrepancy between Self-Report and Official Measures." *American Sociological Review* 44 (6): 995–1014.

Hing, Bill Ong. 2017. "Entering the Trump Ice Age: Contextualizing the New Immigration Enforcement Regime." *Texas A&M Law Review* 5:253.

Ken Paxton Attorney General of Texas. 2021. "AG Paxton: Texas Lawsuit Results in Court Upholding Federal Law, Halts Biden Administration's Unlawful Freeze of Deportations." News Release, January 26, 2021. https://www.texasattorneygeneral.gov/news/releases/ag-paxton-texas-lawsuit-results-court-upholding-federal-law-halts-biden-administrations-unlawful#:~:text=%E2%80%9CThe%20Court's%20decision%20to%20stop,%2C%E2%80%9D%20said%20Attorney%20General%20Paxton.

Lee, Matthew T., and Ramiro Martinez Jr. 2002. "Social Disorganization Revisited: Mapping the Recent Immigration and Black Homicide Relationship in Northern Miami." *Sociological Focus* 35 (4): 363–80.

Light, Michael T., Jingying He, and Jason P. Robey. 2020. "Comparing Crime Rates between Undocumented Immigrants, Legal Immigrants, and Native-Born US Citizens in Texas." *Proceedings of the National Academy of Sciences* 117 (51): 32340–47.

Light, Michael T., and Ty Miller. 2018. "Does Undocumented Immigration Increase Violent Crime?" *Criminology* 56:370–401.

Light, Michael T., and Jeffery T. Ulmer. 2016. "Explaining the Gaps in White, Black, and Hispanic Violence since 1990: Accounting for Immigration, Incarceration, and Inequality." *American Sociological Review* 81 (2): 290–315.

Lyons, Christopher J., María B. Vélez, and Wayne A. Santoro. 2013. "Neighborhood Immigration, Violence, and City-Level Immigrant Political Opportunities." *American Sociological Review* 78 (4): 604–32.

Martinez, Ramiro, Jr., and Matthew T. Lee. 2000. "Comparing the Context of Immigrant Homicides in Miami: Haitians, Jamaicans and Mariels." *International Migration Review* 34:794–812.

Miles, Thomas J., and Adam B. Cox. 2014. "Does Immigration Enforcement Reduce Crime? Evidence from Secure Communities." *Journal of Law and Economics* 57:937–73.

Motomura, Hiroshi. 2011. "The Discretion That Matters: Federal Immigration Enforcement, State and Local Arrests, and the Civil-Criminal Line." *Immigration & Nationality Law Review* 32:167.

Nielsen, Amie L., Matthew T. Lee, and Ramiro Martinez Jr. 2005. "Integrating Race, Place and Motive in Social Disorganization Theory: Lessons from a Comparison of Black and Latino Homicide Types in Two Immigrant Destination Cities." *Criminology* 43 (3): 837–72.

Ousey, Graham C., and Charis E. Kubrin. 2009. "Exploring the Connection between Immigration and Violent Crime Rates in US Cities, 1980–2000." *Social Problems* 56:447–73.

———. 2018. "Immigration and Crime: Assessing a Contentious Issue." *Annual Review of Criminology* 1:63–84.

Rima, Dzhansarayeva, Alimkulov Yerbol, Shopabayev Batyrbek, Tlepbergenov Orynbassar, and Kevin M. Beaver. 2019. "Examining the Potential Association between Immigration and Criminal Involvement Using a Nationally Representative and Longitudinal Sample of Youth." *Journal of Interpersonal Violence* 36 (21–22): NP12155–NP12175.

Rumbaut, Rubén G., Douglas S. Massey, and Frank D. Bean. 2006. "Linguistic Life Expectancies: Immigrant Language Retention in Southern California." *Population and Development Review* 32 (3): 447–60.

Sampson, Robert J. 2008. "Rethinking Crime and Immigration." *Contexts* 7:28–33.

Sampson, Robert J., Jeffrey D. Morenoff, and Stephen Raudenbush. 2005. "Social Anatomy of Racial and Ethnic Disparities in Violence." *American Journal of Public Health* 95:224–32.

Stowell, Jacob, and Stephanie DiPietro. 2014. "Ethnicity, Crime, and Immigration in the United States Crimes by and against Immigrants." In *The Oxford Handbook of Ethnicity, Crime, and Immigration*, edited by Sandra Bucerius and Michael Tonry, 505–28. New York: Oxford University Press.

Tostlebe, Jennifer J., David C. Pyrooz, Richard G. Rogers, and Ryan K. Masters. 2021. "The National Death Index as a Source of Homicide Data: A Methodological Exposition of Promises and Pitfalls for Criminologists." *Homicide Studies* 25:5–36.

Ulloa, Jazmine. 2017. "California Becomes 'Sanctuary State' in Rebuke of Trump Immigration Policy." *Los Angeles Times*.

15

Studying Demographic Shifts and Homicide

The Case of Texas and Immigration Status

Erin Orrick, Chris Guerra, and Alex R. Piquero

Introduction

The relationship between age and crime has been one of the most consistently documented of all criminological facts. Beginning with the plotting of police data in France by Quetelet, followed by the pioneering birth cohort study by Wolfgang et al., and continuing with numerous longitudinal studies examining the relationship between age and crime, it has been observed that "age is everywhere correlated with crime. Its effects on crime do not depend on other demographic correlates of crime" (Hirschi and Gottfredson 1983, 581). In its aggregate form, offending begins in early adolescence, rises to a peak in mid to late adolescence, and drops precipitously in early to mid-twenties. To be sure, it is the case that some crime types do not perfectly mimic the trend described. Acts such as tax evasion, intimate partner violence, and homicide—the focus of this chapter—show some variability to this trend. In particular, the late teens to mid-twenties appears to be the peak age range for homicide offenders, with Black males as the largest group of such offenders (cf. Sharkey and Friedson 2019).

Much has been written about demographic characteristics—especially age—regarding homicide, including cross-national comparisons (Santos, Lu, and Fairchild 2021), demographic changes and forecasting trends (Fox and Piquero 2003; Rosenfeld and Fox 2019; Santos et al. 2019), risk factors associated with homicide perpetration (Loeber et al. 2005), as well as structural correlates associated with homicide rates (cf. McCall, Land, and Parker 2010) and many others. Noticeably absent in this area of research, however, has been an in-depth investigation of homicide, demographic characteristics, and immigration status. In this chapter, we undertake a deep dive into these issues using data from Texas, an American state at the center of the immigration and crime issue (Martinez, Stowell, and Lee 2010; Ousey and Kubrin 2014).

Homicide in Texas

Over the last two decades, homicide rates in the state of Texas have remained lower than at any other period in recent history (see fig. 15.1). During the mid-1960s, homicide rates rose until peaking in the early 1980s, with a second peak in the early 1990s. The last major decrease in homicide rates started in 1992; rates remained stable from the early 2000s and declined even further in 2011. In 2015, many parts of the country started to experience a slight rise in homicide rates (McDowall 2019). Texas was no exception, and reports in 2020 suggested that four large cities in Texas experienced some of the largest increases in homicide rates (Hilsenrath 2020). Still, compared to historic peaks, rates have stayed low, and it remains difficult to predict future trends with a great degree of accuracy (McDowall 2019).

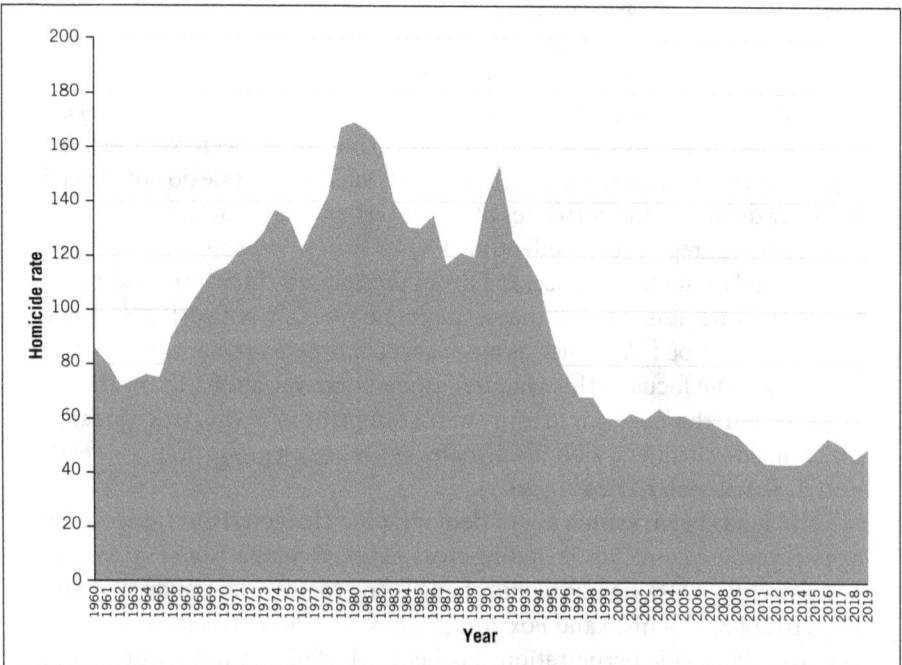

Figure 15.1 Homicide Rate in Texas 1960–2019

Case Study of Incarcerated Sample in Texas

The current case study presents a descriptive analysis of administrative record data from the Texas Department of Criminal Justice (TDCJ). A Public Information Act[1] request was submitted to TDCJ to obtain data on all individuals incarcerated for homicide. TDCJ provided a computerized data file containing individual-level records of all 16,189 individuals held in Texas correctional facilities incarcerated for the offense of homicide as of March 23, 2018. These data were filtered in two ways to obtain the sample presented here. First, only individuals incarcerated for intentional homicide were included;[2] this reduced the sample to 14,442 individuals. Figure 15.2 shows the full distribution of individuals incarcerated by offense year for the full sample.

Second, we focused only on individuals whose homicide offense was committed between 2005 and 2015, resulting in a final sample of 6,484 individuals. We limited the estimates to homicides committed in this time frame to provide a reasonable estimate of the number of individuals ultimately incarcerated for committing homicide during those years. This lag allows enough time for individuals to be processed through the criminal justice system from the time of the offense and still be incarcerated for a homicide committed during the included offense year. To visualize this differently, figure 15.3 overlays the number of homicide offenses reported to the UCR, the number of

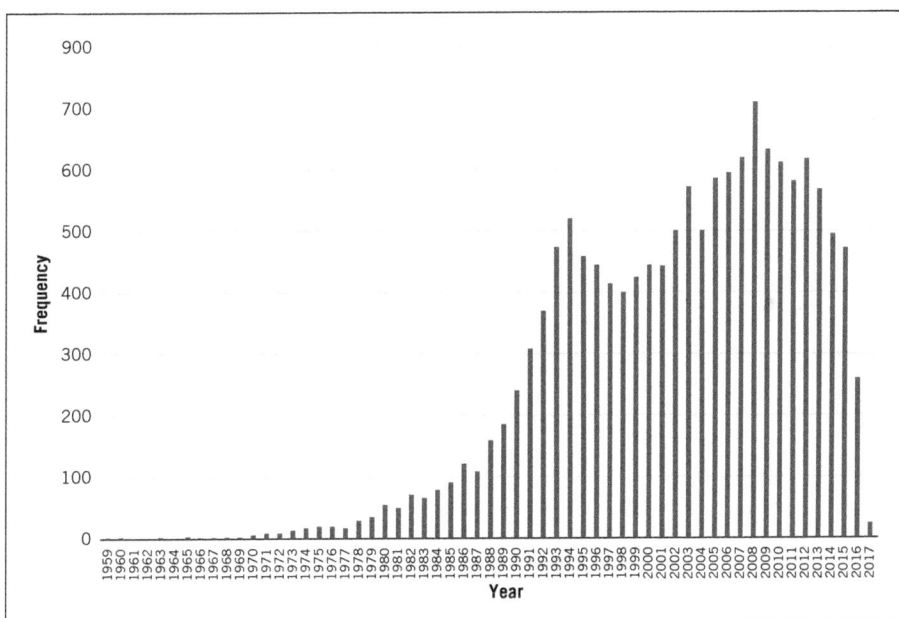

Figure 15.2 Frequency of Individuals Incarcerated Based on Offense Year

individuals incarcerated for a homicide that year, and the rate of incarcerations per homicide. It is important to note that this rate should not be interpreted as the clearance rate for homicides. While TDCJ records indicate the date the offense took place, data limitations preclude connecting homicides reported to the UCR to individuals incarcerated in TDCJ facilities. Further, due to the nature of a cross-sectional snapshot of incarceration data, individuals who committed a homicide during a particular year may already have been released from TDCJ custody or have a case that is still pending. Some individuals may have been incarcerated for multiple homicides. However, the relationship between the percent of individuals incarcerated for homicide compared to the number of reported homicides acts as a proxy for how representative the group of individuals incarcerated might be of those responsible for committing the homicides reported each year. The intention here is to provide a general estimate of the timeframe in which a stock of incarcerated individuals best represent homicides that occurred during a particular point in time.

As seen in figure 15.3, for the years between 2005 and 2015, relative incarcerations to reported homicides is consistently above 40 percent, provid-

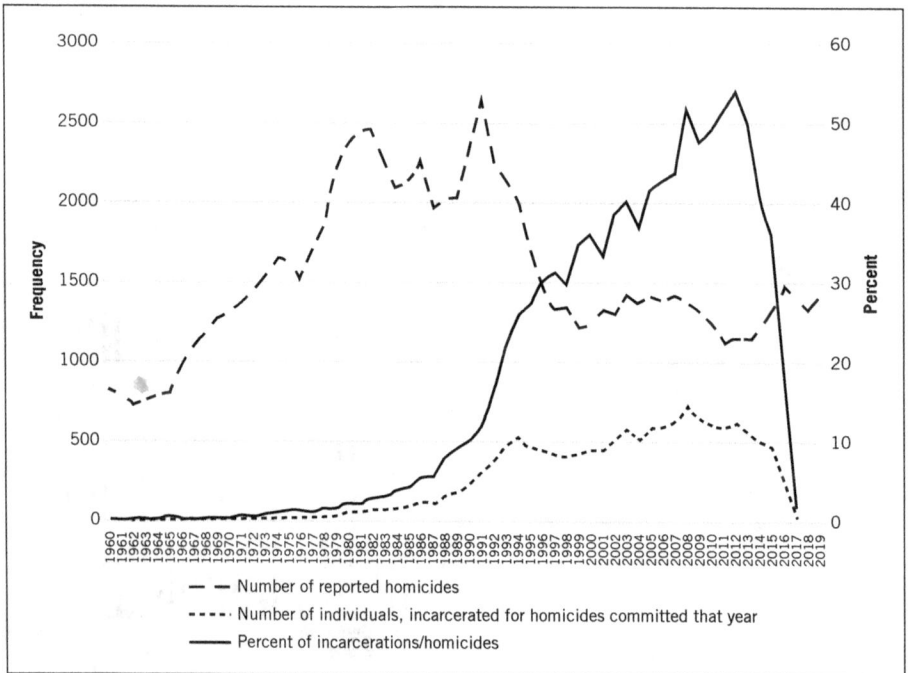

- - Number of reported homicides

----- Number of individuals, incarcerated for homicides committed that year

—— Percent of incarcerations/homicides

Figure 15.3 Number of Homicide Offenses and Individuals Incarcerated by Offense Year

ing some justification for focusing on this time period. Even with homicide historically having the highest clearance rate of all violent crimes, including in Texas, where law enforcement cleared 70.1 percent of homicides in 2015 (Texas DPS 2015), we see the highest percentage of incarcerations compared to homicides in 2012, at 53.75 percent. Again, due to different data sources, the claim here is not that the individuals incarcerated account for 40 to above 50 percent of the homicides committed during this time frame; it provides a means of comparison for how representative the incarcerated population *might* be of all homicides reported.

After the sample was filtered to individuals incarcerated for an intentional homicide committed between 2005 and 2015, descriptive statistics were calculated (see table 15.1). For this sample, the individuals incarcerated for homicide were overwhelmingly male (91.5 percent). This number is in line with national trends showing that males, on average, consistently make up about 90 percent of all perpetrators of homicide (Fox and Fridel 2017). Individuals in the sample were, on average, 28.8 years of age at the time they committed the homicide offense that resulted in their current incarceration. Within the sample, the youngest was 12 years old at the time of their offense, while the oldest was 81 years old. The race/ethnicity of individuals incarcerated was disproportionately Black, at 38.5 percent of the sample, and Hispanic, at 36.6 percent of the sample, compared to white individuals (23.7 percent). This disproportionality continues when examining gender by race. Just over 43.5 percent of females incarcerated were white, whereas approximate-

TABLE 15.1 DESCRIPTIVE STATISTICS FOR SAMPLE (N = 6,484)				
	% / Mean	Std. Dev.	Minimum	Maximum
Male	91.5%		0	1
Age at Offense	28.8	10.87	12	81
Race/Ethnicity				
White	23.7%		0	1
Black	38.5%		0	1
Hispanic	36.6%		0	1
Other Race	0.12%		0	1
High School Degree or GED	73.3%		0	1
Married	18.8%		0	1
Offense/Incarceration History				
Pleaded Guilty	54.6%		0	1
Percent Time Served	26.0%	0.184	0.01	1
Total Previous Prison Stays	1.35	0.755	0	8
Immigration Status				
ICE Verified Foreign Citizen	10.3%		0	1
Mexican Citizen	7.2%		0	1

ly 30 percent were Black and 25.5 percent were Hispanic (1 percent of females were categorized as "other" or "unknown race," see fig. 15.4).

Almost three-quarters (73.3 percent) of the sample were reported to have a high school degree or GED. This relatively high percentage may be a result of the older average age of individuals at the time of the offense or the fact that by the time data were collected, some individuals had earned their GED while incarcerated. Most individuals were unmarried, with less than a fifth of the sample reported to be married or have a common law partner (18.8 percent). Looking at factors associated with an individual's offense or incarceration history, just over half (54.6 percent) had pleaded guilty at trial for the homicide offense they were currently incarcerated for. This is not surprising; due to the severity of the charge, more individuals might choose to go to trial rather than plead guilty. Among those included in the sample, individuals had on average approximately 1.35 previous prison stays and had served just over a quarter of their sentenced time.

Within the sample, there is considerable variability in the length of sentence individuals incarcerated for intentional homicide received. Figure 15.5 displays the frequency of sentence length by category. As expected, the majority of individuals incarcerated were serving a long sentence—usually of eleven years or longer. Texas remains an active capital punishment state, and

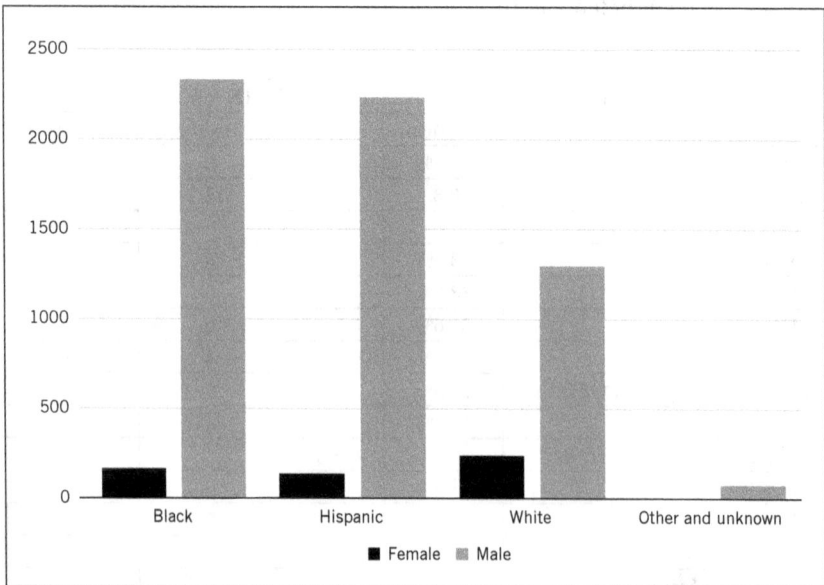

Figure 15.4 Frequency of Individuals Incarcerated by Race/Ethnicity and Gender

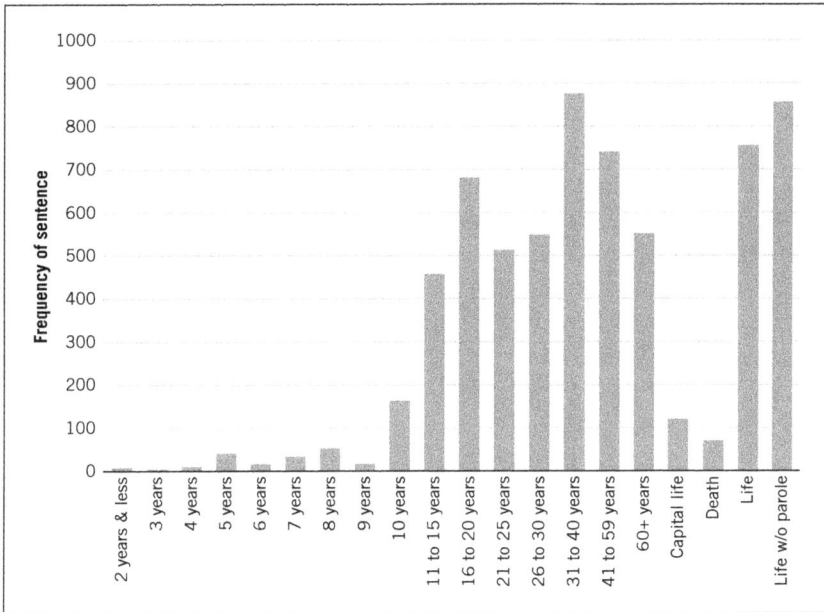

Figure 15.5 Frequency of Sentence Categories

individuals sentenced to death are also included; however, as shown, this group was relatively small.

Immigration and Homicide

Almost twenty years ago, Hagan and Palloni (1999, 618) warned that "recurring political pressures" could lead to a resurgence in the belief that immigrants are more crime prone than individuals born in the United States. This prediction has largely rung true and has been used as a talking point throughout the highly divisive political landscape of the last half decade. While empirical data consistently shows a null or negative relationship between immigration and homicide (Adelman et al. 2017; Bersani et al. 2018; Martinez and Lee 2000; Ousey and Kubrin 2018), it is less clear the extent to which the American public believes that immigrants commit more crime. A 2017 Gallup poll found that 45 percent of Americans believed immigrants made "the crime situation" in the United States worse. When focusing on perceptions of undocumented individuals, the Pew Research Center (2018) published findings revealing that 26 percent of Americans perceived undocumented immigrants as "more likely than U.S. citizens to commit serious crimes." One recent study further probed the correlates associated with perceptions of immigrants as criminogenic, finding measures of Hispanic resentment and white nationalism to be associated with more criminogenic perceptions (Kulig et al. 2020).

A recent meta-analysis of fifty-one macrolevel studies by Ousey and Kubrin (2018, 63) concluded that "the immigration-crime association is negative—but very weak." Studies at both the macro- and microlevels overwhelmingly report either a negative relationship between immigration levels and crime rates (Adelman et al. 2017; Klein, Allison, and Harris 2017; Light and Miller 2018; Lyons, Vélez, and Santoro 2013; MacDonald, Hipp, and Gill 2013; Martinez, Stowell, and Iwama 2016; Wolff et al. 2018) or no relationship at all (Akins, Rumbaut, and Stansfield 2009; Chavez and Griffiths 2009; Emerick et al. 2014; Feldmeyer 2009; Feldmeyer and Steffensmeier 2009; Lee, Martinez, and Rosenfeld 2001; Ousey and Kubrin 2014). Virtually no research has provided evidence of immigration increasing crime rates within specific cities or nationally. Even in a study identifying a significant positive relationship between the number of undocumented immigrants in a state and the number of drug arrests in that state (Green 2016), multiple measures of immigrant status were found to be unrelated to violent crime rates both overall and individually (e.g., murder, rape, etc.). Thus, when positive relationships between immigration and crime do exist, they do so under limited circumstances.

Over the past half century, the American immigration landscape has experienced substantial change. The 1965 Immigration and Nationality Act galvanized a new demographic profile; the proceeding decades saw a greater proportion of immigrants from Asia and Latin America move to the United States (Chishti, Hipsman, and Ball 2015). As a result, many cities became and persevered as immigrant destinations with greater concentrations of immigrants in ethnically cohesive areas and neighborhoods. According to Budiman (2020), the Pew Research Center estimates that there are about 44.8 million foreign-born individuals living in the United States, approximately 13.7 percent of the total U.S. population. In the last decade, while individuals originating from Mexico or other Latin American countries have comprised major immigrant segments, Hispanic immigration has been expected to slow down, with Asian immigration expected to surge by 2065 (Pew Research Center 2015).

What do these shifts in immigration represent for changes in homicide trends? Much of the current political rhetoric surrounding immigration and crime focuses on serious violent crimes, especially homicide, as these capture the public's attention. The research, however, holds important insights regarding this relationship. First, as with the broader relationship between immigration and any crime, it is well supported that greater immigrant concentration is largely associated with a null effect or decrease in violent crime rates, including homicide. This has been found in many peer-reviewed studies focused on major cities across various time periods in the United States (Ousey and Kubrin 2009; 2018), including recent studies that focus on data from the last decade or so (Emerick et al. 2014; Feldmeyer, Harris, and Scroggins 2015; Graif and Sampson 2009; Light and Miller 2018; Xie and Baumer 2019). In other words, even today, researchers find that immigration produces a type of suppression effect for serious types of violent crime. A similar effect is found in research that analyzes crime reporting. According to Xie and Baumer (2019), analysis from the NCVS and census data demonstrates areas with greater levels of immigrant concentration show reduced violent crime reporting. These effects may be somewhat varied regarding homicide. For homicide victimization, heterogeneity among immigrant populations is important to consider. However, a strong empirical base shows that rates and concentration of immigrants, whether authorized or unauthorized, are not related to increases in homicide rates.

As this literature has matured, so have researchers' realizations from assessing the immigrant-crime link. More specifically, immigrants and immigrant groups are far from homogenous, as are the contexts they occupy. Immigrant considerations span historical, legal, social, and acculturative conditions that might inform immigrant influence on homicide. Consistent with work focusing primarily on Latino immigrants (Feldmeyer, Harris, and Scroggins 2015; Shihadeh and Barranco 2013), the degree to which immigration and homicide are linked is particularly place dependent. For example, new immigrant destinations vary substantially on homicide relative to traditional destinations. Places with historically embedded immigrant communities tend to have lower levels of homicide victimization compared to places that began to see greater immigrant migration only as recently as 1990 (Shihadeh and Barranco 2013).

While there are notable trends across the country, it is necessary to consider localized and state-level contexts. Relevant to our focus on homicide in Texas, consider how immigration and homicide trends emerge in locales and at the aggregate level. Texas is home to many immigrant destination cities, like Dallas and San Antonio, and houses the fourth-largest city in the country, Houston. These, combined with localized social conditions, provide reasonable insights into immigrant-homicide trends. For example, Han and Piquero (2022) found that Dallas census tracts with high immigrant concentration experienced increased counts of violent crime (including murder) but only when connected to high disadvantage. But when other immigrant concentration and disadvantage interactions were considered, the relationship yielded unexpected findings regarding how immigrant concentration combines with certain contextual factors. As the authors noted, Dallas can be considered a newer immigrant destination, suggesting that the protective influences involved with having more immigrants in an area (e.g., cohesion, community resources, secure ethnic enclaves) are still developing. Now consider what this relationship would look like in Houston. Given what we know about studies examining immigration and homicide in more traditional immigrant destinations in Texas (Martinez 2000; 2014), we might expect community cohesion and contexts of reception to be underdeveloped in Dallas compared to Houston. In lieu of a recent study to explicitly examine this, prior research demonstrates that there is little to link immigration to homicide in Houston (Stowell et al. 2009).

While these major metropolitan areas each have their own unique history, they embody similar state-level contexts, with close proximity to the U.S.-Mexico border, multicultural influences, and historically dense migratory flows. As Stowell and colleagues (2009) have suggested, border contexts had a greater, albeit decreasing, homicide rate relative to nonborder contexts or sectors through the 1990s and early 2000s. More recently and related to immigrant influence or lack thereof, research from Nowrasteh (2018) has shown that immigrants have a much lower homicide arrest and conviction rate compared to native citizens. Nowrasteh's findings are further supported by a recent study by Orrick and colleagues (2021) examining the average incarceration rate for homicides conditioned by immigrant status using similar data from TDCJ and population estimates from 2013 to 2015. They found that the average incarceration rate for intentional homicide offenders was consistently greater among U.S. born (citizens) compared to the foreign born (noncitizens). Even compared to unauthorized immigrants, the U.S. born still reflected a greater incarceration rate (Orrick et al. 2021).

The case study of individuals incarcerated for homicide in the state of Texas provides a unique opportunity. Information from the incarcerated sample reveals notable trends in the composition of immigrant-related Texas homicides. Approximately 10.3 percent of the total sample are foreign born and verified by Immigration and Customs Enforcement (ICE) as citizens of a non-U.S. country. Moreover, 7.2 percent are verified Mexican citizens, reflecting trends in national figures showing that the majority of immigrants in the United States are of Mexican origin or descent (Budiman 2020).

Immigration Data

During the criminal justice processing of an individual, TDCJ works with federal Immigration and Customs Enforcement (ICE) to identify authorized and unauthorized immigrants incarcerated in Texas (Strayhorn 2006). This process is used to identify those for whom the federal government may ultimately initiate deportation proceedings. The individual identification process begins at intake, while deportation occurs after the completion of the inmate's sentence. The basic process is as follows (Strayhorn 2006): First, TDCJ identifies all individuals who self-report as, or are suspected of, having foreign birth or foreign citizenship. Following this, TDCJ notifies ICE, which interviews identified individuals to verify their citizenship. If ICE verifies an individual as a foreign citizen eligible for deportation, the agency may issue a detainer to assume custody of the individual on release from TDCJ.

An indicator of ICE-verified citizenship is included in the data from TDCJ. As shown in table 15.1, 89.7 percent of those incarcerated for committing homicide between 2005 and 2015 were identified as U.S. citizens, while approximately 10.3 percent were identified as foreign citizens. The availability of ICE-confirmed status allows us to include a more precise measure of immigration status than relying only on self-report or TDCJ-suspected status.[3]

When looking at percentage of individuals incarcerated by offense year and immigration status, the percentage of those verified as foreign citizens ranges between a low of 6.5 percent in 2013 and a high of 12.3 percent in 2005. Figure 15.6 displays the frequency of those incarcerated by immigration status by offense year. The trend line indicating the percentage of those verified as foreign citizens is shown as well. While there are fluctuations in the percent of individuals verified as foreign citizens, the overall trend line remains relatively stable across this ten-year period.

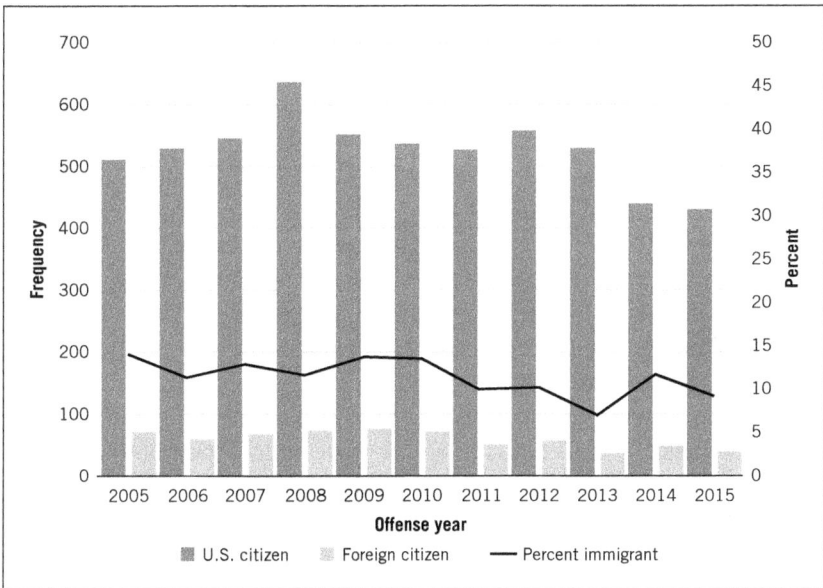

Figure 15.6 Frequency and Percent of Individuals Incarcerated for Homicide by Offense Year and Immigration Status

Almost two-thirds of those verified as foreign citizens reported Mexican nativity, comprising 64.3 percent of all foreign citizens. When other Central and South American countries are included, this number increases to 87.24 percent. This is unsurprising given the proximity of Texas to Mexico and other countries to the south. Table 15.2 displays additional descriptive statistics of available characteristics in the data by immigration status. Foreign citizens incarcerated for homicide are significantly more likely to be male (χ^2 = 15.04, p < 0.000), Hispanic (χ^2 = 946.40, p < 0.000), married (χ^2 = 4.44, p < 0.000), to have pleaded guilty (χ^2 = 10.58, p < 0.000), and to have served a longer portion of their sentence (t = -2.58, p < 0.010). Foreign citizens are significantly less likely than their U.S. citizen counterparts to be of any other race/ethnicity besides Hispanic, have a high school degree (χ^2 = 766.40, p < 0.000), and have previous prison stays (t = 9.93, p < 0.000). While the average age for U.S. citizens is slightly higher than for foreign citizens (29.41 and 28.71 years old respectively), this difference is not statistically significant at the bivariate level.

Discussion and Conclusion

We acknowledged at the outset of this chapter the long-standing relationship between age and crime as well as the specific crime of homicide, with which we have been primarily concerned in this chapter. As there exist several comprehensive overviews of trends and correlates associated with homicide, we sought to provide an in-depth investigation of homicide, demographic characteristics, and, most notably, immigration status in one state that has been at the center of much of the debate surrounding immigration and crime.

Our analysis of the Texas data provides some notable conclusions. First, while the homicide rate in Texas saw a slight increase in homicide after 2015, data from our case study suggest that much of what Texas has experienced in the last decade or so points toward a decreasing trend of homicide, particularly when Texas' incarcerated population is taken into account. When examining demographic characteristics, unsurprisingly, a disproportionate number of individuals incarcerated for homicide are male. Similarly, the sample of individuals incarcerated for homicide is disproportionately Black and Hispanic. Lastly, our sample allows us to examine some immigration status factors. Specifically, foreign citizens—compared to U.S. citizens—represent only a small portion of individuals incarcerated for homicide, making up a relatively stable percentage of that population over an examined ten-year time span (2005–2015). When comparing foreign citizens to U.S. citizens, some factors are more salient for foreign citizens (e.g., being male, married, having pleaded guilty, and having served a longer portion of their sentence). Addi-

TABLE 15.2 DESCRIPTIVE STATISTICS BY IMMIGRATION STATUS

	U.S. Citizen (n=5,818)				Foreign Citizen (n=666)			
	% / Mean	Std. Dev.	Minimum	Maximum	% / Mean	Std. Dev.	Minimum	Maximum
Male	91.1%		0	1	95.5%		0	1
Age at Offense	28.7	10.87	12	81	29.4	9.95	14	65
Race/Ethnicity								
White	26.2%		0	1	1.8%		0	1
Black	42.6%		0	1	3.0%		0	1
Hispanic	30.4%		0	1	91.0%		0	1
Other Race	0.9%		0	1	4.2%		0	1
High School Degree or GED	65.8%		0	1	10.4%		0	1
Married	18.4%		0	1	21.8%		0	1
Offense/Incarceration History								
Pleaded Guilty	53.9%		0	1	60.5%		0	1
Percent Time Served	25.8%	0.18	0.01	1	27.8%	0.19	0.02	0.99
Total Previous Prison Stays	1.38	0.78	0	8	1.07	0.35	0	6
Nativity								
Mexican Born	0.6%		0	1	64.3%		0	1

tionally, being Hispanic, particularly of Mexican nativity, is a persistent, overwhelming characteristic. Overall, when examining the influence of immigration in Texas, homicide rates of foreign citizens do not generally conform to those of the general population (see Orrick et al. 2021). The primary difference between groups found here, at least for our Texas sample, centers Hispanics in the discussion of issues related to immigration and crime. This is important to note as, even within the broader classification of ethnicity, it is a diverse group, and further research is needed to better understand differences based on the heterogeneity present within this group. Even with overwhelming empirical evidence disputing a causal relationship between immigration and violent crime, the debate will likely continue in the political and public discourse until better and more complete data are widely available across the United States. The Texas data used herein offer an opportunity for a detailed case study on individuals incarcerated for homicide; systematic record keeping that keeps track of immigration status allows for further examination by immigration status. We encourage researchers interested in immigration and crime more generally to gather the necessary data to replicate and extend our descriptive work to add not only to the knowledge base but also to the larger public and policy discussions at the fore of many debates in the United States today.

NOTES

1. Available at https://www.tdcj.texas.gov/divisions/es/exec_services_public_information_act.html.

2. Offenses corresponding to the Texas Department of Public Safety (DPS) definition of homicide were included, thus excluding individuals incarcerated for attempted murder, intoxication manslaughter, and criminal negligent murder.

3. To be clear, we are not claiming that all those who have been confirmed by ICE as noncitizens are unauthorized; however, it is among this group that estimates of unauthorized immigrants are derived. Passel and Cohn (2018) published estimates of the unauthorized percent of the total population in Texas (5.7 percent) and the unauthorized percent of the immigrant population in Texas (33 percent). These percentages were used to calculate the estimated unauthorized incarcerated.

REFERENCES

Adelman, Robert, Lesley Williams Reid, Gail Markle, Saskia Weiss, and Charles Jaret. 2017. "Urban Crime Rates and the Changing Face of Immigration: Evidence across Four Decades." *Journal of Ethnicity in Criminal Justice* 15 (1): 52–77. https://doi.org/10.1080/15377938.2016.1261057.

Akins, Scott, Rubén G. Rumbaut, and Richard Stansfield. 2009. "Immigration, Economic Disadvantage, and Homicide: A Community-Level Analysis of Austin, Texas." *Homicide Studies* 13 (3): 307–14. https://doi.org/10.1177/1088767909336814.

Bersani, Bianca E., Adam D. Fine, Alex R. Piquero, Laurence Steinberg, Paul J. Frick, and Elizabeth Cauffman. 2018. "Investigating the Offending Histories of Undocumented

Immigrants." *MIGRATION LETTERS* 15 (2): 147–66. https://doi.org/10.33182/ml.v15 i2.366.

Budiman, Abby. 2020. "Key Findings about U.S. Immigrants." *Pew Research Center* (blog). 2020. https://www.pewresearch.org/fact-tank/2020/08/20/key-findings-about-u-s -immigrants/.

Chavez, Jorge M., and Elizabeth Griffiths. 2009. "Neighborhood Dynamics of Urban Violence: Understanding the Immigration Connection." *Homicide Studies* 13 (3): 261–73. https://doi.org/10.1177/1088767909337701.

Chishti, Muzaffar, Faye Hipsman, and Isabel Ball. 2015. "Fifty Years On, the 1965 Immigration and Nationality Act Continues to Reshape the United States." *Migration Information Source*, October 15, 2015. https://www.migrationpolicy.org/article/fifty -years-1965-immigration-and-nationality-act-continues-reshape-united-states.

Emerick, Nicholas A., Theodore R. Curry, Timothy W. Collins, and S. Fernando Rodriguez. 2014. "Homicide and Social Disorganization on the Border: Implications for Latino and Immigrant Populations: Homicide and Social Disorganization on the Border." *Social Science Quarterly* 95 (2): 360–79. https://doi.org/10.1111/ssqu.12051.

Feldmeyer, Ben. 2009. "Immigration and Violence: The Offsetting Effects of Immigrant Concentration on Latino Violence." *Social Science Research* 38 (3): 717–31. https://doi .org/10.1016/j.ssresearch.2009.03.003.

Feldmeyer, Ben, Casey T. Harris, and Jennifer Scroggins. 2015. "Enclaves of Opportunity or 'Ghettos of Last Resort?' Assessing the Effects of Immigrant Segregation on Violent Crime Rates." *Social Science Research* 52 (July): 1–17. https://doi.org/10.1016/j .ssresearch.2015.01.003.

Feldmeyer, Ben, and Darrell Steffensmeier. 2009. "Immigration Effects on Homicide Offending For Total and Race/Ethnicity-Disaggregated Populations (White, Black, and Latino)." *Homicide Studies* 13 (3): 211–26. https://doi.org/10.1177/1088767909336089.

Fox, James Alan, and Emma E. Fridel. 2017. "Gender Differences in Patterns and Trends in U.S. Homicide, 1976–2015." *Violence and Gender* 4 (2): 37–43. https://doi.org/10 .1089/vio.2017.0016.

Fox, James Alan, and Alex R. Piquero. 2003. "Deadly Demographics: Population Characteristics and Forecasting Homicide Trends." *Crime & Delinquency* 49 (3): 339–59. https://doi.org/10.1177/0011128703049003001.

Graif, Corina, and Robert J. Sampson. 2009. "Spatial Heterogeneity in the Effects of Immigration and Diversity on Neighborhood Homicide Rates." *Homicide Studies* 13 (3): 242–60. https://doi.org/10.1177/1088767909336728.

Green, David. 2016. "The Trump Hypothesis: Testing Immigrant Populations as a Determinant of Violent and Drug-Related Crime in the United States: The Trump Hypothesis." *Social Science Quarterly* 97 (3): 506–24. https://doi.org/10.1111/ssqu.12300.

Hagan, John, and Alberto Palloni. 1999. "Sociological Criminology and the Mythology of Hispanic Immigration and Crime." *Social Problems* 46 (4): 617–32. https://doi.org /10.2307/3097078.

Han, Sungil, and Alex R. Piquero. 2022. "Is It Dangerous to Live in Neighborhoods with More Immigrants? Assessing the Effects of Immigrant Concentration on Crime Patterns." *Crime & Delinquency* 68 (1): 52–79. https://doi.org/10.1177/00111287211007736.

Hilsenrath, Jon. 2020. "Homicide Spike Hits Most Large U.S. Cities." *Wall Street Journal*, August 2, 2020, sec. US. https://www.wsj.com/articles/homicide-spike-cities-chicago -newyork-detroit-us-crime-police-lockdown-coronavirus-protests-11596395181.

Hirschi, Travis, and Michael Gottfredson. 1983. "Age and the Explanation of Crime." *American Journal of Sociology* 89 (3): 552–84. https://doi.org/10.1086/227905.

Klein, Brent R., Kayla Allison, and Casey T. Harris. 2017. "Immigration and Violence in Rural versus Urban Counties, 1990–2010." *Sociological Quarterly* 58 (2): 229–53. https://doi.org/10.1080/00380253.2017.1296339.

Kulig, Teresa C., Amanda Graham, Francis T. Cullen, Alex R. Piquero, and Murat Haner. 2020. "'Bad Hombres' at the Southern US Border? White Nationalism and the Perceived Dangerousness of Immigrants." *Australian & New Zealand Journal of Criminology* 54 (3): 283–304. https://doi.org/10.1177/0004865820969760.

Lee, Matthew T., Ramiro Martinez, and Richard Rosenfeld. 2001. "Does Immigration Increase Homicide? Negative Evidence from Three Border Cities." *Sociological Quarterly* 42 (4): 559–80. https://doi.org/10.1111/j.1533-8525.2001.tb01780.x.

Light, Michael T., and Ty Miller. 2018. "Does Undocumented Immigration Increase Violent Crime?" *Criminology* 56 (2): 370–401. https://doi.org/10.1111/1745-9125.12175.

Loeber, Rolf, Dustin Pardini, D. Lynn Homish, Evelyn H. Wei, Anne M. Crawford, David P. Farrington, Magda Stouthamer-Loeber, Judith Creemers, Steven A. Koehler, and Richard Rosenfeld. 2005. "The Prediction of Violence and Homicide in Young Men." *Journal of Consulting and Clinical Psychology* 73 (6): 1074–88. https://doi.org/10.1037/0022-006X.73.6.1074.

Lyons, Christopher J., María B. Vélez, and Wayne A. Santoro. 2013. "Neighborhood Immigration, Violence, and City-Level Immigrant Political Opportunities." *American Sociological Review* 78 (4): 604–32. https://doi.org/10.1177/0003122413491964.

MacDonald, John M., John R. Hipp, and Charlotte Gill. 2013. "The Effects of Immigrant Concentration on Changes in Neighborhood Crime Rates." *Journal of Quantitative Criminology* 29 (2): 191–215. https://doi.org/10.1007/s10940-012-9176-8.

Martinez, Ramiro. 2000. "Immigration and Urban Violence: The Link between Immigrant Latinos and Types of Homicide." *Social Science Quarterly* 81 (1): 363–74.

———. 2014. *Latino Homicide: Immigration, Violence, and Community.* New York: Routledge.

Martinez, Ramiro, and Matthew T. Lee. 2000. "On Immigration and Crime." In *Criminal Justice 2000*, 485–524. Washington, DC: U.S. Department of Justice, Office of Justice Programs, National Institute of Justice.

Martinez, Ramiro, Jacob I. Stowell, and Janice A. Iwama. 2016. "The Role of Immigration: Race/Ethnicity and San Diego Homicides since 1970." *Journal of Quantitative Criminology* 32 (3): 471–88. https://doi.org/10.1007/s10940-016-9294-9.

Martinez, Ramiro, Jacob I. Stowell, and Matthew T. Lee. 2010. "Immigration and Crime in an Era of Transformation: A Longitudinal Analysis of Homicides in San Diego Neighborhoods, 1980–2000." *Criminology* 48 (3): 797–829. https://doi.org/10.1111/j.1745-9125.2010.00202.x.

McCall, Patricia L., Kenneth C. Land, and Karen F. Parker. 2010. "An Empirical Assessment of What We Know about Structural Covariates of Homicide Rates: A Return to a Classic 20 Years Later." *Homicide Studies* 14 (3): 219–43. https://doi.org/10.1177/1088767910371166.

McDowall, David. 2019. "The 2015 and 2016 U.S. Homicide Rate Increases in Context." *Homicide Studies* 23 (3): 225–42. https://doi.org/10.1177/1088767919847236.

Nowrasteh, Alex. 2018. "Criminal Immigrants in Texas: Illegal Immigrant Conviction and Arrest Rates for Homicide, Sex Crimes, Larceny, and Other Crimes." SSRN Scholarly Paper ID 3501078. Rochester, NY: Social Science Research Network. https://papers.ssrn.com/abstract=3501078.

Orrick, Erin A., Alexander H. Updegrove, Alex R. Piquero, and Tomislav Kovandzic. 2021. "Disentangling Differences in Homicide Incarceration Rates by Immigration

Status: A Comparison in Texas." *Crime & Delinquency* 67 (4): 523–50. https://doi.org /10.1177/0011128720940963.

Ousey, Graham C., and Charis E. Kubrin. 2009. "Exploring the Connection between Immigration and Violent Crime Rates in U.S. Cities, 1980–2000." *Social Problems* 56 (3): 447–73. https://doi.org/10.1525/sp.2009.56.3.447.

———. 2014. "Immigration and the Changing Nature of Homicide in US Cities, 1980–2010." *Journal of Quantitative Criminology* 30 (3): 453–83. https://doi.org/10.1007 /s10940-013-9210-5.

———. 2018. "Immigration and Crime: Assessing a Contentious Issue." *Annual Review of Criminology* 1 (1): 63–84. https://doi.org/10.1146/annurev-criminol-032317-092026.

Pew Research Center. 2015. "Selected U.S. Immigration Legislation and Executive Actions, 1790–2014." Pew Research Center's Hispanic Trends Project. https://www.pewre search.org/hispanic/2015/09/28/selected-u-s-immigration-legislation-and-executive -actions-1790-2014/.

———. 2018. "Shifting Public Views on Legal Immigration Into the United States." Pew Research Center's Immigration Attitudes Project. https://www.pewresearch.org/pol itics/2018/06/28/shifting-public-views-on-legal-immigration-into-the-u-s/

Rosenfeld, Richard, and James Alan Fox. 2019. "Anatomy of the Homicide Rise." *Homicide Studies* 23 (3): 202–24. https://doi.org/10.1177/1088767919848821.

Santos, Mateus Rennó, Yunmei Lu, and Rachel E. Fairchild. 2021. "Age, Period and Cohort Differences between the Homicide Trends of Canada and the United States." *British Journal of Criminology* 61 (2): 389–413. https://doi.org/10.1093/bjc/azaa080.

Santos, Mateus Rennó, Alexander Testa, Lauren C. Porter, and James P. Lynch. 2019. "The Contribution of Age Structure to the International Homicide Decline." *PLOS ONE* 14 (10): e0222996. https://doi.org/10.1371/journal.pone.0222996.

Sharkey, Patrick, and Michael Friedson. 2019. "The Impact of the Homicide Decline on Life Expectancy of African American Males." *Demography* 56 (2): 645–63. https://doi .org/10.1007/s13524-019-00768-4.

Shihadeh, Edward S., and Raymond E. Barranco. 2013. "The Imperative of Place: Homicide and the New Latino Migration." *Sociological Quarterly* 54 (1): 81–104. https://doi .org/10.1111/tsq.12009.

Stowell, Jacob I., Steven F. Messner, Kelly F. Mcgeever, and Lawrence E. Raffalovich. 2009. "Immigration and the Recent Violent Crime Drop in the United States: A Pooled, Cross-Sectional Time-Series Analysis of Metropolitan Areas." *Criminology* 47 (3): 889–928. https://doi.org/10.1111/j.1745-9125.2009.00162.x.

Strayhorn, Carole Keeton. 2006. *Undocumented Immigrants in Texas: A Financial Analysis of the Impact to the State Budget and Economy.* Austin, TX: Office of the Comptroller.

Texas Department of Public Safety (DPS). 2015. "Chapter 3: Index Crime Analysis." 2015 Crime in Texas. https://www.dps.texas.gov/sites/default/files/documents/crimereports /15/citch3.pdf.

Wolff, Kevin T., Jonathan Intravia, Michael T. Baglivio, and Alex R. Piquero. 2018. "The Protective Impact of Immigrant Concentration on Juvenile Recidivism: A Multilevel Examination of Potential Mechanisms." *Crime & Delinquency* 64 (10): 1271–305. https:// doi.org/10.1177/0011128717739608.

Xie, Min, and Eric P. Baumer. 2019. "Neighborhood Immigrant Concentration and Violent Crime Reporting to the Police: A Multilevel Analysis of Data from the National Crime Victimization Survey." *Criminology* 57 (2): 237–67. https://doi.org/10.1111/1745 -9125.12204.

IV

Preventing and Responding

16

Solving Homicide

WENDY REGOECZI AND JOHN JARVIS

Introduction

While a great deal of time and resources are devoted to the investigation and prosecution of homicide cases, many homicides remain unsolved. This fact has prompted researchers to study trends and patterns in solving homicides and to assess explanations for why some cases are solved while others are not. The result is a sizable body of literature that has contributed significantly to our understanding of homicide investigations and clearances. This chapter takes stock of that literature and discusses in detail the challenges remaining in this area of research.

Law enforcement uses the term *clearance* for solving homicides and/or closing cases. There are two ways a case can be cleared. A homicide can be cleared by the arrest of one or more suspects believed to have committed murder. These cases are *cleared by arrest* and make up the bulk of clearances. In some cases, the police know who committed the homicide but cannot physically arrest the suspect for a number of reasons—for example, if the suspect committed suicide, was killed in another homicide, died from some other cause, fled the country, or is serving a prison sentence in another jurisdiction. In these circumstances, homicides can be *cleared by exceptional means*. The FBI defines exceptional clearances as follows:

> In certain situations law enforcement is not able to clear offenses known to them. Many times all leads have been exhausted and ev-

erything possible has been done in order to clear a case. If the following questions can all be answered "yes," the offense can be cleared "exceptionally" for crime reporting purposes: 1) Has the investigation definitely established the identity of the offender? 2) Is there enough information to support an arrest, charge, and turning over to the court for prosecution; 3) Is the exact location of the offender known so that the subject can be taken into custody now? 4) Is there some reason outside law enforcement control that precludes arresting, charging, and prosecuting the offender? (FBI 2011)

Exceptional clearances occur far less frequently than clearances by arrest. A study examining exceptional clearances among law enforcement agencies submitting data to the National Incident-Based Reporting System (NIBRS) found exceptional clearances make up approximately 10 percent of U.S. homicide clearances among those agencies (Jarvis and Regoeczi 2009). A similar percentage was found in a study of Chicago homicides from 1988 through 1995 (Riedel and Boulahanis 2007).

Improving our understanding of trends, patterns, and explanations in solving homicides is important for a number of reasons. First, the United States has experienced a dramatic decline in percent of homicides cleared from the early 1960s to now. In 1961, 93 percent of homicides resulted in the arrest of a suspect; by 2019, this percent had dropped to 61.4. This decline is puzzling given changes occurring during this period that may have been expected to increase the ability of police to solve cases, such as improved scientific technology and the adoption of community policing strategies.

Second, fairly or not, clearances are often used as a measure of police effectiveness (Baughman 2020; Jarvis and Regoeczi 2009; Wellford and Cronin 1999). High clearance rates are frequently touted as evidence that police/investigators are doing a good job, while low clearance rates are seen as reflecting badly on both individual units (such as homicide) as well as departments as a whole. By examining what factors influence whether homicides are solved, researchers can identify changes in policies and procedures that could improve solve rates.

Low homicide clearance rates have a significant negative effect on family members of homicide victims as well as entire communities. Unsolved homicides make it difficult for family members and friends to get closure after the murder of a loved one (Cardarelli and Cavanagh 1992). Families are prevented from having their day in court and seeing an offender brought to justice. Family members and friends can suffer tremendous fear for their safety with the offender still on the street. The deterrent value of arrest is also negatively impacted when more than one-third of individuals committing homicide are never held accountable for their crimes.

Patterns in Clearing Homicide Cases

A number of different factors that may influence whether a case will be solved have been examined. These can be grouped into the following categories: characteristics of the victim, the offense, the investigation, and the neighborhood/community. What we know about how these various factors influence homicide clearances is described next.

Victim Characteristics

A number of studies have examined homicide victim characteristics to assess association with homicide clearance, including the victim's age, gender, and race. One of the more consistent findings is the high likelihood of clearing cases involving child victims and the greater difficulty of clearing cases involving the elderly (Addington 2006; Puckett and Lundman 2003; Regoeczi, Kennedy, and Silverman 2000; Riedel and Rinehart 1996). These patterns are best explained in relation to victim/offender relationships and circumstances surrounding homicides of children and the elderly. Children are most often killed by parents or other family members. Young children are normally under the surveillance of caregivers, reducing the chance they will be killed by a stranger (Cardarelli and Cavanagh 1992). Thus, these cases tend to be more easily solved. In contrast, elderly persons are disproportionately involved in robbery-related homicides and killed by strangers (Abrams et al. 2007; Falzon and Davis 1998; Fox and Levin 1991; Nelson and Huff-Corzine 1998), reducing the likelihood of identifying a suspect.

No clear pattern has emerged as to whether homicide cases involving female or male victims are more likely to be solved. A couple of studies report a higher likelihood of clearance for female victim cases (McEwen and Regoeczi 2015; Regoeczi, Kennedy, and Silverman 2000) while others find no gender differences (Addington 2006; Mouzos and Muller 2001) or a greater likelihood of clearance for male victims (Litwin and Xu 2007). These mixed findings are somewhat surprising given that women have a greater likelihood of being killed by an intimate partner, and intimate partner homicides are generally more easily solved. However, women are also more likely to be victims in types of homicides that are generally difficult to solve, such as killings occurring during the commission of a rape (Petersen 2017).

Findings with respect to whether the victim's race impacts the likelihood the case will be solved are mixed and show no clear pattern. Some research finds cases involving non-White victims are more likely to be solved (Mouzos and Muller 2001; Regoeczi, Kennedy, and Silverman 2000), while other studies find the opposite (Litwin and Xu 2007; McEwen and Regoeczi 2015; Petersen 2017). The handful of studies examining victim ethnicity find cases involving Hispanic victims less likely to be cleared (Alderden and Lavery 2007; Litwin 2004; Roberts and Lyons 2011), consistent with Black's (1976) theory of the behavior of law that lower status victims are devalued by police (discussed in more detail later in the chapter).

Incident Characteristics

Incident characteristics associated with the likelihood of solving a homicide include the circumstances surrounding the case, weapon use, location, and time of occurrence. A number of studies find felony-related homicides, such as those committed during a robbery or rape, harder to solve than homicides resulting from other circumstances (Cardarelli and Cavanagh 1992; Lee 2005; Litwin 2004; Mouzos and Muller 2001; Regoeczi, Kennedy, and Silverman 2000; Riedel and Rinehart 1996; Roberts 2007). Robbery and rape offenses, which have the potential to produce lethal outcomes, are characteristically hit-and-run in nature and therefore less likely to produce on-scene arrests (Black 1970). They are more likely to involve strangers, making it more difficult to identify the perpetrator. Drug and gang-related homicides also generally have lower clearance rates (Jiao 2007; Lee 2005; Pastia, Davies, and Wu 2017).

Homicides involving firearms are generally less likely to be cleared (Braga, Turchan, and Barao 2019; Litwin 2004; Litwin and Xu 2007; Mouzos and Muller 2001; Regoeczi, Kennedy, and Silverman 2000; Rydberg and Pizarro 2014). In contrast, killings committed with weapons that bring the victim and offender into contact with each other (such as fists, knives, or blunt instruments) have higher solve rates, possibly due to increased transference of evidence (Addington 2006; Mouzos and Muller 2001; Puckett and Lundman 2003; Roberts 2007).

Among the more consistent findings concerning clearance is the greater likelihood of solving homicides that take place in residences (Addington 2006; Litwin and Xu 2007; Mouzos and Muller 2001; Wellford and Cronin 1999). This may be due to homicides in homes more often occurring between intimate partners, family members, or individuals known to one another more generally, making it easier to identify the perpetrator. In addition, there may be better preservation of forensic evidence when the incident occurs in a home than in a place where it may be contaminated by people or weather (Addington 2006; Regoeczi, Jarvis, and Riedel 2008).

Characteristics of the Investigation

Less is known about the impact of aspects of homicide investigation on the likelihood of solving cases. Access to this kind of information necessitates cooperation from individual law enforcement agencies, which can be challenging to obtain. Even where access is granted, researchers typically have to code data themselves, as it is not routinely gathered by agencies. Mixed findings have emerged from the small group of studies examining characteristics of homicide investigations. This is the case with respect to the impact of manpower, even though one would expect having more detectives assigned to investigate a homicide case would make it more likely to be solved. It is perhaps surprising that the findings with respect to the influence of manpower on solving homicides are somewhat mixed. Wellford and Cronin (1999) found that cases are more likely to be solved if three, four, or eleven detectives are assigned to the case compared to one detective. In his study of Rochester homicides, LoFaso (2020) found the odds of clearance decline as the number of open cases carried by investigators increase. In contrast, Rinehart's study (1994) found no effect of detective manpower levels on murder clearances in Chicago. Consistent with these studies, Petersen (2017) found homicide clearances in Los Angeles County were not significantly impacted by police workload as measured by the number of homicides per sworn officer. So, at best, the totality of evidence seems to show equivocal to negligible impacts of manpower on homicide clearances.

The process of the investigation itself has received the least attention in terms of how it influences the solvability of cases, as significant case-level detail is required to examine this aspect. A few studies have examined the impact of specific investigative processes, including the collection and testing of forensic evidence, on the likelihood of clearing homicide cases. For example, Schroeder and White (2009) found very large effects on clearances of Manhattan homicides of detectives generating new leads through follow-ups on witness information and computer checks on suspects. Detectives running computer checks on witnesses and being present at postmortem examinations were negatively associated with case clearance. Wellford and Cronin (1999) explain these findings by asserting that such measures are rare and illustrate that other productive leads have been exhausted, presupposing the case is unlikely to be solved. Such contentions have not been borne out in subsequent studies. For example, studying homicide clearances in Boston, Braga, Turchan, and Barao (2019) found that investigative resources (a combined measure that includes factors like the number of detectives on the case, response time of detectives to the initial crime scene, number of patrol officers canvassing the initial crime scene for witnesses and physical evidence, and amount of time spent by the Crime Scene Response Unit processing the scene) have both a direct positive impact on homicide clearances as well as an indirect effect through positive impacts on crime scene results, subsequent investigative actions, and forensic tests.

Research by Wellford et al. (2019) indicates the likelihood of homicide case clearance increases as more agency employees respond to the scene and with investigative supervisors on scene. In addition, agency-level best practices such as performance metrics and goals; structured oversight, procedures, and supervision; and increased investigative experience, expertise, and training have a positive effect on clearances.

Counter to existing research illustrating attenuated clearance rates for homicides involving firearms, the sheer prevalence of firearm-related homicides has sparked various approaches to identifying firearms used in violent crimes. One such effort, the National Integrated Ballistic Information Network (NIBIN), established in 1999, helps identify links between violent crimes committed with firearms. However, an evaluation of NIBIN's use across one hundred fifty sites revealed that while the program has generated a very large number of hits (more than fifty thousand), hits are seldom used to identify unknown suspects and infrequently contribute to suspect arrests (King et al. 2013).

According to the small number of studies examining the impact of forensic evidence on investigations, forensic evidence is collected in a majority of homicide cases (McEwen 2010). In their exploration of the use of DNA evidence by homicide detectives in the New York City Police Department from 1996 to 2003, Schroeder and White (2009) reported that detectives rarely used DNA evidence. Further, they did not find a relationship between DNA evidence and whether cases were cleared. They concluded that investigators used DNA only as a final option, after other investigative measures had been exhausted. However, research by McEwen (2010) indicates that the bulk of forensic evidence testing in homicide cases solved by arrest occurs after the arrest has taken place. In other words, forensic evidence appears to play a bigger role in assisting police and prosecutors with building cases than in initial identification of the suspect. In cases where the investigation has stalled, matches of DNA or fingerprints through the Combined DNA Index System (CODIS) or Automated Fingerprint Identification System (AFIS) have been shown to be important in revitalizing the investigation (McEwen 2010).

An examination of the impact of forensic evidence on homicide investigations and prosecutions in Cleveland, Ohio, found collection of knives, gunshot residue kits, and clothing at the scene increased the odds of clearance, while DNA and ballistics evidence were associated with lower clearance rates (McEwen and Regoeczi 2015). In the bulk of cases, probative results were obtained after the suspect's arrest. Cases with probative results from forensic analysis resulted in more severe charges against defendants, greater likelihood of trials, and higher conviction rates.

A National Institute of Justice study on the impact of forensic evidence on the investigation and prosecution of five major offenses—including homicide—reported no effect of the collection of evidence at homicide scenes or examination of evidence by the crime laboratory on arrests, referrals to prosecutors, or convictions (Peterson et al. 2010). The collection of evidence (but not its examination) was related to the likelihood of pressing charges. Forensic analysis linking the defendant to the crime resulted in longer sentences.

The community context in which homicide investigations take place may have a significant impact on investigation outcomes. Eyewitnesses are present for a significant number of homicides (McEwen 2009; Regoeczi and Jarvis 2013), and the presence and/or number of eyewitnesses significantly increases the likelihood of clearing homicides (LoFaso 2020; McEwen and Regoeczi 2015; Wellford et al. 2019). Residents may be privy to information about the murder through informal neighborhood networks. The cooperation of community residents is critical to the success of many homicide investigations. Whether or not they are willing to cooperate with police in the search for suspects may be influenced by a variety of factors. Recent research on homicide investigations in Cleveland neighborhoods reveals the success of investigations is influenced by views of street justice and self-help as well as fear of retaliation (Regoeczi and Jarvis 2013). This study found that while the presence of third-party witnesses in general increases the likelihood of clearing cases, this effect varies by neighborhood. For example, having witnesses to the homicide is less helpful in solving the case if the homicide occurred in a disadvantaged neighborhood (i.e., high levels of poverty, unemployment, and female-headed households with children). This finding was replicated by LoFaso (2020) in his study of Rochester homicides. LoFaso also found the odds of clearing homicides involving Black victims increases in more disadvantaged neighborhoods. In Los Angeles County, California, Petersen (2017) found homicides are less likely to be cleared in areas with larger Black and Latino populations but more likely to be cleared in neighborhoods with greater concentrated disadvantage. Kennedy and colleagues' (2020) study of New York City homicides found lower clearance rates in socially disadvantaged communities, noting that areas lacking resources may suffer from low trust and cooperation with police. At the city level, Ousey and Lee (2010) reported that cities experiencing increased income, employment, and education boast increased clearance rates.

Challenges in This Area of Research

Inability to Test Theoretical Explanations

Theoretical frameworks for understanding police processes involved in solving homicide are elusive. There are two predominant perspectives. The first is found in Donald Black's *The Behavior of Law* (1976), which is often used to examine the mobility of law (the police) to solve homicide and explain differential outcomes. The second is found in the work of Gottfredson and

Hindelang (1979), which argues that the gravity of the crime (homicide) dictates the procedures employed and overall likely outcomes. Other perspectives appearing in the literature focus on routine practices of the police and have found anchors in such notions as bounded rationality (Jensen 2003), political agency (Davies 2007), or more mainstream criminological theories such as routine activities theory (Roberts 2007) as reflective of police investigative practices. Even social disorganization theory (Regoeczi and Jarvis 2013) has been applied to examine dynamics at the neighborhood level. Several studies support the role of poverty, access to the law, and concentrated disadvantage in explaining homicide clearance outcomes. Yet these contributions generally recognize that the practical, day-to-day decision-making of police executing investigative strategies escapes an adequate singular theoretical framework fully explaining dynamics of homicide clearance and poses significant problems with respect to measuring key variables.

Limited Range of Variables in National Datasets

The range of variables available to study factors impacting homicide resolution processes poses several challenges. Age, sex, and race of the homicide offender and victim, weapon use, location of the reported crime, and relationship (if known) between disputants are the most prevalent in national databases. Data on the circumstances involved in the criminal incident are also available, but broad response categories leave little precision as to the actual nature of circumstances and relationships. Moreover, in instances when cases are unsolved, relationship and circumstance are likely unknown. Data such as how a weapon was used, whether the weapon was brought to the scene or was a weapon of opportunity, whether drugs or alcohol were involved, past history between offender and victim, and even the exact nature of injuries sustained by the victim in the altercation remain altogether missing or not collected. NIBRS provides limited insights along some of these lines, but the lack of precision in reporting categories hampers the utility of these variables to truly measure potential explanatory factors.

City-Level Analyses Hold Promise

Numerous city-level or jurisdiction-specific studies have been conducted that overcome some of the shortcomings of national datasets. These efforts include but are not limited to studies of homicide clearance dynamics in Boston (Braga, Turchan, and Barao 2019), Chicago (Rinehart 1994; Riedel and Boulahanis 2007), Cleveland (McEwen and Regoeczi 2015; Regoeczi and Jarvis 2013), Columbus (Puckett and Lundman 2003), Los Angeles County (Petersen 2017), New York City (Kennedy et al. 2020), and Rochester (LoFaso 2020), among others. Many of the insights yielded by these studies are noted in this chapter. These locality-specific approaches reveal intricacies of clearance processes that multicity studies and national datasets do not. They also tend to include a wider range of variables than are available at the national level—including information on prior criminal histories, forensic evidence, investigative activities, and detective workload—and can assess neighborhood variation in the impact of these predictors on homicide clearance. An open question remains as to the extent to which practices and challenges investigating homicides in one locality are typical of other localities. The willingness of researchers to engage in the time-consuming work of original data collection is critical to building knowledge from these detailed city-level studies and assessing concerns regarding the generalizability of results.

Homicide Clearances: Measurement as a Dependent Variable

Solving homicide is usually equated to the police initiating an investigation that ultimately leads to the arrest of the individual or individuals responsible for the crime and successful prosecution and conviction. However, as noted earlier, arrests only occur about 66 percent of the time, with smaller percentages resulting in successful prosecutions and convictions. This arrest rate has import not only for deterrence of such incidents but also for how best to measure the dependent variable. Most commonly used throughout the literature is the percentage of homicides resulting in arrest. However, the available data reflecting this metric is anything but straightforward. The difficulty lies in variance in how agencies record results of their investigations. Clearly, investigations that result in arrests of suspects fit the mainstream understanding of clearing cases. However, other processes and ambiguity surround how cases that do not result in arrest are recorded and reflected in available data. The most visible of these are exceptional clearances of homicide cases, rooted in FBI definitions dating back to 1929 that permit such outcomes when no actions by the police are found lacking but prosecution cannot proceed due to specific extenuating circumstances.

As noted earlier, the specific investigative circumstances that allow for exceptional clearance reporting include the offender dying (through suicide, by accident, or at the hands of the police before an arrest can be made), being unavailable for arrest (extradition or concurrent prosecutions are typical in these cases), being a young juvenile and perhaps not appropriate for prosecution, or other procedural barriers that prevent an arrest from occurring. The number of exceptionally cleared cases is complicated by a number of ambiguities, as the UCR provides for agency discretion in determining when exceptional clearances are appropriate, explicitly stating that this list of exceptional clearance circumstances is "not all-inclusive, and there may be other circumstances when a law enforcement agency is entitled to report an exceptional clearance" (FBI 2011).

This ambiguity manifests in ongoing debates about the utility of existing data. For example, this distinction cannot be examined in traditional UCR data as crimes cleared and cleared by exceptional means are reported together rather than as two different values. This was the case until about 1995, when NIBRS became more widely available. Additionally, number of crimes cleared and arrest numbers often do not match, as agencies use the provision for agency discretion to close cases, many of which presumably do not meet the explicit conditions set out in UCR for such reporting. Why does this occur? Investigations that do not yield meaningful information, are lacking in adequate evidence to support an arrest, or have no further leads to pursue are often closed *administratively*. That is, there is no further apparent investigative work for the case, and the police move on to other cases where activity may yield an arrest. Second, discrepancies between UCR-reported arrests and arrests reported by local agencies in year-end reports to local administrative authorities (city or state) yield concern even when variance may result from administrative reporting processes rather than true differences in investigative efforts.

This leaves the research community with considerable ambiguity as to which, if any, of the dependent variables available to capture police clearances of homicide adequately measure outcomes. Clearance by arrest, exceptional clearance, and administrative clearance are all distinct but related processes, and aggregated clearance data available to researchers may or may not reflect some or all of these processes. Overwhelmingly, the existing literature uses clearance by arrest and ignores these potential sources of mismeasurement. While the literature is thin on the substantive differences between these methodological variations, there is at least some research that shows that including or excluding exceptional clearances makes a difference (Jarvis and Regoeczi 2009; Riedel and Boulahanis 2007; Roberts 2007).

Lack of Forensic and Evidence-Related Variables

Most of what is known about homicide is drawn from national datasets that contain variables such as the nature of relationship between offender and victim and timing of the incidents. However, neither the UCR or NIBRS contains information about the types of evidence collected and/or analyzed during the investigation, although DNA evidence, blood, fingerprints, relevant electronic data (emails and cell phones) and a host of other forensic data are often considered essential to solving cases. Some cases do not involve such evidence; such evidence may be corrupted, absent, or not otherwise relevant to investigative processes (Hawk and Dabney 2019; Keel, Jarvis, and Muirhead 2009). A few isolated studies argue that forensic evidence (especially

DNA) does not significantly assist in the investigative process (Schroeder and White 2009). Unfortunately, such studies fail to fully consider both the investigative processes employed by the police and uses of such evidence to leverage not only suspects but also witnesses to provide information that will assist in solving the homicide.

Lack of Insightful Data on the Investigation Process

Much is known about procedural aspects that should be followed for successful investigations (Carter and Carter 2016; Keel 2008), but little data are actually captured as to how often such procedures are followed and what each procedure yields in terms of helping investigators solve a homicide (Carter 2013). This lack of data on how different localities go about homicide investigative processes hampers research efforts to understand how the police investigate and respond to homicides and other serious crimes such as rape, robbery, and aggravated assault. Few if any of the variables in national datasets pertain to actual police actions taken in an effort to solve cases. To examine such investigative variables, city-level or locality-specific data collection such as recent work by Hawk and Dabney (2019) must be relied on to illuminate how and why the police succeed or fail to solve homicides.

Alternatively, some researchers have gained access to archived individual case files documenting not only police work but also medical reports, photos, records of criminal justice personnel, and judicial proceedings for previously investigated homicides. Again, there are advantages and disadvantages to these types of data. The most common limitations are lack of generalizability to a wider variation of cases, data collection variability (as there are rarely fixed protocols for contents of these files), and missing data. Nonetheless, many valuable insights can be gained from using these data about what increases the odds of solving homicides. Complicating efforts to understand what the police do to solve homicides and other crimes, as well as lack of data for researchers to study such dynamics, is variation in public willingness to cooperate with the police in efforts to investigate homicides. The research findings on this point are equivocal, but most police and investigators insist that the ability of the public to assist the police and vice versa are essential to the effectiveness of the police to provide public safety. Many studies support this notion, but the police vary widely in their ability to engender trust in the communities they serve (see Riedel and Jarvis 1998).

Suggestions for Future Research

While national datasets reflecting crimes that come to the attention of the police remain limited, some enhancements to such data collection efforts hold promise for studying homicide solvability. Among these welcome additions are specificity regarding circumstances involved, availability of witnesses and whether witnesses provide useful information, and details on how weapons were used to inflict injuries, among a host of other variables describing how police go about responding to cases. However, difficulties in obtaining such information abound, including lack of uniform national guidelines and training on how data elements should be collected and reported. As such, jurisdictional-level datasets rather than national-level collections show more promise for studying homicide clearances. City-level analyses often reveal the idiosyncrasies of investigative practices—more is known about the socioeconomic factors that influence crime generally, and there is less variance in legal and administrative variables than in multicity studies. In addition, original data collection can significantly reduce the amount of missing data, since information can be obtained from the full set of investigative reports in the file, many of which are completed after data on the incident are submitted through the UCR or NIBRS.

Along these lines, both recent research (Hawk and Dabney 2019) as well as the evidence provided in this chapter illustrate that ethnographic studies of investigative procedures and investigator behaviors can yield insights into difficulties and successes in trying to solve homicides. Specifically, the actions of investigators as they encounter suspicious deaths and how and why they employ certain investigative strategies are often revealed using the qualitative approaches common to ethnographic studies.

Increased quantity and quality of available data alone will not suffice in advancing our understanding of the dynamics leading to higher rates of homicide solvability. This field of research would benefit from an expansion of statistical methods beyond traditional multiple and logistic regression models to methods that can better model the complexity of relationships among factors impacting homicide solvability. This would promote a better understanding of why, for example, homicides involving minority victims are less likely to be solved in some situations while in others, they have a greater likelihood of being solved. The predominance of additive, direct effects models in the existing literature prevents the exploration of the likely conditional nature of the impacts of some factors on homicide clearances.

Conclusion

While a sizeable body of literature has emerged examining the investigation and prosecution of homicide cases, approximately one-third of all cases remain unsolved. Improvements in the quality and quantity of data on victims, incidents, and police practices could yield important discoveries as to why some cases are solved while others are not. Additionally, better access to and understanding of contemporary police practices and especially investigative procedures may yield important future insights. We encourage researchers to seek funding to conduct multijurisdictional studies with detailed original data collection in order to simultaneously examine the impacts of victim, incident, investigation, witness, evidence, and community characteristics on solving homicides. More research on the role of technology, including cell phones, shot spotters, and surveillance cameras, is also needed. Finally, it will be important to assess the ongoing impact of existing tensions between law enforcement and the communities they serve on the ability of police to solve homicides.

REFERENCES

Abrams, Robert C., Andrew C. Leon, Kenneth Tardiff, Peter M. Marzuk, and Kari Sutherland. 2007. "'Gray Murder': Characteristics of Elderly Compared with Nonelderly Homicide Victims in New York City." *American Journal of Public Health* 97 (9): 1666–70.

Addington, Lynn. 2006. "Using National Incident-Based Reporting System Murder Data to Evaluate Clearance Predictors: A Research Note." *Homicide Studies* 10 (2): 140–52.

Alderden, Megan A., and Timothy A. Lavery. 2007. "Predicting Homicide Clearances in Chicago: Investigating Disparities in Predictors across Different Types of Homicide." *Homicide Studies* 11 (2): 115–32.

Baughman, Shima Baradaran. 2020. "How Effective Are Police? The Problem of Clearance Rates and Criminal Accountability." *Alabama Law Review* 72:47–130.

Black, Donald J. 1970. "Production of Crime Rates." *American Sociological Review* 35 (4): 733–48.

———. 1976. *The Behavior of Law*. New York: Academic Press.

Braga, Anthony A., Brandon Turchan, and Lisa Barao. 2019. "The Influence of Investigative Resources on Homicide Clearances." *Journal of Quantitative Criminology* 35 (2): 337–64.

Cardarelli, Albert P., and David Cavanagh. 1992. "Uncleared Homicides in the United States: An Exploratory Study of Trends and Patterns." Paper presented at the annual meeting of the American Society of Criminology, New Orleans, LA.

Carter, David. 2013. *Homicide Process Mapping: Best Practices for Increasing Homicide Clearances*. Washington, DC: U.S. Department of Justice, Bureau of Justice Assistance.

Carter, David L., and Jeremy G. Carter. 2016. "Effective Police Homicide Investigations: Evidence from Seven Cities with High Clearance Rates." *Homicide Studies* 20 (2): 150–76.

Davies, Heather J. 2007. "Understanding Variations in Murder Clearance Rates: The Influence of the Political Environment." *Homicide Studies* 11 (2): 133–50.

Falzon, Andrew L. and Gregory G. Davis. 1998. "A 15 Year Retrospective Review of Homicide in the Elderly." *Journal of Forensic Sciences* 43 (2): 371–74.

Federal Bureau of Investigation (FBI). 2011. "Offenses Cleared, in Uniform Crime Report, Crime in the United States 2010." https://ucr.fbi.gov/crime-in-the-u.s/2010/crime-in-the-u.s.-2010/clearancetopic.pdf.

———. n.d. *Integrated Automated Fingerprint Identification System*. Accessed January 28, 2013. http://www.fbi.gov/about-us/cjis/fingerprints_biometrics/iafis/iafis.

Fox, James Alan, and Jack Levin. 1991. "Homicide against the Elderly: A Research Note." *Criminology* 29 (2): 317–27.

Gottfredson, Michael R., and Michael J. Hindelang. 1979. "A Study of the Behavior of Law." *American Sociological Review* 44 (1): 3–18.

Hawk, Shila R., and Dean A. Dabney. 2019. "Shifting the Focus from Variables to Substantive Domains When Modeling Case Outcomes." *Homicide Studies* 23 (2): 93–125.

Hawk, Shila R., Dean A. Dabney, and Brent Teasdale. 2020. "Reconsidering Homicide Clearance Research: The Utility of Multifaceted Data Collection Approaches." *Homicide Studies* 25:195–219. https://doi.org/10.1177/1088767920939617.

Jarvis, John P., and Wendy C. Regoeczi. 2009. "Homicide Clearances: An Analysis of Arrest versus Exceptional Outcomes." *Homicide Studies* 13 (2): 174–88.

Jensen, Carl. 2003. *A Test of Bounded Rationality on Police Investigative Decision-Making*. Doctoral diss., University of Maryland.

Jiao, Allan Y. 2007. "Explaining Homicide Clearance: An Analysis of Chicago Homicide Data 1965–1995." *Criminal Justice Studies* 20 (1): 3–14.

Keel, Timothy G. 2008. "Homicide Investigations: Identifying Best Practices." *FBI Law Enforcement Bulletin* 77 (2): 1–9.

Keel, Timothy G., John P. Jarvis, and Yvonne M. Muirhead. 2009. "An Exploratory Analysis of Factors Affecting Homicide Investigations: Examining the Dynamics of Murder Clearance Rates." *Homicide Studies* 13 (1): 50–68.

Kennedy, Leslie W., Joel M. Caplan, Eric L. Piza, and Amanda L. Thomas. 2020. "Environmental Factors Influencing Urban Homicide Clearance Rates: A Spatial Analysis of New York City." *Homicide Studies* 25 (4): 313–34. https://doi.org/10.1177/10887679 20976183.

King, William R., William Wells, Charles Katz, Edward Maguire, and James Frank. 2013. *Opening the Black Box of NIBIN: A Descriptive Process and Outcome Evaluation of the Use of NIBIN and Its Effects on Criminal Investigations*. Washington, DC: U.S. Department of Justice, National Institute of Justice.

Lee, Catherine. 2005. "The Value of Life in Death: Multiple Regression and Event History Analyses of Homicide Clearance in Los Angeles County." *Journal of Criminal Justice* 33 (6): 527–34.

Litwin, Kenneth J. 2004. "A Multilevel Multivariate Analysis of Factors Affecting Homicide Clearances." *Journal of Research in Crime and Delinquency* 41 (4): 327–51.

Litwin, Kenneth J., and Yili Xu. 2007. "The Dynamic Nature of Homicide Clearances: Multilevel Model Comparison of Three Time Periods." *Homicide Studies* 11 (2): 94–114.

LoFaso, Charles A. 2020. "Solving Homicides: The Influence of Neighborhood Characteristics and Investigator Caseload." *Criminal Justice Review* 45 (1): 84–103.

McEwen, Tom. 2009. *Evaluation of the Phoenix Homicide Clearance Project*. Washington, DC: U.S. Department of Justice, National Institute of Justice.

———. 2010. *The Role and Impact of Forensic Evidence in the Criminal Justice System*. Washington, DC: U.S. Department of Justice, National Institute of Justice.

McEwen, Tom, and Wendy C. Regoeczi. 2015. "Forensic Evidence in Homicide Investigations and Prosecutions." *Journal of Forensic Sciences* 60 (5): 1188–98.

Mouzos, Jenny, and Damon Muller. 2001. *Solvability Factors of Homicide in Australia: An Exploratory Analysis*. Canberra: Australian Institute of Criminology.

Nelson, Candice, and Lin Huff-Corzine. 1998. "Strangers in the Night: An Application of the Lifestyle-Routine Activities Approach to Elderly Homicide Victimization." *Homicide Studies* 2 (2): 130–59.

Ousey, G. C., and M. R. Lee. 2010. "To Know the Unknown: The Decline in Homicide Clearance Rates, 1980–2000." *Criminal Justice Review* 35 (2): 141–58.

Pastia, Cristina, Garth Davies, and Edith Wu. 2017. "Factors Influencing the Probability of Clearance and Time to Clearance of Canadian Homicide Cases, 1991–2011." *Homicide Studies* 21 (3): 199–218.

Peterson, Joseph L., Ira Sommers, Deborah Baskin, and Donald Johnson. 2010. *The Role and Impact of Forensic Evidence on the Criminal Justice Process*. Washington, DC: U.S. Department of Justice, National Institute of Justice.

Petersen, Nick. 2017. "Neighbourhood Context and Unsolved Murders: The Social Ecology of Homicide Investigations." *Policing and Society* 27 (4): 372–92.

Puckett, Janice L., and Richard J. Lundman. 2003. "Factors Affecting Homicide Clearances: Multivariate Analysis of a More Complete Conceptual Framework." *Journal of Research in Crime and Delinquency* 40 (2): 171–93.

Regoeczi, Wendy C., and John P. Jarvis. 2013. "Beyond on the Social Production of Homicide Rates: Extending Social Disorganization Theory to Explain Homicide Case Outcomes." *Justice Quarterly* 30 (6): 983–1014.

Regoeczi, Wendy C., John Jarvis, and Marc Riedel. 2008. "Clearing Murders: Is It about Time?" *Journal of Research in Crime & Delinquency* 45(2): 142–62.

Regoeczi, Wendy C., Leslie W. Kennedy, and Robert A. Silverman. 2000. "Uncleared Homicide: A Canada/United States Comparison." *Homicide Studies* 4 (2): 135–61.

Riedel, Marc, and John Boulahanis. 2007. "Homicides Exceptionally Cleared and Cleared by Arrest: An Exploratory Study of Police/Prosecutor Outcomes." *Homicide Studies* 11 (2): 151–64.

Riedel, Marc, and John Jarvis. 1998. "The Decline of Arrest Clearances for Criminal Homicide: Causes, Correlates, and Third Parties." *Criminal Justice Policy Review* 9 (3–4): 279–306.

Riedel, Marc, and Tammy Rinehart. 1996. "Murder Clearances and Missing Data." *Journal of Crime and Justice* 19 (2): 83–102.

Rinehart, Tammy. 1994. *An Analysis of Murder Clearances in Chicago: 1981–1991*. Unpublished MA thesis, Southern Illinois University.

Roberts, Aki. 2007. "Predictors of Homicide Clearance by Arrest: An Event History Analysis of NIBRS Incidents." *Homicide Studies* 11 (2): 82–93.

Roberts, Aki, and Christopher Lyons. 2011. "Hispanic Victims and Homicide Clearance by Arrest." *Homicide Studies* 15 (1): 48–73.

Rydberg, Jason, and Jesenia M. Pizarro. 2014. "Victim Lifestyle as a Correlate of Homicide Clearance." *Homicide Studies* 18 (4): 342–62.

Schroeder, David A., and Michael D. White. 2009. "Exploring the Use of DNA Evidence in Homicide Investigations: Implications for Detective Work and Case Clearance." *Police Quarterly* 12 (3): 319–42.

Wellford, Charles, and James Cronin. 1999. *An Analysis of Variables Affecting the Clearance of Homicides: A Multistate Study*. Washington, DC: Justice Research and Statistics Association.

Wellford, Charles A., Cynthia Lum, Thomas Scott, Heather Vovak, and J. Amber Scherer. 2019. "Clearing Homicides: Role of Organizational, Case, and Investigative Dimensions." *Criminology & Public Policy* 18 (3): 553–600.

17

Focused Deterrence, Public Health, and Effective Homicide Prevention

ANTHONY A. BRAGA

Introduction

As part of its sustainable development goals, the United Nations has advanced an outcome target to "significantly reduce all forms of violence and related death rates everywhere," with supporting indicators such as number of victims of intentional homicide per 100,000 population by sex and age.[1] The United Nations Office on Drugs and Crime (2019) highlights both country-level and community-level approaches in its policy recommendations to countries with high levels of homicide. Recommended country-level interventions are not generally focused on homicide prevention itself and instead tend to promote programs mitigating socioeconomic factors that create environments conducive to lethal violence, such as inequality, unemployment, and political instability. Recommended community-level interventions include recognizing that homicides in places with high homicide rates are often committed with guns and driven by gang disputes and organized crime, applying public health principles to prevent homicides rather than simply react to them, and implementing police reforms that engage communities and enhance trust.

Focused deterrence strategies seek to change offender behavior by understanding underlying violence-producing dynamics and conditions that sustain recurring homicide and violent gun injury problems and implementing a blended strategy of law enforcement, community mobilization, and social service actions (Braga and Kennedy 2020). While originating from a problem-oriented policing framework, focused deterrence strategies have been recognized as fitting within public health approaches to preventing serious gun violence (Braga and Weisburd 2015; Welsh, Braga, and Sullivan 2014). Unfortunately, criminal justice and public health approaches have largely been perceived by practitioners, academics, and policy makers as entirely separate approaches to reducing serious violence (Moore et al. 1994; Cerdá, Tracy, and Keyes 2018). For instance, evidence-based policing programs are increasingly recognized as important to the health of citizens, but neither health agencies nor police departments consider policing as part of a public health response to violence (Shepherd and Sumner 2017).

Reducing death rates is a primary concern for both police departments and public health agencies; there have been long-standing calls for greater collaboration between the two disciplines to prevent and respond to homicide and other forms of serious violence (Shepherd and Farrington 1993; Wen and Sharfstein 2015). Consistent with public health practice, the focused deterrence approach identifies underlying risk factors and causes of recurring homicide, develops tailored responses to these underlying conditions, and measures the impact of implemented interventions. Available evaluation evidence suggests that these strategies generate noteworthy violence reduction impacts and should be part of a broader portfolio of homicide prevention strategies available to policy makers and practitioners. This chapter reviews the practice, theoretical principles, and evaluation evidence of focused deterrence strategies, making links between this police-led homicide reduction approach and public health practice and policy.

Focused Deterrence: Practice and Theory

Focused deterrence strategies (sometimes called "pulling levers" policing programs) are usually implemented as problem-oriented policing projects that analyze specific recurring crime problems (such as homicide) and implement interventions tailored to local conditions and operational capacities (Braga and Kennedy 2020). Upfront analyses consistently find that urban homicide problems are highly concentrated among a very small number of chronic offenders involved in ongoing conflicts between gangs and other criminally active groups. For instance, in Chicago, 70 percent of all fatal and nonfatal gunshot injuries occurred in co-offending networks comprising less than 6 percent of the city's total population; the rate of gun homicide in the network was more than nine times higher than the city as a whole (Papachristos, Wideman, and Roberto 2015). Strategic law enforcement, community, and social service agency activities combine to change offender behavior by addressing underlying violence-producing dynamics and conditions that cause homicide to recur. As summarized by Kennedy (2019, 156–57), focused deterrence operations tend to follow this basic framework:

- Selecting a particular crime problem, such as serious gun violence.
- Pulling together an interagency enforcement group, typically including police, probation, parole, state and federal prosecutors, and sometimes federal enforcement agencies.
- Conducting research, usually relying heavily on the field experience of frontline police officers, to identify key offenders—and frequently, groups of offenders, such as street gangs, drug crews, and the like—and the context of their behavior.
- Framing a special enforcement operation directed at those offenders and groups of offenders and designed to substantially influence that context, for example by using any and all legal tools (or "levers") to sanction groups such as drug-selling crews whose members commit serious violence.
- Matching enforcement operations with parallel efforts to direct services and moral voices of affected communities to those same offenders and groups.
- Communicating directly and repeatedly with offenders and groups to let them know they are under particular scrutiny; which acts (such as shootings) will get special attention; when enforcement of the law has happened to particular offenders and groups; and what they can do to avoid enforcement action, emphasizing community norms and specifying the availability of supportive services.

This list provides a clear sense of the steps required to implement a focused deterrence strategy. For instance, putting together a working group of representatives from relevant criminal justice, social service, and community-based organizations who can bring varied incentives and disincentives to influence targeted offender behavior is a key early operational step. Consistent with problem-oriented policing framework, three main operational variations on focused deterrence have developed: group violence intervention (GVI) has been applied to control violent behavior by gangs and other criminally active groups; drug market intervention (DMI) has been implemented to address violence and disorder generated by overt drug markets; and individual offender strategies have sought to control serious violent behavior by individual chronic offenders (Braga, Weisburd, and Turchan 2018). Focused deterrence has been applied to a wider range of problems, such as intimate partner violence, serious violence in maximum security prisons, and covert opioid markets, with some very promising crime reduction impacts (Braga and Kennedy 2020). However, relative to the three core strategies, there is much less practical experience and empirical evidence to consider in these other applications.

The approach has been applied in multiple jurisdictions to control homicide problems. Focused deterrence was first developed in Boston as part of an applied research project that yielded the well-known Operation Ceasefire intervention to reduce an epidemic of youth homicide in the early to mid-1990s (Kennedy, Piehl, and Braga 1996). The Boston experience is extensively documented elsewhere and briefly summarized here. The Boston Police Department (BPD) collaborated with Harvard University researchers to convene an interagency working group comprising criminal justice, social service, and community-based partners to develop policy-relevant insights on the nature of youth homicide in Boston and advance an innovative response to underlying dynamics driving the city's homicide problem. The homicide problem analyses revealed that roughly 1 percent of Boston's youth participated in gangs, but ongoing conflicts among these groups generated at least 60 percent of the city's homicides. Homicide victims and offenders were very well known to the criminal justice system, often under some form of correctional supervision, and had been arraigned for a range of crime types.

The interagency working group used the problem analysis research to frame the Ceasefire gang homicide reduction strategy. This approach involved direct communication with gangs via call ins and street conversations that violence would no longer be tolerated, enforcement responses customized to chronic offending behaviors and criminal-justice vulnerabilities of targeted gangs, and offers of opportunities and services for gang members. Equally important, the inclusion of community partners, such as an influential black clergy group (known as the Ten-Point Coalition), allowed the BPD and their criminal justice partners to develop a mechanism for transparency and accountability very desirable to Boston's minority community. Through these relationships, the BPD created the political support, or "umbrella of legitimacy," that it needed to pursue a more focused intervention than would be possible otherwise (Braga, Turchan, and Winship 2019). A U.S. Department of Justice quasi-experimental evaluation concluded that the Ceasefire focused deterrence strategy was associated with a two-thirds reduction in Boston youth homicide (Braga et al. 2001).

Theoretical Perspectives

Deterrence theory suggests that crime can be prevented when the cost of committing crime is perceived by the offender to outweigh the benefits (Zimring and Hawkins 1973). The available research suggests that deterrent effects are ultimately determined by offender perceptions of sanction risk and certainty (Nagin 2013). Strategies that result in large, visible shifts in apprehension risk are likely to generate deterrent effects large enough to reduce crime and criminal apprehensions (Durlauf and Nagin 2011). Focused deterrence strategies have these characteristics. The approach is targeted on specific behaviors by a relatively small number of chronic offenders who are highly vulnerable to criminal justice sanctions. Working group members confront offenders directly, informing them that continued offending will not be tolerated and about how the system will respond to violations of these behavior standards. Face-to-face meetings with offenders are an important first step in altering perceptions about sanction risk (Horney and Marshall 1992). Direct communication and affirmative follow-up responses may cause offenders to reassess the risks of continuing their criminal behavior.

Focused deterrence program designers and implementers seek to generate large violence reduction impacts from the multifaceted ways in which this strategy influences targeted offenders (Kennedy 2011). As such, there are complementary violence reduction mechanisms at work in focused deterrence strategies. The emphasis is not only on increasing the risks associated with offending but also on decreasing opportunity structures for crime, deflecting offenders away from crime, increasing the collective efficacy of communities, and enhancing the legitimacy of police actions. Situational crime prevention techniques are often implemented as part of the core work of pulling levers in focused deterrence strategies (Braga and Kennedy 2020). Extending guardianship, assisting natural surveillance, strengthening formal surveillance, reducing anonymity of offenders, and utilizing place managers can greatly enhance the range and quality of the varying enforcement and regulatory levers that can be pulled on offending groups and key actors in criminal networks.

The focused deterrence approach also seeks to direct offenders away from violence through the provision of social services and opportunities. Individuals are offered job training, employment, substance abuse treatment, housing assistance, and a variety of other services and opportunities. Communities with strong collective efficacy are characterized as having high capacity for collective action for the public good (Sampson, Raudenbush, and Earls 1997). Focused deterrence strategies strive to enhance collective efficacy in communities by engaging and enlisting community members in activities such as communicating direct messages to offenders to stop behaving violently and start taking advantages of services and opportunities, connecting local community groups to government resources to support antiviolence efforts, and mobilizing residents to increase their presence in public spaces.

Finally, the focused deterrence approach takes advantage of recent theorizing regarding procedural justice and legitimacy. The effectiveness of policing is dependent on public perceptions of the legitimacy of police actions (Tyler 2006). Community involvement increases the transparency of criminal justice decision-making and helps safeguard against indiscriminate and unfocused law enforcement. Targeted offenders are treated with respect and dignity and allowed to choose a different life trajectory by taking advantage of services and opportunities. Police and other criminal justice partners attempt to increase the likelihood that offenders will "buy in" and voluntarily comply with prosocial, antiviolence norms by interacting with offenders in ways that enhance procedural justice in communication sessions.

Linking Public Health and Focused Deterrence Approaches to Homicide Prevention

Public health researchers and practitioners have historically prevented death and illness by applying a fundamental problem-solving capacity to the development of interventions such as water quality control, immunization programs, and food inspection regimes (Institute of Medicine 1988). These success stories provide important examples of the possibilities of intervening in serious problems through organized effort rooted in scientific knowledge. Public health research and practice does not separate scientific consideration of the nature of problems from conversations of how to best remedy those problems. In essence, a public health approach to homicide prevention is action oriented, and its main goal is the analysis of scientific evidence in order to prevent injury and reduce violence (Mercy and Hammond 1999).

The public health approach involves defining the problem, identifying risk factors and causes, developing and implementing interventions, and measuring the effectiveness of these interventions (fig. 17.1). Steps may not follow this linear progression, as on-the-ground conditions may require steps to occur simultaneously, targeted problems to be reanalyzed, and ineffective interventions to be adjusted (Mercy and Hammond 1999). Information systems that define and analyze homicide problems are often used to evaluate the impacts of implemented homicide prevention programs. Criminologists will immediately recognize parallels between the public health model and the basic action research model that has grounded applied social science inquiries for many decades (Lewin 1947) and provided structure to problem-oriented policing projects (Goldstein 1990). The fields of criminology and public health now often overlap and intersect in their examination of the nature of serious violence and the development of prevention responses to address it (Welsh, Braga, and Sullivan 2014).

Tertiary prevention attempts to change the trajectory of a homicide problem after it has already been established and caused harm. In public health terms, tertiary prevention efforts intervene after an illness has been contract-

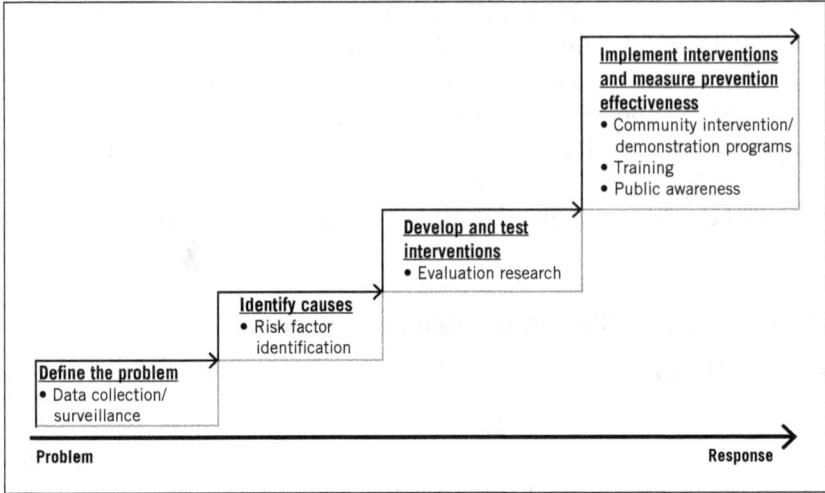

Figure 17.1 Public Health Model as a Scientific Approach to Prevention
(Source: Adapted from Mercy et al. [1993].)

ed or an injury inflicted and seek to minimize long-term consequences of the disease or injury (Institute of Medicine 1988). Criminologists and public health researchers have both contributed to a growing body of evaluation evidence that shows a wide range of effective tertiary treatments (Lipsey 2009). The movement toward the adoption of evidence-based violence prevention programs has been strengthened by these developments (Greenwood 2006). Alongside this movement, criminal justice agencies have launched strategic innovations to solidify the emerging links between public health and criminology in serious violence prevention (Welsh, Braga, and Sullivan 2014).

Focused deterrence strategies complement public health perspectives on homicide prevention. The public health approach generally involves three key elements: (1) a focus on prevention; (2) a focus on scientific methodology to identify risk and patterns; and (3) multidisciplinary collaboration to address the issue (Institute of Medicine 2008). Ecological frameworks that analyze homicide and other serious violence problems, used in both criminology and public health, emphasize designing an appropriate strategy to prevent or reduce the targeted homicide problem. Multidisciplinary collaborations are required to address complex individual, situational, and neighborhood risk factors that comprise persistent homicide problems (Institute of Medicine and National Research Council 2013). Academic-practitioner research partnerships and interagency working groups are two core components of focused deterrence strategies that are complementary to the public health approach and warrant further discussion.

Academic-Practitioner Research Partnerships

The work of academic partners in focused deterrence initiatives deviates from traditional research and evaluation roles usually played by scientific researchers. In working group settings, researcher-practitioner collaborations are integrated in ways that more closely resemble policy analysis exercises blending research, policy design, action, and evaluation (Kennedy and Moore 1995). Academics are important assets in effective focused deterrence projects; they provide real-time social science aimed at refining the working group's understanding of the problem, creating information products for both strategic and tactical use, testing the logic and appropriateness of candidate intervention ideas, maintaining the working group's focus on clear outcomes, and evaluating the performance of implemented interventions. Further, academics have played key roles in framing and organizing focused deterrence projects (Kennedy, Piehl, and Braga 1996; Braga and Kennedy 2020).

Academic research partners in focused deterrence strategies conduct epidemiological inquiries into the nature of local homicide problems so that interventions can be appropriately customized to underlying conditions and situations that cause homicides to recur. Indeed, public health perspectives point to the importance of identifying and understanding problems as they aggregate across individuals or groups (Moore et al. 1994). Frequently, doing so involves analyses of geographic and network-based concentrations of serious violence not unlike public health analyses of the localized transmission of disease. For instance, the Kerani et al. (2005) analysis of the geographic concentration of four different kinds of sexually transmitted diseases shares important parallels with the Braga, Papachristos, and Hureau (2010) study documenting the persistent concentration of fatal and nonfatal shootings at small gun-violence hot spots intersecting with gang and drug turfs in Boston. Sophisticated network analyses of street gangs and high-rate offenders suggest that most of the risk of murder concentrates in small networks of identifiable individuals; homicide risks are not only determined by individual-level risk factors but also the contours of individuals' social network (Papachristos 2009; Papachristos, Braga, and Hureau 2012). The salience of place concentration and social network dynamics in the identification and analysis of homicide problems aligns closely with the social epidemiology of HIV/AIDS problems (Poundstone, Strathdee, and Celentano 2004).

The underlying etiology of homicide problems concentrated among a small number of high-risk people who tend to be involved in violent exchanges at specific high-risk places points to the need for a concerted, targeted prevention strategy. The action-oriented approach applied in focused deterrence programs is congruent with a public health posture toward understanding and intervening in homicide problems (Mercy et al. 1993). In public health models, the first stage involves identifying and tracking the selected problem (e.g., high rates of homicide in a specific community) via mortality and serious injury surveillance systems. Next, the risk factors that contribute to the problem are identified and analyzed (e.g., ongoing violent disputes between rival gangs), interventions are launched to address these underlying factors, and impacts on targeted outcomes (e.g., homicide, fatal and nonfatal shootings) are carefully measured. After homicide reduction impacts are confirmed, the implemented program may be introduced to other areas with similar problems.

Convening an Interagency Working Group with a Locus of Responsibility for Action

Focused deterrence strategies are supported by interagency collaborations that span traditional boundaries separating criminal justice agencies from each other, from human service organizations, and from community groups. These kinds of collaborations are required to legitimize, fund, equip, and operate the complex strategies most likely to succeed in controlling and preventing homicide (Institute of Medicine and National Research Council 2013). Jurisdictions that implement focused deterrence strategies leverage interagency resources to create a very powerful "network of capacity" to prevent homicide (Moore 2002). The creation of this network positions jurisdictions to implement effective responses to homicide problems, as criminal justice agencies, community groups, and social service agencies coordinate and combine their efforts in ways that magnify their independent impacts.

In many cities suffering from homicide problems, criminal justice agencies work independently from each other, often at cross-purposes, without coordination, and in an atmosphere of distrust and dislike (Braga, Kennedy, and Tita 2002). This can also be true of different groups operating within specific organizations. The convening of a focused deterrence interagency working group comprising line-level personnel with resource decision-making authority creates the capacity to assemble the wide range of incentives and disincentives required to deliver a meaningful homicide prevention program. A locus of responsibility for homicide prevention needs to be assigned to this interagency working group because in most cities, no single organization is responsible for developing and implementing a coherent strategy to address persistent homicide problems.

Criminal justice agency partnerships provide a diverse menu of enforcement approaches that can be tailored to gangs and other criminally active groups responsible for generating the bulk of homicide problems. Without collaborative relationships, enforcement levers available to be pulled on offending groups are very limited. The participation of social service and opportunity provision organizations in focused deterrence programs provides "carrots" to balance law enforcement "sticks." The inclusion of street outreach workers and other groups that offer help to offenders by facilitating access to prevention and intervention programming helps secure community support and involvement in focused deterrence programs. Public health research further suggests that street outreach workers may help reduce violent gun injuries by mediating ongoing conflicts among gangs (Webster et al. 2012). Finally, the participation of credible community partners, such as black clergy members, can mobilize communities to exert informal social control in public spaces (through peace walks and the like), communicate antiviolence norms, encourage social service uptake by high-risk gang members, and confer much-need legitimacy to focused deterrence strategies in communities of color concerned about fair and effective policing in their neighborhoods (see Brunson et al. 2015; Braga, Turchan, and Winship 2019).

Evaluation Evidence

An ongoing, systematic review of evaluation evidence provides the most rigorous assessment of the effects of focused deterrence on crime and violence. The most recent iteration of systematic review identified twenty-four quasi-experimental evaluations of focused deterrence programs (Braga, Weisburd, and Turchan 2018). Table 17.1 presents the basic features of the twenty-four evaluations. These studies evaluated focused deterrence programs implemented in small, medium, and large cities. With the exception of an evaluation of a focused deterrence program in Glasgow, Scotland, all included studies were conducted in the United States. Evaluation evidence on the effects of focused deterrence on crime is relatively new, with all twenty-four evaluations completed after 2000 and half released after 2013. Twelve evaluations tested the violence impacts of GVI programs; nine evaluations considered the effects of DMI programs on crime problems connected to street-level drug markets, and three appraised crime reductions generated by focused deterrence programs targeting individual repeat offenders.

All twenty-four studies used varying, quasi-experimental designs to analyze the impact of focused deterrence strategies on crime and violence (Braga, Weisburd, and Turchan 2018). Rigorous quasi-experimental designs with near-equivalent comparison groups created through matching techniques were used in twelve evaluations (50 percent). Quasi-experimental designs with nonequivalent comparison groups based on naturally occurring conditions, such as other cities or areas within the city that did not receive treatment, were

TABLE 17.1 CHARACTERISTICS OF FOCUSED DETERRENCE
EVALUATIONS IN CAMPBELL REVIEW (N=24)

Characteristic	N	Percent
Country		
United States	23	95.8
Other (Scotland)	1	4.2
City Population		
Small (< 200,000 residents)	8	33.3
Medium (200,000–500,000 residents)	6	25.0
Large (> 500,000 residents)	10	41.7
Study Type		
Quasi-experiment with matched comparison group	12	50.0
Quasi-experiment with nonequivalent comparison group	9	37.5
Quasi-experiment with no comparison group (ITS)	3	12.5
Intervention Type		
Gang/group violence	12	50.0
Individual crime	3	12.5
Drug market	9	37.5
Displacement and Diffusion		
Measured displacement/diffusion	5	20.8
Did not measure displacement/diffusion	19	79.2
Publication Type		
Peer-reviewed journal	15	62.5
Grey literature	9	37.5
Published report	2	8.3
Unpublished report	7	29.2
Completion Year		
2001–2004	2	8.3
2005–2008	5	20.8
2009–2012	5	20.8
2013–2015	12	50.0

Source: Braga, Weisburd, and Turchan 2018.

used in nine studies (37.5 percent). One-group-only interrupted time-series designs that used statistical controls to account for trends and seasonal variations were used in three evaluations (12.5 percent). The impacts of crime prevention programs can be limited if the implemented intervention results in crime displacement—associated criminal offenders moving to commit crime in unprotected areas or at unprotected times, committing crime in new ways, or some other variation (see, e.g., Reppetto 1976). Some scholars have observed that crime prevention programs can generate the opposite of displacement—diffusing crime control benefits to unprotected areas or targets—

as criminals overestimate the reach of implemented programs (Clarke and Weisburd 1994). Five focused deterrence studies included in the systematic review considered whether the evaluated program resulted in crime displacement or diffusion of crime control benefits.

Nineteen of the twenty-four focused deterrence evaluations (79.2 percent) included in the review reported at least one noteworthy violence control impact (Braga, Weisburd, and Turchan 2018). None of the five studies that examined possible crime displacement effects noted significant movement of violent offending from targeted areas into surrounding areas or increased violence by untreated gangs socially connected to targeted gangs. Rather, three studies reported noteworthy diffusion of crime control benefits associated with the implementation of focused deterrence strategies in targeted areas. The systematic review used meta-analysis to synthesize crime and violence reduction impacts across the twenty-four focused deterrence evaluations. The "effect size" statistic was used to represent the strength and direction (positive or negative) of each included study in the overall meta-analysis of included program evaluations, and the "mean effect size" represented the average effect of focused deterrence on reported outcomes across all included evaluations (for an extended discussion of meta-analytic techniques, see Lipsey and Wilson 2001). Effect sizes of 0.20 suggest small program impacts on outcomes; 0.50 suggest medium program impacts, and 0.80 suggest large program impacts.

Figure 17.2 presents the effect sizes and 95 percent confidence intervals for all included focused deterrence evaluations. The meta-analysis suggests that focused deterrence programs have an overall statistically significant moderate effect on crime and violence (mean effect size = .383, $p < 0.05$). For focused deterrence evaluations that measured impacts on homicide outcomes, the impacts of the strategies were impressive: 63 percent reduction in Boston youth homicides, 34 percent reduction in total Indianapolis homicides, 25 percent reduction in young black male homicides in Rochester, 37 percent reduction in total Chicago homicides, 42 percent reduction in Stockton gun homicides, 35 percent reduction in Cincinnati group-member-involved homicides, 29 percent reduction in Kansas City total homicides after six months, 17 percent reduction in New Orleans total homicides, and 37 percent reduction in total New Haven homicides (studies reviewed in Braga, Weisburd, and Turchan 2018).

Rigorous program evaluation evidence on the impacts of focused deterrence on targeted crime problems continues to grow. Recently completed quasi-experimental evaluations of GVI in two very challenging urban environments—Oakland and Philadelphia—reported statistically significant reductions in shootings in areas with targeted gangs relative to matched com-

Mean effect sizes for study outcomes

Study name	Outcome	Std diff in means	Standard error	Std diff in means and 95% CI
Lowell PSN	Gun assaults	1.186	0.207	
Indianapolis VRS	Total homicides	1.039	0.283	
NHLongevity	Combined	0.936	0.324	
Nashville DM	Combined	0.838	0.320	
Stockton, CA	Gun homicides	0.763	0.157	
Rochester Ceasefire	Combined	0.675	0.298	
NOLA GVRS	Combined	0.656	0.283	
Boston Ceasefire I	Combined	0.645	0.241	
KC NoVA	Combined	0.607	0.322	
LA Ceasefire	Combined	0.565	0.351	
Rockford DM	Combined	0.521	0.285	
Boston Ceasefire II	Combined	0.503	0.068	
Chicago GVRS	Total gang shootings	0.414	0.157	
Oncima IRV	GM homicides	0.352	0.224	
Glasgow CIRV	Combined	0.298	0.133	
Guntersville DM	Combined	0.248	0.225	
High point DM	Combined	0.243	0.126	
Newark Ceasefire	Gun shot wounds	0.225	0.160	
Chicago PSN	Combined	0.181	0.061	
Roadie DM	Combined	0.079	0.082	
Seattle DM	All crime	0.074	0.035	
Peoria DM	Combined	0.037	0.300	
Ocala DM	All crime	−0.001	0.055	
Montgomery DM	All crime	−0.051	0.116	
		0.383	0.061	

$$-2 \quad -1 \quad 0 \quad 1 \quad 2$$

Favors control   Favors treatment

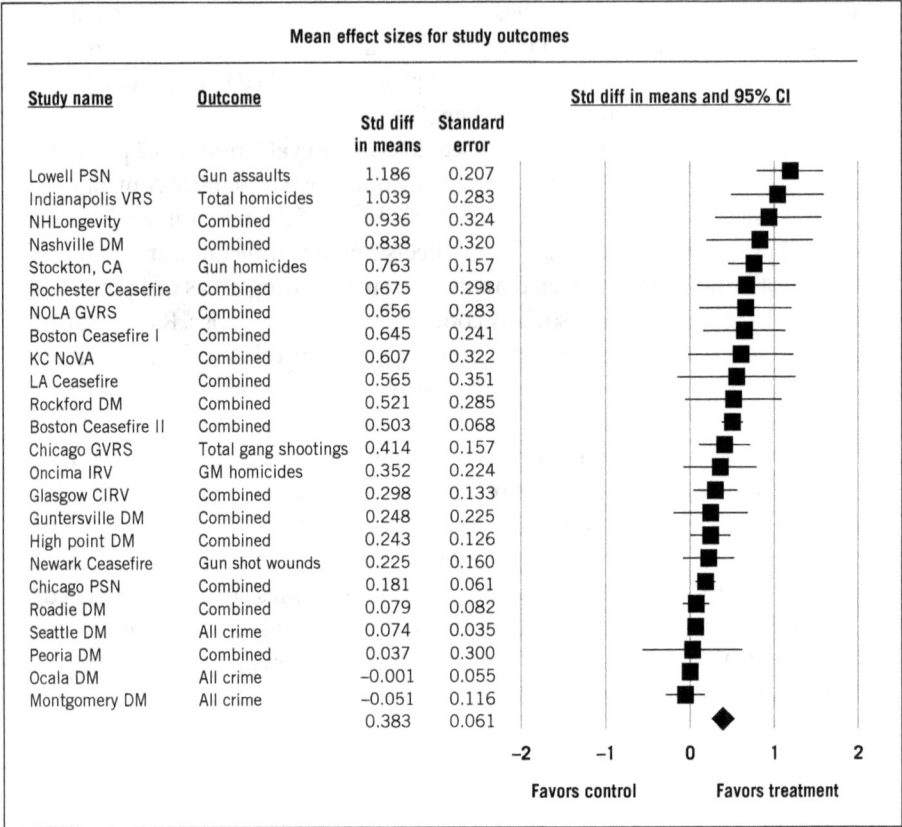

Figure 17.2 Campbell Review Meta-analysis of Included Focused Deterrence Studies (*Source: Braga, Weisburd, and Turchan [2018].*)

parison areas with untreated gangs (Braga, Turchan, and Winship 2019; Roman et al. 2019). The available focused deterrence evaluation evidence is limited by an absence of randomized controlled trials (e.g., see National Academies 2018). After the completion of the most recent Campbell systematic review, the first randomized controlled trial of an individual offender focused deterrence program centered on reducing subsequent recidivism by high-risk probationers and parolees in St. Louis (MO) was finished (Hamilton, Rosenfeld, and Levin 2018). Probationers and parolees were randomly assigned to a treatment group that was invited to attend a focused deterrence notification meeting and a control group that was not invited to attend. The randomized experiment found that the parolees and probationers who did attend the focused deterrence notification meeting were less likely to be arrested over the following seventeen months relative to those who did not attend the meeting.

Conclusion

Consistent with public health practice, the focused deterrence approach identifies underlying risk factors and causes of recurring fatal and nonfatal violent injury problems, develops tailored responses to these underlying conditions, and measures the impact of implemented interventions.

The ultimate target of focused deterrence homicide violence reduction strategies is the self-sustaining dynamic of retaliation that characterizes many ongoing gang and group conflicts. Focused deterrence operations are not designed to eliminate gangs or stop every aspect of gang activity but to control and deter gang-involved homicide. The communication of antiviolence messages attempts to weaken or eliminate the "kill or be killed" norm, as individuals recognize that their enemies will be operating under the new rules as well. Indeed, the term "focused deterrence" is somewhat of a misnomer, as the approach could be referred to as "strategies of fairness and focus" given the attention the work gives to enhancing police legitimacy through highly economical use of criminal justice resources, transparency, respectful treatment of offenders, provision of social services, and community engagement (Kennedy, Kleiman, and Braga 2017).

Focused deterrence fits well with the substance of United Nations–recommended community-level interventions given its focus on reducing homicides committed by gangs and other criminally active groups, adherence to public health principles, and promotion of more legitimate police crime control actions. However, it is important to recognize that further research is required to determine whether homicide prevention policies and practices can be transferred to settings outside U.S. urban environments. Experiences in Glasgow, Scotland, and Malmö, Sweden, suggest that the approach may be beneficial in addressing serious violence problems in other Western countries (Deuchar 2013; *The Local* 2019). Police executives and public officials in Middle Eastern and South American countries such as Turkey, Israel, and Brazil have explored the possibility of implementing focused deterrence strategies to control gang and group-related violence in their cities (Borges, Rojido, and Cano 2019; Braga and Kennedy 2020). The flexible problem-solving framework undergirding focused deterrence strategies suggests that the approach can be tailored to varying international contexts. And, while speculative, the strong scientific evidence showing homicide reductions in U.S. cities clearly supports further experimentation with focused deterrence in international urban settings.

NOTE

1. United Nations, 2023, "The Sustainable Development Goals Report, Special Edition," https://unstats.un.org/sdgs/report/2023/The-Sustainable-Development-Goals -Report-2023.pdf.

REFERENCES

Borges, Doriam, Emiliano Rojido, and Ignacio Cano. 2019. *Avaliação de Impacto do Pacto Pelotas Pela Paz*. Rio de Janeiro, Brazil: Laboratório de Análise da Violência, Universidade do Estado do Rio de Janeiro.

Braga, Anthony A., and David Kennedy. 2020. *A Framework for Addressing Violence and Serious Crime*. New York: Cambridge University Press.

Braga, Anthony A., David M. Kennedy, and George Tita. 2002. "New Approaches to the Strategic Prevention of Gang and Group-Involved Violence." In *Gangs in America*, edited by C. Ronald Huff, 271–86. Thousand Oaks, CA: Sage.

Braga, Anthony A., David M. Kennedy, Elin J. Waring, and Anne M. Piehl. 2001. "Problem-Oriented Policing, Deterrence, and Youth Violence: An Evaluation of Boston's Operation Ceasefire." *Journal of Research in Crime and Delinquency* 38 (1): 195–225.

Braga, Anthony A., Andrew Papachristos, and David Hureau. 2010. "The Concentration and Stability of Gun Violence at Micro Places in Boston, 1980–2008." *Journal of Quantitative Criminology* 26 (1): 33–53.

Braga, Anthony A., Brandon Turchan, and Christopher Winship. 2019. "Partnership, Accountability, and Innovation: Clarifying Boston's Experience with Pulling Levers." In *Police Innovation*, edited by David Weisburd and Anthony Braga, 227–50. New York: Cambridge University Press.

Braga, Anthony A., and David Weisburd. 2015. "Focused Deterrence and the Prevention of Violent Gun Injuries." *Annual Review of Public Health* 36:55–68.

Braga, Anthony A., David Weisburd, and Brandon Turchan. 2018. "Focused Deterrence Strategies and Crime Control: An Updated Systematic Review and Meta-analysis of the Empirical Evidence." *Criminology & Public Policy* 17 (1): 205–50.

Braga, Anthony A., Greg Zimmerman, Lisa Barao, Chelsea Farrell, Rod Brunson, and Andrew Papachristos. 2019. "Street Gangs, Gun Violence, and Focused Deterrence." *Journal of Research in Crime and Delinquency* 56 (4): 524–62.

Brunson, Rod, Anthony A. Braga, David Hureau, and Kashea Pegram. 2015. "We Trust You, but Not That Much: Examining Police–Black Clergy Partnerships to Reduce Youth Violence." *Justice Quarterly* 32 (6): 1006–36.

Cerdá, Magdalena, Melissa Tracy, and Katherine Keyes. 2018. "Reducing Urban Violence: A Contrast of Public Health and Criminal Justice Approaches." *Epidemiology* 29 (1): 142–50.

Clarke, Ronald, and David Weisburd. 1994. "Diffusion of Crime Control Benefits." *Crime Prevention Studies* 2:165–84.

Deuchar, Ross. 2013. *Policing Youth Violence: Transatlantic Connections*. London: IEP Press.

Durlauf, Steven, and Daniel Nagin. 2011. "Imprisonment and Crime: Can Both Be Reduced?" *Criminology & Public Policy* 10 (1): 13–54.

Goldstein, Herman. 1990. *Problem-Oriented Policing*. Philadelphia: Temple University Press.

Greenwood, Peter. 2006. *Changing Lives: Delinquency Prevention as Crime-Control Policy*. Chicago: University of Chicago Press.

Hamilton, Benjamin, Richard Rosenfeld, and Aaron Levin. 2018. "Opting Out of Treatment." *Journal of Experimental Criminology* 17 (1): 1–17.

Horney, Julie, and Ineke Marshall. 1992. "Risk Perceptions among Serious Offenders." *Criminology* 30 (4): 575–94.

Institute of Medicine. 1988. *The Future of Public Health*. Washington, DC: National Academies Press.

———. 2008. *Violence Prevention in Low- and Middle-Income Countries*. Washington, DC: National Academies Press.

Institute of Medicine and National Research Council. 2013. *Priorities for Research to Reduce the Threat of Firearm-Related Violence*. Washington, DC: National Academies Press.

Kennedy, David. 2011. *Don't Shoot*. New York: Bloomsbury.

———. 2019. "Policing and the Lessons of Focused Deterrence." In *Police Innovation*, edited by David Weisburd and Anthony Braga, 205–26. New York: Cambridge University Press.

Kennedy, David, Mark Kleiman, and Anthony Braga. 2017. "Beyond Deterrence: Strategies of Focus and Fairness." In *Handbook of Crime Prevention and Community Safety*, edited by Nick Tilley and Aiden Sidebottom, 157–82. New York: Routledge.

Kennedy, David, and Mark Moore. 1995. "Underwriting the Risky Investment in Community Policing." *Justice System Journal* 17 (3): 271–90.

Kennedy, David, Anne Piehl, and Anthony A. Braga. 1996. "Youth Violence in Boston: Gun Markets, Serious Youth Offenders, and a Use-Reduction Strategy." *Law and Contemporary Problems* 59 (1): 147–96.

Kerani, Roxanne, Mark Handcock, Hunter Handsfield, and King Holmes. 2005. "Comparative Geographic Concentrations of Four Sexually Transmitted Infections." *American Journal of Public Health* 95 (2): 324–30.

Lewin, Kurt. 1947. "Group Decisions and Social Change." In *Readings in Social Psychology*, edited by Theodore Newcomb and Eugene Hartley, 340–44. New York: Atherton Press.

Lipsey, Mark. 2009. "The Primary Factors That Characterize Effective Interventions with Juvenile Offenders." *Victims and Offenders* 4 (2): 124–47.

Lipsey, Mark, and David Wilson. 2001. *Practical Meta-Analysis*. Thousand Oaks, CA: Sage.

The Local. 2019. "Malmö Pushes Ahead with US Anti-gang Method after Shootings." November 13. https://www.thelocal.se/20191113/malm-police-push-ahead-with-anti-gang-method-despite-shootigs.

McGarrell, Edmund, Steven Chermak, Jeremy Wilson, and Nicholas Corsaro. 2006. "Reducing Homicide through a 'Lever-Pulling' Strategy." *Justice Quarterly* 23 (2): 214–29.

Mercy, James, and Rodney Hammond. 1999. "Combining Action and Analysis to Prevent Homicide." In *Homicide*, edited by Dwayne Smith and Margaret Zahn, 297–310. Thousand Oaks, CA: Sage.

Mercy, James, Mark Rosenberg, Kenneth Powell, Claire Broome, and William Roper. 1993. "Public Health Policy for Preventing Violence." *Health Affairs* 12 (4): 7–29.

Moore, Mark. 2002. "Creating Networks of Capacity." In *Securing Our Children's Future*, edited by Gary Katzmann, 338–85. Washington, DC: Brookings Institution Press.

Moore, Mark, Deborah Prothrow-Smith, Benjamin Guyer, and Howard Spivak. 1994. "Violence and Intentional Injuries." In *Understanding and Preventing Violence*, edited by Albert Reiss and James Roth, 4:167–216. Washington, DC: National Academies Press.

Nagin, Daniel. 2013. "Deterrence in the Twenty-First Century." In *Crime and Justice*, edited by Michael Tonry, 42:199–263. Chicago: University of Chicago Press.

National Academies. 2018. *Proactive Policing: Effects on Crime and Communities*. Washington, DC: National Academies Press.

Papachristos, Andrew. 2009. "Murder by Structure." *American Journal of Sociology* 115:74–128.

Papachristos, Andrew, Anthony A. Braga, and David M. Hureau. 2012. "Social Networks and the Risk of Gunshot Injury." *Journal of Urban Health* 89 (6): 992–1003.

Papachristos, Andrew, Christopher Wildeman, and Elizabeth Roberto. 2015. "Tragic, but Not Random." *Social Science & Medicine* 125:139–50.

Poundstone, Katharine, Steffanie Strathdee, and David Celentano. 2004. "The Social Epidemiology of HIV/AIDS." *Epidemiologic Reviews* 26:22–35.

Reppetto, Thomas. 1976. "Crime Prevention and the Displacement Phenomenon." *Crime & Delinquency* 22 (2): 166–77.

Roman, Caterina, Nathan Link, Jordan Hyatt, Avinash Bhati, and Megan Forney. 2019. "Assessing the Gang-Level and Community-Level Effects of the Philadelphia Focused Deterrence Strategy." *Journal of Experimental Criminology* 15 (4): 499–527.

Sampson, Robert, Stephen Raudenbush, and Felton Earls. 1997. "Neighborhoods and Violent Crime." *Science* 277:918–24.

Shepherd, Jonathan, and David Farrington. 1993. "Assault as a Public Health Problem." *Journal of the Royal Society of Medicine* 86:89–94.

Shepherd, Jonathan, and Steven Sumner. 2017. "Policing and Public Health—Strategies for Collaboration." *JAMA* 317 (15): 1525–26.

Tyler, Tom. 2006. *Why People Obey the Law.* Princeton, NJ: Princeton University Press.

United Nations Office on Drugs and Crime. 2019. *Global Study on Homicide.* Vienna: UNDOC.

Webster, Daniel, Jennifer Whitehill, Jon Vernick, and Elizabeth Parker. 2012. *Evaluation of Baltimore's Safe Streets Program.* Baltimore: Johns Hopkins University.

Welsh, Brandon, Anthony A. Braga, and Christopher Sullivan. 2014. "Serious Youth Violence and Innovative Prevention." *Justice Quarterly* 31 (3): 500–23.

Wen, Leana, and Joshua Sharfstein. 2015. "Unrest in Baltimore: The Role of Public Health." *JAMA* 313 (24): 2425–26.

Zimring, Franklin, and Gordon Hawkins. 1973. *Deterrence.* Chicago: University of Chicago Press.

Conclusion

The Future of Homicide Research

KAREN F. PARKER AND RICHARD STANSFIELD

Homicide Today

The writing of this book occurs on the back of grim records set by many American and European cities beginning in 2020. While the rate of homicide remains relatively low by historical standards, and across-the-board crime increases were not witnessed in most countries, several data sources confirm focused increases in murders. From 2019 to 2020, the U.S. murder rate increased approximately 30 percent according to mortality data published by the Centers for Disease Control and Prevention (CDC), the highest year-on-year increase for a century. Considerable variation within and across places exists. While large cities like New York have less than a fifth of the homicides they had thirty years ago, other metropolitan areas have considerably higher homicide rates, seeing acceleration in a gradual trend of rising gun violence across the country since 2014 (Sharkey and Marsteller 2022). Homicides increased more modestly, and from a lower baseline, in some European countries including Germany and England. Homicides also remained high in many central and southern American countries, albeit with large variation between countries.

These very real spikes in murder, absent from increases in other crimes, call to attention the constellation of homicide research described in this volume that carefully details what we know about victims and perpetrators, individual and structural drivers of homicide, and how law enforcement and community-based resources can be leveraged for homicide reductions. Researchers in this volume critically emphasize the need for research that details the unique predictors of criminal and interpersonal homicide that receive less attention. Namely, the role of growing inequality and racial disadvantage throughout our neighborhoods, an opioid epidemic, and in the United States, the rise in the number of firearms owned both legally and illegally.

This volume reiterates that homicide globally continues to be largely male perpetrated. Younger men are at particular risk for early death from gang and gun violence, while women are far more likely to be victims of intimate partner related homicide, and communities facing significant economic disadvantages may experience higher rates of homicide. Although much of the work on predictors of violence remains focused on individual-level correlates, McCall and colleagues remind us that certain ecological risk factors consistently predict rates of homicide, including population structure, concentrated poverty, unemployment, racial inequality and segregation, and family disruption. These factors collectively contribute to the persistent concentrated disadvantage that exposes communities to greater risk for gun violence than their nondisadvantaged counterparts.

While individual demographic risk factors and community characteristics may vary from country to country, one common thread linking homicides throughout the world is the role of firearms. As described by Semenza and Griffiths in this volume, shootings are the most common cause of death worldwide, accounting for more than half of all homicides globally. While the proportion of homicides committed with a firearm varies across the globe, the prominence of firearms in homicide is undeniable. More than three quarters of the murders in the United States in 2020 were perpetrated with firearms, while just over half of all murders were cleared. Thus, while the evidence around investigative techniques and violence prevention through focused deterrence are particularly compelling, a research agenda pursuing efforts to prevent homicide must also take seriously the actions (and inactions) in the ability to limit the spread of illegal guns in the United States. Although a recent study found that the increase in gun purchases in 2020 did not correlate with gun violence (Schleimer et al. 2021), others have noted that more people may have been carrying guns in 2020 (Arthur and Asher 2021).

As discussed by Semenza and Griffiths, homicide researchers have grappled with ways to capture firearm availability in their research. While evidence suggests that some proxies for legal gun availability (Haviland et al. 2021) and illegal ownership (Kleck and Paterson 1993) may exist, the millions of firearms processed in the United States each year are largely under the radar. Historically the ATF has been severely underfunded, such that only 7 percent of licensed gun dealers may get inspected in a year. The ability to trace and track illegal guns also remains hampered. Researchers can aid in this important aspect of homicide prevention by continuing to assess the role of guns, gun flow, and purchase locations and laws in their role in homicide changes. Undoubtedly, one of the most effective ways to prevent homicide is to prevent criminals from obtaining guns in the first place (Braga et al. 2021). Homicide research could also be influential in examining the impact of new legislation, including laws designed to strengthen penalties for stealing firearms from stores and enable law enforcement to track and reduce the number of illegal firearms in circulation more effectively.

Guns are certainly not the only story when it comes to homicide. Maybe a testament to strong gun control laws in other parts of the world, the proportion of homicides in the U.K. caused by firearms fell to just 8.3 percent in 2021, down from 11.4 percent in 2020. But the threat of knife-perpetrated homicide in England's major cities has increased since the pandemic. It is also a more common method of killing between intimate partners. It is notable that much like homicide in the United States, gun- and knife-perpetrated homicide disproportionately affects communities of color, with higher rates concentrated in places with higher poverty and more people in low-income or temporary housing, in addition to histories of strained community-police relations. Indeed, other scholars have argued that gun or knife carrying are legitimate responses to perceived threats and perceptions that police are incapable of addressing local issues, with the added benefit of garnering respect and displaying "masculinity" in the community (Anderson 1999).

Despite some variation in methods of homicide across countries, the recent trends in homicide in the United States and parts of Europe flag two important additions to the valuable work collated in this volume. First, violence during the pandemic has drawn significant attention to the role of police, community-police relations, and its role in homicide. Policing undoubtedly has a role in homicide, with some studies finding that increases in police force size can help abate homicide (Chalfin et al. 2022). The impact of changes in police-community relations and their impact on homicide is more debated and in need of study. Some studies following the killing of Michael Brown in 2014 by a Ferguson, Missouri police officer suggested that a pulling back of law enforcement activity, combined with people being less willing to call the police to resolve disputes, created more situations conducive to violence escalation (Pyrooz et al. 2016). The relationship between police use of excessive force and criminal homicide has long been theorized in the homicide literature (MacDonald et al. 2003), but after the killing of George Floyd in May 2020, the role of police-community relations and excessive police force remains a key point of inquiry for homicide in communities of color. While there remains a lack of reliable data on the killings by and of police officers globally, homicide researchers may continue to consider how lethal violence involving police is caught up in the complex pathways between community conditions and violence.

Second, while the focus of homicide research often details the prevalence and causes of such violence, homicide impacts families, local residents, social service workers, and the city or nonprofit workers aiming to keep people safe and prevent further violence. This was even more heightened during the pandemic, when this work became harder, yet the combined trauma faced by some communities became greater. Homicide research increasingly must consider the health burden faced by people affected by homicide. This may include studies on the impact on child schooling, the health and anxiety of family members with teenage sons, business owners in high crime areas, or the evaluation of programs aimed at supporting people exposed to homicide. While services for victims of violence and family members losing loved ones to homicide are largely nonexistent in many communities, research must continue to study how the leveraging of local resources, strengths, and networks can help ensure the organization and service of communities. Considered in tandem with the reality that Black and minority residents disproportionately experience homicide, a future avenue of homicide research is assessing the racial and cultural grief of survivors of homicide victims (see Sharpe et al. 2022).

This focus on health also should occur alongside continued studies of homicide prevention and novel investigative techniques that can increase the likelihood of offender identification, uncovering of motive, and informing future violence prevention efforts. As detailed in Braga's chapter, we have mounting evidence that focused deterrence programs may work. Other programs, like Cure Violence, aim to prevent homicide by using similar methods combining community engagement, intervention, and outreach. Cure Violence has seen successful implementation in very complex cultures of violence, such as Honduras (Ransford et al. 2017), in addition to the United States.

While these are programs designed to target people and communities at high risk for homicide incidents, Charlotte Gill (2016) reminds us that there is a distinction between programs focused on at-risk people living in communities and those focused on treating the community as a whole. While there is certainly value in after-school programming and early interventions for their ability to prevent some amount of crime, police-led initiatives, including focused deterrence, have much stronger empirical evidence for homicide prevention (Braga, this volume). Homicide researchers still have much to offer in delineating the role of various actors in violence suppression, including police, residents, government officials, and local property owners who may or may not reside in communities of high crime (Linning et al. 2022).

This research remains critical at all policy levels. At a local level, there remains a lot of debate about the reason for homicide spikes and drops, and best practices to reduce the burden of homicide on communities. As an example, some cities may experience rises in homicide due to uniquely high numbers of distributions of drug markets (e.g., Rabolini et al., this volume). Other places may see low levels of homicide due to unique contexts of incorporation and reception for immigrant groups (Light et al., this volume; Orrick et al., this volume). And rising homicide in other countries may have different originations, with recent reports documenting significantly higher proportions of homicide deaths in Sweden linked to organized crime. Studying and informing these complex problems requires attention to unique histories, legal contexts of countries, and organizations of local neighborhoods.

The Future of Homicide Research

Within this volume, discussions of trends in homicide largely end toward 2019 and 2020. This is particularly true for studies rooted in the United States, where The Uniform Crime Report program and the related Supplementary Homicide Reports—so long a reliable source of homicide data—ended at the national level with 2020. In January 2021, while still voluntary, submission of crime data using the National Incident Based Reporting System (NIBRS) became mandatory. This resulted in a decrease in the number of agencies reporting, from over 90 percent to 66 percent. At the time of publication, those not reporting are some of the largest cities. Thus, while eventually this new series may be a much better tool for analysis—as discussed in the chapter in data sources—current data challenges to studying homicide in the United States are real. At the same time, open access data from individual police agencies are increasing the opportunities to understand homicide trends at a local level in quicker fashion, often at the specific geo location of an incident. As an example, Rosenfeld and Lopez's (2021) influential reports on unrest and crime in the United States during the pandemic relied on data from individual police agencies who make their data publicly available online. These data help confirm sharp increases in homicide in 2020 and 2021. Broadly, the accessibility of such data also promises to aid in the identification of local homicide trends in the United States, in addition to the evaluation of strategies designed to reduce violence.

Recent changes in data collection aside, the current volume offers a comprehensive and systematic look at the key areas of emerging homicide research and offers a dialogue with key scholars on how they propose the field can address some of these methodological issues or challenges. This volume focuses most broadly on the social science study of criminal and interpersonal homicide. Sociopolitical homicide perpetrated due to discrimination, political agendas, and civil unrest are largely out of the purview of this book. The same can be said for homicide because of organized crime, and the homicide of people killed by law enforcement and other state actors. Even so, many of the issues addressed in this book have global resonance; the use of firearms as the predominant method for homicide perpetration; the interplay of drugs and alcohol with some types of homicide; that over half of women and girls murdered are at the hands of partners or other family members.

This volume also reaffirms that our greatest understanding of homicide, and the potential for prevention, comes from subnational studies of homicide where data are the most complete and patterns can be identified. Even within the context of the United States, however, there is significant variation in what we know and do not know. Open data initiatives have transformed our understanding of homicide spatially, and in terms of motivations, perpetrators, and victims. Yet many victims may continue to evade researchers' purview. Kenna Quinet (2007) points out that populations of female prostitutes, teenage runaways, or other transient populations may be drastically undercounted and understudied as these victims were never reported missing or identified as missing prior to their homicide. The case of "missing missing," as Quinet details, provides a stark reminder of the challenges ahead for information sharing and linking across systems.

As detailed in the chapter on data sources, our understanding as researchers is being bolstered by the advent of new linked systems (such as NamUs— the National Missing and Unidentified Persons System). Increasingly, crowd-funded sources of data are emerging as critical tools for researchers looking to understand previously understudied topics of homicide. This includes several well-known sources of data on police-perpetrated homicides. While most macrolevel studies of homicide to date have occurred at the city level, public sources such as the American violence project by Patrick Sharkey and colleagues are helping researchers gain a better understanding of homicide at lower levels of aggregation. Sociologists James Densley and Jillian Peterson launched the Violence Project, a database of mass shootings in the United States, the shooters, their backgrounds, guns, and motivations. And the Center for Homeland Defense and Security maintains a K–12 school-shooting database that serves as a comprehensive tool for researchers of homicides in and near schools.

With these new sources of homicide data displayed over time, researchers will be able to continually improve our understanding of homicide in two ways. First, this will help study the causes of change in different types of homicide over time, considering multifactorial predictors of homicide. Second, researchers will be able to understand the reciprocal relationship between homicide and a constellation of local conditions, including population health. Many researchers have focused on the ecological "causes" of homicide from a unidirectional perspective without considering how homicide also contributes to the cyclical worsening of neighborhood conditions. This necessarily requires a reciprocal analytic approach to consider how structural conditions increase the risk for violence and conversely, how violence exacerbates structural conditions over time.

While aspects of concentrated disadvantage like residential segregation, family disruption, unemployment, and low educational attainment are all known predictors of community violence, each of these is likely to be further exacerbated by violent contexts. The loss of local community members, persistent communal fear, and the mental health consequences of gun-violence exposure all make it harder for communities to address other neighborhood issues, contributing to ongoing cycles of disadvantage and violence that become increasingly difficult to alter (Currie 2020). The cyclical dynamics are particularly acute in historically disadvantaged communities of color composed predominantly of Black and Hispanic residents. The reciprocal analyses required to parse out these dynamics necessitate longitudinal data and the capacity to measure complex bidirectional relationships.

Researchers from the social sciences are also just beginning to help empower communities to prevent mass homicide. In the wake of several school shootings in recent years, worrying behavior and direct threats have been found days prior on perpetrators' social media platforms. A big role for homicide researchers moving forward may be to assist in the evaluation of software that tracks a person's connection to extremist groups online. A recent review suggested that more than half the perpetrators of mass homicide in the United States leak information about their intentions to friends and associates (Silver et al. 2018), with many other examples of worrisome behavior and overt threats along the pathway towards violence. Such information sources have been central to the development of a mass-shootings database in the United States (The Violence Project). Similar projects and data collection efforts have the potential to significantly improve the understanding of risk factors that shape neighborhood rates of gun violence at the local, city, and state levels of the social ecology, in addition to aiding in directing funding to address the most salient combinations of risk factors for homicide.

Homicide researchers can also continue to inform and improve policies addressing violence against girls and women through research. Whether through risk-assessment development that can help distinguish key factors in the likelihood that violence escalates into homicide, or through rigorous evaluations of programs engaging men in healthy masculinity and promotion of gender equality, homicide research within the social sciences continues to play a critical role in prevention. This should be seen as a common goal with medical scholars studying variations in perpetrator neurology and other biological markers. While the field of neurocriminology was out of the purview of this volume, its goals in risk identification and prevention are shared and echoed.

Within this volume alone, the complexity of the homicide problem and the multifactorial nature of the solution is evident. This volume serves as a reminder for the need for comprehensive data behind homicide perpetration that can guide decision-makers in targeted interventions, whether they be law enforcement driven, or legal interventions designed to reduce firearms in the hands of prohibited buyers. It also highlights the need to strengthen education and opportunities for young people in communities, to strengthen community organizations, and to repair community and law enforcement relationships. A diversification of homicide research can serve to further *prioritize* violence prevention agendas for local and city governments by providing insight into the most promising avenues for funding and programming to reduce fatal events. This research can also aid in prioritizing funding and programming decisions for historically underfunded communities of color that have experienced the greatest levels of homicide, in the United States and globally.

REFERENCES

Anderson, Elijah. 1999. *Code of the Street: Decency, Violence, and the Moral Life of the Inner City.* New York: W. W. Norton & Company.

Arthur, Rob, and Jeff Asher. 2021. "One Possible Cause of the 2020 Murder Increase: More Guns." *Vox,* June 12, 2021. https://www.vox.com/22529989/2020-murders-guns.

Braga, Anthony A., Elizabeth Griffiths, Keller Sheppard, and Stephen Douglas. 2021. "Firearm Instrumentality: Do Guns Make Violent Situations More Lethal." *Annual Review of Criminology* 4 (1): 147–64.

Chalfin, Aaron, Benjamin Hansen, Emily K. Weisburst, and Morgan C. Williams Jr. 2022. "Police Force Size and Civilian Race." *American Economic Review: Insights* 4:139–58.

Currie, Elliott. 2020. *A Peculiar Indifference: The Neglected Toll of Violence on Black America.* New York: Metropolitan Books.

Gill, Charlotte. 2016. "Community Interventions." In *What Works in Crime Prevention and Rehabilitation: Lessons from Systematic Reviews,* edited by David Weisburd, David Farrington, and Charlotte Gill, 77–109. New York: Springer.

Haviland, Miriam J., Emma Gause, Frederick P. Rivara, Andrew G. Bowen, Amelia Hanron, and Ali Rowhani-Rahbar. 2021. "Assessment of County-level Proxy Variables for Household Firearm Ownership." *Preventive Medicine* 148:106571.

Kleck, Gary, and E. Britt Patterson. 1993. "The Impact of Gun Control and Gun Ownership Levels on Violence Rates." *Journal of Quantitative Criminology* 9 (3): 249–87.

Linning, Shannon J., Ajima Olaghere, and John E. Eck. 2022. "Say NOPE to Social Disorganization Criminology: The Importance of Creators in Neighborhood Social Control." *Crime Science* 11:1–11.

MacDonald, John, Patrick Manz, Geoffrey Alpert, and Roger Dunham. 2003. "Police Use of Force: Examining the Relationship between Calls for Service and the Balance of Police Force and Suspect Resistance." *Journal of Criminal Justice* 31:119–27.

Pyrooz, David, Scott Decker, Scott Wolfe, and John Shjarback. 2016. "Was There a Ferguson Effect on Crime Rates in Large U.S. Cities?" *Journal of Criminal Justice* 46:1–8.

Quinet, Kenna. 2007. "The Missing Missing: Toward a Quantification of Serial Murder Victimization in the United States." *Homicide Studies* 11 (4): 319–39.

Ransford, Charles, R. Brent Decker, Guadalupe M. Cruz, Francisco Sánchez, and Gary Slutkin. 2017. "The Cure Violence Model: Violence Reduction in San Pedro Sula (Honduras)." *Revista Cidob D'afers Internacionals*: 179–204.

Rosenfeld, Richard, and Ernesto Lopez. 2021. "Pandemic, Social Unrest, and Crime in U.S. Cities." September 2021 Update. Washington, DC: Council on Criminal Justice.

Schleimer, Julia, Christopher McCort, Aaron Shev, Veronica Pear, Elizabeth Tomsich, Alaina De Biasi, Shani Buggs, Hannah Laqueur, and Garen Wintemute. 2021. "Firearm Purchasing and Firearm Violence during the Coronavirus Pandemic in the United States." *Injury Epidemiology* 8:1–10.

Sharkey, Patrick, and Alisabeth Marsteller. 2022. "Neighborhood Inequality and Violence in Chicago, 1965–2020." *University of Chicago Law Review* 89:3.

Sharpe, Tanya, Derek Kenji Iwamoto, Kerry Lee, and Jheanelle Anderson. 2022. "Development and Validation of the Inventory of Stress and Coping for African American Survivors of Homicide Victims." *Psychological Trauma: Theory, Research, Practice, and Policy* 15 (5): 791–99. https://doi.org/10.1037/tra0001246.

Silver, James, John Horgan, and Paul Gill. 2018. "Foreshadowing Targeted Violence: Assessing Leakage of Intent by Public Mass Murderers." *Aggression and Violent Behavior* 38 (2018): 94–100.

Contributors

Mark T. Berg is Professor in the Department of Sociology and Criminology at the University of Iowa. His primary research and teaching interests include criminology and social determinants of health. His recent research examines interpersonal disputes, developmental pathways of antisocial behavior, and life-course determinants of physical health and well-being. He has received funding from the National Institute of Justice (U.S. Department of Justice), the Centers for Disease Control, and the National Science Foundation; recent work on opioid mortality trends is supported by the United States Department of Agriculture.

Laura Boisten is a PhD candidate in the Department of Economics at the University of Wisconsin-Madison. Her research focuses on topics in labor economics, with a primary interest in economics of crime and a secondary interest in education and inequality.

Anthony A. Braga is the Jerry Lee Professor of Criminology and Director of the Crime and Justice Policy Lab in the Department of Criminology at the University of Pennsylvania. He collaborates with criminal justice, social service, and community-based organizations to produce high impact scholarship, randomized field experiments, and policy advice on the prevention of crime at problem places, control of gang violence, and reductions in access to firearms by criminals.

Fiona Brookman is Professor of Criminology and member of the Centre for Criminology at the University of South Wales, UK. Her research examines homicide, violence, and major crime investigation using qualitative research methods. She has over twenty-four years of experience in teaching and research in the fields of policing, violence, and homicide. Her research is helping to enhance police practice and directly inform violence reduction initiatives. In 2011, Fiona established the Criminal Investigation Research Network (CIRN) to generate international research collaboration between detectives, researchers, and policy makers.

Shytierra Gaston is Assistant Professor in the Department of Criminal Justice and Criminology at Georgia State University. Her research and teaching expertise center on two broad areas: the intersection of race/ethnicity, racism, crime, and criminal justice and the U.S. correctional system. Her recent research has examined sources of race disparities in policing, long-term mental health consequences of parental incarceration, and intergenerational consequences of historical racist violence among families of lynching victims. Dr. Gaston is an active member of the American Society of Criminology and the Racial Democracy, Crime, and Justice Network.

Veronica Valencia Gonzalez is a doctoral candidate in the social ecology program at the University of California, Irvine (UCI). Veronica has taken social ecology's approach to heart by seeking to include the voices and opinions of community members in research that focuses on gender violence and intimate partner violence (IPV) within Latine/x communities.

Elizabeth Griffiths is Associate Professor at the School of Criminal Justice at Rutgers University-Newark. Her research focuses broadly on the influence of place on the distribution and movement of crime across space. Her scholarship also explores how system actors and policy officials substantively shape case processing and criminal justice outcomes. In a large, multidisciplinary, mixed-method project funded by the National Science Foundation, Dr. Griffiths examined how race, space, and geography conditioned the policing, prosecution, and punishment of felony drug crimes over a decade in one Southern metropolitan county.

Chris Guerra is Assistant Professor in the Department of Criminal Justice at the University of Texas at El Paso. His primary research focuses on immigration and antisocial behavior. More specifically, he aims to provide nuance to the host of mechanisms involved in examining the immigrant experience (e.g., immigrant generations, statuses, day-to-day behavior) and a variety of negative life outcomes such as criminal offending, victimization, and alcohol use.

John R. Hipp is Professor in the Departments of Criminology, Law and Society, and Sociology at the University of California, Irvine. His research interests focus on how neighborhoods change over time, how that change both affects and is affected by neighborhood crime, and how networks and institutions play a role in that change. He approaches these questions using quantitative methods as well as social network analysis.

John Jarvis is Academic Dean for the FBI Training Division and former Chief Criminologist in the FBI's Behavioral Science Unit. He served as a Senior Scientist and Chief Criminologist in the Behavioral Science Unit at the FBI Academy for about twenty years and chaired the Futures Working Group, which was devoted to examining issues confronting the future of law enforcement and national security. His academic and criminological work focuses on evidence-based policing strategies, crime analysis, crime trend research, and the initiation and support of research efforts by local, state, and federal law enforcement.

Helen Jones is a full-time research fellow at the University of South Wales, UK. Her research generally involves qualitative methods, and her research interests include homicide, the role of forensic science and digital technology in homicide investigation, missing people, major crime investigation, cold case reviews, policing, and vulnerability. Prior to joining the University of South Wales, Helen worked for Leicestershire Police for over twelve years, including as a review officer (2010–2015) and intelligence analyst (2007–2010).

Sharon D. Jones-Eversley is Professor of Family Studies and Community Development at Towson University. As a professor, scholar, researcher, and author, she focuses on social justice, equity, organizational capacity building, planning, and evaluation. Dr. Jones-Eversley brings a lens of racial equity, diversity, justice, and inclusion to her work. Her research examines social and legal determinants of health and death for vulnerable populations such as racial and ethnic persons of color, low-income families, and communities.

Jungmyung Kim is a PhD candidate of the Department of Sociology at the University of Wisconsin-Madison. He studies how organizations and occupations intersect with social stratification systems such as gender, race, and citizenship. His dissertation is an ethnography project examining relationships between police officers and care workers. Mainly through collaborative efforts, he also studies impacts of public policies on social inequalities, such as the influence of sanctuary policies on citizenship disparities in criminal case outcomes.

Kenneth C. Land is the John Franklin Crowell Distinguished Professor Emeritus of Sociology in the Department of Sociology at Duke University. His main research interests are contemporary social trends and quality-of-life measurement, social problems, demography, criminology, organizations, and mathematical and statistical models and methods for the study of social and demographic processes.

Marieke Liem is Professor of Violence and Interventions at Leiden University, where she and her team conduct research on interpersonal violence—with specific research projects on drug-related violence.

Michael T. Light is Professor of Sociology and Chicano/Latino Studies at the University of Wisconsin-Madison. His research primarily focuses on crime, punishment, and immigration.

Xiaoshuang Iris Luo is a PhD student in the Department of Criminology, Law, and Society at the University of California, Irvine. Her primary research interests include the community context of crime, criminal justice, mass incarceration and prisoner reentry, and social networks.

Amy Magnus is Assistant Professor in the Department of Political Science and Criminal Justice at California State University, Chico. Her scholarship centers rural social inequality and activism, gendered violence and other forms of interpersonal violence, and access to justice. She is the most recent recipient of Chico State's Early Career Community Engagement Award, awarded by the university's Office of Civic Engagement.

Ashley M. Mancik is Assistant Professor in the Department of Criminology and Criminal Justice at the University of South Carolina.

Patricia L. McCall is Professor Emerita of Sociology in the Department of Sociology and Anthropology at North Carolina State University. Her research is embedded in the study of crime and social control, including ecological analyses of homicide and suicide identifying the social and economic factors that explain variations in these phenomena across geographic locations and over time—most recently studying European homicide. Other areas of research include latent trajectory analyses modeling criminal careers; country, city, and macrolevel homicide trends; juvenile justice program effectiveness; and projections of juvenile violent crime rates.

Erin Orrick is Associate Professor and Chairperson of the Department of Criminal Justice and Criminology in the School of Criminal Justice at Sam Houston State University. She specializes in the field of corrections, including contemporary issues, prisoner reentry, and recidivism as well as criminal careers and criminal justice policy. She has recently published articles in several leading journals and, in 2012, was awarded the William L. Simon/Anderson Publishing Outstanding Paper for her research titled "Do Parole Technical Violators Pose a Public Safety Threat? An Analysis of Prison Misconduct."

Karen F. Parker is Professor in the Department of Sociology and Criminal Justice at the University of Delaware. Her current research interests include exploring the influence of macrolevel constructs on urban homicide, particularly labor markets, racial segregation, and concentrated disadvantage. Much of her recent work has examined racial threat arguments and incorporated change models to examine how shifts in local economy differentially influence race-specific homicide rates, including the crime drop.

Alex R. Piquero is Director of the Bureau of Justice Statistics in the Department of Justice. He is also Professor and Chair of the Department of Sociology and Criminology and Arts and Sciences Distinguished Scholar the University of Miami and Professor of Criminology at Monash University in Melbourne, Australia. He has published over 475 peer-reviewed articles in the areas of criminal careers, race/immigration and crime, crime prevention, criminological theory, and quantitative research methods and has authored several books.

William Alex Pridemore is SUNY Distinguished Professor in the School of Criminal Justice at University at Albany–SUNY. He was dean of the school from 2015 to 2020. His primary research interests include (1) the effects of social structure, alcohol, and policy on homicide and suicide rates; (2) measurement and method; and (3) rural criminology. His research is interdisciplinary, and he has published more than one hundred peer-reviewed articles, with many appearing in leading journals in criminology, sociology, public health, and substance use.

David C. Pyrooz is Associate Professor in the Department of Sociology at the University of Colorado Boulder. He is interested in why people violate laws, norms, and rules, what happens to them when they do, and how to increase safety and justice in our communities. Most of his research is aimed at the criminology of social groups, particularly gangs. His current research projects involve advancing the science of gang intervention in the Denver area and beyond.

Arnaldo Rabolini is a former PhD student at Leiden University, focusing on drug-related violence.

Kasey Ragan is a PhD candidate at the University of California, Irvine, in the Department of Criminology, Law and Society. Her research focuses on gendered violence, justice alternatives for survivors, crimes of the powerful, and state-corporate crimes. She is currently researching the #MeToo movement, exploring survivor justice, legal consciousness of due process, and the backlash of #MeToo.

Wendy Regoeczi is Professor and Chairperson in the Department of Criminology and Criminal Justice at South Carolina University. For the past two decades, she has been a Criminology faculty member at Cleveland State University and also served as Director of Cleveland State University's Criminology Research Center for fourteen years. The bulk of her research is on homicide, including homicide trends and patterns, police investigation of homicides, homicide followed by suicide, and methodological issues in studying homicide.

Jacqueline Rhoden-Trader is Associate Professor in the Department of Criminal Justice at Coppin State University. She is an applied social science researcher and policy analyst in the field of criminology. Dr. Rhoden-Trader has conducted qualitative and quantitative research on disadvantaged populations, written several articles published in scholarly journals, and trained thousands of individuals nationally and internationally. Specific research interests include geospatial analysis of criminal events from a social structural lens, race and gender disparities across the globe, human trafficking, at-risk/disadvantaged youth, crime and delinquency prevention, and youth development policy.

Johnny Rice II is Assistant Professor and Chairperson in the Department of Criminal Justice at Coppin State University in Baltimore. Before joining Coppin, he worked as a senior program associate with the Supervised Visitation Initiative (SVI) at the Vera Institute of Justice. He has spent the past twenty-two years providing leadership, technical assistance, and support to organizations that serve low-income fathers and families in the areas of child welfare, youth development, and criminal justice in an effort to create safe and stable communities.

Ethan M. Rogers is Assistant Research Scientist in the Public Policy Center at the University of Iowa. His research is primarily focused on criminology, health, and criminal justice policy. The core of Rogers's work focuses on interpersonal disputes and violence. He has published several findings on individual and situational factors associated with the escalation of conflict and the victim-offender overlap. He is currently studying the extent to which homicide booms, including the increase since 2014, are concentrated among demographic groups and geographic places.

Meghan Rogers is Assistant Professor of Sociology and Criminology at the University of Iowa. She received her PhD in Criminal Justice from Indiana University. Dr. Rogers's research interests include cross-national homicide research, measurement of crime and its correlates, and social structures and crime.

Randolph Roth is Professor of History and Sociology at Ohio State and Fellow of the American Association for the Advancement of Science. He specializes in the history of the United States from colonial times to the present, with an emphasis on social and cultural history, the history of crime and violence, environmental history, the history of religion, the history of democracies, global history, quantitative methods, and social theory.

Jose Antonio Sanchez is a doctoral candidate in the Department of Sociology at the University of Colorado Boulder. He received a BS and MS from California State University, Los Angeles, and his research interests include gangs and criminal networks, criminological theory, and international comparative criminology. Currently, he is working as a graduate research assistant for a National Institute of Justice (NIJ)–funded randomized control trial evaluation of the Gang Reduction Initiative of Denver.

Daniel Semenza is Assistant Professor in the Department of Sociology, Anthropology, and Criminal Justice at Rutgers University–Camden. He is also Director of Interpersonal Violence with the New Jersey Gun Violence Research Center and jointly appointed Assistant Professor in the Department of Urban-Global Health in the School of Public Health at Rutgers University. Broadly speaking, his research examines the causes and consequences of community gun violence and the connections between health, criminal justice exposure, and violent victimization.

Richard Stansfield is Associate Professor of Criminal Justice in the Department of Sociology, Anthropology, and Criminal Justice at Rutgers University–Camden. His research is animated by a broad focus on policy-relevant issues, particularly related to violence prediction, assessment, and prevention. This includes work in the area of gun violence prevention, community violence, and risk assessment of domestic violence, in addition to work on risk factors related to reoffending after incarceration. He has published extensively on these topics, spanning journals in public health, criminology, and sociology.

James Tuttle is Assistant Professor of Sociology at the University of Montana. His previous research concentrates on theoretical and empirical issues involving cross-national variation in homicide rates. His current research builds on these areas of inquiry, examining correlates of homicide trends, government use of coercive social control, and the impact of economic deprivation on aggregate crime rates.

Jolien van Breen is Assistant Professor at Leiden University. Her current research focuses on intergroup conflict and violence. She is specifically interested in how people understand and navigate conflict and violence.

Kirk R. Williams is Professor Emeritus, Department of Criminology, Law, and Society at the University of California, Irvine. He has authored or coauthored over ninety peer-reviewed journal articles, book chapters, and technical reports on the causes and prevention of violence, particularly involving youth and adult intimate partners, garnering over eleven thousand citations. He also coedited a book on violence in schools. He has received over 10 million dollars in grants from federal and state funding sources in addition to private foundations. He works extensively with community-based groups, schools, and agencies in violence prevention planning, implementation, and evaluation.

Index

www.ingramcontent.com/pod-product-compliance
Lightning Source LLC
Chambersburg PA
CBHW060145280326
41932CB00012B/1637